Policing International Trade
in Endangered Species

The Sustainable Development Programme is the new name (from February 2002) for the Energy and Environment Programme of the Royal Institute of International Affairs at Chatham House. The Programme works with business, government, and academic and NGO experts to carry out and publish research and stimulate debate across a wide variety of energy, environment and business topics with international implications, particularly those just emerging into the consciousness of policy-makers. Research by the Programme is supported by generous financial and intellectual contributions from its core supporters:

- Amerada Hess Ltd
- Anglo American plc
- BG Group
- BP Amoco plc
- British Nuclear Fuels plc
- Department for Environment, Food and Rural Affairs (UK)
- Department of Trade & Industry (UK)
- ExxonMobil
- Foreign & Commonwealth Office (UK)
- Osaka Gas Co. Ltd
- Powergen plc
- Saudi Petroleum Overseas Ltd
- Shell UK
- Tokyo Electric Power Co. Inc.
- TXU Europe Group plc

Policing International Trade in Endangered Species

The CITES Treaty and Compliance

Rosalind Reeve

THE ROYAL INSTITUTE OF INTERNATIONAL AFFAIRS | Sustainable Development Programme

Earthscan Publications Ltd, London

First published in the UK in 2002 by
The Royal Institute of International Affairs, 10 St James's Square, London SW1Y 4LE
(Charity Registration No. 208223)
and
Earthscan Publications Ltd, 120 Pentonville Road, London N1 9JN

Distributed in North America by
The Brookings Institution, 1775 Massachusetts Avenue NW,
Washington, DC 20036-2188

A catalogue record for this book is available from the British Library.

ISBN   1 85383 880 2 paperback
         1 85383 875 6 hardback

The Royal Institute of International Affairs is an independent body that promotes the rigorous study of international questions and does not express opinions of its own. The opinions expressed in this publication are the responsibility of the author.

Earthscan Publications Ltd is an editorially independent subsidiary of Kogan Page Ltd and publishes in association with the WWF-UK and the International Institute of Environment and Development.

Typeset by Denis Dalinnik
Printed and bound by Creative Print and Design Wales, Ebbw Vale
Original cover design by Visible Edge
Cover by Yvonne Booth
Cover photo by Steve Jackson

Contents

List of figures, tables and boxes

Figures

Tables

Boxes

Foreword

The regulation of international trade in wildlife and wildlife products has never been emotionally neutral. Facing an unprecedented 'tragedy of the commons', ethical value positions in this field confront theories of sustainable development; biologists clash with economists, lawyers with policy scientists; and the North–South divide looms large in the whole debate. Against this background, Dr Rosalind Reeve's book offers intellectual relief, both sobering and refreshing: sobering because its subject is the predominantly technical issues of compliance and enforcement, where ideological disputes may seem less ominous; refreshing because the author does not hesitate to ask controversial questions – such as the rationale of a Compliance Committee – regardless of their current 'political correctness'.

CITES (the 1973 Washington Convention on International Trade in Endangered Species of Wild Fauna and Flora) has indeed played a pilot role among international environmental regimes – as one of the most innovative multilateral treaties in the post-Stockholm era of environmental law, and as the starting point of a new dynamic process of global decision-making for the conservation of natural resources. Significantly, though, much of what is really new about CITES is hardly even mentioned in the text of the treaty, but instead was developed almost entirely by subsequent organizational practice – including most of the regime's present institutional framework; the procedure of majority voting; the technique of periodic implementation reviews; the active participation of non-governmental organizations in compliance monitoring; and the effective use of trade sanctions against non-complying governments. Not least among the merits of Dr Reeve's analysis, therefore, is the fact that rather than expounding 'law on the books', its focus is the accumulated lessons of 30 years of regime *praxis* – 'rules in use', as it were. That is why I am confident that this study will make a lasting contribution to our understanding of what works – and what doesn't work – in global environmental governance.

Peter H. Sand
Institute of International Law
University of Munich

About the author

Dr Rosalind Reeve is an Associate Fellow of RIIA's Sustainable Development Programme. She has worked on wildlife trade issues for 16 years, gaining a masters degree in environmental law in 1999. During that time she has travelled extensively investigating wildlife trade for different NGOs, most recently for the International Fund for Animal Welfare (IFAW) in connection with the reptile trade; has participated in CITES meetings on behalf of the David Shepherd Wildlife Foundation and as a Party representative; was Campaign Director for the Environmental Investigation Agency (EIA); was a member of the UK delegation to the International Whaling Commission; was a consultant to UNEP for the Lusaka Agreement negotiations; and worked as a campaigner for Greenpeace International. She is a member of IUCN's Environmental Law Commission and the international consultant network of the Verification, Training and Information Centre (VERTIC), and has written or contributed to numerous reports and articles on wildlife trade.

Acknowledgments

Since the idea for this book was conceived four years ago many have travelled with me on its journey of realization, some just briefly, others for the whole way. In particular I would like to thank Duncan Brack, Peter Sand and Melanie Shepherd for their belief in the book and for their constant support and encouragement; the David Shepherd Wildlife Foundation for enabling my attendance at CITES meetings; Jake Werksman for his inspiration as an outstanding teacher; James Cameron whose achievements and encouragement convinced me to study law; Rob Hepworth for his valued advice, comments and insight; and staff of the CITES Secretariat – especially Jim Armstrong, Jonathan Barzdo, Malan Lindeque, John Sellar, Juan Carlos Vasquez, Marci Yeater and Willem Wijnstekers – for their patience and helpfulness in the face of endless requests. I am grateful to Duncan Brack, Robert Lamb, Jason Lowther, Ron Orenstein, Peter Pueschel, Martin Roberts and Peter Sand for reviewing and commenting on the text; to the many others who have taken time to respond to requests for information and advice, especially John Caldwell, Esmond Martin and Kal Raustiala; and to staff of the UK Global Wildlife Division (DEFRA) for their assistance in the early days of the book's evolution. For ensuring its professional publication on a tight schedule I am indebted to Margaret May at the Royal Institute of International Affairs, and Sue Hughes, the copy-editor. Last but never least I would like to thank my family, Gordon and Rosemary Bull, Steve Jackson, Gerd Leipold, and Brendan, Bruno, Leona, Maya, Nikhil, Sean and Tara, for their support and understanding.

August 2002   Rosalind Reeve

Acronyms and abbreviations

AC	Animals Committee (CITES)
AC-IMPEL	An environmental compliance and enforcement network of central and eastern European countries targeted for future accession to the EU
AFCD	Agriculture, Fisheries and Conservation Department (Hong Kong)
Basel Convention	Convention on the Control of Transboundary Movements of Hazardous Wastes and their Disposal (1989)
BIDS	Bad Ivory Database System (forerunner of ETIS)
Cartagena Protocol	Cartagena Protocol on Biosafety to the Convention on Biological Diversity (2000)
CBD	Convention on Biological Diversity (1992)
CEC	Commission for Environmental Cooperation (NAAEC)
CEPF	Critical Ecosystem Partnership Fund
CETF	CITES Enforcement Task Force
CFC	chlorofluorocarbon
CITES	Convention on International Trade in Endangered Species of Wild Fauna and Flora (1973)
CLIO	CITES Liaison and Intelligence Officer (now CWESO)
CMS	Convention on the Conservation of Migratory Species of Wild Animals (1979)
COP	Conference of the Parties (to CITES)
COP/MOP	Conference of the Parties serving as the Meeting of the Parties (to the Kyoto Protocol)
COTES	Control of Trade in Endangered Species (Enforcement) Regulations (UK)
CTE	Committee on Trade and Environment (WTO)
CWESO	Customs Wildlife and Endangered Species Officer (UK)
DEFRA	Department for the Environment, Food and Rural Affairs (UK)

DETR	Department of the Environment, Transport and the Regions (UK) (predecessor of DEFRA)
DNPWC	Department of National Parks and Wildlife Conservation (Nepal)
DSB	Dispute Settlement Body (WTO)
DSU	Dispute Settlement Understanding (WTO)
DSWF	David Shepherd Wildlife Foundation
DWNP	Department of Wildlife and National Parks (Malaysia)
ECJ	European Court of Justice
EIA	Environmental Investigation Agency
ERM	Environmental Resources Management
ESPU	Endangered Species Protection Unit (South African Police)
ETIS	Elephant Trade Information System
EU	European Union
EWG	North American Working Group on Environmental Enforcement and Compliance Cooperation
FAO	Food and Agriculture Organization (of the United Nations)
GATT	General Agreement on Tariffs and Trade
GEF	Global Environment Facility
IATA	International Air Transport Association
ICPO–Interpol	International Criminal Police Organization
IDR	in-depth review (under the Climate Change Convention)
IFAW	International Fund for Animal Welfare
IIASA	International Institute for Applied Systems Analysis
ILO	International Labour Organization
IMPEL	European Network for Implementation and Enforcement of Environmental Law.
IMS	information management strategy
INECE	International Network for Environmental Compliance and Enforcement
IUCN	World Conservation Union (formerly International Union for Conservation of Nature and Natural Resources)

IUCN/SSC	IUCN Species Survival Commission
JWCS	Japan Wildlife Conservation Society
KSBK	Konservasi Satwa Bagi Kehidupan (Animal Conservation for Life, Indonesia)
Kyoto Protocol	Kyoto Protocol to the UN Framework Convention on Climate Change (1997)
LATF	Lusaka Agreement Task Force
LRTAP	Convention on Long-Range Transboundary Air Pollution (1979)
Lusaka Agreement	Lusaka Agreement on Cooperative Enforcement Operations Directed at Illegal Trade in Wild Fauna and Flora (1994)
MARPOL	International Convention for the Prevention of Pollution from Ships
MEA	multilateral environmental agreement
MIKE	Monitoring the Illegal Killing of Elephants
MOP	Meeting of the Parties (to the Montreal Protocol on Substances that Deplete the Ozone Layer)
MOU	memorandum of understanding
MTS	multilateral trading system
NAAEC	North American Agreement on Environmental Cooperation
NAFTA	North American Free Trade Agreement
NAWEG	North American Wildlife Enforcement Group
NCB	Interpol National Central Bureau
NCIS	National Criminal Intelligence Service (UK)
NCP	non-compliance procedure
NGO	non-governmental organization
NWCIU	National Wildlife Crime Intelligence Unit (UK)
ODS	ozone depleting substances
OECD	Organisation for Economic Co-operation and Development
PAW	Partnership for Action against Wildlife Crime (UK)
PWLO	Police Wildlife Liaison Officer (UK)
PPMs	process and production methods
Ramsar Convention	Convention on Wetlands of International Importance, especially as Waterfowl Habitat (1971)
RIIA	Royal Institute of International Affairs

Rotterdam Convention   Rotterdam Convention on the Prior Informed
                         Consent Procedure for Certain Hazardous
                         Chemicals and Pesticides in International Trade
                         (1998)
RSPCA   Royal Society for the Prevention of Cruelty to
                         Animals
SADC   Southern African Development Community
SC   CITES Standing Committee
Second Sulphur Protocol Protocol to the Convention on Long-Range
                         Transboundary Air Pollution on Further
                         Reduction of Sulphur Emissions (1994)
SSC   Sub-regional Steering Committee (for MIKE)
SSN   Species Survival Network
SSO   Sub-regional Support Officer (for MIKE)
Stockholm Convention   Stockholm Convention on Persistent Organic
                         Pollutants (2001)
TAG   Technical Advisory Group (for MIKE)
TEC   Technical Expert Committee
TED   turtle excluder device
TETF   Tiger Enforcement Task Force
TIGERS   Trade Infraction and Global Enforcement
                         Recording System
TM   traditional medicine
TRAFFIC   Trade Records Analysis of Fauna and Flora in
                         Commerce
TREM   trade-related environment measure
UAE   United Arab Emirates
UNDP   United Nations Development Programme
UNEP   United Nations Environment Programme
UNFCCC   1992 United Nations Framework Convention on
                         Climate Change
UNIDO   United Nations Industrial Development
                         Organization
UNOIOS   United Nations Office of Internal Oversight
USFWS   United States Fish and Wildlife Service
VERTIC   Verification, Research, Training and Information
                         Centre (UK)
VOC Protocol   Protocol to the 1979 Convention on Long-range
                         Transboundary Air Pollution Concerning the

	Control of Emissions of Volatile Organic Compounds or their Transboundary Fluxes (1991)
WCMC	World Conservation Monitoring Centre (now known as UNEP–WCMC)
WCO	World Customs Organization
WPSI	Wildlife Protection Society of India
WSSD	World Summit on Sustainable Development (2002)
WTMU	Wildlife Trade Monitoring Unit (part of WCMC)
WTO	World Trade Organization
WWF	World Wide Fund For Nature

In memory of
Nick Carter, Adan Dullo, Roy Jackson,
Bruno Manser, Jack Nilles and Michael Werikhe

Three decades and hundreds of studies later, scholarship has unequivocally shown that it is not legislation alone, but rather the implementation process, that determines whether a commitment has any practical influence.

David Victor, Kal Raustiala and Eugene Skolnikoff,
in D. G. Victor, K. Raustiala and E. B. Skolnikoff (eds),
The Implementation and Effectiveness of International Environmental Commitments
(IIASA, 1998).

The gap between law in books and how states act may now appear wider than at any other time in history – the more rules there are, the more occasion there is to break them.

Martti Koskenniemi,
in J. Werksman (ed), *Greening International Institutions* (Earthscan, 1996).

Lack of political will rather than the lack of capacity generally seems to be the most common reason for non-compliance.

CITES Secretariat

Part I
Setting the scene

1 Introduction

Rationale and structure of the book

One of the greatest challenges facing us today is to ensure that the rapidly evolving legal rules in multilateral environmental agreements (MEAs) are applied – to close the gap between the law in books and the law as it is practised by states and followed by individuals. In the last 30 years, MEAs have proliferated in response to the growing international environmental crisis. Well over 200 MEAs have been negotiated, addressing a wide range of environmental problems.[1] As this is a relatively new area of international law, more agreements can be expected in the coming years, either regional or global protocols to implement existing MEAs, or new conventions addressing issues sparsely covered by existing international legal rules, such as forest exploitation and timber trade. Meanwhile, the substantive provisions and procedures in existing MEAs will continue to be elaborated to meet new challenges. This will inevitably involve a growth in complexity as MEAs age and mature.

The 1973 Convention on International Trade in Endangered Species of Wild Fauna and Flora (CITES) is one of the oldest MEAs. A specific tool rather than a global solution, it addresses one of the many threats to Earth's biological diversity – international trade in endangered species. Since its inception, CITES has been seen as the flagship wildlife agreement.[2] It is a cornerstone MEA, lying at the nexus of international trade and species conservation, and largely respected among the conservation community. Most *perceive* it as effective,[3] although this perception must be qualified by saying that there has

---

[1] UNEP lists 216 MEAs in its 1996 *Register of International Treaties and Other Agreements in the Field of the Environment.*

[2] John Lanchbery, 'Long-Term Trends in Systems for Implementation Review in International Agreements on Fauna and Flora', in David G. Victor, Kal Raustiala and Eugene B. Skolnikoff (eds), *The Implementation and Effectiveness of International Environmental Commitments* (International Institute for Applied Systems Analysis, 1998) (hereinafter 'Lanchbery'), at p. 69.

[3] A study by Environmental Resources Management (ERM) found that 74% of respondent parties believe CITES has been effective in deterring illegal trade in wildlife, while 26% do not: see *Study on How to Improve the Effectiveness of the Convention on International Trade in Endangered Species of Wild Fauna and Flora (CITES),* (ERM/ CITES Standing Committee, Sept 1996). See also Peter H. Sand, 'Commodity or Taboo?

never been a thorough empirical assessment of the effectiveness of CITES. Nevertheless, the specific and detailed provisions of this MEA compare farourably with the general and heavily qualified provisions of the1992 Convention on Biological Diversity (CBD). As a framework agreement in all but name, the CBD is an attempt to provide a global solution but so far has proved disappointing as a tool to arrest the decline in biodiversity. Its most practical realization is likely to be through protocols addressing specific threats to biodiversity, such as the Cartagena Protocol on Biosafety adopted in February 2000, as yet untested. By contrast, CITES has 27 years of experience on which to draw since it entered into force. Not only are there lessons to be learned from its system to promote compliance and deal with non-compliance by parties, but now is the time to examine how the system works in light of modern compliance theory and practice in order to identify weaknesses and lessons for the future.

This book therefore provides a comprehensive analysis of the system that has evolved over more than a quarter of a century to implement and enforce CITES, and to achieve compliance with its provisions – otherwise known as a self-policing system. It grew from a thesis submitted for a Masters' degree in environmental law. The four years of research on which the book is based led the author to a firmly held conviction that strengthening MEA compliance systems is one of the most important tasks facing international environmental law today. A global enforcement agency to oversee compliance with international treaties, or, to quote Professor Christopher Stone,[4] an 'international sheriff with badge and pistol', does not exist and would be out of the question in a global political order based on sovereign states. Instead, treaty-specific compliance systems and non-compliance procedures have evolved to fill the void. For regulatory MEAs such as CITES which place specific obligations on parties, it is particularly important that these self-policing systems are effective.

Since existing literature was found to be rather sparse and lacking in detail, much of the information for the book has been compiled from original CITES documents dating back to the first meeting of the Conference of the Parties

---

[3] (cont)
International Regulation of Trade in Endangered Species', *Green Globe Yearbook 1997* (hereinafter 'Sand (1997)'), at p. 26 and n. 138; and *Experience with the Use of Trade Measures in the Convention on International Trade in Endangered Species of Wild Fauna and Flora (CITES)* (OECD, 1997) (hereinafter 'OECD'), at p. 48.
[4] Christopher Stone, 'The Question of Compliance', in *The Gnat is Older than Man* (Princeton University Press, 1993), p. 100.

(COP1) in 1976. Where possible, this source material has been supplemented with personal experience gained in the field or from participation in CITES meetings. Setting the scene for the book, this introduction includes an outline of the problem CITES exists to address. Then, to assist readers unfamiliar with the subject of compliance control, Chapter 2 contains a brief overview defining the main terms and outlining the necessary elements of compliance systems as well as the main schools of thought. The CITES compliance system is then reviewed in Parts II and III under three separate sub-systems: primary rules, compliance information, and – the main substance of the book – non-compliance response. Under 'primary rules' (Chapter 3) have been included the origin and objectives of the Convention, its principles and provisions, national measures, institutions, financial system and strategic vision. Under 'compliance information' (Chapter 4), the mechanisms used to collect, analyse and disseminate information are discussed. The section on non-compliance response is divided into chapters dealing with country-specific, issue-specific and species-specific mechanisms, followed by a discussion of enforcement, technical assistance and capacity-building. Chapter 5 on country-specific responses contains a detailed review of case studies involving individual problem countries. In Part IV, weaknesses in the CITES compliance system are identified, other compliance systems are analysed for lessons to improve the CITES system, and the potential for conflict with the multilateral trading system (MTS) and its implications for CITES are examined. Finally, in Part V, conclusions are drawn and recommendations made for the future.

The book does not attempt to review the effectiveness of CITES, a concept quite distinct from compliance. To do this would involve an assessment of whether CITES has succeeded or failed in reducing pressure from trade on endangered species and ultimately enabling their populations to increase, a huge task given the thousands of species covered by the Convention, and beyond the scope of an essentially desk-based study.

Disappearing wildlife

Biodiversity crisis

The Earth is currently experiencing mass extinction on a scale potentially akin to the disappearance of the dinosaurs. If it continues unchecked, we may lose up to 50% of species by the end of this century.[5] This dramatic loss of Earth's

---

[5] Richard Leakey and Roger Lewin, *The Sixth Extinction* (Doubleday, 1995), pp. 232 onwards.

biological diversity – the variety of all living organisms in terrestrial and aquatic ecosystems – is well documented. But assessing the rate of extinction is fraught with difficulty. One estimate predicted the loss of 20–75 species per day by 2040,[6] while a study by the United Nations Environment Programme (UNEP) estimated that between 2% and 25% of surveyed species in tropical forests might become extinct by 2020.[7] In its most recent state of the environment report, GEO-3, UNEP states that 24% of all mammals (1,130 species), 12% of birds (1,183 species) and 5,611 species of plants are currently regarded as globally threatened. The true figure for plants is probably higher, since only 4% of known plant species have been properly evaluated.[8]

Threats

Wild species face many threats, most of which are attributable to human activity. Destruction of natural habitats is recognized as the greatest threat.[9] Others include the introduction of alien invasive species, pollution, intensive agriculture and over-exploitation through domestic commercial use (e.g. the bushmeat trade) and international trade, not to mention climate change and ozone depletion.[10] But even if wildlife trade is not the main cause of biodiversity loss, the pressure of international consumer demand adversely affects many individual species. Collection and harvest from the wild for trade can also cause collateral damage to ecosystems through the removal of keystone species, specific age classes or sexes; the removal of plants providing a food supply for wild fauna; or the use of destructive collection techniques such as cyanide and dynamite fishing.

Nature and role of international trade

Wildlife trade involves live animals and plants as well as a wide variety of their by-products, including hides, furs, ivory, timber, bark, fish products and a host of other derivatives. Only a proportion of the trade is subject to CITES regulations – many wildlife species in trade are not listed in the CITES Appendices

---

[6] Philippe Sands, *Principles of International Environmental Law* (Manchester University Press, 1995) (hereinafter 'Sands (1995)') at p. 369, referring to *Global Biodiversity: Status of the Earth's Living Resources* (World Conservation Monitoring Centre, 1992), pp. 192–247.

[7] OECD n. 2, p. 65, quoting UNEP study.

[8] *Global Environmental Outlook-3, GEO-3* (UNEP/Earthscan, 2002).

[9] Sand (1997), p. 19.

[10] Sands (1995), p. 369; OECD, p. 11.

and so fall outside its remit. From an economic viewpoint, the most significant sectors are the fisheries and timber industries. But despite heavy exploitation, most fish and timber-producing species in international trade are not listed, though pressure is increasing to subject some of them to regulation under the Convention.

Wildlife is traded legally within CITES trade rules and national laws, and illegally in contravention of those rules and laws. Deliberate violations of national laws governing wildlife capture and trade amount to wildlife crime. Consumer markets drive the demand. They include the fashion, food and pet industries; traditional medicine; medical and pharmaceutical research; zoos; and private collectors of rare and exotic animals and plants. Much of CITES trade is characterized by its 'luxury orientation, reflecting consumer patterns often ranging from the non-essential to the perverse'.[11] The trade flows mainly from developing countries rich in biodiversity to affluent developed countries or regions, particularly Japan, the United States and the European Union (EU). Some countries, however, such as Australia, China, Indonesia and South Africa, are both consumers and *range states* (producer countries where species are indigenous).

Consumer demand in many sectors of the wildlife trade has increased in the last 20 years. The fall of the Iron Curtain proved to be a significant event: since then there has been a huge rise in wildlife trade in Eastern Europe and an increase in smuggling, particularly of live animals, into the EU.[12] Interest in exotic species in Europe appears to be increasing significantly, reflected in regular seizures of live reptiles from travellers entering both eastern and western European countries.[13] Demand for exotic pets has intensified in other parts of the world, notably the United States and Japan, but also in producer/consumer countries such as Indonesia and South Africa.[14] Tropical ornamental plants are also in great demand, fuelled by the proliferation of garden centres.[15] Rising

---

[11] Sand (1997), p. 19.

[12] CITES Doc. SC.36.10, 'Enforcement Issues', prepared by the Secretariat for SC36 (Jan/Feb 1996). For more recent CITES documents see <www.cites.org>. Older documents are to be gradually posted on the CITES website to build up an archive.

[13] CITES Doc. 11.20.,1 'Review of Alleged Infractions and Other Problems of Implementation of the Convention', prepared by the Secretariat for COP11 (Apr 2000) (hereinafter 'COP11 Infractions Report').

[14] CITES Doc. 42.10.4, Tiger Technical Missions report prepared for SC42 (Sep/Oct 1999); Rosalind Reeve, research on international trade in African reptiles for International Fund for Animal Welfare (2001–2002) (hereinafter 'Reeve/IFAW research').

[15] Patricia Birnie, 'The Case of the Convention on Trade in Endangered Species', in Rudiger Wolfrum (ed), *Enforcing Environmental Standards: Economic Mechanisms as Viable Means* (Heidelberg: Springer, 1996), pp. 233–64: 234.

demand for traditional medicine, not only in China but also in other parts of the world, has fuelled an illegal trade in specimens from endangered species such as tiger bones, rhino horns, musk (from musk deer) and bear bile and gall bladders. Of the eight CITES-listed bear species, only the giant panda is not hunted for its gall bladder.[16] Some rare plants, including certain orchids and ginseng species, are also threatened by collection for traditional medicine. In Asia, escalating demand for freshwater turtles, either for food or traditional medicine, has led in just four years to a doubling of the numbers that are critically endangered.[17] Meanwhile, an increase in demand for live reef fish for food in Hong Kong and China, coupled with an exponential increase in demand for ornamental fish for aquariums in the United States, has depleted fish stocks and reefs in the Philippines and Indonesia.[18] In Africa, increased demand for bushmeat, for subsistence use and for consumption in restaurants and abroad, has now become one of the main factors driving declines in populations of wild fauna.[19]

The shahtoosh trade is a paradigm example of fashion driving extinction. *Shahtoosh*, meaning 'king of wool' and considered the finest natural fibre in the world, is produced from the under-fleeces of the critically endangered Tibetan antelope or chiru, which are killed to collect the wool. It is woven into shawls in Jammu and Kashmir for sale to wealthy consumers, principally in North America, western Europe, Hong Kong and Japan.[20] Meanwhile, the caviar trade, most of which is illegal and which escalated sharply after the fall of the Soviet Union, illustrates how demand for a luxury food item, prompted by a sudden collapse in trade controls, can suddenly accelerate declines in wild populations – in this case sturgeon species – in a short period of time.

The worldwide commercial trade in wildlife, excluding fisheries and timber, has been valued variously at between US$5 and US$50 billion annually. One estimate dating back to the mid-1980s (which also excluded most plant products other than cacti and orchids) placed the fully declared customs value

---

[16] Dee Cook, Martin Roberts and Jason Lowther, *The International Wildlife Trade and Organized Crime: A Review of the Evidence and Role of the UK* (WWF–UK, Jun 2002) (hereinafter 'Cook et al./WWF–UK').

[17] 'Half of Asia's Freshwater Turtles Endangered', TRAFFIC news release (3 Oct 2000), <www.traffic.org/news/turtles.html>.

[18] 'Reef Fish Laundering Hides Pacific Overfishing', *Environmental News Service* (15 Jul 2002).

[19] Rob Barnett, *Food for Thought: the Utilization of Wild Meat in Eastern and Southern Africa* (TRAFFIC East/Southern Africa, 2000); <www.traffic.org/bushmeat>.

[20] Vivek Menon and Ashok Kumar, *Wildlife Crime: an Enforcement Guide* (Wildlife Protection Society of India/Natraj Publishers, 1998), p. 62.

at US\$5 billion and the 'likely retail value' at close to US\$50 billion.[21] Another estimate put the legal and illegal trade at US\$5–8 billion.[22] Global timber trade is estimated to be worth around US\$150 billion a year,[23] while the annual value of the legal trade in caviar alone has been placed at around US\$100 million, with the illegal trade thought to be worth far more.[24] An often-quoted figure for the 'street value' of illegal wildlife trade, attributed incorrectly to Interpol, is US\$5 billion; but the estimate is not based on objective research and could well be higher.[25] The extent and value of the illegal wildlife trade are notoriously difficult to estimate. Nevertheless, it by definition a hidden activity, clearly happens on a significant and damaging scale. In the UK alone, it is considered with some certainty to be worth several million pounds a year.[26]

Individual animals and plants can command high prices. A grey parrot worth US\$20 at the time of capture might retail at US\$1,100.[27] Rare parrots change hands for US\$100,000 per pair.[28] A top-quality bird of prey can fetch more than US\$30,000 in the Middle East where hunting with falcons is popular.[29] In London in 1997, 138 shahtoosh shawls seized from a shop in Mayfair were valued at about US\$4,000 each.[30] Reptile collectors pay high prices for rare species and individual colour variations. A Japanese collector apparently

---

[21] Mark Trexler, 'The Convention on International Trade in Endangered Species of Wild Fauna and Flora: Political or Conservation Success?', PhD thesis (University of California at Berkeley, 1990), p. 9, quoting a 1986 WWF CITES fact sheet.

[22] OECD p. 12, referring to US General Accounting Office, *Wildlife Inspection: Fish and Wildlife Service's Inspection Programme Needs Strengthening*, GAO/RCED-95-8 (1995).

[23] Duncan Brack, Kevin Gray and Gavin Hayman, *Controlling the International Trade in Illegally Logged Timber and Wood Products* (RIIA, Feb 2002) (hereinafter 'Brack et al. (Feb 2002)'); see <www.riia.org>.

[24] 'CITES moves to block caviar smuggling operations', CITES press release (16 Nov 2001).

[25] Report of the CITES Working Group, UNEP Workshop on Enforcement of and Compliance with MEAs, Geneva (12–14 Jul 1999).

[26] Cook et al./WWF-UK.

[27] OECD n. 7, p. 65.

[28] T. De Meulenaer, 'Wildlife Law Enforcement in Europe', in *Proceedings of the EU Wildlife Enforcement Workshop, London 1–2 March 1998* (UK DETR, 1998), pp. 84–8: 86.

[29] Matthew McAllester, 'Tough Times for Afghan Animal Traders', *Newsday* (10 Feb 2002).

[30] A. Kumar, 'Shahtoosh Trade and the Tiger Connection', in *Proceedings of the EU Wildlife Enforcement Workshop, London 1–2 March 1998* (UK DETR, 1998), pp. 104–106: 106.

paid US\$175,000 for the first albino reticulated python caught in Southeast Asia.[31]

Not all species command such high prices. Taking the live reptile trade as an example, the majority is made up of lower-value species traded in high volumes. Between 1995 and 2000, global imports of live reptiles whose trade is controlled by CITES numbered between 1.5 and 2 million annually, three to four times higher than in 1989.[32] The total number of live reptiles traded globally every year is much higher than this, since many species in demand, particularly snakes, are not covered by CITES; they are therefore not subject to international trade controls and do not appear in international trade statistics. Retail prices of these lower-value species can range from US\$2 for a gecko (*Hemidactylus* species) to US\$50 for an African savannah monitor lizard (*Varanus exanthematicus*). But profit margins are high. For example, a ball python (*Python regius*) worth US\$2 to a trapper in Ghana retails for between US\$25 and US\$50 in the United States, while a common green iguana (*Iguana iguana*) worth between US\$1.80 and US\$2.50 to the exporter in Columbia or El Salvador retails overseas for US\$12–29.[33]

The potential profits and low risks of detecting illegal wildlife trade provide an incentive for smugglers and dealers prepared to bend and break the rules. Different levels of organization can be identified, ranging from 'organized' crime to 'major and organized crime groups'.[34] At one end of the spectrum are small networks of collectors, enthusiasts and family members; at the other are groups such as the 'red mafia' from the former Soviet Union and drugs cartels. The large-scale legal trade is also used as a cover for organized illegal wildlife trade offences. A proportion of legal traders and wildlife experts are involved in the parallel illegal trade, which draws on their skills and expertise. Recent research has suggested that major organized crime groups are engaged in wildlife trade in two main areas: the former Soviet Union, where they are involved in the illegal caviar trade, and key drug production and distribution states, which coincide with major range states for wildlife. The illegal wildlife and drugs trade are linked in three ways: by parallel trafficking along shared smuggling routes; by the use of 'legal' wildlife shipments to conceal drugs; and by the use of wildlife products to barter for drugs, and the exchange of

---

[31] Personal communication from reptile trader (Nov 2001).

[32] Reeve/IFAW research. Figures based on UNEP–WCMC CITES trade statistics.

[33] Joseph Franke and Teresa Telecky, *Reptiles as Pets: An Examination of the Trade in Live Reptiles in the United States* (Humane Society of the United States, 2001).

[34] For a full discussion of this see Cook et al./WWF-UK from which information in this paragraph is drawn.

drugs for wildlife to launder the proceeds of drug trafficking. In one case, boa constrictors imported to the United States from Colombia with valid CITES documents were found stuffed with cocaine-filled condoms; all the snakes died. In another, the US Fish and Wildlife Service discovered heroin-filled condoms in the stomachs of goldfish.[35] Criminals have used tigers, crocodiles and venomous snakes as deterrents to guard or conceal drug stashes and consignments.[36] Meanwhile, 'plane loads' of smuggled birds from Australia have apparently been exchanged for heroin in Bangkok and the drugs flown back to Australia for sale.[37] In Brazil, police estimates suggest perhaps 40% of all illegal drugs shipments are combined with wildlife traffic.[38]

Violence is associated with aspects of illegal wildlife trade. There have been deaths linked with caviar, tiger and shahtoosh trafficking and with the protection of rhino and elephant populations in Africa. A press release from the UK National Crime Intelligence Service stated:

> The last two leaders of the Chinese anti-poaching team in Tibet have been murdered and anti-poaching teams in source countries are regularly the targets of assassinations.[39]

Controlling wildlife trade in the face of strong market forces and organized crime is a monumental task. Smugglers and traders who bend the rules and exploit loopholes are invariably several steps ahead of authorities handicapped by lack of resources and political backing. An argument often used to support the trade is the economic benefit accruing to range states and in particular to rural communities. But the reality is that those who benefit most from the wildlife trade are the middlemen and 'kingpins' at the head of the chain. The trappers and poachers at the bottom often put their lives at risk, but receive a relative pittance in return. And revenue from licensing and trade duties is not always ploughed back into conservation and rarely reaches the community level.

---

[35] Cook et al./WWF-UK, quoting S. Galster, S. LaBudde and C. Stark, *Crime against Nature: Organized Crime and the Illegal Wildlife Trade* (Endangered Species Project, 1994).

[36] Cook et al./WWF-UK, quoting a TRAFFIC International Investigator.

[37] Cook et al./WWF-UK, quoting Queensland Police Service, personal communication (Oct 2001).

[38] Cook et al/WWF-UK, quoting A. Faiola, 'Animal Smugglers Sucking Life from the Amazon', *Washington Post* (3 Mar 2002).

[39] 'National Wildlife Crime Intelligence Unit launched at NCIS', NCIS press release (22 Apr 2002), <www.ncis.gov.uk/press/2002/12_02>.

Protection versus sustainable use

Wildlife trade is an emotive issue. Its control has been justified scientifically, economically, ethically and aesthetically, with viewpoints ranging from overtly anthropocentric to overtly biocentric. Conservationists are often placed in two camps: the so-called 'protectionists', who believe wildlife should be protected for its own sake, and those who promote 'sustainable use', i.e. the consumptive use of wildlife at a sustainable level as a means to conserve it. In reality this is an over-simplification, and there are many shades of grey opinions. 'Protectionists' can be pragmatists, and those who promote 'sustainable use' can appreciate the intrinsic value of wildlife. Nevertheless, it is possible to distinguish loosely one group, which perceives international trade as a threat on the basis of its overall track record, from another, which promotes it as a benefit, providing an incentive for good wildlife management.[40] The two groups often pull against each other in their attempts to influence CITES, a dynamic that has caused sharp divisions, most notably over the ivory trade.

The concept of sustainable use has gained considerable support over the last decade. Some promote it in the genuine belief that it provides the only means to save endangered species in the wild. But others undoubtedly misuse it for their own ends. Unscrupulous traders often find it a convenient peg on which to hang their activities and justify what sometimes amounts to little more than habitat-stripping. In practice, sustainable use does not always withstand the test of prevailing conditions in producer and consumer countries. As one commentator pointed out, it 'assumes...that property rights are clearly defined or that in the case of a common property resource good management regimes are in place – conditions which do not in fact always hold'.[41] In many producer countries property rights are poorly defined and wildlife management regimes are under-resourced, while underpaid and under-equipped enforcement officers fight an uphill battle against wildlife crime and corruption with little political backing. In consumer countries controls on wildlife trade may generally be better, but without exception their enforcement is a low priority and is underfunded by comparison with other forms of economic crime prevention.

A common mistake is to assume that experience in the trade in one species can be applied indiscriminately to others. Species are unique. Biological param-

---

[40] See CITES Resolution Conf. 8.3, 'Recognition of the Benefits of Trade in Wildlife' (1992). All CITES resolutions and decisions currently in effect can be found at <www.CITES.org>. Past resolutions that have been repealed can be found in proceedings of COP meetings, except for COP10 resolutions which were published separately by the Secretariat.
[41] OECD, p. 12.

eters such as growth and recruitment rates, habitat requirements and ability to breed in captivity vary enormously, as do market conditions such as prices and demand. Circumstances affecting trade controls such as the ability to identify specimens are also variable between different species. What works for sturgeon or the Nile crocodile will not work for rhinos, sea turtles or certain species of tortoises, for example. Experience with crocodile farms is frequently used to promote sustainable use of other species; but, while Nile crocodiles are relatively easy to breed in captivity, other species cannot sustain captive breeding programmes. A dogmatic application of sustainable use theory also tends to exclude ethical considerations, such as whether consumptive exploitation of certain species should be taboo. Whales, elephants and primates come to mind. Ethics are all too often ignored by conservationists on both sides, who have a tendency to adopt and sometimes misuse scientific arguments to support their case. Few wildlife policy-makers are willing to tackle head-on such issues as whether we have the right to exploit all species, or whether some should simply be left alone and, if so, where the line should be drawn.

An uncontested fact is that uncontrolled international trade has led to drastic depletion of some wildlife species. Under today's conditions, it remains a serious threat demanding attention at an international level. Ensuring that CITES achieves its objective of preventing international trade from threatening the survival of species is in the interest of all – protectionists, supporters of sustainable use and wildlife itself. And this is where the compliance system comes in. Promoting compliance is a cross-cutting task that should not fall prey to the dynamics of protection versus sustainable use. It is in the interest of all – except the perpetrators of wildlife crime – to ensure that the CITES compliance system is as strong and effective as possible.

2 Overview of compliance control

Definitions and distinctions

There is no consensus as to the meaning of 'compliance', 'implementation' and 'enforcement'. The concepts overlap, the terms are used interchangeably, and definitions vary. *Compliance*, perhaps the easiest of the terms to define, is generally understood in international law as 'behaviour that conforms to a treaty's explicit rules'.[1] Failure to so behave is termed *non-compliance*. A *compliance system* has been defined as the 'subset of the treaty's rules and procedures that influence the compliance level of a given rule'.[2] A *non-compliance procedure*, which is concerned with detecting and responding to treaty violations, is one part of a compliance system and therefore a narrower concept.

Guidelines on MEA compliance and enforcement recently adopted under UNEP define 'compliance' differently in two contexts. In relation to enhancing compliance with MEAs, it is defined as 'the fulfilment by the contracting parties of their obligations under a multilateral environmental agreement and any amendments to the multilateral environmental agreement'. In relation to national enforcement and international cooperation to combat violations of laws implementing MEAs, it is defined as 'the state of conformity with obligations, imposed by a State, its competent authorities and agencies on the regulated community, whether directly or through conditions and requirements in permits, licences and authorizations, in implementing multilateral environmental agreements'. The Guidelines justify the two definitions by stating that the term 'compliance' is well known and understood by those in both fields, but with a different understanding.[3]

Implementation tends to be defined variably. In its strictest sense, it refers to 'measures parties take to make international agreements operative in their domestic law'.[4] In a wider definition, three phases in implementation of international

---

[1] Ronald B. Mitchell, 'Compliance Theory: An Overview', in James Cameron, Jacob Werksman and Peter Roderick (eds), *Improving Compliance with International Environmental Law* (Earthscan, 1996) (hereinafter 'Mitchell'), at p. 17.
[2] Mitchell, p. 17.
[3] UNEP Governing Council Decision SS.VII/4, 'Compliance with and enforcement of multilateral environmental agreements', UNEP(DEPI)/MEAs/WG.1/3, annex II (Feb 2002).
[4] *Nordic Research Project on the Effectiveness of International Environmental Agreements: draft report* (Finnish Ministry of the Environment, 1995), at p. 6.

environmental obligations by states have been identified: adopting national implementing measures; ensuring that national measures are complied with by those subject to their jurisdiction (national compliance); and fulfilling obligations to the relevant international organizations.[5] The activities of non-state actors stimulated by an international agreement may also be included.[6] Non-state actors, however, were excluded from the definition of 'implementation' in the UNEP Guidelines, which is '*inter alia*, all relevant laws, regulations, policies, and other measures and initiatives, that contracting parties adopt and/ or take to meet their obligations under a multilateral environmental agreement and its amendments if any'.[7]

Enforcement has been defined as the 'formal, legally circumscribed reaction to a breach of an obligation'.[8] A distinction can be drawn between national and international enforcement. National enforcement is the reaction to breaches of national law, commonly by individuals. The UNEP Guidelines define 'enforcement' within a national context as 'the range of procedures and actions employed by a State, its competent authorities and agencies to ensure that organizations or persons, potentially failing to comply with environmental laws or regulations implementing multilateral environmental agreements, can be brought or returned into compliance and/or punished through civil, administrative or criminal action'.[9] International enforcement, on the other hand, is the response to a lack of fulfilment by states of their international legal obligations. This may occur at the instigation of a state, an international organization or, in a more limited way, non-governmental actors.[10]

Implementation and enforcement are therefore means to achieve compliance with a treaty's rules. Compliance should not, however, be equated with effectiveness.[11] High compliance with low standards will elicit little environmental benefit, as the disastrous history of quotas set by the International

---

[5] Sands (see ch. 1, n. 6), p. 143.

[6] David G. Victor, Kal Raustiala and Eugene B. Skolnikoff, 'Introduction and Overview' in David G. Victor, Kal Raustiala and Eugene B. Skolnikoff (eds), *The Implementation and Effectiveness of International Environmental Commitments* (International Institute for Applied Systems Analysis, 1998) (hereinafter 'Victor et al.'), p. 5.

[7] UNEP Governing Council Decision SS.VII/4 (see n. 3 above).

[8] Martti Koskenniemi, 'New Institutions and Procedures for Implementation Control and Reaction', in Jacob Werksman (ed.), *Greening International Institutions* (Earthscan, 1996), p. 237.

[9] UNEP Governing Council Decision SS.VII/4 (see n. 3 above).

[10] Sands, at pp. 144, 148.

[11] Mitchell, p. 6.

Whaling Commission shows.[12] Low compliance with high standards may prove more effective in practice. Nevertheless, it has been concluded that 'in most instances, compliance will correlate sufficiently with effectiveness to make *more* compliance preferable to *less*'.[13] As one commentator put it, 'compliance is not an end in itself but rather a means to achieve effectiveness, which is in turn a means to manage environmental stresses'.[14]

Another concept that has evolved through the study of mechanisms to achieve compliance with MEA provisions is that of *review institutions*. These have been defined as 'specific institutions, formal or informal, that gather, assess, and take decisions based on information relevant to the implementation of, compliance with, adjustment of, and effectiveness of obligations contained in MEAs, as well as in subsidiary agreements and authoritative decisions of the parties'.[15] 'Institution' in this sense does not connote a formal organization, but a 'persistent and connected sets of rules (formal and informal) that prescribe behavioural roles, constrain activities, and shape expectations'.[16] Thus, the concept of review institutions is a broad one. Though valid and useful in some contexts, confusion may arise in using a term more commonly used to describe a formal organization, of which there are several within the CITES regime. The term 'compliance system' will therefore be used in this book to connote mechanisms that have evolved to induce compliance and address non-compliance with CITES.

Compliance systems (and non-compliance procedures) should not be confused with *dispute settlement*. Dispute settlement mechanisms exist primarily to deal with disputes between two (or more) countries about their obligations under particular international agreements. Typically, some kind of tribunal or court is established to hear the case and reach conclusions, though there is usually a preliminary phase where disputing parties are encouraged to reach an amicable settlement. Dispute settlement mechanisms are most appropriate where the breach of an agreement causes measurable harm to a country (e.g. loss of market access in a trade agreement), and where the case revolves around the interpretation of general rules and principles. Though not always popular with environmentalists, one of the best known and most effective dis-

---

[12] Victor et al., p. 7.

[13] Mitchell, p. 6.

[14] Victor et al., p. 7.

[15] Kal Raustiala, *Reporting and Review Institutions in 10 Multilateral Environmental Agreements* (UNEP, 2001).

[16] Robert O. Keohane, *International Institutions and State Power: Essays in International Relations Theory* (Westview Press, 1989).

pute settlement mechanisms is the one that operates under the World Trade Organization (WTO) to settle disputes over breaches of the WTO agreements.[17]

Compliance systems and non-compliance procedures are most appropriate where a breach of an agreement damages the integrity of the regime itself rather than causing direct and measurable harm to a single country, for example agreements dealing with global environmental issues whose provisions are highly specific. Reference to dispute settlement need only be a last resort in the event the compliance system fails. Thus, compliance systems and non-compliance procedures are important devices to avoid disputes. Almost all MEAs contain a clause providing for dispute settlement; but to date there has been no case of such a clause being invoked. The multilateral nature of issues dealt with by MEAs renders a bilateral dispute settlement procedure largely irrelevant, particularly where an effective compliance system exists.[18]

Elements of a compliance system: the necessary tools

Compliance systems and non-compliance procedures vary in form from treaty to treaty, but the following essential elements for a satisfactory system of compliance control can be identified:

- procedures to monitor and gather information;
- procedures to evaluate the information by a body of experts competent to request additional information and assess the overall implementation of the agreement as well as the compliance record of specific parties;
- if necessary, supplementary ad hoc procedures, such as inspection, inquiry or fact-finding;
- compliance-related response and follow-up measures;
- strong, effective and efficient international institutions.[19]

---

[17] Duncan Brack, *International Environmental Disputes: International Forums for Non-compliance and Dispute Settlement in Environment-related Cases* (RIIA/UK DETR, Mar 2001) (hereinafter 'Brack (2001a)'); see <www.riia.org/Research/eep.eep.html>.

[18] Winfried Lang, 'Compliance Control in International Environmental Law: Institutional Necessities', *Heidelberg Journal of International Law*, 1996, 56, pp. 685–95 (hereinafter 'Lang'), at p. 695; Brack (2001a), p. 3.

[19] K. Sachariew, 'Promoting Compliance with International Environmental Standards: Reflections on Monitoring and Reporting Mechanisms', *Yearbook of International Environmental Law*, 2 (1991), pp. 31–52; Lang, p. 685.

Minimum institutional requirements (using the term in the sense of formal organizations) have been identified by Winfried Lang as:

- an institution, usually a secretariat, to collect governmental and non-governmental information and transform it into a comparable set of data and facts;
- a separate body to evaluate and interpret the data and facts, comprising individual experts or governmental representatives, which may be selective in membership or open-ended;
- a main political body to 'take measures', which acts on its own or on the recommendation of the 'reviewing' and/or 'recommendatory' body.[20]

A treaty's compliance system can be broken down into three sub-systems:

1 the *primary rule system,* consisting of the actors, rules and processes related to the behaviour targeted by the regime. An MEA's primary rule system generally attempts to alter the actions of private, sub-national actors (be they organizations or individuals) through the implementation activities of national governments;
2 the *compliance information system,* consisting of the actors, rules and processes that collect, analyse and disseminate information on violations and compliance. This generally comprises self-reporting by parties, independent monitoring, data analysis and publishing activities;
3 the *non-compliance response system,* consisting of the actors, rules and processes governing the formal and informal responses undertaken to induce those in non-compliance to comply.[21]

For the purposes of this book, these three component sub-systems have been used as a framework to analyse the CITES compliance system, paying attention to the essential elements of a satisfactory system of compliance control and minimal institutional requirements identified above. The primary rule system has been interpreted broadly to include the origin, objectives, institutional and financial structure, national measures and strategic vision of the Convention.

Non-compliance response measures vary depending on the nature of the regime. They may be punitive – 'sticks' – or involve incentives – 'carrots'.[22]

---

[20] Lang, p. 694.

[21] Mitchell, p. 17.

[22] For more information see Peter H. Sand, 'International Economic Instruments for Sustainable Development: Sticks, Carrots and Games', *Indian Journal of International Law*, 36/2 (1996), pp. 1–16 (hereinafter 'Sand 1996').

Sticks usually take the form of trade or financial sanctions, and in the case of MEAs tend to evolve subsequent to treaty adoption in the light of practical experience and the political dynamics of each regime. Trade restrictions may be applied multilaterally under a treaty regime, or on a unilateral basis as under the Pelly Amendment in the United States,[23] though the potential exists for conflict with international economic law, especially the 1947/94 General Agreement on Tariffs and Trade (GATT), which forms one of the central pillars of the World Trade Organization (WTO). This potential with respect to CITES is examined in more detail towards the end of the book.

Carrots have been described as 'payoffs to other countries to cooperate'.[24] They take the form of access to natural resources (e.g. fisheries quotas, or access to genetic resources used in the CBD); access to markets (e.g. by the CITES permit system); access to technology; and access to funding, either bilateral or multilateral.[25] Access to funding is becoming the most important incentive for compliance with MEAs. Bilateral funding may be instituted through intergovernmental foreign aid, non-governmental donors or debt-for-nature swaps. Multilateral funding may be instituted through trust funds, such as the UNEP convention trust funds of which the CITES Trust Fund is an example.[26] The 1990s, however, saw the emergence of new financial mechanisms which have been used both to encourage membership in MEAs and to secure compliance with treaty obligations such as the Montreal Protocol Multilateral Fund and the Global Environment Facility (GEF), which provides the 'financial mechanisms' for the UN Framework Convention on Climate Change (UNFCCC) and the CBD.[27]

---

[23] 1971 amendment to the 1967 Fishermen's Protective Act (85 *Stat.* 786, 22 U.S.C.A. 1978). After Congressman T. M. Pelly's death in 1973, the provisions were extended to other fisheries and wildlife legislation; see Steve Charnovitz, 'Encouraging Environmental Cooperation Through the Pelly Amendment', *Journal of Environment and Development*, 3/1 (1994), pp. 3–28.

[24] Charnovitz, 'Encouraging', p. 5.

[25] Sand (1996), p. 9.

[26] Peter H. Sand, 'Trusts for the Earth: New International Financial Mechanisms for Sustainable Development', in Winfried Lang (ed.), *International Law and Sustainable Development* (Kluwer, 1996), pp. 167–84: 172.

[27] Article 21.3, UNFCCC; Article 39, CBD; Article I, para. 6, Instrument for the Establishment of the Restructured Global Environment Facility. See also R. Mott, 'The GEF and the Conventions on Climate Change and Biological Diversity', *International Environmental Affairs*, 5 (1993): 299.

Management versus enforcement

There are two schools of thought on compliance theory: the 'managerial' school and the 'enforcement' school.[28] The *managerial school* holds that states tend to make efforts to comply with their treaty obligations and sees non-compliance as a problem of capacity, treaty ambiguity and/or uncontrollable social or economic change. Its proponents oppose the use of coercive sanctions, viewing them as ineffective and unsuitable. They advocate a non-confrontational, non-punitive approach to enhance compliance, involving increased transparency and what they term 'active treaty management'. The elements of active treaty management are: regular review and assessment of the performance of treaty obligations; non-adversarial dispute settlement; capacity-building; treaty adaptation; and robust international organizations.[29]

The *enforcement school* argues that states calculate the costs and benefits when they choose whether or not to comply. Its proponents criticize the policy inferences of the managerial school as 'dangerously contaminated' by restricting the selection of treaties on which to base them to those that contain obligations that are easily achieved. They stress that, as MEAs become more ambitious in their obligations, the likelihood of intentional non-compliance will increase, requiring more coercive enforcement strategies, which will raise the cost of non-compliance. They illustrate their point with agreements on trade liberalization, economic integration and arms control, noting the conspicuous absence of enforcement in failed regimes such as fisheries agreements and the Mediterranean Action Plan, and partly attributing to potent sanctions 'almost perfect' compliance with equipment measures under the International Convention for the Prevention of Pollution from Ships (MARPOL).[30]

Research carried out under the auspices of the International Institute for Applied Systems Analysis suggests that, while most implementation problems

---

[28] Kal Raustiala, and David G. Victor, 'Conclusions', in David G. Victor, Kal Raustiala and Eugene B. Skolnikoff (eds), *The Implementation and Effectiveness of International Environmental Commitments* (International Institute for Applied Systems Analysis, 1998) (hereinafter 'Raustiala and Victor'), at p. 681.
[29] Antonia H. Chayes, Abram Chayes and Ronald B. Mitchell, 'Active Compliance Management in Environmental Treaties', in Winfried Lang (ed.), *International Law and Sustainable Development* (Kluwer, 1996).
[30] George W. Downs, David M. Rocke and Peter N. Barsoom, 'Is the Good News about Compliance Good News about Cooperation?' *International Organization*, 50/3 (1996), p. 379; George W. Downs, 'Enforcement and the Evolution of Cooperation', *Michigan Journal of International Law* (1998), p. 319.

are not wilful violations, both 'managerial' and 'enforcement' instruments (i.e. 'carrots' and 'sticks') are necessary for dealing with non-compliance.[31]

---

[31] Raustiala and Victor, p. 682.

Part II

CITES compliance system: primary rules and information

3 Primary rules

Origin and objectives[1]

The origin of CITES lies in a 1963 resolution of the General Assembly of the International Union for Conservation of Nature and Natural Resources (IUCN), now the World Conservation Union, calling for 'an international convention on regulation of export, transit and import of rare or threatened wildlife species or their skins and trophies'.[2] Successive draft texts were prepared and circulated by the IUCN Environmental Law Centre in Bonn, then revised in 1969 and 1971 in light of comments received from 39 governments and 18 non-governmental organizations (NGOs).

The IUCN initiative coincided with a US prohibition of imports of wildlife 'threatened with worldwide extinction', except for scientific or breeding purposes, under the 1969 Endangered Species Conservation Act.[3] The species affected were included on a list promulgated by the US Department of the Interior. But the move sparked complaints of competitive disadvantage from the American leather and fur industries and the pet trade. So the US government was directed to encourage the enactment of similar laws by other countries and to 'seek the convening of an international ministerial meeting' to conclude 'a binding international convention on the conservation of endangered species'.[4]

Meanwhile, preparations were underway for the 1972 UN Conference on the Human Environment in Stockholm. However, since negotiations for CITES were not completed in time, Recommendation 99 of the Stockholm Action Plan called for 'a plenipotentiary conference to be convened as soon as possible, under appropriate governmental or intergovernmental auspices, to prepare and adopt a convention on export, import and transit of certain species of wild animals and wild plants'.[5]

---

[1] Most of the information on the origin of CITES is drawn from Sand (1997) (see ch. 1, n. 3).

[2] Willem Wijnstekers, *The Evolution of CITES: A Reference to the Convention on International Trade in Endangered Species of Wild Fauna and Flora* (CITES Secretariat/ IFAW, 2001) (hereinafter 'Wijnstekers'), at p. 15.

[3] Public Law No. 91-135, US Statutes 83. 275, entry into force on 3 Jun 1970; superseded by a comprehensive new Endangered Species Act after the adoption of CITES in 1973.

[4] Public Law No. 91-135 (1969), sects. 5(a) and (b).

[5] Sand (1997), n. 28.

All these initiatives converged in a conference of 80 plenipotentiaries, held at the Pentagon in Washington DC from 12 February to 3 March 1973. Coincidentally, immediately before the Conference one of the largest cases of illegal wildlife imports in New York – the Vesely–Forte case – was uncovered and prosecuted, focusing public attention on the urgency of the issue. A 1972 draft text put forward by the United States, based on a consolidation of the IUCN text and a counter-proposal from Kenya, served as the working document for the Conference. The initial IUCN drafts had been based on control of wildlife trade through global lists of threatened species, to be drawn up and updated on the advice of an international expert committee. But the counter-proposal by Kenya, which led developing country opposition to such an approach, insisted on the right of each range state to determine its own list of tradable species.

The outcome of the Conference was CITES, composed of 25 articles and four appendices. Also known as the Washington Convention, it was originally signed by 21 countries on 3 March 1973 and entered into force after the tenth ratification on 1 July 1975.[6] It subjected imports of species listed in three appendices to mandatory licensing with permits and certificates – in effect, 'passports' – to be issued by trading countries in accordance with criteria in Appendix IV (now superseded by a resolution[7]). As of August 2002, there were 158 parties with two more due to join in November 2002.[8]

Initially hailed as the 'Magna Carta for Wildlife',[9] CITES is both a conservation and a trade instrument which attempts to reconcile the two often competing values. Its objectives, not explicitly stated in the Convention, have to be derived from the preamble, which recognizes, *inter alia,* that:

> wild fauna and flora…are an irreplaceable part of the natural systems of the earth which must be protected for this and the generations to come.[10]

The primary objective has been identified in literature produced by the CITES Secretariat as ensuring 'the international cooperation of parties to prevent international trade in specimens of wild animals and plants from threatening their survival'.[11] Therefore the three key concepts are *international cooperation,*

---

[6] Wijnstekers, p. 16.

[7] Resolution Conf. 10.2 (Rev.), 'Permits and Certificates' (2000).

[8] CITES website <www.cites.org>.

[9] Elizabeth N. Layne, 'Eighty Nations Write Magna Carta for Wildlife', *Audubon Magazine*, 75/3 (1973), p. 99.

[10] See <www.cites.org> for the full text of CITES.

[11] OECD, p. 30 (see ch. 1, n. 3), quoting from 'A brief introduction to CITES', by the CITES Secretariat.

trade controls and *species survival*. While some try to argue that sustainable use is an objective, it has been concluded that:

> This is probably not the case. CITES is not *per se* a treaty to promote trade and use of wildlife. The principal objective of CITES is and has always been to ensure that international trade does not lead to species extinction.[12]

In other words, CITES seeks to prevent unsustainable use, not to promote sustainable use over non-use.

Principles and trade provisions

The following description of the principles and trade provisions of CITES will be restricted to the elements necessary to understand the compliance system. For a more detailed treatment of this subject, readers are referred to *The Evolution of CITES*, a handbook by the current CITES Secretary General, Willem Wijnstekers.

CITES Appendices: definitions and trade controls

The three CITES Appendices contain over 30,000 species of fauna and flora, over 25,000 of which are plants. Most listed species are on Appendix II.[13]

Appendix I of CITES includes 'all species threatened with extinction which are or may be affected by trade'.[14] In effect, this is a 'black list' of species, in which trade for 'primarily commercial purposes' is prohibited. Other trade, largely confined to specimens required for scientific and educational purposes and hunting trophies, is subject to the grant of both an import and an export permit (or a re-export certificate) under specific conditions.[15] These include, *inter alia*, the grant of the import permit *before* the export permit (or re-export certificate); determination by the exporting state that the specimens were not illegally obtained; and advice by Scientific Authorities concerning states of both export and import that trade will 'not be detrimental to the survival of that species' – the so-called 'non-detriment' finding. The Convention stresses that

---

[12] OECD, p. 32.
[13] For Appendices I–III, see <www.cites.org/eng/append>. The current Appendices I and II entered into force on 19 Jul 2000, while Appendix III (as of 13 May 2002) was valid from 29 Oct 2001.
[14] Article II.1.
[15] Article III.

trade in Appendix I species must be subject to 'particularly strict regulation…and must only be authorized in exceptional circumstances'.[16]

Appendix II includes 'all species which although not necessarily now threatened with extinction may become so unless trade in specimens of such species is subject to strict regulation'.[17] In effect, it is a 'grey list' of controlled species for which commercial trade is allowed subject to conditions. 'Look-alike' species are also listed, to prevent trade under the guise of non-threatened species. Appendix II trade is subject to the issue of an export permit (or re-export certificate) under specific conditions, including, *inter alia*, a determination by the exporting state that the specimens were not illegally obtained and a non-detriment finding by the Scientific Authority.[18] An import permit is not required.

Commercial trade is not defined in the treaty itself, but was subsequently defined by resolution as an activity whose 'purpose is to obtain economic benefit, including profit (whether in cash or in kind) and is directed toward resale, exchange, provision of a service or other form of economic use or benefit'. In deciding whether a transaction is for 'primarily commercial purposes', importing parties are to define it 'as broadly as possible so that any transaction which is not wholly "non-commercial" will be regarded as "commercial"'.[19]

The parameters for non-detriment findings, an important means to control trade, are not specified in the Convention or in any resolutions currently in effect. The nearest to a specification is a recommendation concerning the role of Scientific Authorities that 'the findings and advice of the Scientific Authority of the country of export be based on the scientific review of available information on the population status, distribution, population trend, harvest and other biological and ecological factors, as appropriate, and trade information relating to the species concerned'.[20] According to one commentator, biological parameters that should be looked at in non-detriment findings include principally the age at first reproduction, growth and recruitment rates, and distribution and abundance in the country of origin. In addition to the volume exported, Scientific Authorities should take into account collateral damage at collection sites and mortality before export, as well as the level of domestic use for subsistence or commercial purposes and other threats such as habitat destruction and pollution.[21]

---

[16] Article II.1.

[17] Article II.2.

[18] Article IV.

[19] CITES Resolution Conf. 5.10, 'Definition of "Primarily Commercial Purposes"' (1985).

[20] CITES Resolution Conf. 10.3, 'Designation and Role of Scientific Authorities' (1997).

Appendix III includes species listed unilaterally by parties as being subject to regulation within their jurisdiction and for which international cooperation is needed to control trade.[22] Permits differ depending on whether exports originate in the listing country or in another range state. In the former case, trade requires an export permit granted subject to a finding that the specimen was legally obtained, and a certificate of origin. In the case of other range states, trade is subject to the grant of a certificate of origin (or re-export certificate).[23] There is no requirement for a non-detriment finding, as for Appendix I and II species.

To provide for the welfare of live wildlife in trade, before issuing export permits for live animals and plants on all Appendices (and re-export certificates for those on Appendices I and II), the Management Authority of the state of export/re-export must be satisfied that they will be 'so prepared and shipped as to minimize the risk of injury, damage to health or cruel treatment'.[24] In addition, before issuing an import permit for a live Appendix I animal or plant, the Scientific Authority of the state of import must be satisfied that the recipient is 'suitably equipped to house and care for it'.[25] Parties are also recommended to apply the International Air Transport Association (IATA) Live Animals Regulations for transport of live animals by air (and where appropriate to apply them to other means of transport) and incorporate them into their domestic legislation.[26]

Amending Appendices I and II

Amendments to Appendices I and II are decided at each meeting of the Conference of the Parties (COP), with a postal procedure for urgent cases.[27] Proposals for amendments must be submitted by parties at least 150 days before a COP meeting. The Secretariat then consults other parties and interested bodies and

---

[21] Caroline Raymakers, 'Biodiversity and Wildlife Trade: From Fauna and Flora in Trade to Sanctions', in Monika Anton, Nicholas Dragffy, Stephanie Pendry and Tomme Rozanne Young (eds), *Proceedings of the International Expert Workshop on the Enforcement of Wildlife Trade Controls in the EU, 5-6 Nov 2001* (TRAFFIC/IUCN, 2002).

[22] Article II.3.

[23] Article V.

[24] Articles III.2(c), III.4(b), IV.2(c), IV.5(b), V.2(b).

[25] Article III.3(b).

[26] CITES Resolution Conf. 10.21 'Transport of Live Animals' (1997).

[27] Article XV.

communicates the response, as well as its own recommendations, at least 30 days before the meeting. Guidelines for the Secretariat when making recommendations are provided in Resolution Conf. 5.20. The IUCN Species Survival Commission and TRAFFIC International are commissioned to conduct technical reviews of the proposals, which are distributed separately from the Secretariat's comments and recommendations. Some months before the eleventh meeting of the COP in April 2000 (COP11), the Secretariat also circulated 'provisional' assessments of the listing proposals, including statements that it supported or did not support them. The move attracted criticism for pre-empting the IUCN/TRAFFIC peer review as well as potentially prejudicing parties against some of the proposals (discussed further under Chapter 10 on weaknesses in the CITES compliance system).

A two-thirds majority of parties present and voting at the COP meeting is required to adopt amendments (i.e. those casting a positive or negative vote, not those abstaining). Adopted amendments enter into force 90 days after the meeting, except for those parties entering a reservation within the 90-day period. Amendments approved at COP11 entered into force on 19 July 2000. Criteria for the amendment of Appendices I and II, and a format for proposals, are provided in Resolution Conf. 9.24. The criteria, currently undergoing a review, are based on biological and trade parameters, and include the precautionary measure that 'parties shall, either as regards the status of a species or as regards the impact of trade on the conservation of a species, *act in the best interest of the conservation of the species*' (emphasis added).

Split-listing different populations of the same species on different Appendices is becoming increasingly common (the African elephant being the best known example). Justification is found in Article I, which defines a species as 'any species, sub-species, or geographically separate population thereof'. Although the amendment criteria advise that 'Listing of a species in more than one appendix should be avoided in general in view of the enforcement problems it creates',[28] this seems to have done little to deter the practice.

Tracking shipments: permits, certificates and marking systems

The primary mechanism to track CITES shipments, and the central pillar of the CITES trade control system, is the scheme of permits and certificates. General requirements for these documents are laid out in Article VI, but have

---

[28] CITES Resolution Conf. 9.24, 'Criteria for Amendment of Appendices I and II' (1994).

been elaborated in detail over the years.[29] Some of the more pertinent requirements are:

- the restriction of issuing authorities to national CITES Management Authorities designated by parties;
- a separate permit or certificate for each consignment of specimens;
- a maximum validity of six months for export permits and re-export certificates and 12 months for import permits;
- the use of security stamps cancelled by an authorized signature and a stamp or seal, preferably embossed;
- the restriction of authorized signatures to those notified by parties to the Secretariat;
- the restriction of permit and certificate numbers to 14 digits, to assist tracking and reporting;
- the recommended use of security paper for trade in wildlife specimens of exceptional value;
- the statement on permits and certificates of both the source of specimens (e.g. wild caught, captive bred, ranched or artificially propagated) and the purpose of the transaction (e.g. commercial, scientific or educational);[30]
- the use of standard nomenclature adopted by CITES for names of species and specific numbers of specimens or units of measurement.

Permit fraud and inattention to these requirements by Management Authorities have proved to be a persistent problem. To counter this, in 2001 the CITES Secretariat issued additional advice on permits and certificates (which indicates some of the problems encountered) by notification to parties:

- that traders be encouraged to apply for permits and certificates shortly before the time of export, not at the beginning of a year, the harvest season or at a time when annual export quotas are established;

---

[29] The most recent requirements for CITES permits and certificates are contained in CITES Resolution Conf. 10.2 (Rev.) 'Permits and Certificates' (2000).

[30] Source codes currently in use are: W (wild caught), R (from a ranching operation), D (Appendix I animals/plants bred in captivity/artificially propagated for commercial purposes), A (artificially propagated plants), C (captive bred animals), F (animals bred in captivity, F1 or subsequent generations, not fulfilling the definition of captive bred), U (source unknown, which must be justified), I (confiscated or seized specimens). Purpose codes currently in use are: T (commercial), Z (zoos), B (botanical gardens), Q (circuses and travelling exhibitions), S (scientific), H (hunting trophies), P (personal), M (biomedical research), E (educational), N (reintroduction or introduction into the wild), B (breeding in captivity or artificial propagation).

- that quantities to be exported are exact, since permits and certificates are commonly issued with quantities in round figures;
- that no replacement be issued until the original permit or certificate is returned to the issuing authority;
- that, if a trader claims that the quantities actually exported were smaller than authorized, the original document should be inspected and proof of the number exported should be obtained;
- that document and shipment inspections should be conducted at the time of export, particularly for live animal shipments;
- that the original copy of a permit or certificate be collected by customs or other border control authorities of the importing country, endorsed to show completion of the trade and forwarded to the Management Authority.[31]

There is, however, no system to verify that the advice has been implemented. (Parties are required to provide biennial reports on their measures to implement and enforce CITES, but, as discussed further below, the requirement is virtually moribund.) Research by the author in East and southern Africa in connection with the reptile trade indicates that measures recommended for permits and certificates are frequently not complied with.[32]

Specimens may also be marked, for example by using indelible ink, tags, rings or microchips, to assist with identification and tracking.[33] Marking systems are increasingly being used as additional means to control and track trade. Examples are the universal tagging system for crocodile skins, the implantation of microchips into live animals and, most recently, a universal labelling system for caviar.[34] Nevertheless, the majority of wildlife in trade is unmarked, and controls are still largely dependent on permits and certificates alone.

Trade with non-parties

Trade with non-parties is regulated by Article X, which requires 'comparable documentation' issued by 'competent authorities' in the non-party state. This

---

[31] Notifications to the Parties, No. 2001/044, 'Management of Export Quotas and Combating Fraudulent Use of Permits and Certificates' (9 Jul 2001), and No. 2001/072 'Fraudulent Use of Permits and Certificates' (5 Nov 2001).

[32] Reeve/IFAW research (see ch.1, n. 14).

[33] Article VI.7.

[34] CITES Resolutions Conf. 8.13 (Rev.), 'Use of Coded-Microchip Implants for Marking Live Animals in Trade'; Conf. 11.12, 'Universal Tagging System for the Identification of Crocodilian Skins', and Conf. 11.13, 'Universal Labelling System for the Identification of Caviar'.

basic provision to prevent 'free-riders' has been elaborated and tightened through resolutions.[35] Parties can accept permits and certificates only from non-party states whose competent authorities and scientific institutions are included in the most recent version of an updated list compiled by the Secretariat, or after consultation with the Secretariat. Parties importing Appendix I and II species must also require certification that the competent scientific institution in the non-party state has made a non-detriment finding and that the specimens were not illegally obtained. Before allowing trade in Appendix I species with non-party states, parties are also required to consult with the Secretariat, and to allow the trade of wild specimens only in special cases for conservation or welfare purposes.

Exemptions, special provisions and export quotas

CITES incorporates several provisions enabling parties to bypass the permit requirements. This has been referred to as 'deviation tolerance' from full compliance.[36] The exemptions include:

- specific reservations enabling parties to opt out of a species listing, giving it the status of a non-party with respect to that species;[37]
- exceptions or 'loopholes', including: a 'grandfather clause' for specimens acquired before CITES provisions applied (pre-Convention specimens); specimens in transit; specimens that are household or personal effects; specimens either bred in captivity or artificially propagated; the non-commercial loan, donation or exchange of herbarium specimens and live plant material between registered scientific institutions or scientists; and travelling exhibitions such as zoos and circuses.[38]

The rationale for these exemptions is to give CITES flexibility; but, not surprisingly, they have been greatly abused.[39] As a result, there have been successive

---

[35] The most recent requirements for trade with non-parties are contained in CITES Resolution Conf. 9.5 'Trade With States not Party to the Convention' (1994).

[36] Sand (1997), p. 22.

[37] Article XXIII.

[38] Article VII.

[39] Simon Lyster, *International Wildlife Law* (Grotius, 1985), p. 256; Sand (1997), p. 22; Gwyneth G. Stewart, 'Enforcement Problems in the Endangered Species Convention: Reservations Regarding the Reservation Clauses', *Cornell International Law Journal*, 14 (1981), p. 429; Paul Matthews, 'Problems Related to the Convention on the International

interpretations and elaboration by the COP through resolutions. Sometimes these have narrowed the exemptions. Examples include transit shipments, pre-Convention specimens, travelling live animal exhibitions and parties who enter reservations with respect to Appendix I species.[40] (These parties are recommended to treat the species as if it were listed in Appendix II, and to report trade in their annual reports.) Often, however, interpretations through resolutions have accommodated special interests and enabled legitimate trade in Appendix I species through definitions for 'captive breeding' and 'artificial propagation' and the introduction of new terms such as 'ranching'.[41]

In the case of 'ranching', trade controls have only been elaborated for species transferred from Appendix I to II (developed for crocodile ranching operations). Although significant numbers of Appendix II species in trade that have never been on Appendix I are described as 'ranched' (source code 'R'), there is no clear definition or trade provisions that apply to these species. The same applies to fauna described by the source code 'F' (animals born in captivity not fulfilling the definition of captive bred). Consequently, use of these terms has been abused, notably in the live bird and reptile trade. Parties tend to treat these 'in between' specimens (i.e. not wild caught and not captive bred) more leniently, for example by exempting them from export quotas, which encourages traders to misrepresent wild caught specimens as ranched or 'F' to circumvent trade controls.

Although there is no reference to a quota system in the Convention, the setting of export quotas, initially introduced as exceptional measures for leopard skins and African elephant ivory, has evolved to become standard practice.[42] Without any specific mandate, it has begun to replace the case-by-case non-detriment

---

[39] (cont)
Trade in Endangered Species', *International and Comparative Law Quarterly*, 45 (1996), p. 421; Valerie Karno, 'Protection of Endangered Gorillas and Chimpanzees in International Trade: Can CITES Help?' *Hastings International and Comparative Law Review*, 14 (1991), pp. 989-1015: 1002.

[40] CITES Resolutions Conf. 4.25, 'Effects of Reservations' (1983); Conf. 5.11, 'Definition of the Term "Pre-Convention Specimen" ' (1985); Conf. 8.16, 'Travelling Live-animal Exhibitions' (1992); and Conf. 9.7, 'Transit and Transhipment' (1997).

[41] Sand (1997), p. 22; CITES Resolutions Conf. 10.16 (Rev.) 'Specimens of Animal Species Bred in Captivity' (2000); Conf. 11.11, 'Regulation of Trade in Plants' (2000); and Conf. 11.16, 'Ranching and Trade in Ranched Specimens of Species Transferred from Appendix I to Appendix II' (2000).

[42] Wijnstekers, p. 387; Sand (1997), p. 22; Martijn Wilder, 'Quota Systems in International Wildlife and Fisheries Regimes', *Journal of Environment and Development*, 4/2 (1995), p. 55.

finding provided for in Articles III and IV.[43] But the system as it stands is uncontrolled, has no scientific basis and is wide open to abuse. While the COP can set quotas, it usually does so only for species of special concern, such as those on Appendix I (e.g. leopard or markhor for hunting trophies), or those that have been transferred from Appendix I to II. The Animals and Plants Committees can also recommend quotas, but this is usually done within the context of reviews of significant trade in selected Appendix II species, a process limited by the number of species that can be reviewed at any one time. In practice, most quotas are set voluntarily by the parties. There is no agreed uniform quota-setting framework that bases quotas on non-detriment findings, includes regular monitoring and annual reviews and addresses quota overages. Currently, quotas can be monitored only retrospectively, through parties' annual trade reports, which are often delayed (see more below on reporting).[44] The 'non-system' as it stands results in delayed detection of quota overages, wide variations between parties in quota-setting and 'bureaucratic' rather than biologically sound quotas. Quotas have been regularly exceeded. In 1999 (the most recent year for which complete data are available), 67 quotas were potentially exceeded for fauna and two for flora. About half of the overages were serious, i.e. exceeded the reported quota by at least 150%, with two exceeding it by 1000%.[45]

The problems with quota-setting have been recognized by certain parties, notably the United States and Germany, and the issue is due to be discussed at the 12th meeting of the COP (COP12) in Chile in November 2002. The United States has proposed establishing an Export Quota Working Group to develop a quota-setting framework for adoption at COP13, while Germany (on behalf of the EU) has proposed an amendment to the resolution on permits and certificates that would introduce regulations on quota-setting.[46]

International institutions

The main international institutions established under CITES comprise the Conference of the Parties (COP), the Secretariat, the executive Standing Com-

---

[43] Sand (1997), p. 23.

[44] CITES Doc. 11.19 'Report on National Reports Required under Article VIII, paragraph 7(a), of the Convention', prepared by the Secretariat for COP11 (Apr 2000); Kim Howell and Michael Griffin, 'Regional Reports: Africa', CITES AC18 Doc. 5.1 (Rev. 1), prepared for AC18 (Apr 2002).

[45] CITES COP12, Doc. 50.2, 'Implementation and Monitoring of Nationally Established Export Quotas for Species Listed on Appendix II of the Convention', prepared by the USA for COP12 (Nov 2002).

[46] CITES COP12, Docs. 49, 50.1 and 50.2.

mittee, and three functional subsidiary or technical committees: the Animals, Plants and Nomenclature Committees. Only the COP and the Secretariat are provided for by the Convention, the other committees having been established by resolution subsequent to the treaty's entry into force. The Secretariat and all four permanent committees inform the COP of their actions through reports. 'If so requested', the Animals and Plants Committees also report to the Standing Committee.[47]

Conference of the Parties

Functions and structure   The Conference of the Parties, as the supreme decision-making body, meets every two and a half years. Eleven meetings have been held between 1976 and 2000, the most recent (COP11) at UNEP headquarters in Nairobi, Kenya, with COP12 due to be held in Chile in November 2002. Functions of the COP include, *inter alia*, adopting amendments to Appendices I and II, reviewing progress on restoring species, and making recommendations 'for improving the effectiveness' of the Convention. Observers have the right to participate in meetings of the COP but not to vote. They include: non-parties; the United Nations and its specialized agencies; and international and national governmental and non-governmental organizations 'technically qualified in protection, conservation or management of wild fauna and flora...unless at least one-third of the parties present object' to the participation of a particular organization.[48]

In practice, NGOs are active participants in COP meetings. They make verbal interventions, suggest amendments to COP recommendations and participate in working groups at the discretion of the chairs of the sessional committees which conduct business at COP meetings prior to plenary sessions. At COP11, over 130 national and international NGOs were registered as observers, numbering nearly 400 people and representing a wide spectrum of conservation, sustainable use and trade interests. The most strongly represented NGOs on an individual basis were TRAFFIC, with 34 representatives, followed by IUCN with 21, IWMC–World Conservation Trust with 18 and Worldwide Fund for Nature with 16. Species Survival Network (SSN), an international coalition of 65 conservation and animal welfare NGOs and individual members, was the most strongly represented on a collective basis.

---

[47] CITES Resolution Conf. 11.1, 'Establishment of Committees' (2000).
[48] Article XI.

The COP conducts its work in plenary and committee sessions. To date there have been four sessional committees: Committee I, which makes recommendations on proposals to amend the Appendices and other biological matters; Committee II, which deals with implementation, enforcement and other issues; the Budget Committee, which makes recommendations on financial matters; and the Credentials Committee, which reviews credentials of party delegates. For COP12 it is proposed to abolish the Budget Committee and add financial matters to the Committee II agenda, reducing the sessional committees to three.[49]

Participation in COP meetings by parties with least available resources is encouraged through the Sponsored Delegates Project, the funds for which are derived from party contributions to the CITES Trust Fund and accumulated unspent balances from externally funded and completed projects. (See more on CITES funding below.) At the time of writing, the funds available will support the participation in COP12 of two delegates from just 23 parties. The CITES Standing Committee has agreed to accord priority to least developed countries, followed by other developing countries and countries with economies in transition, using the UN Development Programme list.[50] Clearly, the limited funds will not support participation by all developing country parties and those with economies in transition, risking precluding their involvement in COP12. Even if they do attend, their delegations will generally be smaller than those from developed countries. The two countries fielding the largest delegations at COP11 (aside from Kenya, where the meeting was held) were Japan and the United States, enabling them broader participation in sessional committees and working groups.[51] This inevitably introduces inequity into COP proceedings, an inequity that will be hard to counter unless parties increase their contributions and enable the expansion of the Sponsored Delegates Project.

Following COP10, held in Harare, Zimbabwe, in 1997, many observers complained about attempts to limit their participation in the meeting, particularly in Committee I. In particular, NGOs complained they were given inadequate seating space and were severely restricted in their ability to participate and to make interventions. Even parties were restricted, in particular in their ability to comment on draft conditions drawn up by a working group to enable the sale of ivory to Japan from Botswana, Namibia and Zimbabwe (the host country). Israel later pointed out that the restriction of observers' rights to participate

---

[49] CITES COP12 Doc. 1, 'Rules of Procedure', prepared for COP12 (Nov 2002).
[50] SC46: Summary Report (Mar 2002), p. 7.
[51] COP11 List of Participants.

contravened the Convention and that the conduct of the meeting violated the rules of procedure.[52] Although no overt response was made by the Secretariat to the criticisms, they appear to have been heard. COP11, hosted by UNEP at its headquarters in Nairobi, Kenya, proved to be a far more congenial and smoothly run affair. Negotiations took place in a neutral atmosphere and efforts were made to facilitate NGO participation and to ensure that the rules of procedure were adhered to. At COP11, the United States expressed its sympathy with concerns expressed by observers at COP10 and proposed a number of recommendations on observer participation which were all agreed as COP decisions. The Secretariat and host government are now instructed to make every effort to ensure there is enough space for observers, with at least one seat per organization on the floor of the plenary and sessional meetings (unless a third of parties present and voting object). The presiding officers are to allow them time for interventions and 'when possible' to invite 'knowledgeable observers' to participate in working groups of Committees I and II.[53]

COP recommendations: resolutions and decisions   COP recommendations, which since 1994 have taken the form of 'resolutions', 'revised resolutions' and 'decisions', have played an extremely important role in the evolution of CITES. Over the years they have grown into a whole new body of rules which have reshaped the regime in a way that was unforeseeable in 1973. At the time of writing, there are 77 resolutions and revised resolutions in force and 170 decisions approved at COP11, giving some indication of the extent and complexity of the regime. The Convention does not indicate the form of COP recommendations. Until COP9 in 1994, they simply took the form of resolutions, though certain decisions could also be found in COP proceedings. In 1994 it was decided to compile all COP decisions not recorded in resolutions into a document that was to be updated after each meeting of the COP.[54] The two types of COP recommendation are differentiated on the basis that resolutions are designed to be of long-term effect, remaining valid until the COP either revises or repeals them, while decisions are valid only for a short term, generally from one meeting of the COP to the next. COP decisions should be deleted by the Secretariat when they

---

[52] Israel National Report to the UNEP Workshop on Enforcement of and Compliance with Multilateral Environmental Agreements (Jul 1999).

[53] See CITES Decisions 11.14, 11.70, 11.71, 11.73, 11.127 and 11.128 (2000) for rules on observer participation in COP meetings.

[54] Decision 11.123 (ex 9.28 and 10.114); see Wijnstekers, p. 339.

have been implemented or have become redundant or obsolete; but in practice decisions designed to be of long-term effect are increasingly being approved. The Secretariat is therefore in the process of undertaking a review and will propose to the COP that certain decisions be incorporated into resolutions.[55]

The recommendations contained in resolutions and decisions become effective from the date on which they are sent out by notification to the parties, unless otherwise specified.[56] After COP11, there was a delay of several months before they were sent out, causing potential problems with implementation of more urgent recommendations. Until COP5 in 1985, resolutions were adopted by a simple majority of the parties present and voting. But with the rationale that a greater majority of support would mean better implementation, a two-thirds majority of votes cast (i.e. excluding abstentions) is now required to adopt resolutions, revised resolutions and decisions, though as far as possible attempts are made to agree them by consensus.[57] Draft resolutions, decisions and other documents to be considered by the COP need to be communicated to the Secretariat at least 150 days before the meeting. Only in exceptional cases, such as an urgent enforcement problem, can they be accepted after the deadline.[58] Guidelines on the submission of draft resolutions and decisions are issued to parties, most recently in March 2002.[59]

Referred to by some as 'soft' law, resolutions and decisions have made the CITES regime dynamic and flexible. In effect, they circumvent the delay imposed by treaty amendments. Article XVII requires two-thirds of the parties to deposit an instrument of acceptance of an amendment to the Convention before it enters into force for those parties that have accepted it. The Gaborone amendment to allow the EU to accede to CITES provides an example of the delay this can incur. Approved at COP4 in 1983, at the time of writing it has still not entered into force. However, despite their necessity to the evolution of the regime, the legal character of COP resolutions and decisions remains undecided. 'Soft' law is a highly controversial subject, not even considered as

---

[55] CITES Decisions: Introduction (2000), <www.cites.org>.

[56] CITES Decision 11.9, 'Regarding Entry into Force of Resolutions and Decisions of the Conference of the Parties' (2000).

[57] Wijnstekers, p. 342; CITES Doc. 11.1 (Rev. 1), 'Rules of Procedure', prepared for COP11 (Apr 2000).

[58] CITES Resolution Conf. 4.6 (Rev.), 'Submission of Draft Resolutions and Other Documents for Meetings of the Conference of the Parties'.

[59] Notification to the Parties No. 2202/006, 'Guidelines for the Submission of Draft Resolutions and Decisions' (6 Mar 2002).

law by some international lawyers because of its non-binding nature.[60] One commentator poses the question, 'Can a decision adopted by the COP by consensus be considered legally binding upon the parties if the COP is not explicitly empowered by the treaty to legislate?' He points out that, while COP decisions (and, by implication, resolutions) have been used to great effect, notably under the Montreal Protocol on Substances that Deplete the Ozone Layer, controversy over their legal effect can cause problems, as in the Basel Convention on the Control of Transboundary Movements of Hazardous Wastes and their Disposal.[61] In CITES, the legal basis of COP recommendations has been questioned occasionally; but so far real controversy has been avoided.[62] A proposal to amend the US Endangered Species Act, which would have prevented enforcement action based 'solely on a notification under the Convention or on a resolution of the Conference of the Parties to the Convention', was fortunately unsuccessful.[63]

Secret ballots   Until 1994, voting at COP meetings on proposals to amend the Appendices and on COP resolutions was always by a show of hands. But at COP9 an option for a secret ballot was introduced, despite objections by parties concerned about the resultant loss of transparency. The rules of procedure now provide that a vote shall be by secret ballot if a request is seconded by ten party representatives. Although the rules state that 'it shall not normally be

---

[60] See Patricia W. Birnie and Alan E. Boyle, *International Law and the Environment* (Clarendon Press, 1992), at p. 26; and M. N. Shaw, *International Law* (Cambridge University Press, 1997), at p. 92.

[61] Jacob Werksman, 'The Conference of Parties to Environmental Treaties', in Jacob Werksman (ed), *Greening International Institutions* (Earthscan, 1996), pp. 55–68: 63.

[62] Sand (1997), p. 29, notes two cases where France and Austria stated that resolutions had no legal effect. France, in its defence in the Bolivian fur skins case (see case study of the EU), argued that CITES Resolution Conf. 5.2 (1985) 'was only a recommendation without any legal effect' (*European Court Reports*, 1 (1990), 4344). In a letter circulated to COP7, the Austrian government, in response to the COP6 Infractions Report (CITES Doc. 6.19), stated that resolutions had no legal standing and that interpretation of the Convention was a matter for Austria's internal legislation. The Italian government also questioned the legal basis of Standing Committee measures recommended on the basis of a COP resolution in response to Italian non-compliance (see case study below).

[63] Ron Orenstein, personal communication (2002), referring to Young–Pombo proposal to amend the US Endangered Species Act (*HR 2275, The Endangered Species Conservation and Management Act of 1995*), in S. 201(b)(6), proposed amended section 11(e)(7)(B).

used',[64] in practice the secret ballot is becoming the norm for votes on controversial amendment proposals. At COP10 it was used 'relatively frequently',[65] and at COP11 most of the votes on strongly contested proposals, such as those concerning whales, sharks and the hawksbill turtle, were by secret ballot. On all matters, a two-thirds majority of votes cast (excluding abstentions) is now required for adoption, with the exception of votes on procedural matters relating to the conduct of the COP meeting, which are decided by a simple majority.

Secretariat and partner NGOs

The CITES Secretariat, provided by UNEP, is located in Geneva. The establishment of a professional full-time Secretariat was unusual in an international environmental instrument at the time when CITES was drafted.[66] The legal basis for its role is found in Article XII, which outlines its functions, together with Article XIII, on International Measures (see Box 3.1). In addition to information-gathering and review, the Secretariat is mandated to undertake scientific and technical studies that will contribute to implementation; to prepare reports and make recommendations on implementation; and 'to perform any other function as may be entrusted to it by the parties'.[67] It is also required to draw instances of non-compliance to the attention of the national Management Authorities concerned, and then, together with any follow-up information and comments received, to the attention of the COP, 'which may make whatever recommendations it deems appropriate'.[68]

At the time of writing, the Secretariat numbers 28 professional and support staff organized into five functional work units:

1 *Policy and Management Unit (PMU)*, responsible for planning, directing, coordinating and administering the work and resources of the Secretariat;

---

[64] CITES Doc. 11.1 (Rev. 1), 'Rules of Procedure', prepared for COP11 (Apr 2000), p. 11.
[65] Stephanie Pendry, 'CITES Meeting Reflects Shift towards Sustainable Use', *Oryx*, 31/4 (1997), p. 229.
[66] Laura H. Kosloff and Mark C. Trexler, 'The Convention on International Trade in Endangered Species: No Carrot, but Where's the Stick?' *Environmental Law Reporter*, 14 (1987), p. 10222–36: 10225.
[67] Article XII.
[68] Article XIII.

Box 3.1: Articles governing the Secretariat's operation

Article XII.2: Functions of the Secretariat

The functions of the Secretariat shall be:

(a) to arrange for and service meetings of the parties;

(b) to perform the functions entrusted to it under the provisions of Articles XV and XVI of the present Convention [concerning amendments of the Appendices, and including recommendations on proposals by parties];

(c) to undertake scientific and technical studies in accordance with programmes authorized by the Conference of the parties as will contribute to the implementation of the present Convention, including studies concerning standards for appropriate preparation and shipment of living specimens and the means of identifying specimens;

(d) to study the reports of parties and to request from parties such further information with respect thereto as it deems necessary to ensure implementation of the present Convention;

(e) to invite the attention of the parties to any matter pertaining to the aims of the present Convention;

(f) to publish periodically and distribute to the parties current editions of Appendices I, II and III together with any information which will facilitate identification of specimens of species included in those Appendices;

(g) to prepare annual reports to the parties on its work and on the implementation of the present Convention and such reports as meetings of the parties may request;

(h) to make recommendations for the implementation of the aims and provisions of the present Convention, including the exchange of information of a scientific or technical nature;

(i) to perform any other function as may be entrusted to it by the parties.

Article XIII: International Measures

1 When the Secretariat in the light of information received is satisfied that any species included in Appendices I or II is being affected adversely by trade in specimens of that species, or that the provisions of the present Convention are not being effectively implemented, it shall communicate such information to the authorized Management Authority of the party or parties concerned.

2 When any party receives a communication as indicated in paragraph I of this Article, it shall, as soon as possible, inform the Secretariat of any relevant facts insofar as its laws permit and, where appropriate, propose remedial action. Where the party considers that an inquiry is desirable, such inquiry may be carried out by one or more persons expressly authorized by the party.

3 The information provided by the party or resulting from any inquiry as specified in paragraph 2 of this Article shall be reviewed by the next Conference of the parties which may make whatever recommendations it deems appropriate.

---

2 *Capacity-building Unit (CBU),* responsible for matters concerning external funding support, training and public awareness and national capacity-building to improve implementation;

3 *Convention Support Unit (CSU),* responsible for monitoring implementation of the Convention, providing information and documentation to parties in all working languages, ensuring that provisions are clear to parties, and organizing and supporting meetings of the COP and committees;

4 *Legislation and Compliance Unit (LCU),* responsible for assisting parties with implementation, national legislation and enforcement of the Convention, implementing Article XIII and related resolutions, and developing international cooperation on enforcement with international enforcement agencies;

5 *Scientific Support Unit (SSU),* responsible for providing parties with relevant information concerning implementation of Articles III and IV of the Convention (concerning regulation of trade in species listed on Appendices I and II) and related resolutions, and for assisting parties to develop management programmes for CITES listed species.[69]

At COP1, it was recognized that 'a strong Secretariat is essential to the proper implementation of the Convention'.[70] As case studies concerning non-compliance demonstrate below, the Secretariat has proved remarkably strong, despite its shoestring budget of around US$5 million annually. This strength has led on occasions to a perception that the Secretariat is not as neutral as it could be. This can be attributed in part to the Secretariat's role as a recommendatory body, unusual among MEAs whose secretariats are generally more restricted in their functions. But it can also be attributed to the Secretariat's turbulent history and its tendency at times to push its recommendatory role to a level of involvement rarely witnessed in international fora, an issue discussed further in Chapter 10, which addresses weaknesses in the CITES compliance system.

The Secretariat's relationship with UNEP has not been smooth. When the UNEP Executive Director replaced the CITES Secretary General in 1990 in the wake of a dispute over a ban imposed on international ivory trade at COP7, he ran into conflict with the Standing Committee. As a result, an agreement was approved at COP8, defining the relative roles of UNEP and the Standing Committee and providing for prior consultation in financial and staff matters.[71] In essence, the UNEP Executive Director is responsible for appointing the

---

[69] CITES Doc. 11.9.2, 'Staffing of the Secretariat', prepared by the Secretariat for COP11 (Apr 2000); 'Staff of the CITES Secretariat', <www.cites.org/eng/disc/sec/chart.shtml>.
[70] CITES Resolution Conf. 1.8, 'Resolution Concerning the Secretariat of the Convention' (1976).
[71] Wijnstekers, p. 310.

CITES Secretary General, following consultation with the Standing Committee; while the Standing Committee oversees the development and execution of the Secretariat budget. Other Secretariat staff members are appointed in consultation with the Secretary General. All staff fall under UN personnel rules.

From the beginning, certain NGOs have played an important role in the functioning of the CITES Secretariat, a legacy of IUCN's involvement in preparing the Convention and administering the Secretariat in its early days. The legal basis for this is to be found in Article XII, which enables the UNEP Executive Director, in his/her role of providing the Secretariat, to be 'assisted by suitable inter-governmental or non-governmental, international or national agencies or bodies technically qualified in protection, conservation and management of wild fauna and flora'. In practice, this has led to a close relationship between the Secretariat and certain organizations that are contracted to carry out specific tasks, particularly the various specialist groups of the IUCN Species Survival Commission (a 'knowledge network' of around 7,000 volunteer members), the IUCN Environmental Law Centre, the UNEP–World Conservation Monitoring Centre (formerly the IUCN Conservation Monitoring Centre and an NGO before joining UNEP) and TRAFFIC. TRAFFIC, an acronym for Trade Records Analysis of Fauna and Flora in Commerce, began in 1976 as an IUCN Species Survival Commission Specialist Group but is now a joint programme of WWF and IUCN. Its 22 offices, organized in regional programmes, monitor and investigate wildlife trade, providing information to the Secretariat and national CITES authorities. Occasionally other NGOs are contracted by the Secretariat for specific tasks. The Africa Resources Trust developed a guide to the review and control of significant trade in Appendix II listed species for COP11, while the International Fund for Animal Welfare (IFAW) is assisting with producing a list of species and products used in traditional medicine. IFAW also funded the Secretariat's publication of *The Evolution of CITES*.

Numerous other NGOs representing a spectrum of opinions are involved in CITES, but their involvement is generally restricted to participation in the COP and meetings of the permanent committees. They do not have as close a relationship with the Secretariat as IUCN and TRAFFIC, which consequently exert considerable influence on the regime. Where NGOs overtly represent trade interests, this is for good reasons. But there is a case for diversifying the Secretariat's NGO partnerships with other conservation groups offering legal, scientific and animal welfare expertise. An example is the Species Survival Network (SSN). Formed in 1992 for 'the promotion, enhancement and strict enforcement' of CITES, SSN is active at COP and permanent committee meetings, and has recently been approved by the Standing Committee as a donor for externally funded projects.

Standing Committee

The Standing Committee evolved from an advisory Steering Committee, established at COP1 in 1976 to coordinate a special session of the COP and assist with organizing COP2. In 1979, on the recommendation of the Secretariat, the Steering Committee was re-established by resolution as a permanent executive Standing Committee. From the outset, one of its functions was to provide 'guidance and advice' to the Secretariat on the implementation of the Convention, now phrased as 'general policy and general operational direction'.[72]

In effect, the Standing Committee oversees the operation of the Convention between meetings of the COP. This includes overseeing the Secretariat's budget and all financial activities; coordinating working groups set up by the COP; providing coordination and advice to other committees; drafting potential COP resolutions; and performing 'any other functions as may be entrusted to it' by the COP.[73] Over the years its terms of reference have evolved, and participation in its meetings has expanded to the point where it has become a 'mini-COP'. A Finance Subcommittee, established in response to a COP10 decision, meets immediately prior to Standing Committee meetings to consider budgetary matters.

The Standing Committee is composed of 14 regional party representatives, plus Switzerland (as the depositary government), the previous host country and the next host country (see Table 3.1).[74] Six geographic regions are represented by between one and four members, depending on the number of parties in the region. For each regional representative, there is an alternate member who acts in their absence. With the revision of the Committee's terms of reference at COP11, Africa, as the region with the most parties, gained a fourth

---

[72] CITES Resolutions Conf. 2.2, 'Establishment of the Standing Committee of the Conference of the Parties' (1979), and Conf. 11.1 Annex 1, 'Establishment of the Standing Committee of the Conference of the Parties' (2000). For a history of the Standing Committee, see Wijnstekers, p. 453.

[73] CITES Resolution Conf. 11.1, Annex 1, 'Establishment of the Standing Committee of the Conference of the Parties' (2000).

[74] The number of regional representatives was increased from 12 to 14 at COP11.

Table 3.1: Composition of the Standing Committee, 2000–2002

Members	Alternates	End of member's term
Regional representatives		
Africa: 49 parties,* 4 representatives		
Burkina Faso	Cameroon	2002
South Africa	Zambia	2004/5
Tanzania	Kenya	2004/5
Tunisia	Ghana	2004/5
Europe: 42 parties,* 3 representatives		
France	Portugal	2004/5
Italy	Czech Republic	2002
Norway	Turkey	2004/5
Central and South America and the Caribbean: 31 parties,* 3 representatives		
St Lucia	St Vincent &	
	the Grenadines	2004/5
Ecuador	Chile	2004/5
Panama	Nicaragua	2002
Asia: 28 parties,* 2 representatives		
China	Thailand	2004/5
Saudi Arabia	India	2002
North America: 3 parties,* 1 representative		
United States (Chair)	Canada	2004/5
Oceania: 5 parties,* 1 representative		
Australia	Vanuatu	2004/5
Depositary government		
Switzerland (permanent member)		
Previous host party		
None		
Next host party		
Chile		2004/5

* Number of parties in the region as of August 2002.

representative. The geographic representation differs from the UN caucus system, which consists of five regions.[75]

Regional representatives are elected for a term lasting from the close of the COP meeting at which they are elected to the close of the second COP meeting thereafter (about five years). The chair, currently Kenneth Stansell of the

---

[75] The regions in the UN caucus system for geographic representation consist of West European and Other (WEOG–EU, USA, Australia, New Zealand and Canada), eastern Europe (including Russia), Latin America and the Caribbean (GRULAC), Africa and Asia.

United States, and vice-chair are chosen from among the regional representatives, who are the only voting members, the depositary voting to break a tie. In practice, however, decision-making is by consensus.

Other parties may participate as observers in standing committee meetings, but they cannot vote. Other organizations may also be invited by the chair to participate as non-voting observers; but in practice until now this privilege has been extended only to IUCN, UNEP–WCMC and TRAFFIC. Historically, the Standing Committee has lacked transparency in its operation. With the exceptions noted, NGOs have been excluded, restricted to a formal presentation to Standing Committee members scheduled outside the meeting. Until recently preparatory documents and proceedings could be obtained only by visiting the Secretariat offices in Geneva. But times are changing (noticeably since the current Secretary General took office). Documents are now published on the website – preparatory documents since February 1999 and proceedings since November 2001 (though delays in posting proceedings are problematic). And, in a surprising move that will greatly increase transparency, at its forty-sixth meeting in March 2002 the Standing Committee agreed to open participation to other NGO observers in future meetings, subject to an invitation from the chairman.

Technical committees

The first committee of experts to be established under CITES was the Technical Expert Committee (TEC). Originally set up at COP2 in 1979 to harmonize permit requirements, its mandate was immediately expanded to 'deal with control over trade in Appendix II and III species'.[76] At COP3 in 1981 the Committee was confirmed as permanent and its mandate expanded to cover, *inter alia,* implementation and enforcement issues. Along the lines of the International Labour Organization's Committee of Experts on the Application of Conventions and Recommendations (discussed in chapter 11), the TEC was charged to undertake a periodic review of annual reports, as well as to:

> identify…problems with enforcement of the Convention and provide guidance to the Secretariat and the parties on measures that may be undertaken to remedy these problems

and

---

[76] CITES Resolutions Conf. 2.5, 'Harmonization of Permit Forms and Procedures' (1979), and Conf. 2.6, 'Trade in Appendix II and III Species' (1979).

review the implementation of the Convention by the parties and make recommendations for harmonization of documents and procedures.[77]

In effect, the TEC constituted the third leg of a 'three-legged institutional stool' responsible for CITES implementation, under guidance of the COP, together with the Secretariat and Standing Committee. At COP4 in 1983 the TEC was renamed the Technical Committee, and, in response to widespread concern about lack of controls on Appendix II trade, was charged with ensuring implementation of Article IV for significantly traded Appendix II species for which scientific information was lacking.[78]

Initially, the TEC worked well as a limited forum for exchange of enforcement information; but participation in its meetings gradually expanded to the point where it became a mini plenary session, a situation apparently considered unmanageable by the Secretariat.[79] In 1987 an extensive reorganization of CITES committee structure and functions was undertaken. The Technical Committee was abolished, leaving the Secretariat and Standing Committee as the primary institutions dealing with implementation and enforcement issues. Meanwhile, four functional committees (Animals, Plants, Identification Manuals and Nomenclature) were established to provide technical and scientific advice to the COP in their respective areas, in cooperation with external scientific bodies such as the IUCN/SSC specialist groups.[80] Reviews of significantly traded Appendix II listed animals and plants were allocated to the Animals and Plants Committees respectively.[81]

Following the review of committee structure and functions at COP11 in 2000, the Identification Manual Committee responsible for preparing manuals for the identification of species was abolished. Its functions were transferred to the Secretariat, assisted by the Animals and Plants Committees, which, together with the Nomenclature Committee, remain operational. The Nomenclature Committee consists of just two scientists, a zoologist and a botanist appointed by the COP, who serve in their individual capacity to ensure that correct, standardized

---

[77] CITES Resolutions Conf. 3.5, 'Technical Expert Committee' (1981), and Conf. 3.10, 'Review and Harmonization of Annual Reports' (1981).

[78] CITES Resolutions Conf. 4.4, 'Amendment to the Name of the Technical Expert Committee' (1983), and Conf. 4.7, 'Regulation of Trade in Appendix II Wildlife and Implementation of Article IV, paragraph 3, of the Convention' (1983).

[79] Peter Sand, personal communication (2000).

[80] Sand (1997), p. 21.

[81] CITES Resolution Conf. 6.1, 'Establishment of Committees' (1987). See Resolution Conf. 11.1, 'Establishment of Committees' (2000) for current terms of reference.

and up-to-date nomenclature is used for the Appendices. They also review proposals for amendment of the Appendices, at the request of the Secretariat to check that the names of species and taxa are correct.[82] In practice, open meetings of the Committee are held during the course of the Animals and Plants Committee meetings, chaired by the appropriate committee representative, to discuss nomenclature issues.

The Animals and Plants Committees are now the main technical committees operating under CITES. Their functions include:

- reviewing significantly traded Appendix II species and formulating recommendations for remedial measures (an important part of species-specific non-compliance response as discussed below);
- advising other CITES institutions on all matters relevant to international trade in CITES listed animals and plants, which may include proposals to amend the Appendices;
- cooperating with the Secretariat to assist Scientific Authorities;
- advising range states that request assistance on management techniques and procedures;
- developing regional directories of botanists and zoologists;
- assessing information on other species for which a review is indicated, e.g. if there is a change in volume of trade;
- undertaking a periodic review of CITES-listed species leading to the submission of amendment proposals through the depositary government;
- drafting resolutions for consideration by the COP;
- reporting to the COP, and 'if requested' to the Standing Committee; and
- performing any other functions entrusted by the COP or Standing Committee.[83]

Unlike the Standing Committee, the regions choose individuals to serve as members of the Animals and Plants Committees. North America and Oceania elect one person each, while the other four regions elect two. Each committee therefore numbers ten members in all. No expertise is specified in the terms of reference, but members tend to be from Scientific Authorities. They serve from the close of the COP meeting at which they are elected to the close of the second meeting thereafter (about five years). They have a duty, *inter alia*, to maintain communication with parties in their regions, as well as to request their opinions prior to Committee meetings and to inform them of the results.

---

[82] CITES Resolution 11.1, 'Establishment of Committees', Annex 3 (2000).
[83] CITES Resolution 11.1, 'Establishment of Committees', Annex 2 (2000).

As with the Standing Committee, observers may attend the meetings at the discretion of the chairs. Traditionally this discretion has been exercised more liberally than it has by the Standing Committee, with a wider range of NGOs and individuals being admitted to meetings. This has resulted in greater transparency, and has enabled the Animals and Plants Committees to benefit from a broad range of NGO expertise.

National measures

CITES is a non-self-executing treaty, meaning that national legislation is required to implement several of its provisions.[84] Parties are required to take measures to prohibit trade in specimens violating the Convention, and to provide for penalties for violations and for the confiscation of specimens.[85] Parties are also required to designate 'one or more Management Authorities competent to grant permits or certificates' and 'one or more Scientific Authorities'.[86] They are obliged to care properly for living specimens in transit, and 'may' designate ports of entry and exit for clearance of CITES-listed species.[87] Confiscated living specimens are to be returned to the state of export at the expense of that state, or located in an appropriate facility such as a rescue centre.[88] Parties must also maintain records of trade in species listed on all three Appendices, including names and addresses of exporters and importers, details of permits and certificates issued, the numbers, quantities and names of species traded and the states with which trade occurred.[89] Annual reports on trade and biennial reports on measures taken to enforce CITES are to be submitted to the Secretariat and made publicly available unless this is inconsistent with a party's laws.[90] (Reporting is discussed in the following chapter.)

The above are all binding provisions laid down in the Convention. Resolutions and decisions elaborate many more provisions which require national measures to be effective. To enable compliance with CITES provisions, it is

---

[84] Cyrille de Klemm, *Guidelines for Legislation to Implement CITES*, IUCN Environmental Policy and Law Paper No. 26 (IUCN–World Conservation Union, 1993).
[85] Articles II.4 and VIII.1.
[86] Article IX.1.
[87] Article VIII.3.
[88] Article VIII.4.
[89] Article VIII.6.
[90] Article VIII, paras. 6, 7 and 8.

considered that national legislation should encompass the following key elements:[91]

- list of species (not equivalent to domestic fauna and flora);
- general provisions: purpose, definitions, specimens regulated (including all parts and derivatives), scope and links to related legislation;
- institutions: explicitly designated, powers and relationship to each other described *vis-à-vis* implementation of CITES, and provision for a coordination mechanism;
- regulation of trade:
  - permits, certificates, marking;
  - licensing, registration;
  - border and internal trade control (limited entry points);
  - special provisions, e.g. control of shipments in transit, introduction from the sea, personal effects;
  - breeding operations and nurseries;
- compliance measures: offences to encompass:
  - prohibition of possession, transport and trade without proof of legal acquisition;
  - punishment of fraud and non-compliance;
  - confiscation of specimens illegally traded and/or possessed.

In designing national legislation to implement CITES, consideration also needs to be given to:

- the adequacy of penalty in relation to offence;
- increased penalty on subsequent offences;
- the imposition of fines as well as imprisonment, a ban on future trade activities and forfeiture;
- corporate liability;
- national and regional harmonization;
- fines directed towards environmental enforcement or management.[92]

---

[91] Marceil Yeater, 'Enforcement and the CITES National Legislation Project', and Caroline Raymakers, 'Biodiversity and Wildlife Trade: From Fauna and Flora in Trade to Sanctions' both in Monika Anton, Nicholas Dragffy, Stephanie Pendry and Tomme Rozanne Young (eds), *Proceedings of the International Expert Workshop on the Enforcement of Wildlife Trade Controls in the EU, 5-6 Nov 2001* (TRAFFIC/IUCN, 2002).

[92] Marceil Yeater, 'Enforcement and the CITES National Legislation Project'.

Article XIV.1 confirms the right of parties to adopt 'stricter domestic measures' than provided for in the Convention. Many do this; a notable example is the European Union (discussed in Chapter 5). While national measures are the cornerstone of CITES, they are often woefully inadequate in practice, as the programme to improve national legislation for implementing CITES has revealed (discussed in detail in Chapter 6). National institutions generally lack capacity and are chronically underfunded and under-supported. Many countries have failed to designate scientific authorities; coordination between national authorities, enforcement agencies and the prosecution service is often lacking; enforcement agencies lack specialized training, equipment and staff; penalties are often inadequate, and even if they are sufficient the judiciary often fails to apply them, not recognizing cases involving wildlife crime as matters of importance. These issues are discussed further in the context of non-compliance and weaknesses in the CITES compliance system.

Funding

CITES has no additional funding mechanism equivalent to those with which some modern MEAs have been equipped to secure compliance with their obligations. Instead, its operating costs are met by a special trust fund, with supplementary external funding sought on a project basis.

CITES Trust Fund

Initially, the Secretariat was funded by UNEP and administered by IUCN. But in 1978 the UNEP Governing Council decided to phase out its funding over a four-year 'sunset period', during which parties were expected to take over with direct contributions for Secretariat and Conference costs.[93] Article XI was formally amended in 1979 to confer financial powers on the COP (though the amendment did not enter into force until 1987), and a CITES Trust Fund was established under UNEP auspices with an agreed scale of contributions based on the UN scale. With the new arrangements, the regime became financially self-supporting and no longer dependent on UNEP fund grants.[94]

The Trust Fund covers, *inter alia*, Secretariat costs, support for committee meetings, technical support from UNEP–WCMC, and technical assistance to

---

[93] Sand (1997), p. 21; UNEP Governing Council decision 6/5/D, 24 May 1978.
[94] Sand (1997), p. 21; CITES Resolution Conf. 2.1 (1979). Amendment adopted by a plenipotentiary meeting in Bonn, 22 June 1979, entry into force 13 April 1987 for those accepting the amendment.

parties. For the triennium 1997–9 the average annual budget was US$4.7 million. (The actual amount spent, however, was US$4.2 million, part of the shortfall in spending being accounted for by delayed recruitment of new personnel.[95]) The average annual budget for the period 2001–2005 is US$5.5 million.[96] Non-payment of contributions by parties is a persistent problem, to the extent that the Secretariat warned the Standing Committee in March 2002 that, if 50% of contributions were not received by the end of May, the 2002 work programme would have to be curtailed. Recently non-payment has begun to be addressed within the context of a discussion of possible measures for non-compliance, though some parties view payments to the trust fund as voluntary and are reluctant to agree the use of sanctions to induce payment (discussed further in Chapter 6).

Parties are reluctant to approve any increase in their contributions. At the Standing Committee's March 2002 meeting (SC46), they objected to increases in either the budget or their contributions when faced with the need for a 10% increase to maintain the current level of activities (a 'no-change option'). They asked the Secretariat to prepare a budget for COP12 in November 2002 reflecting a zero growth in parties' contributions, indicating which activities could not be executed.[97] While the budget stands still, the Convention is growing, with nine new parties since COP11. High expectations are placed on an over-burdened Secretariat. The Legislation and Compliance Unit, for example, numbers just three professional staff, only one of which is an experienced enforcement officer. Plans to hire an officer with customs experience were shelved for budgetary reasons. Yet the workload ascribed to the Secretariat on enforcement and compliance by the COP and Standing Committee could fully occupy a sizeable team of professionals. While parties profess to support measures to improve implementation, enforcement and compliance, it is clear that they are not prepared to pay for it with increased contributions to the trust fund.

External funding

External funding for specific CITES-related projects is received mostly in the form of bilateral aid. This dates back to COP2, when the Secretariat was requested

---

[95] CITES Doc. 11.10.1 (Rev.1), 'Financial Report for 1997, 1998 and 1999', prepared by the Secretariat for COP11 (Apr 2000).

[96] CITES Resolution Conf. 11.2, 'Financing and Budgeting of the Secretariat and of Meetings of the Conference of the Parties' (2000). The Secretariat may draw additional funds from the CITES Trust Fund balance.

[97] SC46: Summary Report (Mar 2002), p. 6.

to draw up proposals for specific programmes or projects which would 'assist in the effective implementation of the Convention' for submission to funding institutions, after consultation with the Standing Committee.[98] In addition to bilateral donations from parties, there have been contributions over the years from NGOs, including wildlife trade and industry groups. This has led to controversy more than once. Following a debate about this at COP7 in 1989, monitoring of the Secretariat's budget process was strengthened by enhancing the oversight powers of the Standing Committee.[99] In April 1991 the Committee agreed guidelines for developing proposals and seeking funds external to the Secretariat's core budget, and directed the Secretariat to maintain a list of acceptable non-governmental donors, to be reviewed by the Standing Committee. The approved list excludes:

- sources that have been involved in illegal trade of CITES-listed species or other relevant wildlife conservation infractions, whether convicted or not;
- individual companies directly involved in legal commercial CITES trade, which should channel funds through trade associations or conservation organizations;
- any organization that 'deliberately brought the Convention into public disrepute'.[100]

An analysis of external funding from 1994 to 2002 reveals a change in the nature of donors, with less money being accepted from trade and industry organizations over 1997–9 than in the previous triennium. A more recent change in priorities for funding from species-specific studies to implementation, enforcement and capacity-building is also evident. The exception is the species-specific system being developed to Monitor Illegal Killing of Elephants (MIKE), which is claiming a rapidly increasing proportion of funds. (See the following chapter on the compliance information system for a discussion of MIKE.)

For the triennium 1994–6, more than US$4 million was received in external funding from 33 donors. Major donors included the United States, the European Union (through the European Commission), several EU countries, Japan, Switzerland and a number of NGOs. Among the NGO donors were several wildlife trade/industry organizations, which contributed over

---

[98] CITES Resolution Conf. 2.3, 'External Funding of Special Programmes' (1979).
[99] David S. Favre, 'Trade in Endangered Species', *Yearbook of International Environmental Law*, 1 (1990), p. 193: 195.
[100] Wijnstekers, p. 332.

US$160,000. Belgium was the largest donor, through a fund established for elephant conservation in Tanzania, with money from an auction of 9.6 tonnes of African elephant ivory confiscated in 1986; at US$1.4 million, this amounted to a third of the total funds received over the triennium. Japan was the second largest donor, followed by France, the United States and the United Kingdom.[101]

During the triennium 1997–9, US$1.6 million was received in external funding, down by 60% compared with the previous triennium. The major donor was Japan, followed by the United Kingdom, China and the United States. During this period the only donation from wildlife trade/industry organizations was US$1,500 from the International Wood Products Association, down by 99% compared with funds received from trade and industry in the previous triennium. An analysis of the types of project that were ongoing, completed or started between 1997 and 1999, and their costs, is contained in Table 3.2. (The analysis excludes the Belgian-funded elephant conservation project in Tanzania, which was started in the previous triennium and suspended for delays and non-justification of expenses.)

The largest proportion of external funding between 1997 and 1999 was allocated to meetings (48%), most of which went towards funding COP10, including sponsoring delegates.[102] Species-related studies of trade and status accounted for 29% (US$503,913), while capacity-building through training seminars amounted to 7% (US$119,050) of the spending from external funds. This compared with 5% (US$90,000) spent on developing MIKE. The total allocated to implementation and enforcement-related activities was US$256,300 (15% of total expenditure), approximately half the expenditure on species-related studies.[103]

Table 3.3 contains an analysis of externally funded projects to be implemented in 2001 and 2002, sent out by the Secretariat to potential donor organizations. The largest proportion of estimated expenditure was allocated to MIKE, which at more than US$4 million represents 55% of the total projected expenditure of US$7.2 million. Species-specific projects accounted for 6% of projected expenditure (US$431,607), down by 14% compared with the amount spent on similar projects in 1997–9. Implementation and enforcement-

---

[101] See CITES Doc. 10.14, 'External Funding', prepared by the Secretariat for COP10 (Jun 1997).
[102] CITES Doc. 11 10.4, 'External Funding', prepared by the Secretariat for COP11 (Apr 2000).
[103] Including three training seminars, the *Identification Manual* and the information management project.

Table 3.2: Analysis of externally funded CITES projects on-going, completed or started, 1997–1999[a]

Project type	Number	Costs (US$)	% total costs
Meetings			
COP10	1	773,838	44.1
SIDS [b]	1	30,000	1.7
Tibetan antelope	1	41,000	2.3
Sub-total	3	844,838	48.2
Species-related studies of trade/status			
For sustainable use/conservation	9	421,837	24.0
For future listing	1	82,076	4.7
Sub-total	10	503,913	28.7
Training seminars			
CITES	1	46,500	2.7
Plants	1	17,550	1.0
Enforcement	1	55,000	3.1
Sub-total	3	119,050	6.8
Monitoring			
MIKE [c]	3	90,000	5.1
Identification manual	3	87,250	5.0
IUCN review of listing proposals	2	58,333	3.3
Information management	1	50,000	2.9
Totals	25	1,753,384	100

[a] Information has been taken from CITES Doc. 11.10.4, 'External Funding' (2000). Note this analysis excludes a project on elephant conservation funded by Belgium prior to 1997.
[b] SIDS = Small Island Developing States.
[c] MIKE is a programme for Monitoring the Illegal Killing of Elephants.

related activities accounted for 17% of projected expenditure (US$1.2 million),[104] *nearly five times the amount spent in 1997–9, and three times the projected expenditure on species-specific projects in 2001 and 2002.* Capacity-building

---

[104] Including 13+ training seminars and workshops, three specific enforcement activities and the *Implementation Manual*. (N.B.: this is a minimum figure since it excludes two projects whose budget was unspecified.)

Table 3.3: Analysis of externally funded CITES projects to be implemented, 2001–2002[a]

Project type	Number	Estimated budget (US$)	% total budget
Meetings			
COP12	1	1,000,000	13.75
Hawksbill turtle	2	323,550	4.45
Mahogany	1	90,000	1.24
Freshwater turtles & tortoises	1	90,000	1.24
Syngnathidae (sea horses)	1	90,000	1.24
Sub-total	6	1,593,550	21.92
Species projects			
Status surveys	7	357,000	4.91
Management plan	1	24,607	0.34
Synthesis of studies	1	50,000	0.69
Sub-total	9	431,607	5.94
Training seminars and workshops			
CITES	1	44,000	0.61
National legislation	9	687,000	9.45
Sturgeon anti-poaching	1	60,000	0.83
Scientific authorities	[unspecified]	300,000	4.13
Tiger conservation	1	[unspecified]	
Sub-total	13+	1,091,000+	15.02
Enforcement activities			
TETF[b]	1	60,000	0.83
Coral trade	1	[unspecified]	
Tibetan antelope mission	1	15,000	0.21
Sub-total	3	75,000+	1.03
Monitoring			
MIKE	4	4,030,440	55.43
Implementation manual	1	50,000	0.69
Totals	36	7,271,597	100

[a] Information has been taken from a CITES circular to potential funding organizations, 19 April 2001.
[b] Tiger Enforcement Task Force.

through training seminars and workshops accounted for 15% (US$1.1 million),[105] nine times the amount spent in 1997–9. While these comparisons are qualified by the fact that some of the proposed 2001–2002 projects may not have found donors, conclusions can still be drawn concerning an apparent change in priorities compared with the period 1997–9. It is clear that implementation, enforcement and capacity-building are assuming more importance, while MIKE has now become the largest externally funded project by far.

Strategic Vision through 2005

Following COP9, the Standing Committee commissioned a consultancy organization, Environmental Resources Management (ERM), to study ways to improve the effectiveness of CITES.[106] ERM's report contained 25 recommendations covering five areas: fundamental policy; scientific issues; administrative and implementation issues; institutional issues; and relations with other organizations. Eight recommendations were then selected as priorities for action (though the rationale for their choice is somewhat obscure[107]), including the preparation of a strategic plan for the Convention.

Following the agreement at COP10 of an action plan to implement some of ERM's recommendations, the Standing Committee established a Strategic Plan Working Group. The Group produced the 'Strategic Vision through 2005', consisting of both a Strategic Plan and an Action Plan for its implementation, which was approved at COP11. The purpose of the Strategic Vision is stated as being 'to ensure that no species of wild fauna or flora becomes or remains subject to unsustainable exploitation because of international trade'.[108] Seven goals are identified by the Strategic Plan:

1 to enhance the ability of each party to implement the Convention;
2 to strengthen the scientific basis of the decision-making process;

---

[105] This is a minimum figure since it excludes one project whose budget was unspecified.
[106] Environmental Resources Management (ERM), *Study on How to Improve the Effectiveness of the Convention on International Trade in Endangered Species of Wild Fauna and Flora (CITES),* attached to CITES Doc. SC.37.6 (ERM/CITES Standing Committee, Sep 1996) (hereinafter 'ERM report').
[107] For example, interpretative resolutions on sustainable use and stricter domestic measures are considered greater priorities than financial and institutional support for training and equipping personnel in developing countries and countries with economies in transition. See ERM report, Table A and Box A, for the 25 recommendations and eight priority recommendations.
[108] CITES Decision 11.1 and Annex 1, 'Strategic Vision through 2005' (2000).

3 to contribute to the reduction and ultimate elimination of illegal trade in wild fauna and flora;
4 to promote greater understanding of the Convention;
5 to increase cooperation and conclude strategic alliances with international stakeholders;
6 to progress towards global membership;
7 to provide the Convention with an improved and secure financial and administrative basis.

Each goal is expanded into several objectives, totalling 38 in all. The objectives are expanded further into 139 action points comprising the Action Plan. Generally pragmatic, if implemented these action points could make a contribution towards strengthening aspects of the CITES compliance system, for example through improving cooperation to combat illegal trade and coordination between national CITES authorities, and accessing more funds. But the success of the Action Plan will depend on the political will of parties, and on the extent to which they are prepared to match the rhetoric with adequate funding and direct it towards action that genuinely enhances the implementation and enforcement of CITES provisions. (See section on 'Funding mechanism' in Chapter 10.)

4 Information system

A compliance system is only as good as its information base. The collection, analysis and dissemination of information on violations and compliance are therefore essential. CITES was one of the first MEAs to provide for an information system.[1] The regime relies largely on self-reporting by parties, but also on information provided by NGOs and other inter-governmental organizations such as Interpol and the World Customs Organization (WCO, formerly Customs Cooperation Council, CCC). In addition, the Secretariat may be asked to visit parties on an ad hoc basis to verify specific information, such as the recent verification of ivory trade controls in parties wishing to trade in raw ivory, or in relation to cases of serious non-compliance such as Italy in the early 1990s or more recently the United Arab Emirates (see Chapter 5). The collection, review and dissemination of information, the substance of this chapter, are responsibilities of the Secretariat. The response to non-reporting, a long-standing problem which seriously undermines implementation of CITES, is dealt with in Chapter 6, and liaison with Interpol and WCO is covered in Chapter 9.

National reporting

On the basis of records that they are obliged to keep on importers, exporters and trade in all CITES-listed species, parties are required to prepare annual reports and transmit them to the Secretariat.[2] These annual reports are to contain information on permits and certificates granted as well as a list of the states with which trade occurred and details of traded specimens listed in the Appendices, including the names of species, types of specimens and numbers or quantities.[3] In addition, parties are required to provide biennial reports containing information on 'legislative, regulatory and administrative measures taken to enforce the provisions of the present Convention'.[4]

---

[1] Farhana Yamin and Annabella L. Gualdoni, 'A Case Study of a Regional Approach to Compliance with CITES in Southern Africa', in James Cameron, Jacob Werksman and Peter Roderick (eds), *Improving Compliance with International Environmental Law* (Earthscan, 1996), pp. 187–218: 188.

[2] Articles VIII.6 and 7; Wijnstekers, p. 270 (see ch. 3, n. 2).

[3] Articles VIII.6(b) and 7(a).

[4] Article VIII.7(b).

Annual reports have two primary purposes:

1 to provide the basis for monitoring trade in listed species, including reviews of significant trade in Appendix II species by the Animals and Plants Committees;
2 to provide information on implementation of the Convention, including detection of illegal trade, by highlighting discrepancies between reported imports and exports and assessment of compliance with quotas. [5]

The requirements for annual reporting have been greatly elaborated over the years through a series of resolutions.[6] Guidelines have also been provided since 1982 for their preparation and submission.[7] The deadline for submission of annual reports is 31 October of the year following that in which the trade took place. The Secretariat, however, may approve a valid request for an extension, provided the party submits a written request containing adequate justification before the 31 October deadline.[8] Extensions were granted to ten parties between 1995 and 1998.[9]

The Secretariat's functions include 'studying' parties' reports; requesting any further information it deems necessary to ensure implementation of the Convention; and preparing annual reports on, *inter alia,* implementation.[10] Some of these functions are contracted out. Under an annual consultancy contract, data from annual reports are maintained in a computerized database by the World Conservation Monitoring Centre (UNEP–WCMC) based in Cambridge, UK. Formerly a NGO, WCMC now falls under UNEP as part of its

---

[5] John Caldwell and Lorraine Collins, 'A Report on Annual Reports Submitted by the Parties to CITES', CITES Doc. 10.26 Annex, prepared for COP10 (Jun 1997) (hereinafter 'WCMC report (1997)'). Updated by Jonathan Harwood, 'A Report on Annual Reports Submitted by the Parties to CITES', CITES Doc.11.19 Annex 2, prepared for COP11 (Apr 2000) (hereinafter 'WCMC report (2000)').

[6] All recommendations on annual reporting are now consolidated in CITES Resolution Conf. 11.17, 'Annual Reports and Monitoring of Trade' (2000); see also Wijnstekers, p. 271.

[7] Guidelines on reporting were first prepared by the Secretariat in 1982 in compliance with CITES Resolution Conf. 3.10 (1981). They have since been revised and updated, the most recent revision taking place at SC45 in June 2001. See Wijnstekers, p. 275, for Guidelines; and CITES SC45 Doc. 13.2 'Guidelines for the Preparation of Annual reports', prepared by the Secretariat for SC45 (Jun 2001), and Summary Record of SC45, p. 12, for amendments.

[8] CITES Resolution Conf. 11.17, 'Annual Reports and Monitoring of Trade' (2000).

[9] WCMC report (2000).

[10] Article XII.

environmental monitoring and assessment system. The database, which goes back to 1975 and to which half a million trade records are added every year, allows import and export records to be cross-matched. It also enables export records to be compared with export quotas. Where the records do not match, or parties report possible illegal trade, UNEP–WCMC informs the Secretariat.[11]

In 1981 the mandate of the TEC was expanded to include 'undertaking a periodic review of annual reports'.[12] Since the Committee's abolition, this expert review has been assumed by the Secretariat, in association with UNEP–WCMC.

The importance of accurate, complete and timely reporting cannot be overstressed. The COP has recognized 'the importance of the annual reports as the only means of monitoring the implementation of the Convention and the level of international trade in specimens of species included in the appendices'.[13] Trade data from annual reports comprise an essential tool in assessing the volume of world trade in CITES-listed species and their individual conservation status. It is the basis for selecting significantly traded species for review (culminating in species-specific responses to non-compliance), and is used increasingly to single out countries with significant trade for action in cases of non-compliance, for example under the national legislation project. The database is therefore a fundamentally important part of the CITES compliance system. Yet reporting information for the database has proved to be a persistent problem.[14] Many parties have not taken the issue seriously enough, variously failing to submit reports, or submitting them late, or failing to comply with the guidelines on reporting, rendering data 'more or less useless', or submitting incomplete or inaccurate data.[15]

At COP10, WCMC reported that, while quality of reporting, particularly for animals (except invertebrates), had improved, non-reporting and lateness of submissions still presented serious problems.[16] Comprehensive CITES data

---

[11] Lanchbery, p. 71 (see ch. 1, n. 2), quoting John Caldwell, WCMC, in a personal communication.

[12] CITES Resolution Conf. 3.10, 'Review and Harmonization of Annual Reports' (1981).

[13] CITES Resolution Conf. 11.1, 'Annual Reports and Monitoring of Trade' (2000).

[14] The many resolutions on reporting testify to this. See CITES Resolutions Conf. 2.16 on 'Periodic Reports' (1979), Conf. 3.10 on 'Review and Harmonization of Annual Reports' (1981), Conf. 5.4 on 'Periodic Reports' (1985), and Conf. 8.7 on 'Submission of Annual Reports' (1992); see also Resolution Conf. 11.17 'Annual Reports and Monitoring of Trade' (2000).

[15] CITES Doc. 8.17 (Rev.), 'Report on National Reports Under Article VIII, Paragraph 7, of the Convention', prepared by the Secretariat for COP8 (Mar 1992).

[16] WCMC report (1997).

Figure 4.1: Submission of annual reports to CITES, 1975–1998

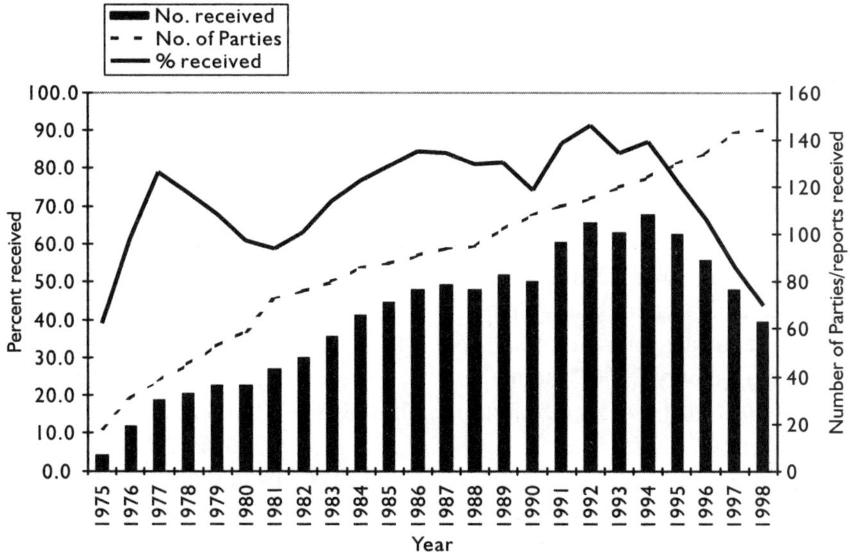

Source: 'A Report on Annual Reports Submitted by the Parties to CITES', CITES Doc. 11.19, Annex 2, prepared by Jonathan Harwood, UNEP-WCMC, for COP11, April 2000.

are normally three years out of date.[17] In February 1999 the Secretariat reported to the Standing Committee a 'continued deterioration in the timely submission of reports'. Only 30% of the annual reports for 1997 had been received by the deadline.[18] The situation had not improved significantly by COP11 in 2000. UNEP–WCMC's analysis showed a trend towards a reduced number of parties reporting (see Figure 4.1). Since 1995 there had been a steady decline, while at the same time the number of parties had increased. They concluded that, while there is a core of parties that report regularly and with improved timeliness, outside this core the frequency of reporting is declining, *making accurate and confident analysis of world trade in CITES-listed*

---

[17] Ibid.

[18] CITES Doc. SC.41.16, 'Late Submission of Annual Reports', prepared for SC41 (Feb 1999). The proportion of parties submitting reports on time averaged 42% until 1993, when it increased to 60% (probably because of the timing of COP9), declining to under 50% for 1994 and 1995. See WCMC report (1997).

species increasingly difficult.[19] Action taken at COP11 has since spurred several parties into producing their backlogged reports (this is discussed in more detail below in relation to non-compliance response); but it is questionable whether the action will have any consistent long-term effect, given that the Standing Committee has failed to implement the COP's directive to apply trade sanctions to non-compliers.

Non-compliance with reporting guidelines is also a persistent problem. Parties are requested to record the *actual trade* that took place (i.e. the quantity of specimens exported or imported). Reporting on the basis of permits issued, while allowed under the terms of the Convention, can lead to overestimates of trade volume, since permits are frequently issued for quantities in excess of those actually traded. While there has been an improvement in the number of parties reporting on actual trade (but only from 14 to 35 between February 1997 and January 2000), the majority of parties still fail to communicate the relevant information to the Secretariat. They also fail to report all the information required.[20]

Failure to report, as well as inaccurate and incomplete reporting, was highlighted by the Secretariat as one of 'two major areas of concern' at COP11, along with apparent non-compliance with export quotas.[21] The lack of timely and accurate reporting seriously undermines the quality of reviews of significant trade in Appendix II species (a major CITES programme, discussed in greater detail in Chapter 7), and means that 'a large part of the usefulness' of comparative tabulation of exports and imports for detecting illegal trade is lost.[22] It also limits the scope for monitoring compliance with quotas at an international level, which has become more important with the increasing use of quotas as a trade control tool. UNEP–WCMC compared quotas for 1997 with quantities reported as traded, and found 'some significant examples where trade has apparently been conducted in excess of established quotas'.[23] As already noted in Chapter 3, in 1999 (the most recent year for which complete data are available), out of 67 quotas potentially exceeded, about half of the overages were serious.[24]

---

[19] WCMC report (2000).

[20] Ibid.

[21] Ibid.

[22] CITES Doc. 8.17 (Rev.), 'Report on National Reports Under Article VIII, Paragraph 7, of the Convention', prepared by the Secretariat for COP8 (Mar 1992).

[23] WCMC report (2000).

[24] CITES COP12 Doc. 50.2, 'Implementation and Monitoring of Nationally Established Export Quotas for Species Listed on Appendix II of the Convention', prepared by the USA for COP12 (Nov 2002).

The biennial reporting requirement has been largely unimplemented by parties and little time has been devoted to following it up.[25] The ERM study found that few parties were even aware of the requirement.[26] But difficulties in obtaining current information on national legislation for the national legislation project (detailed in Chapter 6) have drawn attention to the lack of biennial reporting, leading to notifications and a COP decision calling on parties to submit reports.[27] The Secretariat reported 'some improvement' in biennial reporting to COP10 in 1997, but stated that most parties still did not comply with the requirement.[28]

While CITES reporting has been noted as being better than that of other MEAs,[29] it compares unfavourably with the Ramsar Convention on wetlands and the Montreal Protocol (discussed in Chapter 11). Information from the trade database underpins many crucial decisions on implementation. As one commentator succinctly put it, 'If garbage is what state parties feed into the reporting system, then garbage is what will come out.'[30]

UNEP is currently engaged in an attempt to harmonize national reporting under five global biodiversity conventions: the conventions on biological diversity (CBD), migratory species (CMS), CITES, wetlands (Ramsar) and world heritage. A pilot project involving seven countries – Belgium, Ghana, Hungary, Indonesia, Panama, Seychelles and the UK – is being undertaken by UNEP–WCMC and UNEP's Division of Environmental Conventions, the findings of which are to be reported to the World Summit on Sustainable Development (WSSD) in Johannesburg in August/September 2002. In the runup to the Summit, the 'clustering' of MEAs to work more closely together is a live topic of discussion, including in inter-ministerial discussions on environmen-

---

[25] Some annual reports contain part of the information required in biennial reports. CITES Doc. 7.19, 'Report on National Reports under Article VIII, Paragraph 7, of the Convention', prepared by the Secretariat for COP7 (Oct 1989); CITES Doc. 9.24 (Rev.), 'National Laws for Implementation of the Convention', prepared by the Secretariat for COP9 (Nov 1994).

[26] ERM report (see ch. 3, n. 106), p. 54.

[27] CITES Decision 11.38 (ex-9.20), 'Regarding Biennial Reports' (2000).

[28] CITES Doc. 10.31, 'National Laws for Implementation of the Convention', prepared by the Secretariat for COP10 (Jun 1997).

[29] Sand (1997) (see ch. 1, n. 3), referring to US General Accounting Office, *International Environment: International Agreements are not well Monitored,* GAO/RCED-92-43 (Washington: GAO, 1992), 23–8.

[30] Thilo Marauhn, 'Towards a Procedural Law of Compliance Control in International Environmental Relations', *Heidelberg Journal of International Law*, 56 (1996), pp. 696–731: 707.

tal governance and reform of environmental institutions convened by UNEP. Yet, while the motive of streamlining and improving the efficiency, and therefore cost effectiveness, of operating the five conventions is sound, UNEP should proceed with caution. Information based on national reporting is the backbone of compliance systems. In an overview of reporting and review institutions, Raustiala has warned:

> the importance of establishing well-functioning, reliable, and comprehensive data gathering systems cannot be over-stated...While attempts to streamline or merge MEA reporting requirements have some potential, MEA commitments show a clear trend toward greater complexity over time. As commitments grow more detailed, efforts to merge reporting requirements are likely to be undermined. Such merging or streamlining efforts may in turn undermine the ability of national reports to provide necessary information for the specific MEAs involved.[31]

Information from NGOs

Non-governmental organizations are an important source of information on compliance. The information enters the system directly through reports from NGOs to the Secretariat, and indirectly in reports from states to the Secretariat that are based on NGO information.[32] Since its founding in 1976, TRAFFIC has collected information on illegal wildlife trade and transmitted it to the Secretariat and national authorities. TRAFFIC informs the Secretariat directly of non-compliance, but also works through its regional offices with national CITES authorities. Some of those authorities report infractions to the Secretariat that were originally reported to them by TRAFFIC.[33] According to Sand, cooperation with the TRAFFIC network has given CITES one of the best operational information sources of any MEA.[34] Information on compliance is also gleaned from literature reviews of significant trade in selected Appendix II listed species, generally conducted by IUCN, TRAFFIC and UNEP–WCMC (see Chapter 7 on the Significant Trade Review).

Other NGOs, such as members of SSN, provide information on an ad hoc basis and through reports of their research, often released and distributed in conjunc-

---

[31] Kal Raustiala, *Reporting and Review Institutions in 10 Multilateral Environmental Agreements* (UNEP, 2001).

[32] Lanchbery, p. 71.

[33] Ibid.

[34] Sand (1997), p. 25.

tion with COP and permanent committee meetings. Their relationship with the Secretariat and some national authorities, however, tends to be more distant and in some cases more guarded than that of TRAFFIC. The Secretariat's chequered history (described in chapter 10 on weaknesses in the CITES compliance system) has made some NGOs wary of providing information directly, a wariness that can also be detected on the side of the Secretariat. As well as inhibiting information-sharing, this wariness ultimately works against the Convention's objectives. While the current Secretariat is more transparent in its dealings than some of its predecessors, and relations with NGOs other than TRAFFIC and IUCN are better than in the past, there is still scope for improvement.

Information on infractions, illegal trade and wildlife crime

The Secretariat receives information on infractions, illegal trade and wildlife crime from parties, Interpol, the WCO and NGOs. A COP resolution dating back to 1994 recommends that parties 'provide to the Secretariat detailed information on significant cases of illegal trade, and…inform the Secretariat, when possible, about convicted illegal traders and persistent offenders'.[35] Since 1997, parties have been urged to supply information on infractions in the format of the Ecomessage.[36] Developed by Interpol as a means of communication for incidents of environmental crime between its National Central Bureaux or NCB (contact points in each country) and the General Secretariat in Lyons, the Ecomessage aims to provide a uniform format for information provision (see Annex 2).

Many parties fail to provide information on illegal trade and wildlife crime. Similarly, many fail to respond to requests for information on alleged infractions made by the Secretariat in accordance with Article XIII and Resolution Conf. 11.3. In its report to COP10 in 1997, the Secretariat expressed concern that this haphazard reporting undermines its coordination function in relation to current infractions cases, prevents accurate analysis of information, and can even lead to cases being lost.[37]

---

[35] CITES Resolution Conf. 9.8 (Rev) (1997), now incorporated into Resolution Conf. 11.3, 'Compliance and Enforcement' (2000). Note that all former resolutions on compliance and enforcement – Conf. 3.9 (Rev) (1994), Conf. 6.3 (1987), Conf. 6.4 (1987), Conf. 7.5 (1989) and Conf. 9.8 (Rev) (1997) – have been consolidated into Resolution Conf. 11.3.

[36] Notification to the Parties No. 966 'ICPO-Interpol, the ECOMESSAGE' (9 Mar 1997).

[37] CITES Doc. 10.28, 'Review of Alleged Infractions and Other Problems of Implementation of the Convention', prepared by the Secretariat for COP10 (Jun 1997) (hereinafter 'COP10 Infractions Report'); COP11 Infractions Report (see ch. 1, n. 13).

The Secretariat disseminates information on infractions and illegal trade to Management Authorities and other enforcement agencies either designated by Management Authorities or with which it has a formal agreement. Information is also shared with Interpol and the WCO when necessary. (Cooperation between the three organizations is discussed in Chapter 9.) Secretariat policy on information dissemination has changed in recent years. Rather than producing detailed and freely available reports on alleged infractions for the COP, in the interests of efficiency and confidentiality effort is now concentrated on a computerized intelligence and information system known as TIGERS (Trade Infraction and Global Enforcement Recording System) and ad hoc CITES Alerts to which access is restricted to parties and cooperating enforcement agencies.

Reports on alleged infractions

Since 1987, the Secretariat has compiled a separate Report on Alleged Infractions for the COP, which until COP11 was lengthy and detailed. (Before 1987, informal reports were attached as annexes to the Secretariat's implementation report.) Prior to COP11, these reports had come 'to be accepted as a reliable and impartial instrument reinforcing national implementation and accountability'.[38]

Until COP11, the objectives of infractions reports were stated as:

1   to provide parties with a record of significant violations;
2   to identify other enforcement problems affecting compliance;
3   to stimulate discussion and seek mechanisms to reduce or eliminate problems identified.[39]

The Secretariat, in response to discomfort on the part of some parties at having their violations placed on record, stressed that their aim was to assist parties in preventing repetition of infractions, *not* to criticize them.[40]

Two types of infraction were covered by the reports:

1   illegal trade, commonly committed by individuals, in general with criminal intent and often without documents, or sometimes with false documents;

---

[38]   Sand (1997), p. 25.
[39]   CITES Doc. 8.19 (Rev.), 'Review of Alleged Infractions and Other Problems of Enforcement of the Convention', prepared by the Secretariat for COP8 (Mar 1992) (hereinafter 'COP8 Infractions Report').
[40]   CITES Com. II 7.11, Committee II report, COP7 (Oct 1989).

2 non-compliance by parties with the provisions of the Convention, either directly or as interpreted by resolutions.[41]

Past reports have revealed widespread and numerous violations by parties and individuals, including:

- issue and acceptance of invalid documents;
- false declaration of Appendix I specimens as bred in captivity;
- use of re-export procedures to 'launder' specimens of illegal origin;
- issue of export permits for more specimens than the established national quota;
- smuggling, including of live specimens, by passengers and crew members of ships and aircraft, and by mail;
- abuse of diplomatic privilege;
- acceptance of documents issued by non-competent authorities in non-party states;
- failure to implement recommendations on transport of live specimens;
- use of transit procedures to commit fraud;
- abuse of exemptions permitted to circuses.[42]

At COP10, following discussion on the format of the infractions report, it was decided that a distinction should be made between alleged infractions of the provisions of the Convention and non-compliance with the provisions laid down in COP resolutions (Decision 10.122). In the event, the Secretariat did not implement this decision. Instead, it altered the whole format of the infractions report, cutting out detail on alleged infractions and drastically reducing the content. For COP11, it was decided to 'report only work by parties that illustrates innovative or particularly significant enforcement action'. The objective of the report was redefined as:

- to provide an 'overview of illicit trade and to identify significant problems relating to the issuance and acceptance of CITES documents'.

In practice, this resulted in six pages of mostly general information, compared with almost 100 pages of detailed infractions in previous years. Only three cases of infractions were mentioned in anything more than general

---

[41] COP10 Infractions Report.
[42] Ibid.

terms.[43] The reasons for this change are discussed below in the section on 'Loss of public access to information'.

The Secretariat declared Decision 10.122 'redundant', given the new format it had adopted for the COP11 infractions report. There is no record of the Secretariat obtaining Standing Committee approval for the change of format, and the chairman at the time cannot recall the subject being raised. Whether formal approval would be needed is a moot point, but, given the significance of the change, it would certainly have been desirable.

TIGERS

In 2000 the Secretariat announced the development of a new computerized system to process reports of wildlife crime and illicit trade, the Trade Infraction and Global Enforcement Recording System (TIGERS).[44] The database is managed by the Secretariat in accordance with standard law enforcement agency protocols. Information is entered from a variety of sources, including Interpol and the WCO, but special emphasis is placed on reports from CITES Management Authorities and parties' enforcement agencies. Each information report in the database has credibility and confidentiality ratings. Management Authorities and their designated enforcement agencies may request information searches, priority being given to parties that routinely contribute data to TIGERS. A range of outputs can be supplied to parties, including:

- the involvement of countries in wildlife crime reports;
- the frequency of specific species occurring in reports;
- the frequency of species categories occurring in reports;
- a search for names of individuals/companies that have been involved in wildlife crime or illicit trade;
- the frequency of particular crime types in reports.

TIGERS is designed to complement the Ecomessage reporting format, which if used facilitates data input.

CITES Alerts

Since September 2000, the Secretariat has supplemented TIGERS with CITES Alerts on specific issues of concern. These are not published on the CITES

---

[43] COP11 Infractions Report.
[44] Information on TIGERS is taken from the COP11 Infractions Report.

website but are sent solely to Management Authorities, Interpol, the WCO and enforcement agencies with which the Secretariat has formal agreements for information exchange.[45] As of June 2002, nine have been issued on an ad hoc basis:

1 Intelligence and Information Relating to Infractions of the Convention and Inputs to the TIGERS Database;
2 Illicit Trade in Caviar;
3 Invalid CITES Documents Issued by Rebel Forces in the Democratic Republic of the Congo;
4 Smuggling of Birds from China;
5 Illegal Fishing of and Trade in *Strombus gigas* (queen conch);
6 Illegal Trade in Bushmeat;
7 Illegal Trade in Caviar and the United Arab Emirates;
8 Fraudulent Use of Genuine Import Permits;
9 Illicit Trade in Plants.[46]

Loss of public access to information

The Secretariat's policy change on information dissemination (to favouring TIGERS and CITES Alerts over infractions reports) is understandable to an extent, given its shortage of human and financial resources and the need for efficiency and confidentiality in intelligence-gathering, analysis and distribution. But it has resulted in a concurrent loss of accountability and access to information. Past infractions reports were invaluable sources of information for the compilation of the country cases cited in this book (see Chapter 5). Although parties disliked being shown up by the reports, in effect they provided the only regularly updated publicly available record of national implementation and enforcement of CITES and acted as an incentive to parties to avoid a repeat of the problems identified.

As justification for changing the infractions report, the Secretariat cited:[47]

1 a report compiled under the auspices of the Interpol Wildlife Crime Subgroup noting that a substantial number of cases detailed in the infractions report are not relevant to an analysis of illegal trade or wildlife crime because they concern technical problems of permits and certificates;[48]

---

45 Notification to the Parties No. 2000/058, 'Alerts' (20 Sep 2000).
46 John Sellar, personal communication (Jun 2002).
47 COP11 Infractions Report.
48 Notification No. 1999/13, concerning 'Review of Alleged Infractions' (29 Jan 1999).

2   comments made by parties at COP10 expressing dissatisfaction with the format of the reports, and the view of 'a significant number of parties' that reporting of incidents of illegal trade provided a negative view of their state;
3   the inadvisability of 'detailed reporting of the various *modus operandi* used by wildlife criminals and illicit traders in a document available to the general public';
4   the lack of available resources to report multiple incidents;
5   the belief that 'it is counter-productive to publicize any analysis of illicit wildlife trade until the majority of parties participate in the established reporting systems'.

With only one enforcement officer in the Secretariat, it is fully appreciated that there are currently inadequate resources to produce a detailed analysis of infractions every two years. But the other reasons given are unconvincing. Parties' concern about a negative view of their state should not deter open reporting and the need for accountability, and it is difficult to see how publicizing an analysis of illicit wildlife trade based on available information could be counter-productive. With the parties' poor record in annual reporting and haphazard reporting of illegal trade, there could be a long wait if such an analysis were dependent on the majority participating in reporting systems. Concerning the comment in the Interpol report on the relevance of cases involving technical problems with permits and certificates, it must be born in mind that 'infractions' and wildlife crime are not one and the same. Violations by parties do not necessarily amount to 'crime'; but, nevertheless, they can seriously undermine the implementation of the Convention and need to be brought to light. Lastly, on the advisability or otherwise of releasing information on the *modus operandi*, there is a case to be made for more extensive public awareness of the methods used by wildlife criminals and illicit traders to promote their detection (through public reporting) and general support for higher penalties and improved enforcement.

The public's access to information on illegal trade, wildlife crime and CITES infractions is now restricted to news reports, TRAFFIC bulletins and ad hoc information released by NGOs. The need for confidentiality for professional enforcement purposes and while a case is *sub judice* goes without saying, but this has to be balanced with the equally important needs; for transparent reporting once it is safe to release information; for general access to information on infractions to assess implementation and enforcement; and for accountability by parties. Instead of drastically reducing public access to information, a balance needs to be struck. The decision by the Secretariat to stop providing a detailed record of infractions was evidently unilateral. While there was a clear need to streamline and improve the system for information processing and dissemination, open discussion in the COP, or at least in the Standing Committee, would have been beneficial. Aside from legitimizing the Secretariat's action, it would have left open the option of finding additional resources to support a regular analysis of infractions, illegal trade and wildlife crime that would serve the purposes of accountability and transparency without jeopardizing confidentiality.

On-site verification through ad hoc missions

The CITES Secretariat has been conducting ad hoc visits, or missions, to parties experiencing implementation problems since the early days of its operation. The country case studies on non-compliance in Chapter 5 include several examples where Secretariat missions have been conducted to gather information, assess problems and/or provide advice and technical assistance to relevant national authorities. Bolivia, Italy and Greece are examples of countries for which Secretariat missions yielded information on non-compliance which contributed in part to eventual recommendations for trade sanctions. Secretariat missions are also used to assess progress with implementing conditions laid down for the lifting of trade sanctions, as was the case with Thailand and Italy.

Missions are usually conducted only with the consent of the country concerned. An exception was the United Arab Emirates, when the government declined to meet a Secretariat staff member sent to open dialogue over recommended trade sanctions. On a second occasion, the Standing Committee gave the UAE little choice, recommending trade sanctions if it failed to invite a mission (see case study in Chapter 5).

Technical expert missions, organized by the Secretariat, have increasingly been used to assess problems in range and consumer states concerning illegal trade in specimens from high-profile endangered species, in particular rhinos and tigers. These have been followed by high-level political missions which have reported with recommendations to the Standing Committee and COP. (This is discussed in detail in Chapter 8.) During the technical missions, other valuable information on implementation and enforcement was gathered and included in the report to the Standing Committee (see Chapter 9).

In the context of the ivory trade, Secretariat missions have been undertaken to verify compliance with conditions in range and consumer states wanting to trade ivory, then later to oversee the sales, assess trade controls and check that revenue was ploughed back into conservation. This intense use of on-site verification is discussed further below.

The most recent development is the conduct of enforcement needs assessment missions by the Secretariat in relation to poaching and trade in specific species. The first was conducted in the Russian Federation on caviar trade in November 2001, and a second is to be carried out in China concerning poaching of Tibetan antelope.[49]

Information management strategy

In its review of the effectiveness of CITES, ERM identified a need to expand assistance provided by the Secretariat in information and communications, and recommended a feasibility study to identify requirements to improve electronic communications between parties. At the request of the Secretariat, endorsed by the Standing Committee, UNEP–WCMC prepared an information management strategy (IMS), which was approved at COP10.

The goals of the IMS are:

1   to build capacity in national CITES authorities to collect, manage, interpret and use relevant information;
2   to ensure the coordinated provision of information services that support the implementation of CITES.[50]

The IMS is being implemented in two phases. Phase I consists of a pilot study of information management needs in a single region – Africa – and Phase II is dependent on its outcome.

As well as implementing the ongoing pilot study, the Secretariat is developing the CITES website, which became operational in 1997, as part of the IMS.[51] The website has fast become the central core for CITES data and information dissemination. Most documents prepared in advance of meetings are now posted on the site, along with reports of committee meetings and regular CITES Notifications to parties, except for those containing sensitive enforcement-related

---

[49] CITES SC46 Doc.11.2, 'Enforcement Matters', and Doc. 15, 'Conservation of and Trade in Specific Species', prepared by the Secretariat for SC46 (Mar 2002).
[50] CITES Doc. 10.82, 'Development of an Information Management Strategy', prepared by WCMC for COP10 (Jun 1997).
[51] CITES Doc. 11.57 'CITES Information Management Strategy', prepared by the Secretariat for COP11 (Apr 2000).

information. The aim is eventually to provide an archive of all CITES documentation, although since early documents were not produced on computers it will take some time to achieve this.[52]

The website undoubtedly has greatly improved the transparency of the regime, enabling wider dissemination of information and increased accessibility; but there is still a problem with delays in posting documents, most notably following COP11 when many months passed before the new resolutions and decisions were available, either in print form or electronically. A second problem is the limited access to the internet for staff in relevant authorities in developing country parties, because of either a lack of computer equipment, the cost of access or poor telecommunications. Even if senior staff do have access, the information may not be passed down to staff at lower levels. The IMS aims to overcome these barriers in time, its long-term goal being a website that services all parties, as well as a wider audience. The Secretariat is aware of the problems faced by developing countries and is conducting a survey of parties to determine how many have poor or no access to the internet. It is also continuing to provide information to parties in printed or e-mail form to ensure that no party is excluded from dissemination of information. But the current reality is that, until all professional staff in relevant authorities in developing country parties have cheap and easy internet access – not just a few at senior level – the gap between the internet-haves and have-nots will increase.

Elephants and ivory: a special case

Verification of the 1999 ivory auctions

The sales of ivory stockpiles from Botswana, Namibia and Zimbabwe to Japan in April 1999 were attended by the most intensive – and controversial – use of on-site verification by the Secretariat to date.[53] At COP10 in Harare in 1997, the African elephant populations from the three range states were transferred from Appendix I to II, subject to certain limitations on trade. In particular, commercial export of raw ivory was limited to 'experimental trade' in declared stocks from the three range states to Japan. The trade was subject to a series of conditions laid down in Decision 10.1, though it must be said that a number of the conditions were badly drafted and ambiguous, and had been agreed in

---

[52] Willem Wijnstekers, personal communication (Nov 2001).

[53] For a description of the sales and verification missions, see CITES Doc. 11.31.1, 'Experimental Trade in Raw Ivory of Populations in Appendix II', prepared by the Secretariat for CITES COP11 (Apr 2000).

questionable circumstances. They had been drawn up by a working group at COP10, but then put to a secret ballot in Committee I without any discussion allowed, even by parties, as part of a package of decisions and proposals relating to the African elephant. The conditions for resuming trade included, *inter alia*:

- remedying deficiencies in enforcement and control measures identified by the CITES Panel of Experts, which reviewed the proposals for downlisting by the three range states (condition (a));
- support and commitment by the three range states to 'international cooperation in law enforcement through such mechanisms as the Lusaka Agreement' (condition (e));[54]
- reinvestment of trade revenues into elephant conservation (condition (f));
- agreement of a mechanism by the Standing Committee to halt trade and immediately re-transfer the three populations to Appendix I in the event of non-compliance with the conditions or an 'escalation' of elephant poaching or illegal trade (condition (g));[55]
- agreement of international systems for monitoring illegal hunting and trade (condition (i)).

The Secretariat was tasked with verifying fulfilment of the conditions.

In November 1998 the Secretariat carried out verification missions to each of the four countries wanting to trade to check compliance with conditions (a), (e) and (f), and reported to the 41st Standing Committee meeting in February 1999 (SC41). All countries except Botswana, with respect to its ivory recording system, were given a clean bill of health. Some of the parties at the Standing Committee meeting, notably Germany, Italy and Kenya, disagreed with the Secretariat assessment and took issue with some of its findings, in particular over the adequacy of trade controls in Japan and whether range states had complied with condition (e) on international cooperation in law enforcement. None of the three range states had joined the Lusaka Agreement, though Botswana did state it was considering whether to become a signatory. Instead,

---

[54] The 1994 Lusaka Agreement on Co-operative Enforcement Operations Directed at Illegal Trade in Wild Fauna and Flora establishes an inter-agency task force to strengthen regional cooperation in Africa on wildlife law enforcement (see Chapter 9).

[55] The Standing Committee cannot agree to transfer species between the Appendices without contravening the terms of the Convention. At SC40 it was decided that, in the event of non-compliance or an 'escalation' in poaching/illegal trade, Switzerland as the depositary government would be requested to propose a retransfer of one or more populations for consideration by postal vote.

they offered as evidence of compliance with condition (e) their involvement in the development of a draft protocol on cooperation in wildlife management under the Southern African Development Community (SADC), together with their engagement in bilateral agreements establishing joint commissions with neighbouring countries on defence and security. The Secretariat verified this as adequate to comply with the condition.[56]

Eight African range states raised serious concerns about compliance with the conditions in Decision 10.1 in a letter to the Standing Committee. In addition to considering that condition (e) had not been complied with, they raised several concerns about the system being developed under the auspices of the Secretariat to monitor illegal elephant hunting, required by condition (i) and dubbed MIKE (Monitoring the Illegal Killing of Elephants).[57] India, as a range state for the Asian elephant, also voiced strong objections. At the time, MIKE was far from being implemented and was the subject of considerable criticism from range states, which felt they had not been consulted, as well as from scientists and NGOs, including WWF International (see more below). Pending MIKE's implementation, the Secretariat had developed, on Standing Committee instruction, an interim monitoring mechanism based on two types of report form to be submitted by range states. But scepticism that this would be effective was eventually borne out. By November 1999, very few responses had been received.[58]

All parties' objections concerning non-compliance with the conditions, which served to contradict parts of the Secretariat's verification, were overridden or countered, either by the Secretariat itself, by IUCN observers involved in developing MIKE or by the states wanting to trade in ivory. Controversial conditions in Decision 10.1 were 'clarified' in a way that was biased towards their fulfilment. One 'clarification' was that implementation of MIKE was not necessary for the ivory sales to go ahead. Instead, a temporary mechanism was agreed which would allow a halt to trade if information from national reporting indicated an 'important increase' in illegal hunting or trade, (though 'important increase'

---

[56] CITES Doc. SC.41.6.1 (Rev) Annex 2, 'Report of the Secretariat's Mission to Verify Compliance with Decision 10.1, Part A by Botswana, Japan, Namibia and Zimbabwe', prepared for SC41 (Feb 1999).

[57] CITES Inf. SC.41.12, Letter to the Standing Committee from Burkina Faso, Chad, Congo-Brazzaville, Ghana, Kenya, Liberia, Mali and Zambia, presented to SC41 (Feb 1999).

[58] Notification to the Parties No. 1999/93, 'Monitoring of Illegal Hunting of Elephants and National Reporting Forms on Illegal Killing of Elephants and Enforcement Actions' (30 Nov 1999).

was not defined).[59] Another 'clarification' was that joining the Lusaka Agreement was not a requirement – it was not even necessary that the mechanism to which range states committed was 'like' the Lusaka Agreement. The Secretariat stated that the Lusaka Agreement was just 'an example' of such a mechanism. After extensive debate, and despite the objections raised, the Standing Committee decided all conditions in Decisions 10.1 (as clarified) had been fulfilled, pending a further verification mission by the Secretariat to Botswana. This was conducted later in February, and the go ahead given for the auctions to take place in April 1999.

More verification missions to the three range states were undertaken to oversee the auctions; then in July 1999 the Secretariat visited Japan to check on the import. A clean bill of health for all four countries was reported to the Standing Committee. In November 1999 yet more verification missions were conducted to check that Botswana, Namibia and Zimbabwe had reinvested revenues into elephant conservation. In December 1999, a final verification mission to Japan concluded that the Secretariat was satisfied with Japan's domestic ivory controls.

This intensive monitoring of the ivory sales through on-site verification was unprecedented in CITES history. Clearly, the reason was the intense controversy surrounding the auctions and the need to demonstrate that the process was strictly controlled. While it is hard to challenge some of the Secretariat's findings through the missions without data from independent on-site visits, parties attending SC41 were not the only ones to express concerns that Decision 10.1 conditions had not been fulfilled. NGOs, in particular the Japan Wildlife Conservation Society and Environmental Investigation Agency (EIA), circulated reports containing evidence that controls in relation to elephant hunting and/or ivory trade in Japan and Zimbabwe were inadequate.[60]

In addition to its verification missions in connection with the ivory sales, in the wake of SC41 the Secretariat conducted visits to no less than 27 elephant range states in Central and West Africa and Southeast Asia to 'secure commitment' to MIKE.[61] Clearly, this was in response to the criticism levelled by range states that they had been largely excluded from the MIKE process.

---

[59] CITES Doc. SC.41.6.4 (Rev 2), 'Operational Procedure Regarding Implementation of Paragraph g) of Decision 10.1, Part A', prepared at SC41 (Feb 1999).
[60] Masayuki Sakamoto, *Analysis of the Amended Management System of Domestic Ivory Trade in Japan* (JWCS, Jan 1999); *Lethal Experiment* (EIA, Apr 2000).
[61] CITES Doc. 11.31.2, 'Monitoring of Illegal Trade and Illegal Killing', prepared by the Secretariat for COP11 (Apr 2000).

ETIS and MIKE

At COP10 in 1997, part of the package of decisions and proposals on the African elephant included Resolution Conf. 10.10 on Trade in Elephant Specimens. It called, *inter alia*, for the establishment of two international monitoring systems:

1 to monitor the illegal trade in elephant specimens;
2 to monitor the illegal killing of elephants.

Various parameters were laid down for the systems. These parameters, as revised at COP11, are:

1 measuring and recording levels and trends, and changes in levels and trends, of illegal hunting and trade in elephant range states, and in trade entrepots;
2 assessing whether and to what extent observed trends are related to changes in the listing of elephant populations in the CITES Appendices and/or the resumption of legal international trade in ivory;
3 establishing an information base to support the making of decisions on appropriate management, protection and enforcement needs; and
4 building capacity in range states.[62]

Thus, the two systems are intended as monitoring tools to assess the effects of CITES decisions concerning the African and Asian elephant.

ETIS The monitoring system for illegal trade was required to include details of law enforcement records for seizures or confiscations of elephant specimens that have occurred anywhere in the world since 1989 (the year the African elephant was listed on Appendix I). TRAFFIC's Bad Ivory Database System (BIDS), established in 1992, was designated for the task, and parties were mandated to communicate information on elephant ivory and other elephant product seizures to TRAFFIC via the CITES Secretariat. With approval of the Standing Committee, BIDS evolved into a more sophisticated monitoring tool and was renamed the Elephant Trade Information System (ETIS). On two occasions before COP11 met in April 2000, the Secretariat circulated an Ivory and Elephant Product Seizure Data Collection Form for parties to submit information, but the response was disappointing (see below). By the time of COP11, US$157,800 had been given to TRAFFIC to

---

[62] CITES Resolution Conf. 10.10 (Rev.) 'Trade in Elephant Specimens' (2000).

implement ETIS, US$20,000 of which came from the CITES Trust Fund. The operational budget for 2000–2002 was estimated at US$303,856.[63]

Parties are required to provide information on seizures of elephant products to the Secretariat within 90 days of their occurrence. TRAFFIC's role is to analyse and interpret the data together with the Secretariat and institutions involved in MIKE, and produce a report for each meeting of the COP. The intention is to produce an ETIS country report for each party on an annual basis to inform parties of their status and provide a feedback loop of information. By COP11, the main features of ETIS had been established with the assistance of consultants from the University of Reading. The core database on ivory seizures was housed at TRAFFIC's office in Lilongwe, Malawi (though it has since moved to Harare, Zimbabwe); a law enforcement effort–effectiveness database was being developed by TRAFFIC International in Cambridge; a link had been established to the main CITES trade database; and subsidiary databases, for example on ivory product markets, were being developed. TRAFFIC was also producing a national-level ETIS workshop 'toolkit' directed at wildlife and law enforcement authorities, with the aim of developing national data collection protocols.

By COP11, it was apparent that the same problems plaguing the CITES trade database – inadequate and tardy reporting by parties – were also affecting ETIS. As of 31 January 2000, with some notable exceptions (France, Namibia, Spain and Switzerland), the response had 'generally been poor'. Most parties were failing to report within 90 days of a seizure. There was also a problem with data quality, which needed to be 'improved greatly for most countries which have records in ETIS'. One of the most common problems was a failure to provide both the weight and the number of tusks or pieces by ivory type. As of 31 January 2000, ETIS contained details of 4,361 ivory seizures that had occurred in 49 countries or territories since 1989 (see Figure 4.2). However, according to TRAFFIC's report, all that could be concluded from the data was that illegal ivory trade continued to occur. No conclusions on levels or trends or any link with the decisions at COP10 could be made, but if parties cooperated with provision of data on seizures, it was hoped to produce more comprehensive data analysis by COP12.[64]

---

[63] CITES Doc. 11.31.2, 'Conservation of and Trade in Elephants: Monitoring of Illegal Trade and Illegal Killing', prepared by the Secretariat for COP11 (Apr 2000).

[64] Tom Milliken and Louisa Sangalakula, 'A Report on the Status of the Elephant Trade Information System (ETIS) to COP11', CITES Doc. 11.31.1, Annex 5 (Apr 2000).

Figure 4.2: Volume of raw, semi-worked and worked ivory seized and number of seizures by year

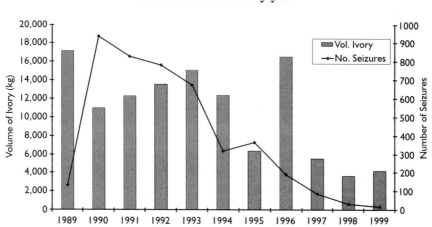

(Source: ETIS 31 January 2000)

Source: ETIS, 31 January 2000, presented in 'A Report on the status of the Elephant Trade Information System to the 11th meeting of the Conference of the Parties', CITES Doc. 11.31.1, Annex 5, prepared by Tom Milliken and Louisa Sangalakula, TRAFFIC East/Southern Africa, April 2000.

As of April 2002, the prognosis for ETIS looked no better, at least with respect to the African region. Africa's regional representatives to the Animals Committee reported that only three African countries had submitted data – Cameroon, Egypt and Namibia. They commented that 'Overall, the region is failing to respond adequately to both the reporting of seizures and feedback from ETIS country reports.'[65] According to the Secretariat, TRAFFIC is in the process of organizing capacity-building workshops on ETIS, but whether these will improve reporting on a consistent basis in the absence of any form of incentives is doubtful.

MIKE The system to monitor illegal killing of elephants – MIKE – is a far more expensive, complex and controversial process than ETIS. Initially developed by IUCN's African and Asian Elephant Specialist Groups, it involves data collection at specific sites in selected African and Asian range

---

[65] Kim Howell and Michael Griffin, 'Regional Reports: Africa', CITES AC18 Doc. 5.1 (Rev. 1), prepared for AC18 (Apr 2002).

states. In the best-case scenario, 60 sites are proposed: 45 in Africa and 15 in Asia. The information to be collected includes: elephant population data; reports of illegal hunting; law enforcement effort deployed in detecting and preventing illegal hunting and trade; other external factors, including civil strife, increased levels of human activity and the proximity of the site to international boundaries; and qualitative data such as changes in elephant behaviour and distribution, poaching camps within the site and intelligence reports from the area. It is proposed to conduct counts of live elephants and/or carcasses every two years on average to provide updated information for COP meetings, and to collect additional data on law enforcement effort, external factors and qualitative information more regularly. The projected cost of the first six years, using the best-case scenario (surveying 60 sites), was US$13.4 million, with an annual recurrent expenditure of US$2.4 million.[66] Startup costs for MIKE were estimated at US$200,000. At SC41 in February 1999, it was agreed to set aside US$100,000 from the Trust Fund to get MIKE off the ground if external funding was not immediately available.[67]

As already noted, MIKE faced considerable criticism from parties, including nine range states, at SC41. Criticisms included the methodology for site selection, the system's inability to demonstrate causality (that poaching was or was not caused by reopening the ivory trade) within a short time frame, its considerable cost (France described it as a Rolls Royce), and the lack of involvement of range states in its development.[68] IUCN and TRAFFIC provided a written response to the criticisms at COP11 in which they explained and defended the choices made in the development of MIKE. On the issue of causality, they stated that 'The most that can be achieved is to statistically assess the evidence relating or correlating illegal trade with elephant mortality.'[69]

---

[66] CITES Doc. SC41.6.3, 'Proposal for Establishing a Long Term System for Monitoring the Illegal Killing of Elephants (MIKE)', prepared by the IUCN/SSC African and Asian Specialist Groups for SC41 (Feb 1999).

[67] SC41 Summary Report (Feb 1999).

[68] CITES Inf. SC.41.12, Letter to the Standing Committee from Burkina Faso, Chad, Congo-Brazzaville, Ghana, Kenya, Liberia, Mali and Zambia, presented to SC41 (Feb 1999); SC41 Summary Report (Feb 1999). For other criticisms of MIKE see *Lethal Experiment* (EIA, Apr 2000).

[69] CITES Doc. 11.31.2 Annex, 'A Written Record of the IUCN/TRAFFIC Responses to Questions on the Design of the System for Monitoring the Illegal Killing of Elephants (MIKE) raised during discussion at the 41st CITES Standing Committee Meeting', prepared for COP11 (Apr 2000).

In the wake of SC41, between February and December 1999, there was an intense flurry of activity to launch MIKE and secure commitment from range states. In addition to the numerous Secretariat visits, a pilot project was launched in Central Africa consisting of three sites in five countries; a second pilot programme for Southeast Asia was launched in Bangkok; a MIKE workshop was conducted in Namibia to initiate MIKE in southern Africa; and a planning meeting for MIKE implementation in West Africa was held in Ghana. Progress was steered by a MIKE subgroup reporting to the Standing Committee, and a Central Coordination Unit for MIKE was established in Nairobi, Kenya.[70]

MIKE faced more criticism at COP11, spearheaded by Kenya and India. Describing the system as 'an academic exercise to collect population data', the two parties attempted to shelve the MIKE programme, replace it with range state reporting and introduce a provision to fund improved enforcement capacity in elephant range states. The attempt largely failed. They had proposed extensive amendments to Resolution Conf. 10.10, including an additional section on 'improving elephant security in range states', which would make future ivory exports conditional on achieving measurable goals in range state enforcement capacity and elephant security, for which funds would be raised. In justifying their proposal, Kenya and India stated that range states 'believe that the urgent funding priority now should be the prevention of elephant poaching rather than the establishment of expensive and inconclusive programmes for monitoring elephant populations'.[71]

Their amendments were vigorously opposed by states wanting to trade ivory and by the Secretariat, which stated categorically that it did not support the Kenya/India proposals.[72] The result of intense negotiations in a working group closed to observers was a decision to continue and expand MIKE, with some relatively minor changes taking on board some of the critics' points. Capacity-building in range states was added as a fourth objective (though its nature was unspecified); reference to causality as an element of the system was removed and replaced with 'establishment of correlations' between relevant parameters and COP decisions on elephants; and provision was included for a MIKE Technical Advisory Group (TAG) which would be involved, *inter alia*, in selecting sites, developing methodology and providing training to officials in

---

[70] CITES Doc 11.31.2, 'Conservation of and Trade in Elephants: Monitoring of Illegal Trade and Killing', prepared by the Secretariat for COP11 (Apr 2000); SC42: Summary Report (Sep/Oct 1999).
[71] CITES Doc. 11.31.3, 'Revision of Resolution Conf. 10.10', submitted by Kenya and India to COP11 (Apr 2000).
[72] Ibid., p. 2.

countries with selected sites and to Management Authorities of elephant range states.[73]

The proposals to condition trade on enforcement and security goals and to raise funds specifically for building enforcement capacity in range states were rejected. They might have gained more support had they been presented as separate initiatives rather than attempting to write them into a comprehensive revision of Resolution Conf. 10.10, which was perceived by its supporters as the 'MIKE resolution', aimed at developing a monitoring system to support decision-making, rather than a system to build enforcement capacity. Given the time, effort and funds invested in MIKE since COP10, efforts to shelve it were unlikely to succeed, but parallel initiatives to negotiate stronger and clearer conditions for future ivory trade, including measurable law enforcement goals, and to provide funds equivalent to those being sunk into MIKE for building enforcement capacity in range states, might have had more success.

The MIKE Technical Advisory Group became operational in December 2000, and the MIKE subgroup was re-established by the Standing Committee after COP11 to reflect its new membership, with South Africa as the chair and Kenya as one of the ten members.[74] For implementation, the MIKE programme has been divided into six sub-regions, four in Africa and two in Asia. The aim is to establish a Sub-regional Steering Committee (SSC) of elected representatives in each sub-region, the SSC chairperson being the contact person for the MIKE director. Full-time sub-regional support officers (SSOs) will provide technical support to the SSCs, as well as to national officers and site officers. While site officers are to oversee data collection and analysis by teams at site level, national officers will coordinate the work at national level and liase with their SSO and national SSC member.

The MIKE programme appears to be at different stages of implementation in each sub-region. As of SC45 in June 2001, a training workshop had been held in South Africa, in addition to meetings in East, Central and West Africa. Progress reports on the pilot phase in Central Africa were posted on the website. About US$3 million had been raised, with funding received from the European Commission, the Critical Ecosystem Partnership Fund (CEPF), the Belgian BEESWAX Fund and the United States. Comprising the World Bank,

---

[73] CITES Resolution Conf. 10.10 (Rev.), 'Trade in Elephant Specimens' (2000).

[74] The MIKE subgroup is composed of Burkina Faso, Cameroon, Kenya, Saudi Arabia, South Africa, Thailand and the United Republic of Tanzania, together with the major donors – the USA, European Commission and Critical Ecosystem Partnership Fund (CEPF).

the Global Environment Facility (GEF), Conservation International and the MacArthur Foundation, the CEPF is providing US$275,000 for MIKE implementation in West Africa while the United States has funded the pilot phase in Central Africa. No funding had been secured for implementation of MIKE in Asia.[75] In April 2002, the Africa regional representatives to the Animals Committee briefly reported that MIKE was operating at different levels of efficiency and commitment within the region and that national implementation ranged from 'total non-compliance to serious commitment'.[76] Botswana was cited as functioning particularly well, but had apparently had no feedback from the regional coordinator (presumably the SSO for the Southern Africa subregion).

At the time of writing, no further information is readily available. The report on MIKE to SC46 was verbal and was not recorded in the meeting's proceedings, and information concerning MIKE on the website has not been updated. This raises the issue of transparency. Lack of transparency in the programme's early development was a major factor behind initial criticisms of MIKE by range states and NGOs. The situation improved for awhile with the publication of detailed information and MIKE meeting reports on the CITES website. But full transparency needs to be maintained, given that this is the most expensive and ambitious project ever undertaken within CITES.

Rationale

On its website, the Secretariat justifies ETIS and MIKE as follows:

> Much is at stake when trade controls for elephants are debated within CITES. The polarity of opinion among the parties on the subject, together with associated passions, has threatened to skew the working of the Convention in practice and challenged the basis on which it operates. For these reasons, as well as for the benefit of elephant conservation itself, it is crucial that the decisions taken by CITES on elephant issues are based, and seen to be based, on the best possible information. MIKE and ETIS have been adopted by CITES as sources of such information, to support its decisions on elephants.

---

[75] CITES SC45 Doc. 22, 'Elephants: MIKE Subgroup Report', prepared by the Secretariat for SC45 (Jun 2001).

[76] Kim Howell and Michael Griffin, 'Regional Reports: Africa', CITES AC18 Doc. 5.1 (Rev. 1), prepared for AC18 (Apr 2002).

The Secretariat is quite right in its assessment of the effects of the elephant issue on CITES. But whether MIKE and ETIS will provide the hoped-for solution is open to question. ETIS is dependent on prompt reporting of seizures by parties whose history of reporting in CITES is poor, and MIKE has a long way to go before it will be able to provide the amount of data needed on a regular basis. From an equitable viewpoint, it is questionable whether the human and financial cost of the two programmes, all to satisfy the desire of a handful of parties to trade in one commodity from one species, can be justified, especially given the limited funds available to CITES. Elephants may be the Convention's 'flagship' species and are undeniably 'special', but thousands of other listed species receive comparatively next to no attention – or funds. And spending such a disproportionate sum on the verification and monitoring of two species (though the Asian elephant has yet to benefit), without even attempting to raise equivalent funds for preventive anti-poaching measures, detracts from other crucial cross-cutting issues, such as improving the capacity for enforcement of CITES at national level.

5 Problem countries

Introduction

The CITES non-compliance response system has evolved over several years through COP resolutions and practice. The system uses 'carrots', mostly in the form of technical assistance, strongly backed by 'sticks', in the form of trade sanctions. Two types of this mixed response can be identified: 'country-specific' and 'species-specific'. Within 'country-specific' response, further distinctions can be made between the basic procedure elaborated in 1989 for problem parties experiencing major problems with implementation of the Convention overall (the subject of this chapter) and other procedures that have evolved to address non-compliance by parties in relation to specific issues, notably, lack of national implementing legislation, non-submission of annual reports and non-designation of Scientific Authorities (Chapter 6). Within 'species-specific' response, a distinction can be made between the review mechanism that has evolved for significantly traded Appendix II species (Chapter 7), and ad hoc responses for high-profile Appendix I species such as the tiger and rhinoceros (Chapter 8). Enforcement, technical assistance and capacity-building, all means to respond to and prevent non-compliance, are addressed separately in Chapter 9.

The institutions at the centre of the non-compliance response system are the Secretariat and the Standing Committee, operating in tandem to effect implementation of the Convention under guidance of the COP, with the Animals and Plants Committees playing a technical role in species-specific response. Measures up to and including suspension of trade in CITES listed species have frequently been recommended against offending countries, using as the legal basis Article XIV, which allows parties to adopt stricter domestic measures than those provided for in the Convention. This has been referred to as the *collective* application of Article XIV on a temporary basis (see Box 5.1).[1]

Procedure for parties experiencing major implementation problems

Until 1989, the basis for action in cases of serious non-compliance was derived solely from Article XIII on International Measures, which:

---

[1] Sand (1997) (see ch. 1, n. 3), p. 21.

Box 5.1: Article XIV: Stricter Domestic Measures

I   The provisions of the present Convention shall in no way affect the right of parties to adopt:
   (a) stricter domestic measures regarding the conditions for trade, taking, possession or transport of specimens of species included in Appendices I, II and III, or the complete prohibition thereof: or
   (b) domestic measures restricting or prohibiting trade, taking, possession or transport of species not included in Appendices I, II or III.

- mandates the Secretariat to inform relevant Management Authorities of instances of non-compliance;
- obliges parties to reply as soon as possible;
- enables the COP to 'make whatever recommendations it deems appropriate'.

At COP7 in 1989, a new procedure was adopted by resolution which was to lead to a more actively applied and significantly stronger response to non-compliance. The originator of the initiative was the World Wide Fund for Nature (WWF), whose 1989 report on 'Problems in CITES Implementation' indicated there were 'major problems in many countries'.[2] WWF proposed an implementation monitoring procedure involving the Secretariat and Standing Committee, along the lines of that used by the Ramsar Convention on Wetlands.[3] It was introduced as an amendment to a draft resolution on enforcement that had been prepared by the Secretariat, which, if adopted as proposed, would have done little if anything to solve enforcement difficulties facing the Convention. Following support for the amendment from the UK, the WWF observer was requested to draw up precise wording. In the event, Resolution Conf. 7.5 on 'Enforcement' (now part of consolidated Resolution Conf. 11.3) included almost verbatim the WWF proposal and detailed a procedure for non-compliance response that elaborated on Article XIII and has remained unchanged through subsequent COP meetings (see Box 5.2).

   The procedure in place since 1989 provides for due notice to be given to the non-compliant party, time to respond in cases of an alleged infraction, the provision of advice and technical assistance by the Secretariat, and notification to parties and the COP. It also mandates the Standing Committee to pursue the

---

[2] CITES Com. II 7.1, Committee II report, COP7 (Oct 1989).
[3] The Convention on Wetlands of International Importance Especially as Waterfowl Habitat (2 Feb 1971, Ramsar).

Box 5.2: Non-compliance response procedure for parties experiencing major implementation problems[a]

Regarding application of Article XIII

(a) when, in application of Article XIII, the Secretariat requests information on an alleged infraction, parties reply within a time-limit of one month or, if this is impossible, acknowledge within the month and indicate a date, even an approximate one, by which they consider it will be possible to provide the information requested;

(b) when, within a one year time-limit, the information requested has not been provided, parties provide the Secretariat with justification of the reasons for which they have not been able to respond;

(c) if major problems with implementation of the Convention in particular parties are brought to the attention of the Secretariat, the Secretariat work together with the party concerned to try to solve the problem and offer advice or technical assistance as required;

(d) if it does not appear a solution can be readily achieved, the Secretariat bring the matter to the attention of the Standing Committee, which may pursue the matter in direct contact with the party concerned with a view to helping to find a solution; and

(e) the Secretariat keep the parties informed as fully as possible, through Notifications, of such implementation problems and of actions taken to solve them, and include such problems in its report of alleged infractions.

[a] From CITES Resolution Conf. 11.3 'Compliance and Enforcement' (2000) (formerly Resolution Conf. 7.5).

---

matter with the party concerned and 'find a solution'. The procedure does not, however, specify the measures to be taken in cases of non-compliance. Instead, these have evolved through practice based on the advice of the Secretariat.

Non-compliance responses that have been used but are not specified in Resolution Conf. 11.3 include:

- provision of security paper for permits and certificates by the Secretariat;
- requirement that the Secretariat confirms permits for a period of time;
- formal warning by the Secretariat;
- suspension of cooperation by the Secretariat;
- verification missions by the Secretariat;
- recommendation by the Standing Committee to suspend trade in CITES-listed species with the non-compliant party;
- specification by the Standing Committee of conditions to be met before a recommended trade suspension is lifted.

Table 5.1: Countries and territories subjected to recommended trade suspensions in CITES-listed species, 1985–2002

Country/territory	Trade suspension recommended	Suspension lifted
Bolivia	1985/6	1987
UAE (withdrew from CITES 1988–1990)	1985 2001	1990 Still in force**
Macau*	1986	1986
El Salvador* (joined CITES 1987)	1986	1987
Equatorial Guinea* (joined CITES 1992)	1988	1992
Thailand	1991	1992
Grenada* (joined CITES 1999)	1991	1992
Italy	1992	1993 (temporary) 1995 (permanent)
Greece	1998	1999
Guyana	1999	1999
Senegal	1999	2000
Democratic Republic of Congo	2001	Still in force**
Fiji	2002	2002 (temporary)
Vietnam	2002	2002
Yemen	2002	Still in force**

* Non-parties.
** As of August 2002.

In practice, only the last two responses require approval by the Standing Committee. Although verification missions are usually carried out at the invitation of the party concerned, recently the Standing Committee directed a party to invite a mission from the Secretariat, recommending trade sanctions if it failed to do so (see the case study of UAE below).

The Secretariat commented, at the time of its adoption in 1989, that the non-compliance response procedure 'simply specified the current practice under CITES'.[4] In some ways this was true. Even though Article XIII mandated the COP to make recommendations in cases of non-compliance, there had only been one case where the COP targeted a non-compliant country with a resolution

---

[4] CITES Com. II 7.1, Committee II report, COP7 (Oct 1989).

recommending trade sanctions – Bolivia in 1985. In other cases prior to 1989, trade restrictions were recommended by either the Standing Committee or the Technical Committee, but were not based on any formally agreed procedure.

Despite the Secretariat's scepticism, formalizing the procedure and the Standing Committee's role as a recommendatory body in addition to the COP had the effect of strengthening 'country-specific' non-compliance response. Prior to 1989, relatively soft targets were chosen for action. Most were non-parties, and there was a distinct reluctance to act firmly against powerful consumer states such as Japan and the European Union (discussed in detail below). Since 1989, several cases of parties with implementation problems have been brought before the Standing Committee by the Secretariat, with the result that sanctions in the form of recommended trade suspensions in CITES-listed species were imposed (see Table 5.1). Among them were two EU members, Italy and Greece. The formalized procedure was also used to strengthen the role of the Secretariat. Between 1990 and 1991, several notifications to parties cited Resolution Conf. 7.5 as a basis for the Secretariat taking a more active role in identifying enforcement problems.[5]

Country case studies

Throughout its history, many countries have been subjected to recommended trade restrictions under CITES. Generally this measure of last resort is reserved for non-compliant parties whose implementation of the Convention is severely deficient and non-parties whose activities seriously undermine the Convention's operation. Through case studies, this section examines how the evolving procedure and responses have been applied to different non-compliant countries, both parties and non-parties, range states and consumers, and where possible assesses their effectiveness.

Bolivia and Paraguay

Bolivia and Paraguay were notorious in the 1980s for their rampant illegal trade in wildlife and lack of implementation of CITES measures, but the response of CITES was different in the two cases. Stricter measures were taken against Bolivia, largely because of its lack of cooperation.

---

[5] See Notifications to the Parties No. 595, 'Secretariat Investigations Officer' (1990); No. 630, 'CITES Enforcement Co-ordination' (1991); and No. 636, 'Thailand: Ban on CITES Trade' (1991).

Problems in Bolivia and Paraguay were first noted following a Secretariat mission to Latin America in 1979. In a report to the Standing Committee, the Secretariat stated:

> The illegal traffic between Brazil–Bolivia; Brazil–Paraguay and Bolivia–Paraguay is enormous, especially when taking into account that the armies of Bolivia and Paraguay collaborate with it, and keeping in mind also that, according to information obtained in Bolivia, cocaine is hidden among smuggled skins.

Of the three countries, it was reported that only Brazil had the administrative structure in place to implement the Convention.[6]

In 1981, the Secretariat reported to COP3 that in its analysis of 1978 trade statistics submitted by parties with their annual reports it had noticed 'an extraordinary increase' in trade, of both skins and live animals, from Paraguay. Since Paraguay did not submit annual reports, the increase had been noted from imports recorded by other parties. Records from the Federal Republic of Germany alone showed that between 1977 and 1978 there had been a 16-fold increase in imports of *Felidae* (cat) skins from Paraguay, a nine-fold increase in imports of crocodilian hides and a two-fold increase in imports of otter skins, over 200,000 skins and hides having been imported altogether in 1978 compared with 20,000 in the previous year. Imports of fur skins and reptile hides to Japan, a non-party until 1980, doubled in the same period. Similar increases were apparent in the trade of live animals out of Paraguay, especially birds and reptiles. The report also detailed specific cases of illegal trade to European countries using forged export permits and involving skins of Appendix I and II listed species, as well as live snakes and parrots. Ocelots, otters, peludo (*Felis wiedii*) and caimans were among the species involved.[7]

In 1982, following reports of increasing illegal activities, the Secretariat, with assistance from the German Fur Trade Association, undertook a mission to both Paraguay and Bolivia, but little action of any real substance resulted. Following the visit, it was clarified by notification to parties that export of Paraguayan wild fauna was prohibited, while re-export of wildlife from Paraguay was allowed under national law. Meanwhile, the German Fur Trade Association paid for the printing of new permits and certificates on security paper in

---

[6] SC2: Summary Report, CITES Doc. 3.5 Annex 4, prepared for COP3 (Feb/Mar 1981).
[7] CITES Doc. 3.6 Annex 3, 'Investigation of Illegal Trade From Paraguay', prepared by the Secretariat for COP3 (Feb/Mar 1981).

Switzerland.[8] In Bolivia, it was discovered that a Management Authority official had collaborated with the Bolivian bird export association to print blank permits. CITES parties were urged by notification to reject old format permits, while new ones were printed in Switzerland.[9]

The problems in Paraguay and Bolivia were raised at COP3 and COP4 with apparently little result.[10] In 1985, however, action was finally taken against Bolivia at COP5, prompted partly by concern expressed by other Latin American countries, particularly Bolivia's neighbours, about the depletion of their wildlife resulting from the 'ever-growing and destructive illegal trade'.[11] In August 1983 countries attending a seminar on CITES Implementation for South and Central America and the Caribbean had approved a resolution urging the Bolivian government to take measures to prevent illegal wildlife trade 'in view of the anxiety expressed by the countries of the area'.[12] But nearly two years later illegal trade from Bolivia was still flourishing. According to a Secretariat report to COP5, the Bolivian government seemed to be 'strongly promoting' the re-export of wildlife hunted illegally in the territory of neighbouring countries. The trade, which used forged or stolen permits, or genuine permits to cover shipments of illegally acquired wildlife, was 'vast', involving tens of thousands of specimens. The Secretariat also reported that it was 'receiving increasingly frequent reports of the devastation of wildlife in the central region of South America (especially the Pantanal)'. It described the situation as 'extreme', requiring an 'extreme' solution'. While a problem of similar scale was still evident in Paraguay, involving the smuggling of primarily fur skins and reptile skins to Europe, the Secretariat had at least received cooperation from the government which had prohibited exports and stopped issuing permits or certificates.[13]

After much debate, and initial objections from Bolivia pleading socioeconomic problems,[14] Resolution Conf. 5.2, proposed by 14 Latin American

[8] CITES Doc. 4.8 'Report of the Secretariat', prepared for COP4 (Apr 1983); Notification to the Parties No. 319 'Situation in Paraguay' (13 Oct 1982).

[9] CITES Doc. 4.8 'Report of the Secretariat', prepared for COP4 (Apr 1983); Notification to Parties No. 224, 'Situation in Bolivia' (16 Sep 1982); Notification to Parties No. 246, 'Situation in Bolivia (continued)' (4 Feb 1983).

[10] CITES Plenary Session Summary Reports: Plen. 3.2 (Rev.), COP3 (Feb/Mar 1981); Plen. 4.2 (Rev.), COP4 (Apr 1983).

[11] CITES Resolution Conf. 5.2, 'Implementation of the Convention in Bolivia' (1985), preamble.

[12] See Notification to the Parties No. 310 (28 Aug 1984).

[13] CITES Doc. 5.8.1, 'International Compliance Control', prepared by the Secretariat for COP5 (Apr/May 1985).

[14] CITES Plen. 5.2 and Plen. 5.9 (Rev.), Plenary Session: Summary Reports, COP5 (Apr/May 1985).

countries (including Bolivia, once the resolution was amended), was approved by 20 votes to 14. It recommended that 'all parties refuse to accept shipments of CITES specimens' from Bolivia if within 90 days Bolivia had not demonstrated 'to the Standing Committee that it [had] adopted all necessary measures to adequately implement the Convention'.[15] The Secretariat objected strongly to the 90-day grace period, but it appears to have been necessary to elicit the support of Chile and Bolivia. Along with the COP recommendation for trade sanctions, the EU offered to provide assistance with a view to 'proper management of wildlife in Bolivia'.[16]

By the time of the first Standing Committee meeting following COP5, some parties had already imposed trade sanctions, the 90-day grace period having expired. However, since Bolivia seemed to be responding, the Standing Committee recommended that parties already imposing a ban on trade should consider suspending it, pending a Secretariat review. Bolivia had reportedly banned the export and re-export of live fauna, established a high-level committee to supervise CITES implementation and entered into an agreement to submit export permits to the Secretariat.[17] Concern was expressed by the Standing Committee about the way Resolution Conf. 5.2 had been worded. Legal aspects were 'subject to lengthy discussion', and, 'resolutions being only recommendations, most of the participants believed that the Committee should be guided mainly by the spirit of the Resolution and should, therefore, help Bolivia in its efforts and then re-examine the situation at the next meeting of the Standing Committee'. Both Argentina and the United States offered assistance to Bolivia – the latter in the form of a seconded enforcement officer.[18]

By the time of the next Standing Committee meeting in November 1986, there was little real progress. The Secretariat had conducted a mission to Bolivia and reported that a total ban on trade in wildlife and wildlife products had been introduced in June 1986 (with the exception of 50,000 caiman skins). Despite the ban, however, export permits equivalent to the annual quota imposed by presidential decree had apparently been sold to a Paraguayan company. It was recommended that action be taken before the COP in 1987. Bolivia had not taken up the offers of assistance from Argentina and the United States, and the Argentine representative complained that they were being affected by illegal trade from both Bolivia and Paraguay. He called for the curtailment of exports

---

[15] CITES Resolution Conf. 5.2 'Implementation of the Convention in Bolivia' (1985).

[16] CITES Plen. 5.9 (Rev.), Plenary Session: Summary Report, COP5 (Apr/May 1985).

[17] Extract from SC13 Summary Report (Oct/Nov 1985), attached to Notification to the Parties No. 370, 'Bolivia' (17 Dec 1985).

[18] SC13: Summary Report (Oct/Nov 1985), p. 9.

from both countries. The Committee agreed that the issues posed by Paraguay and Bolivia be referred to COP6, and that in the meantime 'parties suspend any import of CITES specimens from Bolivia'.[19]

The confirmation of trade sanctions by the Standing Committee was the turning point for Bolivia. In January 1987, shortly after the suspension was imposed, discussions between the Secretariat and the Bolivian President led to a formal agreement 'to ensure proper implementation of CITES in Bolivia', consisting of two phases.[20] Phase I involved an inventory of Appendix II specimens that could then be exported. A temporary suspension of trade was agreed during phase II while a Secretariat consultant, to be funded by the United States, worked with the Bolivian Management Authority to, *inter alia,* train personnel, establish a Scientific Authority and assist with revising laws.[21] At COP6 a further resolution on Bolivia was approved, but this time acknowledging Bolivia's willingness to comply while recommending special provisions for caiman exports from the country.[22] In 1994 the resolution was amended to delete all reference to Bolivia.[23] Thus, on paper at least, it appears that Bolivia, with technical assistance, responded to the trade ban.

Paraguay, however, continued to present a problem. In 1987 the Secretariat reported to COP6 that illegal trade from the country was continuing and criticized importing countries for not making more effort to control the trade or provide assistance to Paraguay.[24] Nevertheless, no resolution equivalent to 5.2 was passed. The turning point did not come until 1990, with a publicized incident in which the Management Authority offered for sale 35,236 caiman skins and 3,480 skins of greater rhea (a flightless bird), claiming they had been confiscated. The Secretariat believed the skins never existed and that the purpose of the advertised sale had been to launder illegal skins from Brazil and/or Bolivia. It warned the Management Authority not to issue export permits until the Secretariat had inspected all documents and obtained details of the alleged confiscation. On receiving no reply, the Secretariat informed the authorities

---

[19] SC14: Summary Report (Oct 1986), p. 5; Notification to the Parties No. 413, 'Bolivia' (28 Nov 1986).

[20] Kathryn S. Fuller, Ginette Hemley and Sarah Fitzgerald, 'Wildlife Trade Law Implementation in Developing Countries: the Experience in Latin America', *Boston University International Law Journal,* 5 (1987), pp. 289–310: 303.

[21] CITES Doc. 6.20 (Rev.), 'Implementation of the Convention in Certain Countries', prepared by the Secretariat for COP6 (Jul 1987).

[22] CITES Resolution Conf. 6.4, 'Implementation of the Convention in Bolivia' (1987).

[23] CITES Resolution Conf. 6.4 (Rev.), 'Controls on Illegal Trade' (1994).

[24] CITES Doc. 6.20 (Rev.), 'Implementation of the Convention in Certain Countries', prepared by the Secretariat for COP6 (Jul 1987).

that it would suspend all cooperation with Paraguay until the matter was clarified.[25]

In August 1990 the Director of TRAFFIC South America visited Paraguay and disclosed the incident at a press conference. Shortly afterwards, the minister responsible was replaced. High-level meetings were held between the Secretariat, the President and the new minister, which resulted in a new Management Authority finally acting against illegal trade and carrying out several successful operations. In June 1991 2 tonnes of confiscated skins, most from Appendix I species, were burned, and a month later live animals, including endemic Brazilian parrots, that had also been confiscated were returned to Brazil, prompting the Secretariat to state that 'a new era has started for the Convention in [Paraguay]'.[26] At COP8, prompted by concerns that its attempts to control trade were being undermined by the EU's lack of controls, Paraguay went a step further and took an active role in an initiative to improve implementation in the EU. It also presented a draft resolution urging trade restrictions against Singapore (see more below).[27]

Japan

The response to Bolivia and Paraguay under CITES contrast starkly with treatment of another case of serious non-compliance in the 1980s – Japan.[28] When Japan, a powerful wildlife consumer, joined CITES in 1980, it entered nine reservations, more than any other signatory at the time of becoming a party. The number reached 14 at one time, but has since reduced.[29] In 1984 the Secretariat reported serious problems with Japan, which at the time was the 'second most important importing country'. The problems included:

- non-communication;
- lack of controls on imports;
- deficient legislation.[30]

---

[25] COP8 Infractions Report.

[26] Ibid.

[27] CITES Doc. 8.18 (Rev.), 'Implementation of the Convention in the European Economic Community', prepared by Paraguay for COP8 (March 1992).

[28] Eric McFadden, 'Asian Compliance with CITES: Problems and Prospects', *Boston University International Law Journal*, 5 (1987), pp. 311–325: 313.

[29] Phyllis Mofson, 'Protecting Wildlife from Trade: Japan's Involvement in the Convention on International Trade in Endangered Species', *Journal of Environment and Development*, 3/1 (1994), pp. 91–107.

[30] SC11: Summary Report (Jul 1984), p. 9.

The Secretariat's first review of alleged infractions from 1985 to 1987, prepared for COP6, criticized Japan for importing 'enormous quantities' of crocodile skins in violation of CITES; for not responding to communications; and for importing 'massive quantities' of Appendix I sea turtle specimens without appropriate documentation. In 1985 Japan had allowed the import of over 48 tonnes of caiman skins from Paraguay alone without CITES documents, and it continued to accept imports of illegally traded crocodilian skins through 1986. Only after preparation of the infractions report, in which the Secretariat recommended that the COP request Japan to stop these imports, did the Secretariat finally receive a response from Japan to its communications, a response it considered unsatisfactory.[31]

With respect to imports of sea turtle specimens, while Japan had reservations on the Appendix I listings of sea turtles, it had not objected to Resolution Conf. 4.25, recommending that only imports with appropriate documents should be permitted. Nevertheless, Japan persistently accepted shipments that had been exported illegally without export documents, or with documents issued in contravention of the Convention. In its infractions report, the Secretariat records 15,209 kg of turtle shell imports to Japan in 1985 and 1986, 81% of which it had confirmed as illegal. A further 90 kg from Panama had been seized in transit in the Netherlands on its way to Japan. Total imports were probably much higher. In previous years, annual imports of over 70,000 kg of shell had been reported.[32] At the Standing Committee meeting in October 1985, the Costa Rica representative on behalf of Panama complained about Japan's persistent imports of illegally exported sea turtle shells with no accompanying CITES documents. He proposed that an immediate explanation be requested of Japan, and that if the situation remained unchanged the Standing Committee should ask parties 'to take strong action against Japan'. The Secretariat, however, in a contradiction of statements in its subsequent infractions report, appears to have diffused his proposal by reporting that 'substantial improvements had been made in Japan's implementation of CITES'. It proposed that it was more appropriate to 'inform Japan of the Standing Committee's deep concern', and that if the situation did not improve to take the matter up again at the next meeting.[33]

The issue of Japan was not raised at the next Committee meeting, and, despite its record of persistent non-compliance, COP6 failed to approve a Latin

---

[31] CITES Doc. 6.19 (Rev.), 'Review of Alleged Infractions', prepared by the Secretariat for COP6 (Jul 1987) (hereinafter 'COP6 Infractions Report').

[32] COP6 Infractions Report; Eric McFadden, 'Asian Compliance with CITES: Problems and Prospects', *Boston University International Law Journal*, 5 (1987), pp. 311–25: 314.

[33] SC13: Summary Report (Oct/Nov 1985), p. 8.

American move for action. A draft resolution on CITES implementation in Japan, France and Austria, prepared by Latin American and Caribbean parties whose CITES controls were being seriously undermined by illegal imports allowed into consumer countries, was severely weakened and in effect nullified by COP amendments. Any reference to specific parties was deleted, and the substance of the operative part – an evaluation of CITES implementation in Japan, France and Austria to be reported to the next COP – was deleted.[34] During a discussion that reflected a producer–consumer country split, Japan stated that it was making improvements, but complained that 'CITES is not a tribunal and such resolutions destroy the spirit of co-operation amongst the parties'.[35]

The problem of permitting imports of illegally exported species continued. TRAFFIC analysed Japan's 1990 annual report and found several irregularities, including permitting imports of species not occurring in the country of origin listed, and allowing imports from countries that prohibited the export of the species in question.[36] But still no overt action was taken against Japan under CITES. Meanwhile, outside pressure from other countries, particularly the United States in relation to Japan's sea turtle imports, was mounting. In March 1991, the US Departments of Commerce and the Interior certified Japan under the Pelly Amendment for trade that threatened the survival of sea turtles and diminished the effectiveness of CITES. The US Pelly Amendment to the Fishermen's Protective Act of 1967 establishes a process that allows any person or entity to petition the US government to certify that nationals of a country are diminishing the effectiveness of an international fisheries programme or an international endangered or threatened species programme. If this determination (formally called a certification) is made, then the US president has discretionary power to impose trade sanctions against that country. In April 1991, a month after the certification, Japan banned imports of Olive Ridley sea turtles and announced its commitment to withdraw its reservation. In June 1991 it announced its intention to phase out imports of hawksbill turtles by the end of 1992, and ultimately to withdraw its reservation as well.

At the time, Japan was the world's largest importer of Olive Ridley and hawksbill turtles. Japanese wildlife exports (including fish) to the United

---

[34] See draft resolution, 'The Implementation of CITES in Japan, France and Austria', CITES Doc. 6.19.1, prepared for COP6 (Jul 1987), and compare with Resolution Conf. 6.3, 'The Implementation of CITES' (1987).

[35] Plenary Session: Summary Report, COP6 (Jul 1987).

[36] Phyllis Mofson, 'Protecting Wildlife from Trade: Japan's Involvement in the Convention on International Trade in Endangered Species', *Journal of Environment and Development*, 3/1 (1994), pp. 91–107.

States earned nearly US$400 million annually. Members of the tortoise shell industry, which employed over 2,000 workers, likened the US action to a 'second atomic bomb'.[37] Following the certification, while President Bush was deciding whether to impose trade sanctions, Japan entered into formal negotiations with the United States. In the event, no sanctions were imposed. In February 1992 Japan finally announced that it would tighten import controls through increased contact with exporting countries to validate documentation, a move undoubtedly prompted by its hosting of COP8 in Kyoto the following month.[38]

United Arab Emirates

The United Arab Emirates (UAE) has proved to be a persistent thorn in the side of CITES. It also has the distinction of being the only country that has been subjected to a recommended trade suspension on two separate occasions, most recently in November 2001.

The UAE, particularly Dubai and Sharjah, increased in significance as centres for trade in endangered species in the middle and late 1980s. Taking advantage of lax customs controls, large shipments of raw ivory, illegally obtained from poached elephants in countries such as Tanzania, Kenya and Zambia, were smuggled into Jebel Ali Free Zone, central Dubai and Ajman, or imported with forged documents. There the ivory was semi-processed into simple jewellery and signature seals ('hanko') for export to the Far East, particularly Japan, Taiwan, Hong Kong and Singapore. Dubai was also a major entrepot for rhino horn smuggled out of East Africa to supply the Yemeni market for traditional dagger ('jambiya') handles. Since all species of rhinoceros were listed on Appendix I, and UAE was a party to CITES, the trade was illegal. The UAE itself was (and still is) also a market for rare live mammals and birds, particularly birds of prey, as well as skins from snakes and wild cats such as tiger, leopard and cheetah.[39]

---

[37] Keith Bradsher, 'Sea Turtles Put New Friction in US–Japan Trade Quarrels', *New York Times* (17 May 1991).

[38] Information on US certification of Japan taken from Elizabeth DeSombre, *Domestic Sources of International Environmental Law: Industry, Environmentalists, and US Power* (MIT Press, 2000) (hereinafter 'DeSombre'); and Phyllis Mofson, 'Protecting Wildlife from Trade: Japan's Involvement in the Convention on International Trade in Endangered Species', *Journal of Environment and Development*, 3/1 (1994), pp. 91–107.

[39] Esmond Martin, 'Ivory, Rhino Horn and other Wildlife Trade in the United Arab Emirates', *Swara Magazine*, 15/4 (East African Wildlife Society, 1992) (hereinafter 'Martin (1992)'), p. 25.

During 1985 and 1986, the Secretariat received several reports concerning the freely occurring illegal trade in CITES-listed species in the UAE. A wide range of species were involved, but there was particular concern about elephant ivory, rhino horn and snake skins. Several major cases were brought to the attention of the UAE, but no action was taken and most Secretariat communications went unanswered. Despite being a party since CITES entered into force, the UAE had made no effort to implement its provisions, and in some instances seemed to be facilitating illegal trade. The matter was raised by the Secretariat with the Standing Committee in October 1985, and a proposal for an immediate prohibition on trade with the UAE in CITES listed species was endorsed.[40] The Secretariat then notified parties, urging them to 'take immediately all possible measures to prohibit and prevent trade with or through the United Arab Emirates in any specimens [of CITES listed species] until such time as the Secretariat is satisfied that adequate steps have been taken in that country to implement CITES'.[41]

The Secretariat subsequently made attempts to open a dialogue with the UAE to assist with establishing CITES controls. In November 1986 a mission was sent to the UAE, but the government declined to meet the Secretariat staff member. While the mission was still there, the Secretariat was informed that a decree to withdraw from CITES, effective from January 1988, had been issued by the UAE President. (There were reports of claims that one of the reasons for UAE's withdrawal was the financial cost of being a party.[42]) The Secretariat requested that the matter be discussed bilaterally before formal finalization, but the request was denied.[43] In response, it issued a notification to parties in March 1987 reiterating a 'total ban on all trade in CITES species with the United Arab Emirates', the strongest wording ever used.[44]

In 1989 the UAE came under strong pressure to stop the trade in ivory, which at the beginning of the year was still flourishing. In early 1989 the UK-based NGO, the Environmental Investigation Agency (EIA), had visited UAE following a field trip to East Africa to investigate ivory shipments being smuggled out by *dhow*. They filmed and documented some of the ivory carving factories set up in the UAE by traders based in the Far East, particularly Hong Kong, and released it to the media. In a report distributed at COP7 in October 1989, EIA claimed that over 1,000 tonnes of illegally obtained ivory

---

[40] COP6 Infractions Report; SC13: Summary Report (Oct/Nov 1985), p. 7.
[41] Notification to the Parties No. 366, 'The United Arab Emirates' (28 Nov 1985).
[42] Esmond Martin, personal communication (Feb 2002).
[43] COP6 Infractions Report.
[44] Notification to the Parties No. 438, 'The United Arab Emirates' (31 Mar 1987).

had passed through Dubai since 1984.[45] According to official figures from Dubai, however, the Emirate had imported 42 tonnes of 'unworked or simply prepared ivory' in 1987, 24 tonnes in 1988 and less than 2 tonnes in 1989.[46]

The UAE had actively facilitated the ivory trade by notifying its withdrawal from CITES just one month after traders from Hong Kong had been issued licences to set up further factories. Its lack of cooperation with CITES extended to range states. In one particular incident, Tanzanian officials visiting the UAE to seek the return of a shipment of 70 tonnes of illegally obtained ivory were stonewalled by the authorities. After Tanzania supplied information to Interpol, the UAE seized the vessel and its shipment, but then released the ivory to the consignee, stating it amounted to only 1,740 kg.[47]

In parallel with NGO pressure, a few parties used diplomatic channels. The issue of ivory carvers moving to the UAE had been raised in the Standing Committee in January 1988. It was agreed that a high-level delegation, which would include the United States as chair of the Standing Committee, one African country and one Arabic country, should be sent there.[48] At the next meeting, however, in March 1989, the Chairman reported that the US Department of State had concluded that a high-level delegation could prove counterproductive, instead favouring a 'quieter approach at the ambassadorial level'; subsequent contacts by US, UK and Netherlands ambassadors were felt to have led to the closure of two ivory carving factories in Dubai and to the possibility of the UAE rejoining CITES.[49] By the end of 1989 all ivory carving factories had been closed down in Jebel Ali, Dubai and Ajman. The Dubai authorities had enacted customs notices prohibiting the transit and import of raw and worked ivory and rhino horn, and had confiscated 12 tonnes of tusks as well as worked ivory items. The raw ivory was later burned, but not before the two companies involved had been compensated at rates higher than the tusks' value.[50]

The UAE rejoined CITES in February 1990 and the recommendation for a ban on trade was lifted.[51] The country's re-adherence to the Convention came shortly after COP7, when the African elephant was transferred to Appendix I following extensive publicity concerning the ivory trade. The UAE's decision

---

[45] *A System of Extinction: The African Elephant Disaster* (EIA, Oct 1989).
[46] Martin (1992), p. 25.
[47] EIA (see n. 45 above).
[48] SC17: Summary Report (Jan 1988), p. 21.
[49] SC18: Summary Report' (Feb/Mar 1989), p. 4.
[50] Martin (1992), p. 25.
[51] Sand (1997), p. 21.

probably had more to do with the negative publicity attracted by its role in the trade and pressure from NGOs than with the trade ban, which had been in effect for over four years, or the 'quieter approach' of the US State Department – or for that matter any genuine political will on the part of the UAE, or at least some of the Emirates, to implement CITES controls.

Reports of illegal trade in defiance of the UAE's new legislation, particularly in Sharjah, where enforcement was poor, continued in the early 1990s.[52] The Secretariat infractions report to COP8 detailed several incidents involving a number of species. In October 1990 a Secretariat representative visiting a market in Sharjah had found many CITES bird species for sale in very poor conditions. In December 1990 Tanzanian police seized 68 raw ivory tusks being smuggled to Dubai by South Koreans. In April 1991 the Secretariat received information that clouded leopards, listed on Appendix I, as well as species of bear, deer and primates, had been seen for sale in the Sharjah market. It was also informed of an illicit trade in ivory, rhino horn, musk and furs. In June 1991, *Gulf News* published an article detailing the sale of CITES-listed cat species in Sharjah pet shops. The Secretariat also received information at the same time on an import, apparently without any CITES control, of 100 African grey parrots by a Sharjah shop, 'which would be receiving "special treatment" from a high dignitary of Dubai, UAE'. Communications to the UAE Management Authority from the Secretariat concerning these reports were met with no response.[53]

In 1992 an expert on endangered species trade, Esmond Martin, visited the Sharjah market, or souk, as well as two large pet shops and discovered falcons on sale for US$1,900 each, an African blue monkey for US$400 and greater flamingos from Tanzania for US$550 a pair. Over the previous three years the shops had sold a wide variety of animals, including dik diks for US$550 a pair, chimpanzees from Uganda for US$5,500 a pair and a cheetah also at US$5,500.[54] In November 1992 Martin returned as UNEP's special envoy for rhino conservation. His high-level visit to the ruler of Sharjah prompted some action. A week before the visit, the Sharjah municipal authorities issued a proclamation banning all trade in 'protected' animals and raided several pet shops, confiscating some rare birds and tortoises.[55] But just six months later

---

[52] Sand (1997), quoting A. Kumar, 'Wildlife Trade in the UAE: April 1991', *TRAFFIC Bulletin*, 12/3 (1991), p. 78; Martin (1992), p. 26.

[53] COP8 Infractions Report.

[54] Martin (1992), p. 26.

[55] Esmond Martin, UNEP Special Envoy for Rhino Conservation, *Final Report* (20 Jan 1993).

the traders opened up again, initially for the sale of birds of prey and later for other species.[56]

Reports of illegal trade involving the UAE subsided for awhile. They were notably absent in the Secretariat's infractions reports to COP9 and COP10. But in the report to COP11 in 2000, the single case mentioned in detail (on the basis that it was the only formal communication made to a party in terms of Article XIII.1 of CITES since COP10) concerned the UAE. It involved the issue of re-export certificates by the UAE Management Authority authorizing shipments of caviar on the basis of forged or false Russian Federation documents (in effect, laundering illegally obtained caviar). The Secretariat communicated its concerns to the UAE, but invalid certificates continued to be issued. After a formal communication from the Secretariat in November 1999, advising the UAE that the provisions of the Convention were not being effectively implemented and recommending that the Management Authority conduct investigations and cooperate with the Russian Federation, the UAE responded that the traders in Dubai who were involved had become bankrupt. Requests for cooperation by the Russian Federation went unanswered.[57]

In February 2001 *Gulf News* reported that a wide range of products from endangered species, including cheetahs, wolves, leopards, tigers, turtles, snakes and crocodiles, were still on sale in Sharjah's central market, the Blue Souq. A salesman in the market apparently boasted that he had been in the business for ten years and 'can get hold of virtually any animal product'. He claimed 'my deliveries are flown in, and I pay around eight people to split the load between them. They bring it through the airports hidden in their luggage like normal passengers'. Problems with UAE policy and legislation were highlighted in this article. Confusion over policy meant that items forbidden under domestic law were openly on sale, and until a new Federal Environment Law became fully operational traders could not be prosecuted. Penalties applied only if wildlife products were caught at the border.[58] In February 2002, in the aftermath of the fall of the Taliban, *Gulf News* reported that traders had been allowed to ship unlimited numbers of falcons and other wildlife from Afghanistan to the UAE. The Afghan government had been charging a tax of US$250 per hooked beak, and traders had been using Ariana Airlines, Afghanistan's national carrier, to smuggle birds to Dubai.[59]

---

[56] Esmond Martin, personal communication (Jan 2002).
[57] COP11 Infractions Report.
[58] Joanna Langley, 'Trade in Endangered Species: For Sale: the World's Wildlife Heritage', *Gulf News* (3 Feb 2001).
[59] Matthew McAllester, 'Tough Times for Afghan Animal Traders', *Newsday* (10 Feb 2002).

In June 2001, at SC45, the Secretariat drew the Standing Committee's attention to its 'increasing concern regarding illegal trade involving the United Arab Emirates'. It was receiving regular reports that endangered species, particularly falcons, were being smuggled into the country, as well as cheetah cubs to be trained for hunting. In late 2000 the Secretariat had learned that shipments of caviar were apparently leaving the UAE using pre-Convention certificates, allegedly issued by the Management Authority in contravention of a CITES notification that pre-Convention declarations of caviar should not be accepted after 1 April 1999. The Secretariat had repeatedly written to the UAE since October 2000, but had received only one response.[60] A statement alleging corruption among CITES officials elicited a denial from the UAE Management Authority.[61]

Interestingly, the Standing Committee appears to have recommended the second trade suspension with the UAE in the absence of a specific recommendation from the Secretariat. The Committee agreed that the UAE 'should' invite a Secretariat mission, and that, if by 31 October 2001 it had failed to do so and the Secretariat was not satisfied that the UAE was adequately implementing the Convention, a notification should be distributed 'recommending that, until further notice, the parties refuse any import of specimens of CITES-listed species from and any export or re-export of such specimens to the United Arab Emirates'.[62]

Following SC45, the Secretariat began an assessment of re-exports of caviar from the UAE, which revealed that caviar with a wholesale value of over US$20 million had been re-exported in the first ten months of 2001. A recommendation that this be investigated was made to the UAE Management Authority. An invitation to send a mission to the UAE was received just before the Standing Committee deadline. The mission, which took place at the end of October 2001, was unable to verify adequate implementation of the Convention. Extensive problems were discovered. Officials were inadequately trained and equipped; border controls were inadequate; permits and certificates were being issued and accepted contrary to CITES provisions; national legislation did not provide for proper enforcement or penalization; and there was evidence of substantial volumes of illicit trade. Following the mission, there was little evidence of promised remedial

---

[60] CITES SC45 Doc. 11.2, 'Enforcement Matters', prepared by the Secretariat for SC45 (Jun 2001).

[61] SC45: Summary Record (Jun 2001), p. 8.

[62] Ibid., p. 9.

action.[63] Notification of the recommended trade suspension was subsequently issued on 20 November 2001.[64]

The suspension has drawn a response. In January 2002 the seizure of two baby chimpanzees, two vervet monkeys and three tamarins from a pet shop in the Pet Souk near Port Zayed, Abu Dhabi, was reported. The owner claimed to have bought them in the Sharjah souq. The UAE Director of WWF was quoted as saying that the federal government was moving to put more restrictions on trade in endangered species. In response to the CITES trade sanctions, he said: 'Efforts are being made at the very highest levels – at government levels – to reorganise the CITES legal framework'.[65] In February 2002, 225 desert tortoises and eight birds, including four peacocks thought to have been smuggled from India, were seized at a border post.[66] At SC46 in March 2002 the UAE submitted an Action Plan for the Implementation of CITES in the UAE.[67] The plan includes: restructuring of the Management Authority; nominating a Scientific Authority; review of all permit requests by the CITES Secretariat; federal legislation to implement CITES; a two-year training and capacity-building programme for relevant agencies and organizations (the first training workshop was in March 2002); a registration system for pet shops and training and awareness workshops targeting their owners; and a system for registering falcons and falcon breeding facilities.

The Secretariat acknowledged the Action Plan, adding that the UAE had ceased authorizing trade in CITES specimens, but reported to SC46 that problems remained regarding illegal trade in caviar and movements of falcons. It proposed a three-phase withdrawal of the recommended trade suspension which was agreed by the Standing Committee:

- Phase 1: an immediate withdrawal of the recommended suspension with regard to trade for non-commercial purposes other than movements of live birds of prey;

[63] CITES SC46 Doc. 11.2, 'Enforcement Matters', prepared by the Secretariat for SC46 (Mar 2002); SC45: Summary Record.
[64] Notification to the Parties No. 2001/079, 'United Arab Emirates: Recommendation to Suspend Trade' (20 Nov 2001).
[65] Nissar Hoath and Mildred Fernandes, 'Endangered Primates Confiscated', *Gulf News* (29 Jan 2002).
[66] 'UAE: Smugglers of Endangered Reptiles Nabbed', WAM/Inter Press/Global Information Network (13 Feb 2002).
[67] CITES SC46 Doc. Inf. 4, 'Enforcement Matters: United Arab Emirates', submitted by the UAE to SC46 (Mar 2002).

- Phase 2: withdrawal of the recommended suspension with regard to trade in live birds of prey for non-commercial purposes when the Secretariat has verified that their registration is complete;
- Phase 3: reconsideration of the recommended suspension with regard to commercial trade at SC47 in November 2002.[68]

This approach means that the recommended suspension will apply to commercial trade in CITES-listed species from the UAE until the next review in November 2002.[69]

Thailand

In April 1991 at SC23, the Secretariat presented a detailed report to the Standing Committee on Thailand's failure to implement the Convention during the period January 1988–March 1991. The report was based on information obtained by the Secretariat and TRAFFIC International and recommended a ban by parties on all trade in CITES-listed species with Thailand. As well as being the focus for a large illegal trade in caiman skins, plants, primates, birds and other CITES listed species, Thailand lacked effective implementing legislation, failed to submit annual reports and was unresponsive to Secretariat enquiries. Owing to its poor legislation and the ease of re-exporting illegally obtained specimens, Thailand had become a centre for 'laundering' CITES-listed species. It was a 'primary centre of the illegal caiman skin trade' and 'a central laundering area for trade in CITES species of birds'. Large quantities of native and non-native CITES Appendix I plants taken from the wild were also being exported as artificially propagated. The Secretariat was receiving numerous requests from other parties to confirm the validity of CITES re-export certificates naming Thailand as the country of origin.[70] The representative for Oceania at SC23 added that in New Zealand illegal trade in crocodile skins through Thailand had been going on since 1986, since when there had been at least 15 cases. Birds from Australia (which bans exports of all its indigenous

---

[68] Notification to the Parties No. 2002/020, 'United Arab Emirates: Partial Withdrawal of Recommendation to Suspend Trade' (9 Apr 2002).

[69] 'Commercial trade' is defined as an activity whose 'purpose is to obtain economic benefit, including profit (whether in cash or in kind) and is directed toward resale, exchange, provision of a service or other form of economic use or benefit' (Resolution Conf. 5.10).

[70] CITES Doc. SC.23.21, 'Implementation of the Convention in Thailand and Grenada', by the Secretariat for SC23 (Apr 1991); COP8 Infractions Report.

wildlife) were also being smuggled out through New Zealand and Thailand, and other countries in the region were complaining about the lack of CITES implementation in Thailand contributing to the draining of their wildlife resources.[71]

The Standing Committee endorsed the Secretariat's recommendation for a ban on trade with Thailand. Citing complaints received over several years from other parties (and Resolution Conf. 7.5), the Secretariat sent out a notification urging parties to 'immediately take all possible measures to prohibit trade with Thailand in any specimens of [CITES listed species]'. The prohibition specifically included 'all future import, export and re-export of CITES specimens, to and from Thailand' and was to remain in effect until the Secretariat was 'satisfied' that adequate measures had been taken to implement the Convention.[72]

By January 1992 the Thai government was demonstrating a more positive attitude. The Secretariat reported to the Standing Committee that new legislation had been drafted, a media campaign had been launched and action had been taken against illegal traders. In its infractions report to COP8, the Secretariat noted that several large seizures of CITES listed species had been made by the Thai authorities since notification of the trade ban. The Secretariat attributed the change directly to the ban, but recommended that it be maintained until legislation had been passed and effective controls were in place. Parties' compliance with the ban could not be assessed, but it was stated that 'letters of concern from traders in Thailand…indicate that the action taken has been effective in either banning or severely limiting trade in specimens of CITES species between Thailand and other parties'.[73] Thailand later acknowledged in its country report to a UNEP enforcement workshop that 'the ban resulted in billions baht lost'.[74]

Following COP8, the CITES Secretary General visited Thailand and was informed that implementing legislation had been passed. In April 1992, a year after its imposition, the Standing Committee approved the lifting of the ban.[75] Recently, however, Thailand has been receiving attention again, this time as a

---

[71] SC23: Summary Report (Apr 1991), p. 9.

[72] Notification to the Parties No. 636, 'Thailand: Ban on CITES Trade' (22 Apr 1991).

[73] CITES Doc. SC 24.6, 'Implementation of the Convention in Thailand and Grenada', prepared by the Secretariat for SC24 (Jan 1992).

[74] Somnuk Rubthong, Thailand country report, UNEP/Env.Law/MEAs/17, prepared for UNEP Workshop on Enforcement of and Compliance with MEAs (12–14 Jul 1999).

[75] Notification to the Parties No. 673, 'Thailand: Lifting of Recommended Ban on Trade in CITES Specimens' (2 Apr 1992).

result of concerns over its controls of trade in tiger specimens and ivory. In 2000, TRAFFIC documented widespread availability of products claiming to be tiger-based in Bangkok pharmacies.[76] A report by EIA, released in June 2001 to coincide with SC45, documented a trade in both the import and export of tiger products and derivatives, and an established domestic industry manufacturing tiger products. [77] In February 2002 over 30 NGOs wrote to the Chairman of the Standing Committee, citing these findings and requesting that a mission be sent to Thailand. They also opposed the advocacy by 'key Thai political figures' of a change in legislation to legalize trade in captive bred tigers.[78] At the same time, the Secretariat reported that it was continuing to receive information raising concerns about Thailand's domestic controls of trade in tiger specimens, and that 'Thailand also appears to be an important transit country for illicit trade in wildlife'.[79] A survey of ivory markets in South and Southeast Asia by the NGO Save the Elephants concluded that 'Thailand has by far the largest domestic market for ivory items with over 80% of the total surveyed', raw ivory being smuggled in from Africa and Myanmar to supply the Thai ivory industry.[80] At SC46 in March 2002, the Standing Committee approved a technical mission to Thailand to assess work on tiger conservation and the combating of illicit wildlife trade (to be conducted in the second half of August). Thailand stated that it welcomed the mission and emphasized to the Standing Committee that the sale of captive-bred tigers or parts and derivatives of tigers is prohibited in Thailand.[81]

European Union

Highly variable implementation of CITES in the European Union presented serious problems throughout the 1980s and early 1990s, despite the enactment of EU legislation containing stricter measures than the Convention. Council Regulation 3626/82 on the implementation of CITES in the European

[76] K. Nowell, *Far from a Cure: The Tiger Trade Revisited* (TRAFFIC International, 2000).

[77] Debbie Banks, Dave Currey and Faith Doherty, *Thailand's Tiger Economy* (EIA, Jun 2001).

[78] Letter to Kenneth Stansell from 33 NGOs 'Re: CITES Tiger Decisions taken at COP11' (19 Feb 2002).

[79] CITES SC46 Doc. 15, 'Conservation of and Trade in Specific Species', prepared by the Secretariat for SC46 (Mar 2002).

[80] Esmond Martin and Daniel Stiles, *The South and South East Asian Ivory Markets* (Save the Elephants, 2002).

[81] SC46: Summary Report (Mar 2002), p. 16.

Community was passed in 1982 and came into force in 1984.[82] Since regulations are directly applicable in member states, and therefore binding in their entirety, it had the beneficial effect of requiring EU states that had not acceded to CITES to impose equivalent, and in many ways stricter, measures. Notable stricter measures included the requirement for an import permit for all CITES specimens (and therefore a non-detriment finding by the importing country), not just those listed on Appendix I (a requirement that was 'borrowed' from Denmark, Germany and the United Kingdom); an expanded list of species to be treated as Appendix I; and a ban throughout the European Union on display for commercial purposes as well as the sale and transport of species on the extended Appendix I list. Member states were allowed to adopt measures stricter than the regulation, and a CITES Committee composed of member state representatives was established.

The legislation also provided the European Court of Justice (ECJ) with jurisdiction over CITES matters in the EU, enabling it to adjudicate serious infractions. In a landmark case brought by the European Commission against France, the only judgment concerning the CITES regulation, the court held that France had failed to fulfil its obligation under the regulation by issuing import permits for 6,000 wildcat skins from Bolivia after the COP had adopted Resolution Conf. 5.2 requesting that parties refuse such shipments.[83] The usefulness of the ECJ for CITES-related cases, however, is limited by the length of the procedure. Nearly five years elapsed between the issue of the import permits by France and the ECJ judgment – far too long to have any practical impact on the protection of the species.

While the 1982 regulation appeared strict on paper, it attracted strong criticism for being unenforceable in practice. Shortcomings that were pointed out included the highly variable implementation of the regulation among member states and the loss of statistical data on trade flows within the Community. Automatic mutual recognition of permits from other EU countries led to the recognition of even manifestly incorrect CITES documents. Significantly, the move towards a boundary-free internal market in 1984 meant that enforcement as a whole depended on the level of control in those member states with the weakest enforcement policy. National border controls were coming down, but they were not replaced by EU-wide control and inspection services. Owing

---

[82] 'Council Regulation (EC) 3626/82, on the Implementation in the Community of the Convention on International Trade in Endangered Species of Wild Fauna and Flora', *Official Journal of the European Communities*, L 384/1 (1982).

[83] Case C-182/89, Commission of the European Communities *v.* France, judgment 29 Nov 1990, *European Court Reports*, 1 (1990), 4337.

to the limited numbers of competent customs authorities and problems with interpreting the law, the outside borders of the Community were especially vulnerable at free ports and transit centres. Overseas territories of member states presented a particular problem. Significant quantities of illegal CITES specimens were entering the EU via places such as French Guyana.[84]

In 1985 the Secretariat reported to COP5 that, while the 1982 regulation had some beneficial effects, they had been relatively minor, and implementation in the EU, in certain countries in particular, was 'extremely poor in some major aspects'. Skins of CITES specimens illegally obtained in South America or Asia were entering the Community in 'vast quantities'. Free ports such as Hamburg, where specimens were entering without CITES documents, were a significant loophole. Illegal trade was 'flooding' in through the weakest entry points.[85] No recommendations were made on the issue at COP5, but Germany responded to criticism by instituting CITES controls in the port of Hamburg from 1 August 1985.[86]

In 1987, at COP6, a resolution was passed requesting, *inter alia,* the establishment of 'full means of Community supervision of its legislation by means of an adequately staffed Community inspectorate', and recommending that movement of CITES specimens between member states be monitored.[87] Neither recommendation was implemented. In 1992, at COP8, the issue of EU CITES implementation was raised again, this time by Paraguay, expressing concerns that its attempts to control trade were being undermined by the EU's lack of controls.[88] This led to another resolution urging member states to develop appropriate legislation and substantially increase resources for enforcement of the Convention. Meanwhile, the Secretariat was requested to evaluate controls in the EU and report to COP9.[89]

---

[84] Godelieve A. Vandeputte, 'Why the European Community should become a Member of the Convention on the International Trade in Endangered Species of Wild Fauna and Flora (CITES)', *Georgetown Environmental Law Review,* 3/2 (1990), pp. 245–65; Sand (1997), pp. 26–7.
[85] CITES Doc. 5.8.1, 'International Compliance Control', prepared by the Secretariat for COP5 (Apr/May 1985); CITES Resolution Conf. 6.5, 'Implementation of CITES in the European Economic Community' (1987); Resolution Conf. 8.2, 'Implementation of the Convention in the European Economic Community' (1992). Both resolutions were revised at COP9.
[86] SC13: Summary Report (Oct/Nov 1985), p. 7.
[87] CITES Resolution Conf. 6.5, 'Implementation of CITES in the European Economic Community' (1987) (still in effect as Res. Conf. 6.5 (Rev.)).
[88] CITES Doc. 8.18 (Rev.), 'Implementation of the Convention in the European Economic Community', prepared by Paraguay for COP8 (Mar 1992).
[89] CITES Resolution Conf. 8.2, 'Implementation of the Convention in the European Economic Community' (1992).

Internal border controls were finally abolished from 1 January 1993. Once shipments entered the Community, they were therefore free to move anywhere. At COP9 in 1994, the Secretariat presented its report on CITES implementation in the EU. It identified several problems, including:

- the issue of export and re-export documents for specimens illegally obtained or imported in contravention of the Convention – laundering;
- insufficient EU legislation, and inadequate or non-existent implementation of that legislation;
- inadequate national legislation, with too much disparity between member states;
- inadequate border controls – the removal of internal border controls had not been compensated by increased internal controls;
- variation in the nature and severity of penalties between member states enabling smugglers to take advantage of States with weak provisions;
- insufficient coordination between member states; and
- variation in the number and degree of authority of Management Authorities.

The Secretariat acknowledged that some of the problems, such as insufficient legislation and inadequate border controls, were common to all parties, but some were peculiar to the European Union because it was implementing CITES as if it were a single state while its Management Authorities were virtually independent, with procedures varying enormously from one state to another. It emphasized the point that the degree of CITES implementation in the EU was that of the state with the lowest implementation level.[90] Despite these severe shortcomings, a proposal at COP9 to develop a resolution from the Secretariat's recommendations was 'strenuously opposed' by the EU and failed to materialize.[91]

Eventually, after five years of preparation, new EU legislation (Council Regulation 338/97) came into force in June 1997, replacing the old 1982 regulation.[92] More comprehensive than its predecessor, the new regulation was a notable improvement on the past. The stricter measures noted above were

---

[90] CITES Doc. 9.23, 'Implementation of the Convention Within the European Union', by the Secretariat for COP9 (Nov 1994).

[91] CITES Com. II 9.4, Committee II: Summary Report, COP9 (Nov 1994).

[92] Council Regulation (EC) No. 338/87 of 9 Dec 1996, on the 'Protection of Species of Wild Fauna and Flora by Regulating Trade Therein', *Official Journal of the European Communities*, L61/1, 40 (3 Mar 1997).

retained and several new provisions were introduced.[93] The principal changes are as follows.

1 CITES is integrated into the regulation rather than being attached as an annex.
2 The inclusion of non-CITES-listed species in Annexes A–D is provided for where they meet specific listing criteria.
3 The control of commercial activities within the EU with regard to Annex A species (an extended Appendix I) is tightened, with a ban on their purchase, offer to purchase and acquisition for commercial purposes.
4 The Commission can amend Annexes B–D, whereas, before, a Council decision was required if listing did not result from an amendment to the CITES Appendices by the COP.
5 The Commission can adopt measures on all aspects of implementation, including CITES recommendations.
6 There is an increased possibility of subjecting species to import restrictions.
7 Provisions for the issue of import permits are clarified, and conditions for the issue of export permits and re-export certificates are introduced. While mutual recognition of permits and certificates still holds, competent authorities, or the Commission, in consultation with the issuing competent authority, can declare void permits and certificates issued on false premises.
8 There must be appropriate housing for Annex A and B species (not just those on Appendix I).
9 Proper transport must be provided for all live specimens.
10 Personal effects and household goods are defined and regulated.
11 There is provision for listing exotic species in Annex B that pose an ecological threat.
12 There are requirements for the designation of a Management Authority with primary responsibility for CITES implementation, and one or more Scientific Authorities whose duties shall be separate from those of the Management Authority.
13 A Scientific Review Group is established, composed of member state representatives.

---

[93] Nicole Magel, 'More than CITES: the EU Wildlife Trade Regulations', in Monika Anton, Nicholas Dragffy, Stephanie Pendry and Tomme Rozanne Young (eds), *Proceedings of the International Expert Workshop on the Enforcement of Wildlife Trade Controls in the EU, 5-6 Nov 2001* (TRAFFIC/IUCN, 2002).

14 Member states are obliged to designate points of entry and exit and to provide adequately trained customs staff.
15 An Enforcement Group is established, consisting of member state authorities responsible for implementation.
16 There is a requirement for monitoring, compliance and investigations. Competent member state authorities are obliged to monitor and ensure compliance with the regulation, to instigate legal action in cases of infringements, and to inform the Commission (and CITES Secretariat) of significant infringements and the outcome of investigations. The Commission is obliged to draw member states' attention to matters needing investigation.
17 There is an obligation to have adequate legislation on sanctions and to take measures to ensure the imposition of sanctions. A minimal list of 13 infringements requiring imposition of penalties is included, with an obligation that penalties be appropriate to the nature and gravity of the infringement. This is unusual, since EU legislation usually leaves it to member states to define sanctions.

The CITES Management Committee or Committee on Trade in Wild Fauna and Flora, established by the 1982 Council Regulation, usually meets three times a year and decides on draft measures proposed by the Commission. It also discusses general issues relating to implementation of the 1997 Council Regulation, as well as the Commission Regulation (1808/2001), which details how to implement the Council Regulation. The Scientific Review Group also meets three times a year to discuss scientific questions relating to application of the Council Regulation. Their discussions feed into the Management Committee and national Scientific Authorities, which decide on the introduction into the Union of Annex A and B specimens after considering the Scientific Review Group's opinion. Import restrictions can be imposed only after consultation with the countries of origin. They are published in the Official *Journal of the European Communities* in the form of a Commission Regulation, the so-called 'Suspensions Regulation'. The mandate of the Enforcement Group is to examine technical questions relating to the Council Regulation's enforcement. By 1998 the EU Enforcement Group was meeting regularly to exchange technical expertise and information on particular cases and problem areas.[94]

The 1997 Council Regulation is extremely detailed and addresses many of the criticisms aimed at its predecessor. In effect, the EU has developed a system

---

[94] Roger Smith, formerly with UK CITES Management Authority, personal communication (1998).

based on internal commerce controls within an external 'wall'. And, to give it its due, while some aspects of CITES implementation have been wanting in the Union, there have been positive elements, such as the willingness to suspend imports of significantly traded species (more than 2,000) on the basis of non-detriment findings, a process which provided a model for the now 'CITES-wide' Significant Trade Review mechanism (discussed in Chapter 7). But fundamental problems remain. Most importantly, there is still no EU-wide system of inspection and enforcement, and the lack of internal border controls means that enforcement is still dependent on the weakest link.

The detrimental effects of this weakness are demonstrated by the case studies of Italy and Greece, both formerly problem countries whose lack of implementation was severely undermining efforts by other EU states until they responded to trade sanctions recommended by the Standing Committee (see below). Italy, as a major conduit for shipments of illegally obtained CITES-listed wildlife, was a particularly weak point in the EU 'wall'. Overseas territories still pose a problem. In June 2002, 1,200 Appendix I-listed radiated tortoises (*Geochelone radiata*) smuggled by boat from Madagascar were seized on the French island of Réunion in the Indian Ocean.[95] It was speculated that they may have been on their way to France, since Réunion–Paris is one of the main routes used by traders for shipping wildlife out of Madagascar.[96]

With the forthcoming enlargement of the EU, poor enforcement at the borders of eastern European member states could lead to traders exploiting the situation to gain easy entry to the Union. CITES trade in eastern European countries increased tremendously during the 1990s, along with the smuggling of CITES specimens (mainly live animals) to the EU, despite serious efforts on the part of several of those countries to implement the Convention.[97] The Czech Republic features notably in the illegal reptile trade, for example,[98] while it seems that Hungary is a collecting point for birds smuggled into Italy from eastern Europe, mainly Romania and Serbia. In November 2001 Hungarian customs officials seized the carcasses of more than 10,000 protected birds in a truck on the Hungarian–Croatian border, and in January 2002 an Italian was caught smuggling 20 birds into Hungary from Romania in his

---

[95] 'Le Port: Trafic d'animaux protégés en provenance de Madagascar, saisies de tortues', *Journal de l'Ile de La Réunion* (20 Jun 2002).
[96] Reeve/IFAW research (see ch. 1, n. 14).
[97] CITES Doc. SC.36.10, 'Enforcement Issues', prepared by the Secretariat for SC36 (Jan/Feb 1996).
[98] Reeve/IFAW research.

car.[99] On the positive side, membership of the Union may encourage eastern European states to raise their standards and improve CITES controls; but a concerted effort will be needed to strengthen enforcement on the eastern borders and ports of entry – preferably before they join – if a repeat of the scenario presented by Italy is to be avoided.

The crux of the problem posed by the European Union is that regional economic integration and the breakdown of trade barriers are fundamentally at odds with the premiss upon which CITES is based: that of controlling trade between sovereign states. To reintroduce internal customs controls for CITES-listed species in the EU is a political non-starter. However, some form of internal 'EU CITES police', though contentious, is essential to compensate for lack of internal border controls and strengthen enforcement at its weakest points. Recent discussions on establishing an EU fisheries inspection body might act as a precedent and make the idea more palatable to its opponents. Additionally, a stronger role for Europol in fighting wildlife crime could be explored. The practical problems still posed by variable implementation and enforcement in EU member states will also need to be addressed seriously with the enlargement of the Union if illegal wildlife trade is to be kept under some sort of control. At a TRAFFIC workshop in November 2001, it was reported that penalties for violations of individual wildlife trade laws still vary considerably among the 15 member states. In some member states illegal wildlife trade is not even considered a criminal offence and is treated under administrative law. In the United Kingdom smugglers can face seven years' imprisonment (though the maximum has never been applied), while in Belgium the maximum penalty for a CITES infringement is three months. In Germany wildlife smuggling can result in up to five years in prison and a fine (prior to introduction of the euro) of DM100,000 (US$45,750). Cases were cited where non-resident smugglers managed to evade punishment in the country where they were apprehended.[100]

Political reality dictates that wildlife trade is likely to be a low priority for the European Union compared with all the other integration and harmonization problems posed by an expanded membership. CITES institutions will therefore need to be especially vigilant with respect to implementation and

---

[99] 'Hungary Gears Up to Fight Italian Bird Poachers', *Reuters* (24 Jan 2002).
[100] 'Europe Seeks Tougher Enforcement of Wildlife Smuggling Law', *Environment News Service* (12 Nov 2001), <www.traffic.org/news/harmony.html>; Monika Anton, Nicholas Dragffy, Stephanie Pendry and Tomme Rozanne Young (eds) *Proceedings of the International Expert Workshop on the Enforcement of Wildlife Trade Controls in the EU, 5-6 Nov 2001* (TRAFFIC/IUCN, 2002).

enforcement in the EU accession states, and to demonstrate a willingness to apply sanctions to any that present serious problems – much the same as they did with Italy and Greece.

Italy   In 1991, and again in 1992, the Secretariat reported 'serious and repetitive problems' concerning Italy's implementation of CITES to the Standing Committee. They included:

*   lack of adequate legislation;
*   lack of inspection of goods on import and export;
*   issuance of documents contravening the Convention;
*   a large number of authorities issuing permits;
*   lack of cooperation between CITES and customs authorities;
*   lack of consultation with the Secretariat.

Italy's non-compliance was being exploited by traffickers to gain access to the EU and obtain legal documents for specimens of illegal origin. A large volume of trade, particularly in reptile skins and live animals, including parrots and Appendix I listed primates, was passing through Italy, seriously compromising the implementation of CITES in Europe and presenting an 'undeniable risk to the implementation of the Convention world-wide'.[101]

The Secretariat had been notifying the Italian Management Authority of all this since 1989, to little effect. It had organized a training seminar in Milan for Management Authority officials, but no one even attended from the ministry primarily responsible for issuing import permits. In one notorious case, four chimpanzees, listed on Appendix I, were exported from Italy in full view of customs officials, despite border posts having been informed that the animals should not be allowed to leave the country. They were seized (with the help of the Italian office of TRAFFIC), but subsequently released because of the lack of legislation to penalise CITES violations.[102]

The Secretariat (citing Resolution Conf. 7.5 as its basis) brought the case of Italy to the attention of the Standing Committee and requested advice. It noted concern by Latin American countries that the situation was undermining their

---

[101] CITES Doc. SC. 24.7, 'Implementation of the Convention in Italy', prepared by the Secretariat for SC24 (Jan 1992); SC23: Summary Report (April 1991), p. 10.
[102] CITES Doc. 9.22 (Rev.), 'Review of Alleged Infractions and Other Problems of Implementation of the Convention', prepared by the Secretariat for COP9 (Nov 1994) (hereinafter 'COP9 Infractions Report'); CITES Doc. SC 24.7 (n. 101).

own attempts to combat fraud, and that they might take the matter to the COP if nothing was forthcoming from the Committee.[103] In the event, the Committee, at its meeting in January 1992, decided to give Italy three months to take appropriate measures to solve the problems raised by the Secretariat and report progress.[104]

In June 1992, following a mission to Italy, the Secretariat reported little progress, and recommended a suspension of trade in CITES specimens with Italy. Interestingly, this was supported by Italian civil servants, who had stated that the government would do nothing without trade restrictions being imposed.[105] The Secretariat also proposed, rather boldly, a 'suspension in all CITES trade with all EC countries' if it was confirmed that EU member states were prevented by EU rules from suspending trade with Italy.[106] Not surprisingly, the Standing Committee agreed to the first recommendation, but appears not to have even discussed the second.[107] A carefully worded notification was sent to the parties stating that:

> the Standing Committee recommends…with immediate effect, to adopt stricter domestic measures in accordance with Article XIV, paragraph 1 of the Convention, in order:
>
> – not to issue any CITES documents for specimens consigned to Italy; and
> – not to accept any CITES documents issued by Italy,
>
> until this country demonstrates to the Standing Committee that necessary steps to ensure adequate implementation of the Convention have been taken.[108]

The wording departs from previous notifications in three respects. First, it is the Standing Committee that is making the recommendation, not the Secretariat on the basis of Standing Committee endorsement. Second, it refers to the application of stricter domestic measures rather than a suspension or ban on

---

[103] CITES Doc. SC. 24.7 (n. 101); SC24: Summary Report (Jan 1992), p. 3.
[104] SC24: Summary Report, p. 4.
[105] SC28: Summary Report (Jun 1992), p. 12.
[106] CITES Doc. SC. 28.5, 'Implementation of the Convention in Italy', prepared by the Secretariat for SC28 (Jun 1992).
[107] SC28: Summary Report, pp. 11–12, 17–19.
[108] Notification to the Parties No. 675, 'Italy: Recommendations of the Standing Committee' (30 Jun 1992).

trade. Third, the Standing Committee, rather than the Secretariat, must verify Italy's progress. This careful wording reflects the sensitive nature of the decision – the first time a suspension of trade had been recommended for an EU state. It may also have been in part response to Italy's questioning the legal basis for the recommendation before the Standing Committee and reserving the right to invoke Article XVIII on dispute resolution, (though not stating against whom).[109]

Despite Italy's objection to the Standing Committee's action, a verification mission by the Secretariat in November 1992 noted great improvement in implementation, particularly with respect to border controls. A hundred student volunteers had been selected from the Corpo Forestale (a police corps), and specially trained and assigned to 12 border posts designated to clear CITES specimens. The Secretariat described inspection procedures developed by Customs officials and new Corpo Forestale officers as 'excellent'. Meeting with the Minister of Environment, the mission was informed that a new law decree had been submitted, and that sanctions were creating a problem for the Italian economy. The Secretariat confirmed, by checking export and re-export documents from other countries, that most parties, except Switzerland and the United States (for legislative reasons), had implemented the recommended sanctions, 'notably those in South and Central America that had asked for the ban'.[110] The 'tremendous work' of the Italian office of TRAFFIC was acknowledged.[111]

As a result of the mission, the Secretariat wrote to the Minister of Environment specifying conditions that still had to be met before they could recommend to the Standing Committee a suspension of the recommended trade restrictions. By February 1993 the Secretariat had received responses on all points. The Standing Committee recommended the suspension of sanctions on the basis of 'considerable progress' by Italy.[112] Their complete withdrawal, however,

---

[109] SC28: Summary Report, p. 21.

[110] SC29: Summary Report (Mar 1993), p. 22. Since US legislation did not enable legal action solely on the basis of a CITES notification, it had conducted bilateral negotiations with Italy (see COP9 Infractions Report). The USA had previously adopted legislation to enable a suspension of trade with Thailand, but then had difficulty reversing it (Willem Wijnstekers, personal communication). Switzerland has stated at several Standing Committee meetings that it cannot implement trade restrictions against an EU member state because of a free trade agreement between Switzerland and the EU: see Summary Reports of SC29, SC37 and SC38.

[111] CITES Doc. SC. 29.17, 'Follow-up of Discussions and Decisions on CITES Implementation: Italy', prepared by the Secretariat for SC29 (Mar 1993).

[112] Notification to the Parties No. 722, 'Italy: Suspension of the Recommendations of the Standing Committee' (19 Feb 1993).

was dependent on approval of the new legislation by Parliament and confirmation by a mission that Italy was implementing the new regulations and procedures correctly. It was emphasized to Italy that the suspension was temporary, and that a failure to approve the law decree would result in an automatic reimposition of sanctions. A year later, Italy commented that the sanctions had been 'very costly, both to its economy and to its image', but that Italy now had 'one of the best implementation systems in the world'.[113]

The Standing Committee recommendations were finally withdrawn in April 1995 on Italy's adoption of CITES legislation, and following a Secretariat mission to conduct a 'thorough review' of implementation in the country. Italy's 'outstanding' control procedures and 'high standards of achievement' were cited.[114]

Greece   Greece became a party to CITES only in January 1993, but within five years it was the subject of two Standing Committee recommendations concerning trade restrictions in CITES-listed species.[115] The Secretariat first raised problems in Greece with the Standing Committee in 1994. Apart from a general lack of implementation, Greece had not designated a Management Authority or a Scientific Authority, and its parliament had adopted a law that included CITES Appendices as they were when the text of the Convention was approved in 1973.[116] This meant that major amendments, such as the African elephant, birds of prey, most parrot species and orchids, were not listed. Acting on the Secretariat's advice, the Standing Committee recommended that parties not accept Greek export documents until a Management Authority was designated, but allowed Greece a month's grace at the request of the EU.[117] Greece responded by designating a Management Authority and undertaking to adopt a new law to update the Appendices.[118]

---

[113] SC31: Summary Report (Mar 1994), p. 41.

[114] CITES Doc. SC. 35.13, 'Implementation of CITES in Italy', prepared by the Secretariat for SC35 (Mar 1995); Notification to the Parties No. 842, 'Italy: Withdrawal of the Recommendations of the Standing Committee' (18 Apr 1995).

[115] Notification to the Parties No. 1998/35, 'Greece: Recommendation to Suspend Trade' (6 Aug 1998).

[116] CITES Doc. SC.31.9.5, 'CITES Implementation in Greece', prepared by the Secretariat for SC31 (Mar 1994).

[117] SC31: Summary Report, p. 36.

[118] CITES Doc. SC. 38.3, 'Implementation of the Convention in Greece', prepared by the Secretariat for SC38 (Jun 1997).

In 1995 the Secretariat undertook a mission to Greece to evaluate progress. It reported to the Standing Committee that there was still inadequate CITES legislation, insufficient border controls and a lack of personnel and training. Greece had been one of the parties named in the first phase of the national legislation project (see Chapter 6) as not having even the basic legislation necessary to implement CITES. In addition, there were at least 120 ports of entry and exit, far too many for proper customs control of wildlife trade; only one person was dealing with CITES issues on a part-time basis; and permits and certificates were being printed in Greek.[119] Unlike the situation in Italy, the volume of trade was not large, but because any specimen entering Greece could move freely in the EU, implementation in the Union as a whole was undermined. Since the Appendices had still not been updated, in theory any species listed after 1973 could enter the EU through Greece without CITES documents. The Standing Committee instructed the Secretariat to continue its dialogue and report back. [120]

The Secretariat had several discussions with the Greek authorities and conducted another mission to Greece in May 1997. Although a new law was being drafted and decisions had been taken on a Scientific Authority and ports of entry and exit, there was no indication of when they would enter into force. On the basis that there had been no real improvements in the law or practices since the previous meeting of the Standing Committee, the Secretariat recommended suspension of CITES trade from 1 January 1998. At the request of Greece, the Standing Committee extended the deadline, agreeing that from 1 March 1998 parties should not issue or accept documents for trade with Greece, unless adequate legislation was implemented and border controls improved.[121] The deadline was later extended again to 1 September 1998, this time at the request of the Secretariat on the basis of a certain amount of progress.[122] But the progress stagnated, so in August 1998 the Secretariat notified parties of the Standing Committee's recommendation 'not to issue permits and certificates for trade to Greece and to refuse to accept documents issued by Greece from 1 September 1998 until further notice'.[123] The recommendation was

---

[119] CITES Doc. SC.36.10, 'Enforcement Issues', prepared by the Secretariat for SC36 (Jan/Feb 1996).

[120] SC37: Summary Report (Dec 1996), pp. 25–6.

[121] CITES Doc. SC.38.3 (see n. 118 above); SC38: Summary Report (Jun 1997), p. 6.

[122] CITES Doc. SC. 40.6.3, 'Implementation of the Convention in Individual Countries: Greece', prepared by the Secretariat for SC40 (Mar 1998); SC40: Summary Report (Mar 1998), p. 27.

[123] Notification to the Parties No. 1998/35, 'Greece: Recommendation to Suspend Trade' (6 Aug 1998).

withdrawn in March 1999, following (paper) verification by the Secretariat and approval by the Standing Committee that Greece had finally complied with the conditions laid down.[124] Measures put in place included adoption of legislation, designation of a Scientific Authority, reduction of the number of customs ports of entry from 127 to nine, and improvement of border controls through training of officials at the ports of entry.[125]

Indonesia

In 1993 the Secretariat, acting on information from TRAFFIC about implementation problems in Indonesia, presented a lengthy report to the Standing Committee on the subject. The report stated that export quotas based on economic and political concerns as opposed to science were being set and in any case exceeded for many species. Examples were given where final capture quotas for several psittacine and reptile species had exceeded those advised by the Indonesian Scientific Authority, or had been established in spite of a recommendation that no trade should occur. Animals Committee recommendations for significantly traded Appendix II species had not been implemented by Indonesia in relation to several species of birds and macaques. And, despite the Scientific Authority's recommending that there be no trade in the majority of the 25 Indonesian psittacine species highlighted by the Animals Committee in a report to COP8, quotas were established, in many cases for hundreds or even thousands of birds. In addition to these problems, the Secretariat also reported insufficient monitoring of trade and inadequate national legislation.[126]

The Secretariat made a number of specific recommendations on export quotas; on the involvement of the Scientific Authority; on suspension of trade in significantly traded species subject to recommendations by the Animals Committee; and on trade in other CITES-listed species. The Standing Committee endorsed these, and Indonesia agreed to report back by January 1994.[127] There was, however, no report, so at the next Standing Committee meeting in March 1994 it was agreed, on the Secretariat's advice, that, if Indonesia did not imple-

---

[124] Notification to the Parties No. 1999/32, 'Greece: Withdrawal of the Recommendation of the Standing Committee' (12 Mar 1999).

[125] SC41: Summary Report' (Feb 1999), p. 19.

[126] CITES Doc. SC.30.8, 'CITES Implementation in Indonesia', prepared by the Secretariat for SC30 (Sep 1993). Much of the information in the report was based on a report by Stephen Nash of TRAFFIC Southeast Asia, 'Problems with Implementation of CITES Article IV in Southeast Asia; Review No. 1: Indonesia'.

[127] SC30: Summary Report' (Sep 1993), p. 7.

ment all of the Secretariat's recommendations by 1 February 1995, parties would be advised to 'suspend the import, for commercial purposes, of any specimens of CITES-listed species that have originated in Indonesia, including such specimens being re-exported by other parties, unless they were legally exported from Indonesia before 1 February 1995'. This last concession was added at the request of Indonesia. The suspension would remain in effect for at least a year, after which the Committee would review progress pending an investigation by the Secretariat.[128]

In the event, the recommended trade suspension did not go into effect. In November 1994 the Secretariat reported that Indonesia had complied with its recommendations, and established a task force on smuggling. The Standing Committee agreed that no further action was needed.[129]

In parallel with the CITES action, the European Union implemented its own measures. In December 1991 it prohibited the import from Indonesia of species listed in Annex C, Part 2, of Council Regulation 3626/82. This included a number of commercially important Appendix II species. As a result of this decision, IUCN was contracted to produce technical advice with a view to re-establishing trade with the EU.[130] Following a consultative meeting in Indonesia in July 1993, a Strategic Action plan was developed (though the existence of the plan, and its endorsement by the Indonesian Ministry of Forestry, did not avert the Secretariat's recommendation for trade sanctions the following year).[131] Trade between the EU and Indonesia has since been reopened on a species-by-species basis.[132]

Although on paper Indonesia appears to be complying with the Secretariat's recommendations, problems with enforcing wildlife trade controls still exist, compounded by corruption in the forestry department. A CITES technical team visiting Indonesia in relation to tiger trade found evidence of collusion between enforcement staff and illegal traders, while CITES-listed species were readily available at a bird market in Jakarta. The team commented that

---

[128] CITES Doc. SC.31.9.1, 'CITES Implementation in Indonesia (Continued)', prepared by the Secretariat for SC31 (Mar 1994), p. 8; SC31: Summary Report (Mar 1994), pp. 29–32.

[129] SC32: Summary Report (Nov 1994), pp. 2–3.

[130] In the Secretariat's report on Indonesia to SC30, it states that *Indonesia* contracted IUCN, but in the report of SC31, the observer from the European Commission is reported as saying *the EU* contracted IUCN.

[131] CITES Doc. SC.30.8, 'CITES Implementation in Indonesia', prepared by the Secretariat for SC30 (Sep 1993); SC31: Summary Report (Mar 1994), p. 30.

[132] Willem Wijnstekers, personal communication (1999).

the 'brazen and open approach' to them indicated that enforcement of the law was 'not common or feared'.[133] An Indonesian NGO, KSBK (Animal Conservation for Life), recently released the results of a 15-month investigation into the Indonesian parrot trade (January 2001–March 2002).[134] It monitored trapping, routes, involvement of government and military officials, and five bird markets in Java (which also sell other species, particularly primates, reptiles and fish). According to the KSBK report, trapping quotas were regularly broken; traders and the local forestry department colluded in violations of trapping permits; trapping and transportation permits were issued for white cockatoos (*Cacatua alba*) on a zero quota; and, while bird exporters in Jakarta and Bali reported most exports as captive-bred, they were known to receive wild caught birds. KSBK also reported that birds are being transported by army troops in warships to Java after the troops' tours of duty in remote provinces. In August 2001 military police seized dozens of rare birds smuggled on board a troop ship to Java, and although officers were questioned none were arrested. KSBK estimates that 47% of parrots traded in the bird markets are protected. After being sold, they are then smuggled to Singapore and Malaysia, some ending up in European pet shops. The chairman of KSBK told a press conference that 'weak law enforcement practices and corruption within Indonesia's forestry department means that officials routinely issue permits allowing private companies to catch and sell protected species'. A senior forestry department official present at the news conference was reported as acknowledging that corruption within his agency allowed illegal wildlife trade to flourish.[135]

Democratic Republic of Congo

In June 2001 the Secretariat reported to the Standing Committee on permit fraud in the Democratic Republic of Congo (DRC). False CITES documents had been issued by rebels and used to transport chimpanzees (listed on Appendix I) to a neighbouring country. It was suspected that the animals were destined for the bushmeat trade. But more importantly, the Secretariat had proof that between 1998 and 2000 large-scale illicit exports involving the alteration of genuine permits issued by the Management Authority had occurred

---

[133] CITES Doc. 42.10.4, 'Tiger Technical Missions', prepared by the CITES Tiger Technical Missions Team for SC42 (Sep/Oct 1999), p. 49.

[134] 'Flying without Wing: Executive Summary' (KSBK, Jul 2002), <www.ksbk.or.id/prog/parrots_fly.htm>.

[135] 'Indonesian Army, Corrupt Officials Involved in Endangered Animal Trade: Report', *Associated Press* (4 Jul 2002).

on a regular basis. In one case, permits authorizing the export of two birds were altered and used to export 1,000 birds to two different countries. During the course of its inquiry, the Secretariat discovered that either someone in the Management Authority was acting improperly, or communications to the office were being intercepted.[136] The nature and scale of the frauds prompted the Secretariat to advise parties not to accept permits or certificates issued by the DRC until their validity had been confirmed.[137]

Following an expression of its concern and the provision of recommendations to the DRC to combat fraud, the Secretariat received assurances from the Management Authority that an investigation had commenced to uncover the culprits and that measures had been put in place to prevent a recurrence of the problems. But by June 2001, no information had been received on the progress of the investigation or on any improvements in export controls.[138]

On the Secretariat's recommendation, the Standing Committee agreed that a notification be distributed 'recommending that, until further notice, the parties refuse any import of CITES-listed specimens from and any export or re-export of such specimens to the Democratic Republic of Congo'.[139] Conditions for withdrawal of the recommendation included adequate investigation of the fraudulent use of permits and certificates, measures to eliminate the abuse, and adequate export controls, particularly for live specimens. The Standing Committee specified that the Secretariat was to verify compliance with the conditions through a mission to the DRC, and to provide technical advice and support. Parties were notified of the decision in July 2001.[140] Following a mission at the end of October, the Secretariat concluded that steps were still needed to make initiatives – including institutional and procedural arrangements – operational. It reported to SC46 in March 2002 that it was not possible to withdraw the Standing Committee's recommendation.[141]

---

[136] CITES SC45 Doc. 11.2, 'Enforcement Matters', prepared by the Secretariat for SC45 (Jun 2001).

[137] Notification to the Parties No. 2001/002, 'Verification of Export Permits' (9 Feb 2001).

[138] CITES SC45 Doc. 11.2 (see n. 136 above).

[139] SC45: Summary Record (Jun 2001), p. 8.

[140] Notification to the Parties No. 2001/039, 'Democratic Republic of Congo: Recommendation to Suspend Trade' (9 Jul 2001).

[141] CITES SC46 Doc. 11.2, 'Enforcement Matters', prepared by the Secretariat for SC46 (Mar 2002).

Non-parties

To date, four non-parties have been subject to recommendations to suspend trade in CITES listed species: Singapore, El Salvador, Equatorial Guinea and, most recently, Grenada. All have since become parties to the Convention – arguably, cases of 'free-riders' becoming 'forced riders', although in Grenada's case its accession came some years after sanctions were recommended. Macau, then a Portuguese territory, was also subject to trade sanctions but responded shortly after their imposition by adopting CITES controls.

Singapore   In 1984, following endorsement by both the Technical Committee and the Standing Committee, the Secretariat requested 'all parties to take immediate action to prohibit and prevent any trade in ivory with and through Singapore', then a non-party. The action was taken based on information received by the Secretariat that 'very large quantities' of illegal ivory had been shipped from Africa to Singapore in 1983 and 1984, including 40 tonnes from Burundi alone in one year. (Burundi had just one wild elephant at the time.) In addition, comparable documentation required under Article X was not being issued by the competent authority for the re-export of ivory.[142]

Singapore drew attention again in 1986, this time in connection with the illegal trade in reptile skins. The Secretariat notified parties of a 'very substantial trade' in skins of Appendix II and III listed species, mainly snakes. There was evidence suggesting that many of the skins had been smuggled from India to Singapore, where the country of origin was falsely declared – often as Indonesia. Also, many documents issued for skin re-exports in Singapore did not meet requirements for comparable documentation. In contrast with the response concerning ivory two years previously, trade restrictions were not recommended. Instead, in its notification the Secretariat listed details for parties to check before accepting documents from Singapore and urged 'vigilance' on their part.[143]

That same year, however, unilateral action was taken by the United States under the Lacey Act. On 25 September 1986 the US Fish and Wildlife Service (USFWS) banned all wildlife imports from Singapore, citing the country's inability to provide 'comparable documentation'. Singapore was not providing information on the origins of wildlife exported. US Department of State officials pointed out the implausibility of Singapore, a small, mostly urban, country exporting a large volume of wildlife, unless it was obtaining it from somewhere

---

[142] Notification to the Parties No. 303, 'Appeal for Prohibition of Ivory Trade with Singapore' (23 Jul 1984); SC11: Summary Report (Jul 1984), p. 10.
[143] Notification to the Parties No. 381, 'Singapore: Trade in Skins' (4 Mar 1986).

else. The USFWS was particularly concerned about exports of pangolin (an anteater-like animal), even though it was not native to Singapore. Sanctions affected Singapore's trade in tropical fish with the United States, which earned US$12 million annually, as well as trade in animal products, amounting to another US$3–5 million. Despite an apparent threat by Singapore to raise the dispute under GATT, it became a party to CITES on 30 November 1986, effective 1 March 1987. It also enacted domestic legislation to ban trade in rhino products. The United States responded by lifting the embargo on 30 December 1986.[144]

Apparently Singapore had announced its intention to accede to the Convention before the US sanctions were imposed. In 1985 the CITES Secretariat had agreed to register undocumented and probably illegal stockpiles of ivory held in countries such as Burundi and Singapore as a precondition for their joining the Convention, a move that was strongly criticized by NGOs since it legitimized vast quantities of suspect raw ivory which could then be traded at quadruple the price.[145] Following Singapore's accession to CITES, the Secretariat cancelled its notifications concerning ivory and reptile skin trade, but drew parties' attention to reservations entered by Singapore with respect to three crocodile species.[146]

Singapore enacted CITES implementing legislation in 1989, but illegal trade appears to have continued. In 1992 Paraguay prepared a document for COP8, citing Singapore as one of the main destinations for illegal shipments of caiman skins from the central region of South America, and complaining that Singapore's reservation on *Caiman crocodilus* was rendering controls in exporting countries ineffective. A draft resolution urging parties to reject export and re-export documents issued by Singapore for trade in any crocodilian products was included in Paraguay's submission. By the time of the Conference, however, Singapore had withdrawn its reservation. In response, Paraguay withdrew its draft resolution urging trade restrictions.[147]

---

[144] DeSombre, p. 173; Sand (1997), p. 22 and n. 59, p. 30; *Straits Times*, 1 Jan 1987 (for reference to GATT threat).

[145] Philippe Sands and Albert Bedecarré, 'Convention on International Trade in Endangered Species: The Role of Public Interest Non-Governmental Organizations in Ensuring the Effective Enforcement of the Ivory Ban', *Environmental Affairs*, 17 (1990). p. 799: 807.

[146] Notification to Parties No. 427, 'Singapore' (3 Mar 1987).

[147] CITES Doc. 8.53, 'Illegal Trade of Singapore', prepared by Paraguay for COP8 (Mar 1992); Committee II: Summary Report, COP8 (Mar 1992).

Macau   In October 1985 the Secretariat reported to the Standing Committee that 'increasingly large volumes of "illegal" trade in rhino horn, musk and ivory were being routed to Macau via Hong Kong'. It stressed that the problem was Macau, then a Portuguese territory, not Hong Kong, which was checking transit shipments and sharing information on illegal trade.[148] Because of its lack of CITES controls and the tightening of controls in Hong Kong, ivory carving factories had moved to Macau.[149] Large quantities of African elephant ivory without CITES documents were being shipped there.[150]

Since it had been heard, albeit informally, that Macau might adopt CITES controls before the end of 1985, the Standing Committee agreed that, if the controls were not introduced before 1 January 1986, 'the Secretariat's request to all parties to prohibit trade in ivory with Macau would have its full support'.[151] In the event, the recommended trade suspension applied to more than just ivory. On 16 January 1986 the Secretariat notified parties that, despite several discussions with the Portuguese Management Authority, the government in Macau had taken no action to implement CITES or control trade. It urged parties to 'prohibit or prevent trade with or through Macau in any specimens of species included in the CITES appendices (including manufactured ivory), until such time as the Secretariat is satisfied that the situation in Macau justifies a reversal of this recommendation'.[152]

Following the imposition of sanctions, the Secretariat sent a mission to Macau. It reported that CITES had come into force in the territory through publication of the Convention's Articles in the official bulletin on 22 February 1986, less than a month after the recommended trade suspension, and regulations to permit its full implementation, including a dual permit system, were being prepared. In May 1986, the Secretariat issued a notification cancelling the recommendation for a trade suspension.[153]

El Salvador   In 1986 the Secretariat raised with the Technical Committee the problem of exports from El Salvador. Apparently El Salvador, whose wildlife was very depleted, had become 'one of the main loopholes in Central America

---

[148] SC13: Summary Report (Oct/Nov 1985), p. 7.
[149] Esmond Martin, personal communication (Feb 2002).
[150] CITES Notification to the Parties No. 371, 'Macau' (16 Jan 1986).
[151] SC13: Summary Report, p. 7.
[152] Notification to the Parties No. 371, 'Macau' (16 Jan 1986).
[153] Notification to the Parties No. 387, 'Macau' (7 May 1986).

with regard to trade in wildlife'. Following Technical Committee endorse-ment, the Secretariat sent out a notification urging parties to prohibit all trade in CITES-listed species with El Salvador until the Secretariat was 'satisfied' that it had 'taken... necessary measures to remedy the situation'.[154] A year later, in 1987, El Salvador became a party, whereupon the Secretariat gave notification that the trade ban was cancelled.[155]

Equatorial Guinea   In 1988 the Secretariat issued a notification to parties stating that it had been informed of several cases of trade in Appendix I species from Equatorial Guinea. In particular, it knew of an animal dealer operating there who had been convicted of illegal trade in gorillas in a neighbouring country. Its communication to the competent authority in Equatorial Guinea elicited no response. The Secretariat therefore urged parties 'either to ban all trade in CITES species from Equatorial Guinea or, at least, not to accept any imports ... without checking carefully their legitimacy'.[156] The decision failed to elicit an immediate response. At SC23 in April 1991, Equatorial Guinea 'still remained a major problem'.[157] In 1992, however, it acceded to CITES and the notification of the ban was cancelled.[158]

Grenada   In April 1991 the Secretariat recommended to the Standing Com-mittee that it should support a ban on *all* CITES trade with Grenada. Since the re-establishment of Grenada Zoo in 1989, there had been a marked increase in illegal trafficking in psittacines from Grenada. Birds allegedly smuggled from Guyana or other countries were illegally entering trade as re-exports with per-mits issued by the chief veterinary officer in Grenada. The Secretariat also had documentation indicating that smuggled birds were being certified as captive-bred at the Grenada Zoo then re-exported to parties and non-parties.[159]

The Grenada government did not respond to Secretariat communications until it received a copy of the report recommending a ban. Just before the Standing Committee meeting at which the report was to be considered, it sent a letter indicating that since December 1990 the chief veterinary officer had been ordered not to issue certificates that would facilitate the export of birds

---

[154] Notification to the Parties No. 398, 'El Salvador' (4 Jul 1986).
[155] Notification to the Parties No. 444, 'El Salvador' (28 Sep 1987).
[156] Notification to the Parties No. 494, 'Equatorial Guinea: Illegal Trade' (5 Sep 1988).
[157] SC23: Summary Report (Apr 1991), p. 9.
[158] Notification to the Parties No. 682, 'Equatorial Guinea' (24 Aug 1992).
[159] CITES Doc. SC.23.21, 'Implementation of the Convention in Thailand and Grenada', prepared by the Secretariat for SC23 (Apr 1991); SC23: Summary Report, p. 9.

(though exports had occurred), and instructions had been issued to airlines, the airline authority, the port and customs to prohibit imports and exports of exotic birds. As a result, the Standing Committee decided to give Granada 90 days to correct the situation before recommending a full ban. In the meantime, it was recommended that parties 'should not authorize any import from or export to Grenada of birds and should not authorize CITES trade with Grenada in other CITES specimens without prior consultation with the Secretariat'.[160]

At the next Standing Committee meeting, it was reported that Grenada had prohibited unauthorized exports of birds and seized animals from the offending Grenada Zoo. No further trade restrictions were proposed, but it was recommended that the existing notification remain in effect for the time being.[161] Grenada finally became a party to the Convention nearly eight years later in 1999, though it appears that the notification on trade restrictions was never formally rescinded with a further notification.

---

[160] Notification to the Parties No. 637, 'Grenada: CITES Trade' (22 Apr 1991); COP8 Infractions Report.
[161] CITES Doc. SC 24.6, 'Implementation of the Convention in Thailand and Grenada', prepared by the Secretariat for SC24 (Jan 1992); SC24: Summary Report (Jan 1992), p. 11.

6 Problem issues

This chapter examines the response to non-compliance that has evolved or is being proposed in relation to specific issues – inadequate national implementing legislation, non-reporting, non-designation of Scientific Authorities, and non-payment of dues to the Trust Fund. It concludes with an analysis of the ongoing debate on non-compliance measures that has been sparked by the large number of parties under consideration for sanctions as a result of decisions on national legislation and non-reporting adopted at COP11.

National legislation project

1992–1994

The national legislation project was initiated at COP8 in 1992, motivated by the belief that many parties had not enacted adequate legislation to implement CITES.[1] Resolution Conf. 8.4 directed the Secretariat to identify parties whose legislation did not enable them to:

1 designate at least one Management Authority and one Scientific Authority; or
2 prohibit trade in specimens in violation of the Convention; or
3 penalize such trade; or
4 confiscate specimens illegally traded or possessed;

and report to the Standing Committee and COP9. These four requirements, laid down in Articles VIII and IX of the Convention, were considered the basic national measures needed to implement CITES.

The project has been divided into four phases, each lasting from one COP to the next. In Phase I, from COP8 to COP9, IUCN's Environmental Law Centre and TRAFFIC USA analysed national legislation from 81 parties and territories, dividing it into three categories:

1 legislation believed generally to meet the requirements for CITES implementation;

---

[1] CITES Resolution Conf. 8.4, 'National Laws for Implementation of the Convention' (1992).

2 legislation believed generally not to meet *all* the requirements (i.e. to meet only some of the requirements);

3 legislation believed generally *not* to meet the requirements.[2]

Only 15 parties (19%) met all the basic requirements, while 27 (one-third) fell in category 3 and the remainder in category 2.[3]

1994–1997

Decisions concerning measures to be taken with respect to parties falling in categories 2 and 3, drafted by the Secretariat, were approved largely un-amended at COP9 in 1994:

- *Phase 1, category 3 parties* These parties 'should' introduce (submit to the legislature) implementing legislation by COP10 and report to the Secretariat before the meeting (Decision 6). With respect to parties that had not taken positive steps to implement this, COP10 'shall consider appropriate measures, which may include restrictions on the commercial trade in specimens of CITES-listed species to or from such parties' (Decision 7).
- *Phase 1, category 2 parties* These parties 'should' take steps to improve their legislation in indicated areas of weakness and report to the Secretariat before COP10 (Decision 8).

Phase II of the project – the analysis of legislation in a further 44 parties – was initiated after COP9,[4] and parties were invited by the Secretariat to send requests for technical assistance in developing legislation.[5]

By COP10 in 1997, although a number of Phase I parties in categories 2 or 3 had enacted new legislation and been re-categorized, the majority had not. Of the 44 Phase II parties, 20 (45%) fell into category 3 and 15 (34%) into category 2. At the suggestion of the Standing Committee, the Secretariat identified

---

[2] CITES Doc. 10.31 (Rev.), 'National Laws for Implementation of the Convention', prepared by the Secretariat for COP10 (Jun 1997).

[3] CITES Doc. 9.24 (Rev.), 'National Laws for Implementation of the Convention', prepared by the Secretariat for COP9 (Nov 1994), p. 575.

[4] Notification to the Parties No. 846, 'Analyses of National Legislation for Implementation of the Convention: Second Phase of the Project' (18 Apr 1995).

[5] Notification to the Parties No. 845, 'National Legislation for Implementation of the Convention' (18 Apr 1995).

[6] CITES Doc. 10.31 (Rev.), 'National Laws for Implementation of the Convention', prepared by the Secretariat for COP10 (Jun 1997).

seven Phase I parties falling in category 3 which also had a significant level of trade: Egypt, Guyana, Indonesia, Malaysia–Sabah, Nicaragua, Senegal and Zaire (now the Democratic Republic of Congo, DRC).[6]

1997–2000

Decisions recommending measures similar to those agreed at COP9 were approved at COP10 for Phase I and II, category 2 and 3 parties:

- *Phase I, category 3 parties with high volumes of trade (Egypt, Guyana, Indonesia, Malaysia–Sabah, Nicaragua, Senegal and DRC)* The COP recommended that 'all parties should, from 9 June 1998, refuse any import from, and export and re-export to, these countries of CITES specimens, if so advised by the Standing Committee' (Decision 10.18). The Secretariat was directed to report to the Standing Committee on progress in the seven parties by 9 June.[7]
- *Other Phase I, category 2 and 3 parties* These parties 'should' ensure that implementing legislation was 'in effect' by COP11 and report to the Secretariat before the meeting (Decision 10.19). With respect to those parties that did not take positive steps to implement this, 'the Conference of the parties at its 11th meeting shall consider appropriate measures, which may include restrictions on the commercial trade in specimens of CITES-listed species to or from such parties' (Decision 10.20).
- *Phase II, category 3 parties* These parties 'introduce' (submit to the legislature) implementing legislation by COP11, and report to the Secretariat before the meeting (Decision 10.21). With respect to those that have not taken positive steps to implement this, COP11 'shall consider appropriate measures, which may include restrictions on the commercial trade in specimens of CITES-listed species to or from such parties' (Decision 10.22).
- *Phase II, category 2 parties* These parties should take steps to improve their implementing legislation in areas of weakness and report to the Secretariat before COP11 (Decision 10.23).

The Secretariat was instructed to begin Phase III – the analysis of legislation in remaining parties – and to provide technical assistance to those parties requesting it, giving priority to Phase I parties still in category 3.[8]

---

[7] CITES Decision 10.115 directed to the Secretariat, 'Regarding Implementation of Resolution Conf. 8.4' (1997).

[8] Ibid.

By June 1998, the deadline for compliance, five of the seven targeted Phase I parties remained in category 3. Nicaragua and Malaysia–Sabah had adopted new legislation, so the Secretariat considered that they could be removed from the list.[9] A postal vote by the Standing Committee on whether trade should be suspended with the remaining five was inconclusive, so the matter was referred to SC41 in February 1999. At SC41 the Committee recommended different measures according to the circumstances of the parties.[10] Since Indonesia had provided the Secretariat with copies of recent legislation, they were removed from the list, along with Nicaragua and Malaysia–Sabah. Egypt and Senegal made strong representations in an attempt to avert trade restrictions, and succeeded in buying some time to comply. Guyana and the DRC did not attend.

The strongest measures were recommended for Egypt and Guyana: that trade in CITES specimens would be suspended from 30 September 1999 unless in the meantime the Secretariat verified that adequate legislation had been enacted. The grace period was approved despite Secretariat advice that COP10 Decisions allowed the Standing Committee little discretion. It was also agreed to defer a suspension of trade in CITES specimens with Senegal until 30 September, but with an opportunity to reassess the situation at SC42. The softer measure recognized potentially adequate draft legislation handed to the Secretariat by Senegal at the meeting. Egypt, however, had clearly made little progress, while Guyana had still not enacted draft legislation for which it had received considerable technical assistance from the Secretariat prior to 1997. The state of war in the DRC led to the deferral of a decision until SC43, prior to COP11, when there was a chance Congo might be represented.

Egypt responded to the threat of sanctions. The Secretariat reported to SC42 that, following high-level consultations with the Secretary General and assistance in drafting a ministerial decree during a Secretariat mission in September 1999, Egypt had managed to enact implementing legislation in time.[11] Furthermore, its representatives attended SC42 as observers,

---

[9] 'Implementation of Decision 10.18', prepared by the Secretariat and circulated to the Standing Committee by the Chairman (19 Jun 1998).

[10] Comments in the following paragraphs on the measures agreed for the DRC, Egypt, Guyana and Senegal at SC41 are taken from the author's notes (as an observer party representative). For the text of the agreed measures, see Notification to the Parties No. 1999/18, 'Executive Summary of Decisions Taken at the 41st meeting of the Standing Committee' (12 Mar 1999). See also SC41: Summary Report (Feb 1999), p. 20.

[11] CITES Doc. SC.42.12.2, 'Implementation of Decisions 10.18 and 10.64', prepared by the Secretariat for SC42 (Sep/Oct 1999); SC42: Summary Report (Sep/Oct 1999), p. 22; CITES Doc. 11.21.2, 'National Laws for Implementation of the Convention: Measures to

tabling a document detailing the legislation and announcing the setting up of an Egyptian CITES Standing Committee, as well as workshops planned for the future.[12] Senegal and Guyana, however, had failed to notify the Secretariat as to whether draft legislation had been passed. The Standing Committee noted that the recommendation to suspend trade in CITES specimens with Guyana would be in effect as of 30 September 1999.[13] It also recommended that, from 30 October 1999, parties should 'refuse any import from and export or re-export to Senegal of CITES specimens until further notice'.[14]

Guyana responded instantly by adopting the Species Protection Regulations on 29 September 1999. After reviewing the legislation, the Secretariat withdrew the recommendation for a trade suspension in November.[15] Senegal adopted ministerial regulations on 28 December 1999, which after review were approved by the Secretariat. A notification was sent out withdrawing the recommendation for a trade suspension on 31 January 2000.[16]

In June 1999 the Secretariat conducted a technical mission to DRC to assist with drafting legislation. In March 2000, DRC enacted a ministerial decree. The Secretariat commented: 'this environmental legislation was one of the most comprehensive in francophone Africa and could serve as a model for future assistance to other parties'. At SC43 the Standing Committee agreed the Secretariat's recommendation that DRC should not be subject to trade sanctions.[17] (Although the subsequent recommendation to suspend trade with DRC because of permit fraud, which must have been ongoing at the time of the Secretariat's visit in June 1999, demonstrates that model legislation is meaningless without proper enforcement.)

In Phase III, from COP10 to COP11, the legislation of 18 parties and 10 overseas territories and crown dependencies of the United Kingdom was

---

[11] (cont)
be Taken with Regard to Parties without Adequate Legislation', prepared by the Secretariat for COP11 (Apr 2000).

[12] Robert Hepworth, personal communication (1999).

[13] Ibid.

[14] Notification to the Parties No. 1999/75 'Senegal: Recommendation to Suspend Trade' (21 Oct 1999).

[15] Notification to the Parties No. 1999/78 'Guyana: Withdrawal of the Recommendation to Suspend Trade' (5 Nov 1999); CITES Doc. 11.21.2 (see n. 11 above).

[16] Notification to the Parties No. 2000/004, 'Senegal: Withdrawal of the Recommendation to Suspend Trade' (31 Jan 2000).

[17] CITES Doc. SC.43.6, 'Implementation of the Convention in Individual Countries: Democratic Republic of Congo', prepared by the Secretariat for SC43 (8 Apr 2000); SC43: Summary Report (Apr 2000), p. 5.

analysed. All 18 parties fell into category 3, while only one British territory fell into category 1, the others being classified in either category 2 or 3. In addition, legislation from 30 parties that had previously been analysed was reviewed and re-categorized. At COP11, in April 2000, the overall breakdown of national legislation in all parties analysed in the first three phases (see Table 6.1) was reported as:

- category 1 – 37 parties (26%);
- category 2 – 52 parties (36%);
- category 3 – 47 parties (32%);

The Secretariat identified four Phase III, category 3, parties that, according to the UNEP–WCMC database, had a high volume of international trade in CITES listed species: Fiji, Turkey, Vietnam and Yemen.[18]

Table 6.1: National legislation project by region, April 2000

Region	Category 1	Category 2	Category 3	Analysis ongoing
Africa	3	20	23	2
Asia	3	9	12	3
Central and South America & the Caribbean	6	15	7	3
Europe	19	7	5	1
North America	3			
Oceania	3	1		1
Total	37	52	47	10

Source: Doc. 11.21.1, Annex 2, prepared by the Secretariat for COP11.

2000–2002

At COP11 in 2000, in a departure from decisions agreed at COPs 9 and 10, the Secretariat submitted a draft resolution recommending that Fiji, Turkey, Vietnam and Yemen should be subject to sanctions if they did not adopt adequate legislation by 31 October 2001. (Previously such parties had been given until the following COP to comply.) While taking a firm line with these four Phase III parties, the draft resolution contained no measures for other Phase III, category 3, parties. Nor did it recommend any sanctions for Phase I and II,

---

[18] CITES Doc. 11.21.1, 'National Laws for Implementation of the Convention: National Legislation Project', prepared by the Secretariat for COP11 (Apr 2000).

category 2 and 3, parties who had not complied with COP10 decisions, decisions that instructed COP11 to consider measures that could include trade restrictions.[19] These inconsistencies, and the inequitable application of measures, were pointed out by Australia (on behalf of Fiji) and Germany. A working group convened to prepare a new draft decision.

The amended decision prepared by the working group retained the Secretariat's recommendation for Fiji, Turkey, Vietnam and Yemen, but balanced it with graded recommendations and measures for all other category 2 and 3 parties. Deadlines to effect legislation were tied to inter-sessional Standing Committee meetings, with the aim of inducing all persistent non-compliers to comply before COP12. The working group proposal was more stringent overall than the Secretariat's initial draft, but nevertheless was considered more equitable by parties and approved by consensus. The decisions adopted were:

- *Phase III, category 3, parties with high volumes of trade (Fiji, Turkey, Vietnam and Yemen)* These parties 'should adopt adequate legislation to implement the Convention' before 31 October 2001. They 'should' report progress to the Secretariat 'no later than 30 April 2001'. If they did not adopt the legislation required, 'all parties should refuse any import from and export and re-export of CITES-listed species to' these parties from 31 October 2001, 'if so advised by the Standing Committee' (Decisions 11.15 and 11.16).
- *Other Phase III, category 3, parties* These parties were advised they 'should' take steps to 'enact' the necessary legislation and 'should' report progress no later than six months prior to SC46 in March 2002 (Decision 11.17).
- *Phase I and II, category 2 and 3, parties with high volumes of trade which have not complied with COP 10 decisions* These parties were to ensure that adequate legislation would be 'in effect' no later than 30 days prior to SC45, and were to report progress to the Secretariat no later than six months before that meeting. With respect to non-compliant parties, 'the Standing Committee, at its 45th meeting [19–22 June 2001], shall consider appropriate measures, which may include restrictions on the commercial trade in specimens of CITES listed species to or from such parties' (Decision 11.18).
- *Phase I and II, category 2 and 3, parties with low volumes of trade which have not complied with COP 10 decisions* These parties were to ensure that adequate legislation would be 'in effect' no later than 30 days prior to SC46,

---

[19] CITES Doc. 11.21.2 Annex, 'Draft Decision of the Conference of the Parties to Replace Decision 10.18 to 10.23 and 10.101', prepared by the Secretariat for COP11 (Apr 2000).

and were to report progress to the Secretariat no later than six months before that meeting. With respect to non-compliant parties, 'the Standing Committee, at its 46th meeting [12–15 March 2002], shall consider appropriate measures, which may include restrictions on the commercial trade in specimens of CITES listed species to or from such parties' (Decision 11.19).

In all cases, parties could request technical assistance from the Secretariat, consisting of guidelines for preparing legislation and training for CITES authorities.

At COP11 a new strategy for the national legislation project was approved for Phase IV (COP11 to COP12). Considering that the indefinite continual review of new legislation is impractical, the Secretariat proposed evolving towards a legal capacity-building strategy (discussed more fully in Chapter 9). This approach was endorsed by the Standing Committee, provided it was made clear that the 'stick' and 'carrot' mechanism to deal with persistent non-compliers was to continue.[20] Through regional models of law developed by regional workshops, this strategy aims to achieve harmonization of laws and procedures implementing CITES. Responsibility for developing national laws will rest not with consultants, but with national experts who will receive training and other technical assistance from the Secretariat. A programme of regional workshops to be held between June 2000 and March 2003 was approved; meanwhile the Secretariat's central role in analysing and categorizing legislation and making recommendations was to continue. It was directed:

- to continue amending ratings of legislation and advising parties of amendments required;
- to provide technical assistance when requested, giving priority to category 3 parties;
- to report to COP12 on legislation adopted, as well as any recommendations relating to parties that have not adopted the required legislation and the conclusions of analyses updated or begun since 1999.[21]

At the time of writing, two regional workshops have been conducted as part of the legal capacity-building strategy, one in West Africa, attended by 18 French-speaking African countries, and one in Hong Kong, for countries in East, South and Southeast Asia.

---

[20] Robert Hepworth, personal communication (1999).
[21] CITES Decision 11.132 directed to the Secretariat, 'Regarding Implementation of Resolution Conf. 8.4' (2000).

At SC45 in June 2001, the Secretariat reported on its communications with non-compliant parties that were required to effect legislation, either before the meeting or before 31 October 2001. Its recommendations for action were somewhat weak. With respect to Fiji, Turkey, Vietnam and Yemen, it advised that the Standing Committee 'may wish to advise' parties that the COP recommendation to suspend CITES trade would automatically apply if implementing legislation were not adopted by 31 October 2001. With respect to ten Phase I and II, categories 2 and 3, parties, identified on the basis of UNEP–WCMC trade data as having high volumes of trade (and therefore required by Decision 11.18 to have legislation 'in effect' before SC45), the Secretariat believed 'some flexibility' was warranted over their deadline, since they had been only given six months' notice of impending action. The ten parties were divided into three groups according to their response to the Secretariat notification, and recommendations were made accordingly. Five parties – Cameroon, the Dominican Republic, Mozambique, Panama and Singapore – had not responded. With respect to these, the Secretariat advised that the Standing Committee 'may wish to consider appropriate measures, which may include restrictions on commercial trade in specimens of CITES-listed species'. The Russian Federation, South Africa and Thailand had all responded to say that they were addressing the situation, so the Secretariat advised merely that the Standing Committee 'may' wish to review their progress at SC46.[22] Poland and Romania had implemented legislation that fulfilled some if not all the requirements for implementing CITES and were removed from category 3.[23]

Given that the text of Decision 11.18 clearly stated that the Standing Committee 'shall' consider appropriate measures for all non-compliant parties, the Secretariat's written recommendations seemed to betray a reluctance to implement the COP11 decisions fully. This was reflected in the Standing Committee's final recommendations. Parties were clearly reluctant to recommend trade suspensions. Although the Secretariat advised verbally that there was no flexibility with respect to Fiji, Turkey, Vietnam and Yemen, the Standing Committee only 'provisionally agreed' that the recommended trade suspension would automatically apply to these four parties if legislation were not adopted by 31 October 2001. The recommendation was subject to the Secretariat's seeking a

---

[22] CITES SC45 Doc. 11.1, 'Implementation of the Convention in Individual Countries: National Legislation Project', prepared by the Secretariat for SC45 (Jun 2001).

[23] At SC46, the Secretariat reported that Poland's new legislation had qualified only for Category 2 (CITES SC46 Doc. 11.1, 'Implementation of the Convention in Individual Countries: National Legislation Project', prepared by the Secretariat for SC46 (Mar 2002)).

legal opinion as to whether the date of entry into effect could be delayed to 31 December 2001. With respect to the other eight non-compliant parties (Poland and Romania were exempted), on the basis of a proposal from the Secretariat, it was agreed to defer a decision until SC46 in March 2002.[24]

The outcome of SC45 was disappointing with respect to the Phase I and II parties with high volumes of trade. On the one hand, there was a failure to implement COP Decision 11.18 on the part of the Standing Committee, and on the other, it begs the question as to why the Secretariat failed to notify affected parties until January 2001, nine months after COP11. Targeting Fiji, Vietnam and Yemen, whose legislation was analysed in Phase III, but not the eight non-compliant parties, whose legislation was analysed earlier in Phases I or II, and which also had high volumes of trade but had been given far more time and due notice to comply, is inequitable.

In August 2001 the Secretariat issued a notification identifying 76 Phase I and II, categories 2 and 3, parties with low volumes of trade that were affected by Decision 11.19 and required to have legislation in effect by SC46 in March 2002. Of these, 45 parties were in category 2 and 31 were in category 3. In contrast to its advice to SC45, the Secretariat took a firm line. It stated that the concerned parties had been aware since COP10 or earlier that they could be subject to recommended trade suspensions, that 'parties have no discretion' in applying the Convention's controls to all listed species except those covered by a reservation, and that a failure to do this through domestic legislation 'constitutes a violation of the Convention'. It further concluded that 'the majority of parties still need to adopt or strengthen their legislative, regulatory and institutional measures to implement the Convention adequately'.[25]

On 14 January 2002 parties were notified by the Secretariat that 'the Conference of the parties recommends that ... all parties should refuse any import from and export or re-export to [Fiji, Vietnam and Yemen] of specimens of CITES-listed species, until further notice'.[26] The deadline for adopting legislation had been delayed until 31 December 2001, but the three parties had still not complied. Four days before the deadline, Turkey had published its new legislation and escaped a recommended trade suspension. Vietnam responded rapidly to the notification with a government decree that came into effect on 7

---

[24] SC45: Summary Record (Jun 2001), p. 7.

[25] Notification to the Parties No. 2001/059 'National Legislation Project: Implementation of Decision 11.19' (10 Aug 2001).

[26] Notifications to the Parties Nos. 2002/003, 004 and 005, 'Fiji: Recommendation to Suspend Trade', 'Vietnam: Recommendation to Suspend Trade', 'Yemen: Recommendation to Suspend Trade' (14 Jan 2002).

February 2002. The recommendation to suspend trade was therefore withdrawn on 11 March 2002.[27]

At SC46 in March 2002 the Secretariat reported that Yemen was revising its legislation but that the recommended suspension remained in effect. Fiji, a major coral exporter, attended the meeting and pleaded its case. Its representative informed the Standing Committee that the CITES trade suspension had had a major socio-economic impact on villages and coastal communities. Meanwhile, the government had pledged to enact CITES legislation before the end of 2002, and prepared a plan of action to address unsustainable coral trade, including a cut in exports by 50% of 2001 levels and a commitment not to export until the quota was in effect. The Standing Committee agreed a temporary suspension of its trade sanctions, but 'if Fiji has not enacted legislation by 31 December 2002, the Secretariat shall notify parties that the recommendation of the Conference of the parties that trade be suspended with Fiji is once again in effect until further notice'.[28]

In its report to SC46 the Secretariat identified eight Phase I and II parties with high volumes of trade that still had legislation in categories 2 and 3: Dominican Republic and Mozambique (category 3), and Cameroon, Panama, Poland, the Russian Federation, South Africa and Thailand (category 2).[29] Since SC45, Singapore had enacted legislation that qualified for category 1, while Romania's legislation was still being assessed. The Secretariat further identified 74 Phase I and II, category 2 and 3, parties with low volumes of trade: 30 in category 3 and 44 in category 2 (implying that two parties had complied since the notification in August 2001).

In a new development in the national legislation project, the Secretariat proposed that all identified parties be required to submit a CITES Legislation Plan by 31 May 2002. The Plans were to include agreed steps needed for each party to adopt adequate legislation by a specified deadline, which varied according to whether the party was in category 2 or 3 and had a high or low volume of trade. A variety of non-compliance measures were suggested for parties that failed to meet the specified deadlines.[30]

---

[27] Notification to the Parties No. 2002/016, 'Vietnam: Withdrawal of the Recommendation to Suspend Trade' (11 Mar 2002).

[28] SC46: Summary Report (Mar 2002), p. 9; 'CITES Incentives Inspire Vital Reforms in Wildlife Management', UNEP news release 2002/17 (15 Mar 2002).

[29] Since Poland was reported at SC45 as having been removed from category 3, it must be surmised that its legislation was not adequate to place it in category 1 (though this is not made clear in the Secretariat's SC46 report).

[30] CITES SC46 Doc. 11.1, 'Implementation of the Convention in Individual Countries: National Legislation Project', prepared by the Secretariat for SC46 (Mar 2002).

For the eight parties with high volumes of trade, the Standing Committee adopted the Secretariat's recommendations almost verbatim. Thus, if the Dominican Republic and Mozambique (Phase I and II, category 3) failed to submit a CITES Legislation Plan by 31 May 2002, or to adopt adequate legislation by 31 October 2002, the Secretariat 'shall issue a Notification recommending a suspension of commercial trade in CITES-listed species'. A similar recommendation was made for Cameroon, Panama, Poland, the Russian Federation, South Africa and Thailand (Phase I and II, category 2), except that they have until 31 March 2003 to adopt adequate legislation before a recommendation to suspend trade is made. (The Secretariat had recommended an earlier deadline of 31 January 2003.[31])

For 68 of the parties identified as having low volumes of trade (implying that six of the 74 identified by the Secretariat in its report had complied by the meeting), the Standing Committee agreed measures that differed from those recommended by the Secretariat. For all 68 (Phase I and II, categories 2 and 3), the Standing Committee decided that the CITES Legislation Plan to be submitted by 31 May 2002 should include agreed steps needed to adopt adequate legislation by 31 December 2003. No measures were recommended for those that fail to submit a Plan. Instead, action was deferred to SC47 (November 2002). For those that fail to adopt adequate legislation by 31 December 2003, it was decided that the Standing Committee 'shall' recommend restrictions on commercial trade at its first meeting after the deadline unless a party can 'show good cause for its lack of adequate progress'.[32] The Secretariat had recommended innovative non-compliance measures for those that fail to submit a Plan or adopt legislation by the deadline – namely, loss of the right to participate in permanent committees and suspension of rights to issue re-export certificates and to export species for which there is no quota – but these were not adopted by the Committee.[33]

Of the Phase III, category 3, parties required to report progress six months before SC46, only six had complied out of the 14 parties and three UK overseas territories affected. Since Decision 11.17 required no specific action by the Standing Committee, the Secretariat will make recommendations for action to COP12.[34]

While the inequity apparent following SC45 has to some extent been rectified with the recommendation of sanctions against the eight non-compliant

---

[31] CITES Notification to the Parties No. 2002/023, 'National Legislation Project: CITES Legislation Plan' (9 Apr 2002).

[32] Ibid.

[33] CITES SC46 Doc. 11.1 (see n. 30 above).

[34] Ibid.

Phase I and II parties with high volumes of trade if they fail to comply by the specified deadlines, it can still be argued that those parties have enjoyed more latitude and due notice than Fiji, Turkey, Vietnam and Yemen, whose legislation was analysed in Phase III and who were targeted almost immediately at COP11.The outcome of SC46 was disappointing with regard to Phase I and II parties with low volumes of trade. By deferring action to SC47, the Standing Committee lessened the chance that these parties would submit a CITES Legislation Plan by 31 May 2002, and once again it failed to fully implement a COP decision which clearly stated that measures 'shall' be considered at SC46. There has also been a weakening of the COP recommendation that legislation be 'in effect' by specified deadlines, the Standing Committee recommending merely that it be 'adopted'.

A closer examination of the parties identified as having low volumes of trade gives cause for concern about the basis on which the Secretariat has grouped them. Among them are several that are known to have high volumes of trade, including Benin, China, Comoros, Ghana, Madagascar, the UAE and Tanzania. Why these parties have been misidentified, and as a consequence escaped sanctions, raises questions about the basis for decision-making in the Project. One party – Comoros – has clearly benefited from non-reporting. A party to CITES since 1995, Comoros did not submit any annual reports until early 2002. Until 2000 there was virtually no CITES-related trade, or at least no such legitimate trade. But in March of that year permits began to be issued for increasingly large and frequent exports of CITES-listed species, particularly reptiles destined mainly for the USA.[35] Since the Secretariat's assessment of the volume of trade for the national legislation project was dependent entirely on UNEP–WCMC data, which would not have reflected the newly opened trade, Comoros has so far escaped sanctions, when in fact it is now one of the largest exporters of reptiles in East and Southern Africa. This illustrates the dependence of decision-making on annual reporting by parties, and the inequity that can result if parties fail to report – and in this case the benefit that non-reporting can confer. For the other parties known to have high volumes of trade, it is unknown why they were misidentified, since, even if they had not reported, import reports from other parties should have provided enough information to place them in the high trade volume group.

---

[35] Rosalind Reeve, 'The Trade in Reptiles from Madagascar and Comoros: Summary Report', for IFAW (2002) (hereinafter 'Reeve/IFAW, 2002'). Information on Comoros is based on field research by Melissa MacDonald in Comoros & R. Reeve in South Africa (Oct–Dec 2001).

Balancing 'carrot' and 'stick'

The national legislation project is unique among MEAs in its use of trade restrictions against parties solely for possessing inadequate implementing legislation. It revealed that about 75% of parties reviewed did not have the full range of national legislative and administrative measures needed to implement all aspects of CITES when their legislation was analysed.[36] The combination of 'stick' and 'carrot' has proved itself effective. All seven parties targeted at COP10 responded either to the threat or to the actual imposition of trade sanctions by the Standing Committee, as have Fiji, Turkey and Vietnam targeted at COP11. But by April 2000 the proportion of parties with category 2 or 3 legislation had declined only to 68% (see Table 6.1). The stringent decisions at COP11, designed to rein in persistent non-compliers, have speeded compliance remarkably. By April 2002 the proportion with category 2 or 3 legislation had declined to 51% (by the author's calculation), despite the Standing Committee's reluctance to implement the COP11 decisions. Had the Standing Committee taken a firmer line, the result could have been even better.

Until COP11, the process followed in responding to non-compliance was equitable. Since then, however, an element of inconsistency and inequity has crept in, leading to the sanctioning of Phase III parties before Phase I and II parties. Given that, at the time of writing, over 50% of parties still possess category 2 or 3 legislation, there is a need to maintain a firm, consistent and equitable approach, and not to lose sight of the importance of trade sanctions as a tool to induce compliance. While parties are gradually improving their national CITES legislation, progress appears to relate directly to the amount of pressure exerted. There is still a considerable way to go. It must also be borne in mind that even category 1 parties do not necessarily have legislation that takes into account COP resolutions and decisions – their legislation may only meet the basic requirements outlined in Resolution Conf. 8.4. While the capacity-building strategy is a welcome development, given the enormous variations in national legislation between parties, it will be a long, long time before its goal of harmonizing laws and procedures implementing CITES is achieved. It would be a mistake to depend on the 'carrot' to the detriment of the 'stick', which has proven its effectiveness.

Non-submission of annual reports

Annual reporting is an issue largely ignored by parties and NGOs alike. Repeated efforts by the Secretariat have failed to produce a consistent improvement

---

[36] CITES Doc. 11.21.1 (see n. 18 above).

in parties' reporting. Yet, as has already been stressed, late, incomplete and inaccurate reporting is a major source of concern, particularly since it undermines the quality and usefulness of reviews of conservation status and trade in CITES-listed species, as well as the decision-making that is dependent on an assessment of trade volume in individual parties, such as in the national legislation project. At COP8 in 1992 a mechanism to respond to late submission of annual reports by parties was provided through Resolution Conf. 8.7 (now 11.17).[37] In effect, the non-compliance response system in Resolution Conf. 7.5 (now 11.3) was extended to cases of late reporting by defining failure by a party to submit a report by a specified deadline as a major problem with implementation of the Convention (see Box 6.1). The Secretariat had initially recommended that failure to submit reports by the specified deadline be considered a possible reason for sanctions,[38] but the COP moderated this to 'allow corrective measures commensurate with the degree of lateness of submission'.[39]

The Secretariat's frustration at the subsequent failure of this mechanism is evident in its 1997 report to COP10. It states that, despite bringing the problem of late submission to the attention of the Standing Committee at five different meetings, the Committee took no action. It notes that 'half of the members of the Standing Committee were among the parties that had neither submitted their annual report for 1995 on time nor sought an extension to the deadline'. Although the Secretariat had offered to help parties by arranging for computerization of their data from export permits, which could then be printed by UNEP–WCMC in the form of an annual report, very few parties had taken up the offer.[40]

At COP10, it was decided that 'punitive action' (presumably referring to trade restrictions) against parties was inappropriate for late submission.[41] In its report on the effectiveness of CITES, ERM had recommended that technical assistance be provided for reporting. As a result, the only provisions approved were assistance to parties that have a problem with annual reporting, and the

---

[37] CITES Resolution Conf. 8.7, 'Submission of Annual Reports' (1992), now consolidated into Resolution Conf. 11.17, 'Annual Reports and Monitoring of Trade' (2000).
[38] OECD (see ch. 1, n. 3), p. 33.
[39] CITES Com. II 8.12 (Rev.) 'Summary Report of the Committee II Meeting', COP8 (Mar 1992).
[40] CITES Doc. 10.26 'Report on National Reports Required under Article VIII, Paragraph 7(a), of the Convention', prepared by the Secretariat for COP10 (Jun 1997).
[41] CITES Doc. SC.41.16 'Late Submission of Annual Reports', prepared by the Secretariat for SC41 (Feb 1999).

Box 6.1: Non-compliance response procedure for late submission of annual reports

From Resolution Conf. 11.17

(a) ... failure to submit a report by 31 October of the year following the year for which the report was due constitutes a major problem with the implementation of the Convention, which the Secretariat shall refer to the Standing Committee for a solution in accordance with Resolution Conf. 11.3';

(b) '... the Secretariat may approve a valid request from a party for a reasonable extension of time to the 31 October deadline for the submission of annual reports provided the party submits to the Secretariat a written request, containing adequate justification, before that deadline.

From Resolution Conf. 11.3

(c) ... if major problems with implementation of the Convention in particular parties are brought to the attention of the Secretariat, the Secretariat work together with the party concerned to try to solve the problem and offer advice or technical assistance as required;

(d) ... if it does not appear a solution can be readily achieved, the Secretariat bring the matter to the attention of the Standing Committee, which may pursue the matter in direct contact with the party concerned with a view to helping to find a solution;

(e) ... the Secretariat keep the parties informed as fully as possible, through Notifications, of such implementation problems and of actions taken to solve them, and include such problems in its report of alleged infractions.

---

inclusion in the information management strategy of a standard computer package for preparing annual reports and managing CITES-related data.[42]

At COP11 the Secretariat once again recommended sanctions for non-reporting. It presented a strongly worded draft decision that, surprisingly, was agreed by consensus and without dissent. On the basis of Secretariat reports, the Standing Committee was directed to:

> determine which parties have failed, without providing adequate justification, to provide the annual reports required...for three consecutive years within the deadline established in Resolution Conf. 11.17, or the extended deadline. (Decision 11.89)

With respect to these non-reporting parties identified by the Standing Committee,

---

[42] CITES Doc. 10.82 'Development of an Information Management Strategy', prepared by WCMC for COP10 (Jun 1997); CITES Doc. SC.41.16, 'Late Submission of Annual Reports', prepared by the Secretariat for SC41 (Feb 1999).

from 1 January 2001, parties should not authorize any trade in specimens of
CITES-listed species. (Decision 11.37)

The wording of the decision left no room for discretion on the part of the
Standing Committee.

In September 2000 the Secretariat sent out a notification naming 34 parties
that had not provided annual reports for 1998, 1997 or 1996, and in some cases
not for previous years either. This was an 'early warning' that, unless annual
reports were received before 1 January 2001, the Secretariat would bring the
matter to the attention of the Standing Committee. An additional 16 parties
were warned that, if their reports were not received by 31 October 2000, they
too would be included in the report to the Committee. The overwhelming majority of the parties named were developing countries.[43]

At SC45 in June 2001 (the first chance to review the COP11 decision) the
Secretariat presented parties' annual reporting records since 1991. The
number of parties potentially affected by the COP decision stood at 29 (significantly fewer than when the warning had been sent out in September
2000). Of these, 20 had failed to provide any justification for failing to report for a period of three consecutive years since 1991. The Secretariat
stated, somewhat ingenuously, that when the decision was agreed by the
COP it 'did not envisage that about 20% of the parties might be potentially
subject to a recommendation to suspend trade by the other 80%', and that it
did 'not think it would be helpful to penalise such a large number of parties'. Using weak language reminiscent of its advice on the national
legislation project, it recommended that the Standing Committee 'may'
wish to consider whether to apply the COP11 decision to the period 1991–9,
affecting 20 parties, or to the period 1997–9, affecting 18 parties including
three Standing Committee members – Burkina Faso, Saint Lucia and Saudi
Arabia.[44]

Predictably, the Standing Committee bridled at the prospect of sanctions for
non-reporting. The Secretariat was encouraged to use diplomatic channels to
obtain missing annual reports. There was debate as to whether 'sanctions'
might be imposed under CITES, or whether the measures taken were 'simply
recommendations to suspend trade that states are free to implement or not'.
The question of compliance with the WTO was also raised. The Chairman
noted that the Standing Committee was 'not comfortable' with the decision of

---

[43] Notification to the Parties No. 2000/057, 'Failure to Submit Annual Reports' (29 Sep 2000).
[44] CITES Doc. SC45 13.1 'Late or Non-submission of Annual Reports', prepared by the
Secretariat for SC45 (Jun 2001).

the COP and 'did not want to proceed to cite countries with which trade should be suspended'.[45]

The disappointing outcome of the Standing Committee meeting was that no determination was made on the issue. However, in what could be an important development for the CITES compliance system as a whole, the Secretariat was instructed to prepare for consideration at SC46:

> [an] analysis of the range of legal technical and administrative actions that might be taken in response to problems of non-compliance with the Convention, Resolutions and Decisions, such as the late or non-submission of annual reports, taking into account the need to ensure that such actions do not have a negative conservation impact.[46]

Given that non-reporting seriously undermines the ability to implement the Convention effectively and equitably, it is hard to envisage any 'negative conservation impact' from trade suspensions that could outweigh this – or, indeed, any negative conservation impact at all. In its analysis presented to SC46, the Secretariat observed that it is 'unaware of situations in which [compliance] measures have had or might have a negative conservation impact' (see more below).[47]

As of 28 January 2002, 17 parties had still failed to provide annual reports, or adequate justification, for three consecutive years between 1997 and 2000. They included the Standing Committee members Burkina Faso and Saudi Arabia, who had announced at SC45 that their missing reports would be submitted shortly after the meeting. St Lucia, however, had complied. By SC46 in March 2002 another four parties had complied, including Burkina Faso, bringing the number down to 14, leaving Saudi Arabia as the only non-compliant Standing Committee member.[48]

The Secretariat advised the Standing Committee that it had no discretion concerning the *type* of non-compliance response measure, since Decision 11.37 only allowed for a recommendation to suspend trade, but that it did have discretion as to *when* it was to determine which parties had not complied under Decision 11.89.[49] There was no mention in the Secretariat report of the un-

---

[45] SC45: Summary Record (Jun 2001), p. 11.

[46] Ibid.

[47] CITES SC46 Doc. 11.3, 'Possible Measures for Non-compliance' prepared by the Secretariat for SC46 (Mar 2002), p. 3.

[48] SC46: Summary Report (Mar 2002), p. 17.

[49] CITES SC46 Doc. 17 'Late of Non-submission of Annual Reports', prepared by the Secretariat for SC46 (Mar 2002).

equivocal decision of the COP that, 'from 1 January 2001, parties should not authorize any trade in specimens of CITES-listed species' with non-reporting parties identified by the Standing Committee. Given that non-reporting for three consecutive years during 1997–2000 is a purely factual determination, there could be no justification for further delay. Yet, once again, the Standing Committee delayed its decision, putting off a determination of which parties were non-compliant until SC47.[50]

The Standing Committee's failure to implement the COP's decision is likely to undermine attempts to improve future reporting on a long-term and consistent basis. The threat of trade sanctions at COP11 has pulled in a considerable number of reports and provided a much needed boost to the database, but if the threat proves to be empty its future use as a non-compliance tool is jeopardized. It is also open to question whether the Standing Committee had the discretion to ignore the COP's direction, particularly since the language was unequivocal. The law may be grey when it comes to COP recommendations, but at the very least the Standing Committee's action, or rather its failure to act, undermines the impact of those recommendations. In effect, a handful of parties have not only ignored a decision subscribed to by all, but have also set in motion a process that may bring into question the strongest card that CITES has in its compliance suit – recommended trade suspensions for non-compliant parties.

Non-designation of Scientific Authorities

National Scientific Authorities play an important role in the implementation of the Convention through monitoring export permits, carrying out non-detriment findings and limiting exports in order to maintain a species throughout its range 'at a level consistent with its role in the ecosystems in which it occurs and well above the level at which that species might become eligible for inclusion in Appendix I'.[51] Yet under-resourced, understaffed and, in some cases, non-existent or marginalized Scientific Authorities have long undermined the implementation of CITES.

In 1997 the United States raised the persistent problem that several parties had not designated Scientific Authorities as required by Article IX. Since the United States had first raised the issue at COP6 in 1987,[52] each infractions report had

---

[50] SC46: Summary Report, p. 17.

[51] Articles III.2(a), III.3(a), IV.2(a), IV.3 and IV.6(a).

[52] CITES Doc. 10.76, 'Designation of Scientific Authorities', prepared by the US for COP10 (Jun 1997).

identified a number of parties that had failed to nominate Scientific Authorities.[53] At COP10, Afghanistan, Belize, Comoros, Eritrea, Panama, Rwanda, Saudi Arabia, Turkey and the UAE were named in the Secretariat's infractions report as not having nominated Scientific Authorities, though Turkey was subsequently removed from the list.[54] In response, the COP approved Resolution Conf. 10.3, noting in the preamble that issuance of permits by a Management Authority without appropriate Scientific Authority findings constitutes lack of compliance with CITES. The Resolution, still in effect, recommends, *inter alia*, that parties not accept export permits from countries that have not informed the Secretariat of their Scientific Authorities for more than one interval between regular meetings of the COP.[55]

In February 1999 the Secretariat reported to the Standing Committee that the time limit specified in Resolution Conf. 10.3 had passed for Afghanistan, Belize, Rwanda and the UAE, and that parties would be reminded not to accept export permits from those four countries. Another four parties – Comoros, Dominica, Eritrea and Jamaica – were warned that they should designate authorities before COP11 in order to avoid rejection of their permits, while Antigua and Barbuda and Mauritania were reminded that they should designate authorities before COP12.[56] In March 1999 the Secretariat notified parties that export permits should not be accepted from Afghanistan and Rwanda until information about their Scientific Authorities had been published in the CITES Directory. The Secretariat went further and also recommended that no permits be issued for the export of Appendix I specimens to these states, since import permits for trade in Appendix I species may be issued only following advice from a Scientific Authority.[57] As of January 2002, Scientific Authorities were still not listed on the CITES website for Afghanistan (not surprisingly) and Rwanda, and the March 1999 notification was still included as valid, indicating that neither party had responded to the sanctions. The omission of Belize and the UAE from the March 1999 notification im-

---

[53] The Infractions Reports prepared for COPs 7, 8 and 9 noted that 15, 5 and 10 parties, respectively, had not identified Scientific Authorities.

[54] See CITES Doc. 10.76 'Designation of Scientific Authorities' (see n. 52 above), and COP10 Infractions Report.

[55] CITES Resolution Conf. 10.3 'Designation and Role of the Scientific Authorities' (1997).

[56] CITES Doc. SC. 41.15, 'Designation of Management and Scientific Authorities', prepared for SC41 (Feb 1999).

[57] Notification to the Parties No. 1999/24 'Parties that have not Designated Scientific Authorities' (12 Mar 1999).

plies that they complied, but as of January 2002, according to the website, Belize had still not designated a Scientific Authority (though one was listed for UAE).

After March 1999 the paper trail goes cold. At COP11 in April 2000 the subject of non-designation of Scientific Authorities was not discussed, though, of the four parties who were warned in February 1999 that they should designate Authorities by this date, only Comoros had complied. By January 2002 Jamaica too had complied, but Dominica and Eritrea still had no Scientific Authorities listed, and no notification had been issued by the Secretariat to recommend non-acceptance of their permits. Antigua and Barbuda had complied in advance of its COP12 deadline, but Mauritania had not. Saudi Arabia – a Standing Committee member – still had no Scientific Authority listed despite being named for that reason in the COP10 infractions report in 1997.

It is interesting to note that this response mechanism is not dependent on approval by the Standing Committee, but is automatic on passage of the specified time limit. It seems, however, for unclear reasons, that implementation of the process by the Secretariat stopped dead in its tracks after March 1999.

The 'stick' in Resolution Conf. 10.3 is balanced by a provision encouraging assistance to Scientific Authorities to improve their implementation of the Convention. Discussed more fully below under the section on technical assistance, a programme to implement this provision is currently being carried out by the Secretariat in association with IUCN. While it is clearly needed, this active capacity-building programme could be the reason why implementation of the 'stick' in Resolution Conf. 10.3 seems not to have been implemented since March 1999. If so, the imbalance between 'carrot' and 'stick' needs to be rectified.

Non-payment of dues to the Trust Fund

A new cause for the possible imposition of sanctions was raised at SC45 in June 2001: non-payment of contributions by parties to the Trust Fund. Amid concerns that the financial liquidity of the Fund would be affected, it was decided to address the issue in the broader context of non-compliance. The Secretariat was instructed to write to all parties in arrears inviting them to propose a schedule for making payments. It was also directed to:

> prepare an analysis of the prior years' dues and to indicate any possible sanctions that might be taken in respect of parties with payments in arrears, taking into account the various procedures established by the Conference of

the Parties, e.g. regarding the national legislation project, the non-submission of reports, etc.[58]

The issue would be discussed again at SC46 and a decision made on whether to draft a resolution for consideration at COP12 in November 2002.

The Secretariat wrote to 63 parties that had fallen into arrears with contributions over the period 1992–2000 asking for a time-frame for payment. In response, seven parties paid up in full and six made partial payments. No response was received from 43 parties (68%). The Secretariat recommended to SC46 that these parties be asked to submit a compliance plan by 30 April 2002 committing to payment by 31 August 2002, unless they provided satisfactory justification for not complying.[59] This was agreed by the Standing Committee, which directed the Secretariat to work with parties to develop the plans and decided that the Standing Committee Chair and Secretary General should intervene in cases where the arrears are particularly large. Decisions on further measures were postponed until SC47, and no resolution was proposed for COP12.[60]

The Secretariat also warned the Standing Committee that, if previous experience was repeated and by the end of May 2002 50% of 2002 contributions had not been received, the work programme would have to be curtailed. (By the end of May 2001, only 27% of contributions for that year had been received.) The Standing Committee agreed to write to the six parties whose contributions account for 72% of the Trust Fund – France, Germany, Italy, Japan, the UK and USA – asking for payment by the end of May.[61] However, there seems to be reluctance in the Standing Committee to agree to sanctions for non-payment of contributions. At SC46 concern was expressed about the possibility of action against non-compliant parties, some delegates stating that contributions are voluntary.[62] Within a wider debate of possible non-compliance measures (see below), the Secretariat suggested that CITES Article XI, paragraph 3(a) authorizing the COP to adopt financial provisions could be used together with Resolution Conf. 11.2 on financing the Secretariat and COP 'as the basis for addressing parties whose payments are in arrears'.[63] The

---

[58] SC45: Summary Record (Jun 2001), p. 3.
[59] CITES SC46 Doc. 9.1.3 (Rev. 1), 'Payments of Contributions by Parties', prepared by the Secretariat for SC46 (Mar 2002).
[60] SC46: Summary Report (Mar 2002), p. 5.
[61] CITES SC46 Doc. 9.1.3 (Rev. 1) (see n. 59 above).
[62] SC46: Summary Report, p. 5.
[63] CITES SC46 Doc. 11.3 (see n. 47 above).

suggestion drew a strong response from Ecuador, as regional representative of Central and South America and the Caribbean, which submitted a formal statement that 'a link should not be established between the failure to pay national contributions to the Trust Fund and the possibility to sanction parties'.[64]

Debate on non-compliance response measures

The number of parties affected by possible trade sanctions for non-compliance since COP11 as a result of non-reporting and the national legislation project has sparked the biggest debate on non-compliance response measures since the procedure for dealing with parties experiencing major implementation problems was passed in 1989 (now in Resolution Conf. 11.3). At SC46 in March 2002 the Secretariat presented its first ever analysis of 'Possible measures for non-compliance' in response to the Standing Committee's instruction to prepare an 'analysis of the range of legal technical and administrative actions that might be taken in response to problems of non-compliance with the Convention, Resolutions and Decisions....'.[65] The analysis contained a pragmatic range of gradual and sequential responses to non-compliance available to CITES, some of which are in use and some of which are new (see Box 6.2). It concluded by recommending that the Standing Committee 'endorse the Secretariat's plan to prepare a revision of Resolution Conf. 11.3, to provide a set of procedures and mechanisms to identify and address cases of non-compliance'. The Standing Committee was reluctant, however, to endorse a revision of Resolution Conf. 11.3.[66] Instead, it instructed the Secretariat to prepare a document for COP12, not requiring a COP decision, elaborating on the Secretariat's analysis and including points made in response by Standing Committee members at SC46 (see Box 6.2). Ecuador (regional representative of Central and South America and the Caribbean) stated that the financial penalties and suspension of rights proposed by the Secretariat should be discarded.[67]

The Secretariat's analysis defends the use of trade suspensions, seeing them as a positive and precautionary measure, which provides a 'breathing space' to enable assistance by other parties and to prevent a continuing violation of the Convention that is detrimental to the survival of CITES-listed species. This is

---

[64] SC46: Summary Report, p. 15.

[65] SC45: Summary Record, p. 11; CITES Doc. SC46 11.3 n. (see n. 47 above).

[66] Resolution Conf. 11.3 will be reviewed for COP12, but only with a view to consolidating it with other resolutions. See CITES Notification to the parties No. 2002/024 'Revision of existing Resolutions' (9 Apr 2002).

[67] SC46: Summary Report, pp. 14–15.

Box 6.2: Possible measures for non-compliance available to CITES

Secretariat suggestions[a,b]

- Advice and/or assistance – *in use but limited by human and financial resources*
- Issuance of an informal warning – *in use*
- Additional self-reporting and/or targeted monitoring (e.g. permit confirmation) – *in use*
- Issuance of a formal caution – *in use*
- Public notification of non-compliance – *in use*
- Verification, by review or on site – *in use, but on-site verification limited by human and financial resources*
- Compliance action plans – *in use, but not formally named as such until the introduction of Legislation Plans under the national legislation project*
- Suspension of rights and privileges
  - recommended suspension of trade in specimens of one or more or all CITES species – *in use*
  - restriction of the right to vote at COP meetings – *new*
  - ineligibility for membership of the Standing Committee – *new*
  - loss of the right of a party and its experts to participate in other permanent committees and working groups – *new*
  - ineligibility of a party to receive documents for meetings – *new*
- Financial penalty
  - ineligibility to receive financial assistance – *new*
  - ineligibility to receive funding for participation in COP meetings – *new*

Standing Committee response[ac]

- Place more emphasis on measures for facilitating compliance and working cooperatively with parties – *more funding will be needed*
- Clarify the legal basis for possible non-compliance measures, referring to the Vienna Convention on the Law of Treaties and indicating whether amendments to CITES provisions are required – *a difficult question, given the controversy over 'soft' law*
- Elaborate on possible reasons for non-compliance – *the Secretariat has already cited lack of political will*
- Elaborate on the respective roles of CITES institutions and whether these are reflected in existing resolutions – *this could sidestep the need for a Compliance Committee*
- Provide incentives for compliance – *more funding will be needed for positive incentives*
- Provide means to ensure that measures to address non-compliance do not have any negative conservation impact – *non-compliance in itself has a negative conservation impact*

[a] Author's comments appear in italics.
[b] CITES SC46 Doc. 11.3, 'Possible Measures for Non-compliance', CITES Secretariat (March 2002).
[c] SC46: Summary Record (March 2002)

encouraging. While a revised compliance procedure would benefit from broadening the range of non-compliance measures, it is important that recommended trade suspensions are retained as a measure of last resort, using them in combination with other measures designed to bring parties back into compliance. There is nothing in the Standing Committee's response that would imply a retreat from the use of trade suspensions, but the emphasis is clearly on the desire for incentives and assistance. While providing more 'carrots' to balance the 'sticks' would undoubtedly improve compliance, this demands more funds, which, given the extent of non-payment of contributions and the reluctance of parties to increase them, is unrealistic. If parties want incentives and assistance, they will inevitably have to pay.

The Secretariat's proposal to bring a revised non-compliance procedure before the COP, specifying and broadening the range of non-compliance measures available, carries the attraction of being able to 'nail down' a procedure that currently depends more on custom than any formal agreement between the parties. But such an important task should be carried out by an expert working group, composed of lawyers with experience of compliance issues, and not by the Secretariat, with minimal oversight. It also carries the danger of opening a can of worms that could ultimately weaken rather than strengthen the system. Recommended suspensions of trade are controversial. Although there appears to be a growing recognition in the WTO of the validity of trade-related environment measures (discussed in Chapter 12), not all stakeholders in CITES support the use of trade suspensions as a non-compliance response, particularly pro-trade NGOs and trade associations, which present a formidable lobby. Codification of non-compliance measures could provoke attempts to weaken the use of trade suspensions and the compliance system as a whole. It must be hoped that, if the current debate on non-compliance measures leads to a revision of the procedure, recognition of the system's proven effectiveness will prevail and trade suspensions will be retained among a broadened and balanced range of measures that draw on experience not only from CITES, but also from other multilateral compliance systems.

7 Significant Trade Review

The main mechanism for species-specific non-compliance response, which relates to problems in implementation with respect to individual CITES-listed species, is found in the increasingly complex process that has evolved to deal with significantly traded Appendix II species – the Significant Trade Review. The other form of species-specific response, involving ad hoc measures to rescue high-profile Appendix I listed species facing imminent extinction, such as the rhino and tiger, is addressed in the following chapter.

1981–1989: first review of fauna

In 1981, at COP3, Australia expressed its concern that:

> the Convention is simply documenting the decline of Appendix II species in spite of the fact that Article IV, paragraph 3, of the Convention should prevent any decline once a species is listed in Appendix II.[1]

Article IV(3) obliges parties to monitor exports in Appendix II species and to limit them as necessary through their Scientific and Management Authorities. This is a key obligation of the Convention, but lack of financial resources and scientific expertise meant that many parties were failing to implement it. Despite this, Australia's proposal to create an expert committee to identify Appendix II species that were traded significantly and advise on management programmes was resisted. At the following COP, in 1983, Australia tried again to introduce a procedure to assist with implementing Article IV(3) and this time succeeded (see Box 7.1).[2]

As a result of Australia's initiative, the Technical Committee was mandated by resolution to identify significantly traded Appendix II species, and to develop and negotiate measures 'at the request of at least one of the countries involved' to ensure that trade was within the terms of Article IV(3).[3]

---

[1] CITES Doc. 3.25, 'Regulation of Trade in Wildlife Listed on Appendix II', prepared by Australia for COP3 (Feb/Mar 1981).

[2] David S. Favre, *International Trade in Endangered Species: A Guide to CITES* (Kluwer, 1989), at p. 115; CITES Doc. 4.20, 'Regulation of Trade in Wildlife Listed on Appendix II', prepared by Australia for COP4 (Apr 1983).

[3] CITES Resolution Conf. 4.7, 'Regulation of Trade in Species Listed in Appendix II and Implementation of Article IV, paragraph 3, of the Convention' (1983).

Box 7.1: Article IV(3): Obligation to monitor and limit exports of Appendix II species

A Scientific Authority in each party shall monitor both the export permits granted by that State for specimens of species included in Appendix II and the actual exports of such specimens. Whenever a Scientific Authority determines that the export of specimens of any such species should be limited in order to *maintain that species throughout its range at a level consistent with its role in the ecosystems in which it occurs and well above the level at which that species might become eligible for inclusion in Appendix I*, the Scientific Authority shall advise the appropriate Management Authority of suitable measures to be taken to limit the grant of export permits for specimens of that species.' (emphasis added)

In 1984 the Technical Committee established a Working Group on Significant Trade in Appendix II Species. The group agreed to limit the work to fauna and developed a strategy and timetable to address the issue, which was subsequently approved at COP5 (see Box 7.2). The process involved the formulation of remedial measures for priority species selected from lists compiled by the Wildlife Trade Monitoring Unit (WTMU) of what was then the IUCN Conservation Monitoring Centre (the forerunner of WCMC, which became UNEP–WCMC). The remedial measures could include, but were not limited to, transfer to Appendix I, hunting controls, trade controls (e.g. export quotas), and listing for look-alike reasons. For priority species considered potentially at risk but for which there was insufficient information available, projects would be established to collect information on biology and management.[4]

Work on the Significant Trade Review commenced between COPs 5 and 6 (1985–7), but funding problems caused delays.[5] Eventually WTMU's results were published in 1988, by which time the trade data that were the basis for species selection were six to eight years old. Some field projects on priority species were undertaken. A few species were listed on Appendix I, and others not registered in trade were removed from Appendix II.[6] With the abolition of

---

[4] CITES Doc. 5.26, 'Significant Trade in Appendix II Species', prepared by the Technical Committee Working Group on Significant Trade in Appendix II Species for COP5 (Apr/May 1985).

[5] CITES Doc. 6.35, 'Significant Trade in Appendix II Species', prepared by the Secretariat for COP6 (Jul 1987).

[6] CITES Doc. 7.31 Annex (Rev.), 'Report of the Working Group on Significant Trade in Appendix II Species', prepared for COP7 (Oct 1989).

Box 7.2: Significant Trade Review mechanism for Appendix II fauna, 1985–1989[a]

Steps 1–3 were carried out by WTMU.

Step 1: Production of List A

A list of candidate Appendix II fauna (more than 100 individuals taken from the wild every year) – List A – was created, using trade levels from 1980–82 submitted by parties in their annual reports.

Step 2: Production of List B

Species for which it was known that no problem existed were removed from List A and others traded in low volume but believed to be in difficulty were added, producing a second list of potential problem species – List B.

Step 3: Production of List C

Available information on List B species was assessed and they were divided into three groups (List C):

- *C1 species*, for which information indicated the population was being detrimentally affected by international trade;
- *C2 species*, for which there was insufficient information available to base a judgment;
- *C3 species*, for which levels of trade were thought not to pose a threat.

Step 4: Development of remedial measures

The Technical Committee (after 1987, the Animals Committee) established priority species in each of lists C1 and C2:

- *Priority C1 species*: workshops were to be convened to formulate remedial measures (e.g. transfer to Appendix I, hunting controls, export quotas);
- *Priority C2 species*: projects were to be established to collect information on biology and management.

Step 5: implementation of remedial measures

Range states were to implement the recommendations from the workshops.

[a] Summarized from CITES Docs. 5.26 and 8.30, 'Significant Trade in Appendix II Species' (1985, 1992).

---

the Technical Committee in 1987, responsibility for the significant trade work was transferred to the Animals Committee. In its terms of reference, the Animals Committee was tasked with listing and reviewing Appendix II fauna significantly affected by trade; recommending remedial measures for species believed to be detrimentally affected; and prioritizing projects to collect information on species for which too little was known.[7]

1990–1992: second review of fauna

In 1990 the Animals Committee approved a second review of trade in Appendix II animal species. The review, which began in 1991, was conducted by WCMC and the IUCN–SSC Trade Specialist Group with assistance from TRAFFIC. Minimum net trade in species was calculated for all Appendix II listed fauna from 1983 to 1988. The information was then sent together with questionnaires to expert reviewers, and (in what seems an unnecessary complication of the process) the species were separated into 6 categories:

A International trade known or strongly suspected to be a threat globally;
B International trade probably a threat globally;
C Trade levels and/or conservation status insufficiently known;
D International trade probably not a threat globally;
D* Populations might be depleting in certain countries;
E International trade not known to be a threat globally.

A 'Preliminary 1991 List of Significant Trade Animal Species in categories A–D*' was drawn up. Twenty-three priority species were initially selected for detailed desk-based literature reviews. The species reviews and their recommendations were examined by the Animals Committee and four additional species selected for literature reviews. The reviews of all 27 were submitted to range states for comment. By COP8 in 1992, the reviews were in the final stage of incorporating comments and revising recommendations.[8]

1992–2000: introduction of continuing review and non-compliance response

The year 1992 marked a turning point in the Significant Trade Review, with the introduction into the process of a non-compliance response mechanism. At COP8 that year the significant trade work was criticized for insufficient studies and non-implementation of recommended remedial measures. Continuing

---

[7] CITES Resolution Conf. 6.1, 'Establishment of Committees' (1987), replaced by Resolution Conf. 11.1 (2000).
[8] CITES Doc. 8.30, 'Significant Trade in Appendix-II Species: Animals', prepared by IUCN/SSC Trade Specialist Group and WCMC for COP8 (Mar 1992).

problems with implementation of Article IV (regulation of trade in Appendix II species, see p. 30) were cited, including non-designation of Scientific Authorities and a lack of technical expertise and information to make non-detriment findings.[9] Proposals were presented by the United States and Honduras for suspending trade in significantly traded birds identified on a 'red list'.[10] Uruguay went even further, and proposed the suspension of trade in all live animals for commercial purposes until Article IV requirements had been met.[11]

IUCN opposed a suspension of trade, considering it punitive and setting a 'dangerous precedent' for a *de facto* Appendix I listing. After a divided debate, the proposals to suspend trade were defeated.[12] Instead, a mechanism for continuing review that could respond to non-compliance with Article IV, based on an Animals Committee proposal,[13] was agreed in Resolution Conf. 8.9. It directed the Animals Committee to make primary (short-term) and secondary (long-term) recommendations for the 27 priority species that had been reviewed within 90 days of the resolution's adoption:

- *Primary recommendations* These included, for example, administrative procedures, quotas (which could be zero) or temporary trade restrictions.
- *Secondary recommendations* These included administrative procedures, field studies or evaluations of threats designed to assist non-detriment findings.

Parties were given 90 days to implement primary recommendations and 12 months to implement secondary recommendations. If they failed to satisfy the Secretariat that they had complied, the Secretariat was to 'recommend to the Standing Committee that all parties immediately take strict measures, including as appropriate suspension of trade in the affected species with that party'. The Standing Committee could decide whether to accept the Secretariat's recommendations at a meeting or by postal procedure.[14]

---

[9] CITES Doc. 8.23, 'The Trade in Wild-Caught Birds for Commercial Purposes' and Doc. 8.35, 'The Trade in Wild-Caught Animal Specimens', submitted by the US to COP8 (Mar 1992).

[10] CITES Doc. 8.23 (see n. 9 above), and Doc. 8.23.1, 'The Trade in Wild-Caught Birds for Commercial Purposes', submitted by the USA and Honduras to COP8 (Mar 1992).

[11] CITES Doc. 8.23.2, 'The Trade in Live Wild-Caught Animals for Commercial Purposes', submitted by Uruguay to COP8 (Mar 1992).

[12] CITES Com. II 8.4, Committee II: Summary Report, COP8 (Mar 1992).

[13] CITES Doc. 8.35, 'The Trade in Wild-Caught Animal Specimens', submitted by the US to COP8 (Mar 1992).

[14] CITES Resolution Conf. 8.9, 'The Trade in Wild-caught Animals Specimens' (replaced by Resolution Conf. 8.9 (Rev.)).

The process was revised again at COP9 in 1994 with Decision 9.25 (see Box 7.3 for details). The amended mechanism specified a procedure for the selection of species for review based on trade data produced by WCMC and the division by the Animals Committee of species that had been subject to literature reviews into three categories:

1   species adversely affected by international trade;
2   species for which insufficient information is available;
3   species for which trade is not a problem.

Decision 9.25 also introduced a period for range state consultation prior to the formulation of primary or secondary recommendations, allowing the early removal of species from the process with respect to the country concerned if a satisfactory response was received; and it specified that the Secretariat was to consult with the Animals Committee when making its determination of whether the recommendations had been implemented. A provision was included to enable reintroduction into the process of species that had been subject to primary recommendations.[15]

By the time of COP11 in 2000, there had been four phases in the implementation of Resolution Conf. 8.9 (Phase IV was ongoing at the time). In Phases I–III, a total of 105 animal species and six genera (groups of species) had been reviewed. The first recommended trade suspensions under the Significant Trade Review were notified to parties in April 1993, a year after COP8. The Standing Committee had recommended the suspension of imports of nine species from 12 different states until the Secretariat had determined that primary recommendations had been implemented.[17] The Committee had also agreed that Secretariat recommendations should be extended to non-parties that had not implemented Animals Committee recommendations.[18] Parties were later notified of four additional states from which imports of specified species should be suspended on the basis that they had failed to implement

---

[15] CITES Decision 10.79 (ex-Decision 9.25), Directed to the Animals Committee 'Regarding implementation of Resolution Conf. 8.9' (1997).

[16] Article IV(2)(a) requires the assurance, from the Scientific Authority of the exporting state, that export of any specimen of a species in Appendix II will not be detrimental to the survival of that species before the grant of an export permit. Article IV(3) obliges parties to monitor and limit exports of Appendix II species (see Box 7.1).

[17] Notification to the Parties No. 737, 'Significant Trade in Animal Species Included in Appendix II: Recommendations of the Animals Committee' (20 Apr 1993).

[18] SC29: Summary Report (Mar 1993), p. 14.

Box 7.3: Significant Trade Review mechanism for Appendix II fauna: 1992–2000[a]

Selection and review of species

1 Using the CITES database on reported trade, WCMC reviewed Appendix II trade over the five most recent years and compiled a list of candidate species for which net trade had exceeded a level determined 'safe' by the Animals Committee (e.g. an average of 100 animals taken from the wild globally and entering international trade each year).

2 The Animals Committee added or deleted species from the list on the basis of common knowledge.

3 Consultants (from WCMC, IUCN and TRAFFIC) conducted desk-based studies of the biology and management of selected species, drew conclusions on the effects of international trade, and divided them into three categories:
   (i) species for which global population, or population in a range state, was being adversely affected by international trade;
   (ii) species for which insufficient information was available to base a judgment;
   (iii) species for which level of trade was not a problem.

4 The Animals Committee revised the categorization and eliminated category (iii) species from the process.

5 Range states that had authorized exports of more than a few specimens were given six weeks to advise on the scientific basis for permitting trade (introduced in Phase III).

6 Species for which a satisfactory response was received were eliminated from the list for the state concerned (introduced in Phase III).

Response mechanism for species in categories (i) and (ii)

1 The Animals Committee made either primary or secondary recommendations for identified species, in consultation with the Secretariat, with the aim of ensuring implementation of Article IV, paragraphs 2(a) and 3.[16]

2 Parties concerned were given 90 days to implement primary recommendations to the Secretariat's satisfaction, which could include zero quotas, specific quotas, temporary export restrictions or administrative procedures.

3 Parties concerned were given 12 months to implement to the Secretariat's satisfaction secondary recommendations such as field studies, reviews of threats or administrative procedures.

4 If a party failed to comply, the Secretariat recommended to the Standing Committee that 'all parties immediately take strict measures, including as appropriate suspension of trade in the affected species with that party'.

5 The Standing Committee, on acceptance of the recommendation, directed the Secretariat to notify parties.

6 Suspended trade would be reinstated when the Standing Committee, advised by the Secretariat, was satisfied that requirements of Article IV, paragraphs 2(a) and 3, had been met.

7 The Secretariat, in consultation with the Animals Committee and Standing Committee, reported to the COP.

8 All species that had been subject to primary recommendations were subject to further review after two consecutive periods between meetings of the COP.

[a] Summarized from Resolution Conf. 8.9 and Decision 10.79 (ex-9.25).

secondary recommendations.[19] Since then, the list of parties subject to trade suspensions with respect to specific Appendix II species has been continually updated as states comply, or fail to comply, with Animals Committee recommendations. In some cases the Standing Committee has recommended cautious export quotas followed by a suspension of trade if the state concerned did not comply.

As of COP11 in April 2000, Standing Committee recommendations for suspension of imports following failure to implement Animals Committee recommendations affected 16 animal species and two genera, and involved 16 countries, three of which were non-parties (see Table 7.1). In some cases, however, captive-bred and/or ranched specimens were exempt from the suspensions. Standing Committee recommendations for export quotas affected eight species and involved five parties. (When it exceeded its export quota for *Psittacus erithacus* by 11,000 specimens in 1996, Cameroon was subject to a suspension for 1997–8). Presumably as a direct result of Animals Committee recommendations (although this is not made clear in the Secretariat report), another 23 species and one genus reviewed were subject to a suspension or prohibition of exports, affecting nine countries, one a non-party, (although in some cases exports of captive-bred and/or ranched specimens were allowed).[20]

2000–2002: inclusion of plants

In April 2000 at COP11, the Significant Trade Review mechanism was revised yet again, in part to include procedures for plants similar to those developed for animals but to be implemented by the Plants Committee (see Box 7.4). The procedure for selecting and reviewing candidate species was also amended. More range state consultation was included at an earlier stage, both before and after the consultants' reviews and categorization. The basis for categorizing selected species following the reviews was also changed from the adverse effect of international trade to non-implementation of Article IV, such that the three categories at the time of writing are:

---

[19] Notification to the Parties No. 775, 'Significant Trade in Animal Species Included in Appendix II: Recommendations of the Animals Committee' (23 Nov 1993).
[20] CITES Doc. 11.41.1 Annex 2, 'Implementation of Recommendations of the Animals Committee made in accordance with Resolution Conf. 8.9', prepared by the Secretariat for COP11 (Apr 2000).

Table 7.1: Summary of results of Significant Trade Review mechanism, as of April 2000[a]

Number of species/genera subject to Animals Committee (AC) recommendations and suspensions of trade recommended by the Standing Committee (SC)

Phase	Species/genera subject to AC recommendations	Species/genera subject to SC trade suspensions	Countries involved
I	27 species	8 species (30%)	10
II	69 species 5 genera	8 species (12%) 2 genera (40%)	4 1
III	9 species 1 genus	1 species (11%)	4

Countries subject to Standing Committee recommended suspensions of trade

Country	Species/genera involved	Country	Species/genera involved
Antigua and Barbuda	1 species	Madagascar	1 species + 2 genera
Argentina	1 species	Mozambique	2 species
Azerbaijan	1 species	Peru	1 species
Barbados	1 species	Republic of Moldova*	1 species
Cameroon	1 species	Solomon Islands*	1 species
China	1 species	Tanzania	8 species
Dominica	1 species	Trinidad and Tobago	1 species
Indonesia	2 species	Ukraine	1 species
Lithuania*	1 species		

[a] Data compiled from table in Doc. 11.41.1, Annex 2, presented at COP11, April 2000.
* Non-party states (Moldova and Lithuania have since joined CITES).

1 species for which available information indicates Article IV is not being implemented;
2 species for which it is unclear whether Article IV is being implemented;
3 species for which level of trade is not a problem.[21]

---

[21] CITES Decision 11.106 Directed to the Animals Committee, 'Regarding implementation of Resolution Conf. 8.9 (Rev.)' (2000).

Box 7.4: Significant Trade Review mechanism for Appendix II fauna and flora, 2000–2002[a]

Selection and review of species

1   Using the CITES database on reported trade, UNEP–WCMC reviews Appendix II trade over the five most recent years and compiles a list of candidate species for which net trade has exceeded a level determined 'safe' by the Animals and Plants Committees.
2   Animals and Plants Committees select species of immediate concern.
3   The Secretariat notifies relevant range states and requests comments.
4   Consultants (from UNEP–WCMC, IUCN and TRAFFIC) conduct desk-based studies of biology and management of selected species 'when necessary', draw conclusions on the effects of international trade, and divide them into 3 categories:
    - *Category 1* species, for which available information indicates Article IV is not being implemented;
    - *Category 2* species, for which it is unclear if Article IV is being implemented;
    - *Category 3* species, for which level of trade is not a problem.
5   Range states are given six weeks to comment on the consultants' studies.
6   Animals and Plants Committees may revise categories and eliminate category 3 species from the process.
7   Range states are given six weeks to comment on Article IV implementation problems identified by the Animals and Plants Committees.
8   Species for which a satisfactory response is received from a range state will be eliminated from the process with respect to the state concerned.

Response mechanism for Category 1 and 2 species

For animal and plant species for which sufficient *information is available on trade and biological status*

1   Animals and Plants Committees make either primary or secondary recommendations for identified species, in consultation with the Secretariat, with the aim of ensuring implementation of Article IV, paragraphs 2(a), 3 and 6 (a).[22]
2   Parties concerned are given 90 days to implement primary recommendations to the Secretariat's satisfaction, which may include zero quotas, specific quotas, temporary export restrictions or administrative procedures.
3   Parties concerned are given 12 months to implement to the Secretariat's satisfaction secondary recommendations, such as field studies, reviews of threats or administrative procedures.
4   If a party fails to comply, the Secretariat recommends to the Standing Committee that 'all parties immediately take strict measures, including as appropriate suspension of trade in the affected species with that party'.

---

[22] Article IV, para. 6(a) requires advice from the Scientific Authority that introduction from the sea of any specimen of a species in Appendix II will not be detrimental to the survival of that species before the Management Authority can grant a certificate to enable the introduction. See n. 16 above and Box 7.1 for Article IV, paras 2(a) and 3.

For animal and plant species for which insufficient information is available on trade and biological status

1 Animals and Plants Committees recommend taxon-specific and country-specific status assessments, to be completed by range states within two years of receiving the recommendation.

2 Animals and Plants Committees recommend the establishment of cautious quotas as an interim measure while the assessments are being carried out, to be implemented within 90 days.

3 Once the assessments are completed, the Animals and Plants Committees make primary or secondary recommendations, in consultation with the Secretariat, to be implemented within 90 days or 12 months respectively.

4 If range states fail to implement the quotas or complete the status assessments or implement the primary or secondary recommendations within the time limits, the Secretariat can recommend to the Standing Committee that 'all parties immediately take strict measures, including as appropriate suspension of trade in the affected species with that party'.

For all species subject to strict measures

1 The Standing Committee, on its acceptance of the recommendation for strict measures, directs the Secretariat to notify the parties.

2 Suspended trade will be reinstated when the Standing Committee, advised by the Secretariat, is satisfied that requirements of Article IV, paragraphs 2(a), 3 and 6(a), have been met.

Reporting procedure

1 The Secretariat reports to the Animals and Plants Committees on parties' implementation of their recommendations, and on species previously reviewed or eliminated from the process for which there are concerns regarding trade, to allow their reintroduction into the review process.

2 Animals and Plants Committees report to the COP.

ᵃ Summarized from Resolution Conf. 8.9 (Rev.) and Decisions 11.106 and 11.117.

The response mechanism was also elaborated to provide for *two different responses*:

1 for species under review for which *sufficient* information is available on trade and biological status;

2 for species under review for which *insufficient* information is available on trade and biological status.

The response mechanism for those species for which sufficient information is available remains unchanged. However, for species under review for which there is insufficient information available on trade and biological status an extra stage has been introduced into the process, involving status assessments by range states, to be completed within two years. Only when the assessments are completed will the Animals and Plants Committees make primary or secondary recommendations. The Committees are also directed to recommend the establishment of cautious quotas as an interim measure while the assessments are being carried out. If parties fail to implement the quotas or complete the status assessments, or to implement the primary or secondary recommendations within specified time limits, the Secretariat can recommend to the Standing Committee that 'all parties immediately take strict measures, including as appropriate suspension of trade in the affected species with that party'.[23]

The inclusion of range state status assessments into the process was prompted in part by concern that population assessments and monitoring programmes necessary to maintain exports of Appendix II species below the level that would be detrimental to their survival (i.e. non-detriment findings) are not being undertaken. It was also prompted by the inclusion of plants in the process, recognizing that information on their biological status is often unavailable and that data in annual reports on trade in plants is frequently incomplete.[24] It was hoped that, by introducing status assessments into the mechanism for species for which there are few data, with a provision for sanctions if they are not undertaken, range states would be induced to implement non-detriment findings. But this extra step has considerably lengthened an already long and increasingly complex process.

The Significant Trade Review is currently completing Phase IV, which straddled COP11, and is in the early stages of Phase V. During Phase IV, 38 species and three genera of fauna were reviewed (four of the species having been reintroduced after previous reviews in Phases I and II). At its 16th meeting in December 2000 (AC16), the Animals Committee categorized remaining species reviewed in Phase IV: *Naja* species (cobras), *Moschus* species (musk deer) and *Acipenseriformes* (sturgeons and paddle fish).[25] It also agreed to restrict species reviewed in Phase V to some additional sturgeon species, some tortoises and freshwater turtles, hard corals and species used in traditional medicines. At AC17, in July/August 2001, *Strombus gigus* (the queen conch),

---

[23] CITES Resolution Conf. 8.9 (Rev.), 'Trade in Specimens of Appendix II Species Taken from the Wild' (2000).

[24] See preamble, CITES Resolution Conf. 8.9 (Rev.) (see n. 22 above).

[25] Summary of results of AC16 (Dec 2000), distributed by Species Survival Network.

previously reviewed in Phase III, was added to the list.[26] At AC18 in April 2002, the first desk-based reviews in Phase V of four species of sturgeon and five species of turtles and tortoises were presented by IUCN and TRAFFIC and initial categorizations were decided by the Committee, while range state responses were considered for *Moschus* and *Naja* species.[27]

The Secretariat presented primary and secondary recommendations for 33 of the species reviewed in Phase IV and placed in categories (1) and (2) to SC45 in June 2001, together with recommendations of species-specific import suspensions with countries that had not responded within the 90-day deadline (which had passed for responses to primary recommendations). Countries required to provide additional information were given until 20 July 2001 before an import suspension would be recommended. Others that had not responded, or had provided an inadequate response, were recommended for immediate suspension (though the immediacy was implied rather than speci-fied).[28] At the meeting itself some countries that had responded since the Secretariat prepared its report were removed from the list. The Standing Committee approved the remaining recommendations, with the exception of those relating to sturgeon species in the Black Sea, Amur River and Caspian Sea basins, for which revised recommendations were agreed after consulta-tion with range states (see more on sturgeon below).[29] Table 7.2 shows the Phase IV species and countries affected by Standing Committee recom-mended import suspensions at the time of writing. Out of 33 Phase IV species subject to primary and secondary Animals Committee recommendations, 14 were subject to recommended import suspensions by the Standing Com-mittee for non-compliance (42%). Out of 38 range states affected by Phase IV primary and secondary recommendations, 12 became subject to recom-mended species-specific import suspensions (32%), including one non-party (the Solomon Islands).

At the end of 2001, taking into account the results of all phases, a total of 25 countries were subject to Standing Committee recommended species-specific import suspensions, affecting 29 species and two genera. By April

---

[26] AC16: Proceedings (Dec 2000); AC17: Summary Record (Jul/Aug 2001).

[27] CITES AC18 Doc. 7.1, 'Progress on the Implementation of the Review of Significant Trade (Phases IV and V), prepared by the Secretariat for AC18 (April 2002); 'Summary of the 18th Meeting of the CITES Animals Committee, 8–12 April 2002' (*Earth Negotiations Bulletin*, 16 Apr 2002), <www.iisd.ca/linkages/cites/cites/CITA2/>.

[28] CITES SC45 Doc. 12, 'Significant Trade in Specimens of Appendix II Species', prepared by the Secretariat for SC45 (Jun 2001).

[29] SC45: Summary Record (Jun 2001).

Table 7.2: Species reviewed in Phase IV of the Significant Trade Review process subjected to trade suspensions

Species	Countries subject to recommended trade suspension at SC45	Countries given until 20 July 2001 to provide additional information	Non-compliant countries under import suspension as of 19 Dec 2001	Non-compliant countries under import suspension as of 9 April 2002
Acipenser gueldenstaedtii	Turkey		✓	✗
A. nudiventris	Turkey		✓	✗
A. stellatus	Turkey		✓	✗
Chamaeleo quadricornis		Cameroon	✗	✗
Cordylus tropidosternum		Mozambique	✓	✓
Corucia zebrata	Solomon Islands (non-party)		✓	✓
Dendrobates auratus	Nicaragua		✓	✓
D. pumilio	Nicaragua		✓	✓
D. tinctorius	Suriname		✓	✓
Geochelone pardalis	Democratic Republic of Congo	Mozambique	✓	✗
Hippopotamus amphibius	Democratic Republic of Congo		✓	✓
	Malawi		✓	✓
	Rwanda		✓	✓
H. huso	Turkey		✓	✗
Poicephalus robustus	Democratic Republic of Congo		✓	✓
	Mali		✓	✓
	Togo		✓	✓
Saiga tatarica	Kazakhstan		✓	✓
	Russian Federation		✓	✓

2002 (the latest information at the time of writing) two countries had complied with recommendations, reducing the number affected by import suspensions to 23 and the number of species and genera affected to 25 and two, respectively. All countries and species under a recommended suspension at the time of writing, together with the date it was imposed, can be found in Annex 3.

New models shaping the review

The last few years have seen new developments in the Significant Trade Review that could shape its future evolution. One is the ecosystem approach used to develop responses to the excessive exploitation of sturgeon species for the caviar trade. Another is a decision to conduct the first country-based review, prompted by concerns that a species-by-species approach not only is inadequate to address the problems with non-implementation of Article IV, but also tends to cause a shift in trade from one species to another once a species-specific import suspension is recommended. The trade in chameleons and day geckos from Madagascar provides a good example (see more below). Traders are also liable to shift to other countries not subject to recommended import suspensions, a trend that was observed with trade in grey parrots. To counter this, the Secretariat has even suggested that regionally based Significant Trade Reviews should be considered.[30]

Sturgeon: the caviar story

The trade in sturgeon has presented the Significant Trade Review mechanism with its biggest challenge. Caviar-producing sturgeon represent highly valued commodities. Until 1991 the USSR and Iran virtually controlled the caviar market, investing heavily in maintaining and controlling fish stocks. The system collapsed with the demise of the USSR. Entrepreneurs replaced the state-owned companies, and many took advantage of the lack of controls.

The Caspian Sea once accounted for 95% of the world's caviar, but the percentage as of June 2001 was closer to 90%. Beluga sturgeon (*Husa husa*), an ancient fish which has been around since the time of the dinosaurs (and the source of beluga caviar), has declined more than 90% in the past 20 years.

---

[30] This suggestion was made informally by the Secretariat at AC18.

Conservation groups believe that it no longer reproduces in the wild.[31] According to TRAFFIC, the Caspian Sea sturgeon catch fell from 22,000 tonnes in the late 1970s to 1,100 tonnes in the late 1990s. Reduced river flow, the destruction of spawning sites, corruption, poaching, organized crime and illicit trade all contributed to the decline.[32] According to the Phase IV review of sturgeon species, based on the number of sets of illegal fishing equipment recorded by enforcement agencies of the Caspian Sea and Sea of Azov, the illegal sturgeon catch has been evaluated at between six and ten times the legal catch. Moreover, in 1997 the estimated volume of the Moscow sturgeon meat market was three times the annual catch quotas for all sturgeon species.[33] Known as 'black gold', the legal caviar trade alone has been valued at some US$100 million annually. An estimate of the value of the illegal trade is difficult because of the variation in prices between different countries; but the Secretariat has stated that it is 'clearly enormous'.[34]

In 1997 the COP listed all sturgeon species on Appendix II. In April 2000 a universal labelling system for caviar exports was adopted by the COP, and several species of sturgeon were introduced into Phase IV of the Significant Trade Review process. The review was effectively fast-tracked to enable the Animals Committee to consider the consultant's report and categorize the different species in December 2000. Its recommendations, sent to range states in February 2001, called on Azerbaijan, Kazakhstan, the Russian Federation and Turkmenistan substantially to reduce their requested 2001 quotas for sturgeon catch and caviar exports.

The Animals Committee also called on the governments to institute a number of reforms, including carrying out assessments of sturgeon population levels (with support from FAO), strengthening their controls over domestic trade in sturgeon and improving their enforcement, licensing, identification, labelling and hatchery production and control systems. The Committee further recommended that all exports be banned until the governments reported satisfactorily on these recommendations; once this had been done, exports could

---

[31] 'CITES Declines to Halt Trade in Caspian Sea Caviar', *Environment News Service* (21 Jun 2001).

[32] 'Caviar-exporting States Consider How to Save Caspian Sea Sturgeon', UNEP news release (12 Jun 2001).

[33] CITES Doc. AC16.7.2, 'Implementation of Resolution Conf. 8.9 (Rev.): Acipenseriformes', prepared by TRAFFIC International in cooperation with IUCN and UNEP–WCMC under contract to the CITES Secretariat for AC16 (Dec 2000).

[34] 'CITES Moves to Block Caviar Smuggling Operations', CITES press release (16 Nov 2001).

proceed but with reduced quotas, in most cases 80% of previous quotas. At SC45 the Secretariat proposed to the Standing Committee a deadline for action by all range states of 20 July 2001 if they were to avoid a recommendation for import suspensions, with the exception of Turkey, for which an immediate import suspension was recommended (and agreed) for four species of sturgeon. But range states objected and opposed further quota cuts.[35]

Responding to range state pressure, the Secretariat was asked by the Standing Committee to meet with the states and formulate revised recommendations. These were agreed basin by basin, as follows.

Black Sea (and Azov Sea) A suspension of imports of four species of sturgeon would be recommended for Bulgaria, Romania and the Russian Federation if these countries failed to establish an agreement for the cooperative management of sturgeon fisheries in the Black Sea by the end of February 2002, and failed to implement all other recommendations of the Animals Committee. Further exports in 2001 would also be restricted to no more than 75% of the published export quotas.

Amur River No further action was required with respect to two sturgeon species until the end of February 2002, provided that no more harvesting was done in 2001 by China and the Russian Federation.

Caspian Sea A 12-month action plan involving a halt to sturgeon fishing in the Caspian Sea for the rest of 2001 was agreed by Azerbaijan, Kazakhstan, the Russian Federation and Turkmenistan. (The fifth Caspian Sea state, Iran, was exempt, since it already had a functioning sturgeon management system.) The four states also had to limit exports to stocks harvested in Spring 2001, and by the end of 2001 to agree a common policy for coordinated management of Caspian Sea sturgeon, conduct a survey of sturgeon stocks, ask Interpol to analyse the illegal sturgeon trade, request the Secretariat (in collaboration with Interpol and the World Customs Organization) to conduct a study of enforcement needs for combating illegal harvesting and trade, and to facilitate on-site inspections by CITES of their sturgeon management activities. A failure to implement these actions would result in a zero quota for 2002 for sturgeon exports. Actions to be undertaken before 20 June 2002 included establishing a long-term survey programme and collaborative basin-level management system, increasing efforts to combat illegal fishing

---

[35] UNEP news release (see n. 32 above); CITES SC45 Doc. 12 (see n. 28 above).

and trade and regulate domestic trade, and implementing the caviar labelling system and all other Animals Committee recommendations. A suspension of imports of the four sturgeon species involved was recommended by the Standing Committee if the Secretariat could not verify that these actions have been undertaken.[36]

These Standing Committee recommendations negotiated with range states fell short of the Animals Committee recommendations and therefore disappointed conservation groups. Caviar Emptor, a joint programme of the Natural Resources Defence Council, the Wildlife Conservation Society and SeaWeb, has recommended a halt to international trade in beluga caviar and the long-term reduction of quotas for other Caspian Sea sturgeon. A representative commented that the measures would 'not by themselves be sufficient to stop the downward spiral of beluga sturgeon toward extinction'.[37]

Following the SC45 recommendations, the Secretariat conducted verification and enforcement-related missions in the Caspian Sea states and the UAE.[38] The Secretariat had been monitoring re-exports of caviar from the UAE for several months following reports that organized crime groups in Dubai were coordinating illegal sales of caviar. The caviar smugglers were using forged documents and making false statements to officials to obtain re-export certificates. In the first ten months of 2001 caviar with a wholesale value of US$20 million left the UAE, most of it of illegal origin and probably from the Russian Federation.[39] (See details above on the trade suspension recommended with UAE in November 2001.) There have also been efforts to crack down on illegal trade in the United States and the Russian Federation. In August 2001 it was reported that Russian border guards had seized nearly 2.5 tonnes of sturgeon and 22 pounds of caviar since commercial fishing had been halted by the Russian Federation in the Caspian Sea in July.[40] Several cases in the United States, often involving Russians, have led to prison sentences and stiff fines. In February 2001 a federal judge levied a record-setting fine of US$10.4 million against a caviar-importing company. Three executives of the

---

[36] Notification to the Parties No. 2001/056, 'Implementation of Resolution Conf. 8.9 (Rev): Recommendations of the Standing Committee (10 Aug 2001).

[37] 'CITES Declines to Halt Trade in Caspian Sea Caviar', *Environment News Service* (21 Jun 2001).

[38] Notification to the Parties No. 2001/085, 'Conservation of Acipenseriformes' (10 Dec 2001).

[39] CITES press release (n. 34 above).

[40] 'Russian Guards Seize Sturgeon', *Associated Press* (13 Aug 2001).

firm US Caviar & Caviar received sentences ranging from 15 months to more then three years in prison.[41]

In March 2002 the Secretariat notified parties of progress in sturgeon conservation.[42] In the Black Sea region, agreement had been reached to form a cooperative sturgeon management body, the Black Sea Management Group. All littoral countries of the Amur River, Black Sea and Caspian Sea had committed to developing regional agreements and conservation strategies, and intergovernmental commissions had been established for the management of sturgeons in the Amur River and Azov Sea. Meanwhile the first assessment of enforcement needs to combat illegal harvesting and trade was conducted by the Secretariat in the Russian Federation in November 2001, and a confidential report was supplied to its Management Authorities with recommendations on caviar exports, the control of domestic trade, anti-poaching, tackling organized crime, the involvement of legal traders in illicit activities, and legislation.[43] The Russian Federation responded at SC46 by pledging to regulate all stages of caviar production and to introduce domestic controls through quotas and licensing.[44]

Despite the progress made in developing unified strategies for management, at the time of writing the Secretariat still considers that 'serious problems' remain to be addressed. Among them are inadequate enforcement, non-deterrent penalties, outdated legislation, lack of regulation of domestic trade and large-scale illegal fishing by communities without alternative income sources. Rural communities are facing severe consequences from CITES trade restrictions, but, as the Secretariat points out, consequences in the longer term will be even worse if stocks are allowed to decline further.[45] These ongoing problems, however, did not deter the Secretariat from recommending at SC46, and the Standing Committee from approving, the resumption of exports of caviar from Caspian Sea sturgeon subject to a quota shared between the five littoral states, Azerbaijan, Iran, Kazakhstan, the Russian Federation and Turkmenistan. The Standing Committee also lifted the recommended import

---

[41] Richard Drew, 'Authorities Target Outbreak of Caviar Crime', *USA Today* (16 Dec 2001).

[42] CITES Notification to the Parties No. 2002/012, 'Conservation of Acipenseriformes' (6 Mar 2002).

[43] CITES SC46 Doc. 11.2, 'Enforcement Matters', prepared by the Secretariat for SC46 (Mar 2002).

[44] 'CITES Incentives Inspire Vital Reforms in Wildlife Management', UNEP press release 2002/17 (15 Mar 2002).

[45] CITES Notification to the Parties No. 2002/012 (n. 42 above).

suspension with respect to Turkey on the basis that it had implemented Animals Committee recommendations.[46]

The approval of quotas for Caspian Sea sturgeon was criticized by the NGO alliance Caviar Emptor, predicting it would bring the beluga sturgeon 'one step closer to oblivion'.[47] The alliance has since brought a court action against the US government for failing to list the beluga sturgeon under the Endangered Species Act and consequently ban imports of beluga caviar.[48]

Madagascar: the first country-based review

In a potentially important development for the CITES compliance system, at AC17 in July/August 2001, the Animals Committee agreed to conduct its first country-based review of significant trade in Appendix II species. This was in response to concern that some countries had not been able to comply with Animals Committee recommendations, with the result that one species after another has been identified as being subject to potentially problematic levels of trade in the same country. The Secretariat considered that a country-based approach would be more appropriate and cost-effective for such countries, and it proposed that a test review be conducted for a party that has 'a significant overall level of trade in specimens of Appendix II species and:

(a) [has] been subject to recommendations in relation to several species for which there continues to be justifiable concern over the implementation of Article IV concerning exports;

(b) [has]experienced problems in establishing and implementing export quotas and in addressing recommendations made by the Committee in accordance with Resolution Conf. 8.9 (Rev.);

(c) [has] experienced problems in the monitoring of trade and meeting CITES reporting requirements;

(d) [has] not adopted adequate legislation to implement CITES and/or [has] experienced problems with the enforcement of legislation (e.g. persistent illegal trade); and

(e) [has] remained subject to trade suspensions recommended by the Standing Committee.'[49]

---

[46] SC46: Summary Report (Mar 2002), p. 17.

[47] Miguel Llanos, 'Ban on Caviar Trade Lifted', MSNBC/Reuters (6 Mar 2002).

[48] 'American Courts Asked to Ban Imports of Beluga Caviar', *Guardian* (6 Jun 2002).

[49] CITES AC17 Doc. 7.5, 'Proposal for the First Country-based Significant Trade Review', prepared by the Secretariat for AC17 (Jul/Aug 2001).

Madagascar was chosen as the test case, and the Secretariat was instructed to develop terms of reference and seek external funding. Consultants were contracted from November 2001.[50]

Madagascar is a country with unique endemic species because of its geophysical history. Malagasy species are highly sought after, particularly for the market in exotic pets and plants in the United States, Europe and Japan. As a result of the Significant Trade Review, since November 1994 Madagascar has been subject to recommendations for import suspensions with respect to the majority of its *Phelsuma* species (day geckos) and *Chamaeleo* species[51] (chameleons) as well as *Coracopsis vasa* (the vasa parrot). Only eight species of *Phelsuma* and *Chamaeleo* are allowed to be exported, subject to an annual export quota of 2,000 each. The quotas were introduced belatedly in 1999 following large increases in exports resulting from the trade suspensions recommended for other species in the genera.[52] At AC17, the United States presented information on trade in live reptiles from Madagascar showing that exports in 1999 had significantly exceeded the export quota for six of the eight species, in one case by 334%. Export quotas had also been exceeded (just with imports to the United States) for two species of tortoise and one species of turtle.[53]

At SC45, in June 2001, Madagascar was considered for another import suspension, this time in connection with its trade in *Mantella aurantiaca* (the golden frog), which had been reviewed in Phase IV. In its document prepared for the meeting the Secretariat had proposed an import suspension, but at the meeting itself it advised that no further action was required provided that Madagascar established a cautious quota and maintained a monitoring system for the sites where the species is harvested.[54] Given Madagascar's record, this advice is surprising, and somewhat contradictory of the subsequent development in the Animals Committee. I visited Madagascar in December 2001 to research the reptile trade for the International Fund for Animal Welfare (IFAW) and discovered enormous problems with

---

[50] CITES SC46 Doc. 21, 'Report of the Chairman of the Animals Committee', prepared for SC46 (Mar 2002).

[51] Alternatively classified as *Calumma* or *Furcifer.*

[52] Reeve/IFAW (2002) (see ch. 6, n. 35). Information on Madagascar is based on on-site research (Dec 2001).

[53] 'Exports of Live Reptiles from Madagascar: Adherence to Reported Quotas and Recommendations of the Standing Committee', information document prepared by the USA for AC17 (Jul/Aug 2001).

[54] SC45: Summary Record (Jun 2001).

CITES implementation and enforcement under the former regime of Didier Ratsiraka, including the circulation of blank permits and uncontrolled exports of species under restricted or zero quotas.[55] That same month the World Bank included improvement in CITES implementation as a conditionality for approving funding for the third phase of Madagascar's Environmental Action Plan.[56]

Following these events, Madagascar descended into political chaos sparked by Ratsiraka's refusal to accept the result of the December 2001 election. The newly inaugurated President Marc Ravalomanana installed his ministers in government offices in the inland capital (including the CITES Management Authority), while Ratsiraka continued to control the ports. The chaos resulted in confusion over the legitimacy of wildlife exports, exacerbated by an unknown number of blank CITES permits in circulation signed under the previous administration.[57]

At AC18 in April 2002 Ravalomanana's new administration announced a six-month moratorium on CITES exports, a much-needed move, but one that is almost impossible to enforce without corresponding action by importing countries. The United States immediately announced a suspension of imports (lifted on 20 September), but the European Union decided against an import ban and no action was taken under CITES, even though the Secretariat was aware of the problems. Meanwhile, the country-based Significant Trade Review, initially frustrated by communication problems, has made a tentative start. But while potentially right for Madagascar, the Review is questionable in the context of the CITES compliance system. A country-based review is crossing into the territory of the non-compliance procedure for countries with major implementation problems. To have parallel non-compliance procedures in the same Convention makes no sense. It would make more sense for CITES to support the trade moratorium announced by the new administration by urging parties to suspend imports, and then to examine ways of building capacity to implement and enforce CITES in Madagascar once the political situation is resolved.

---

[55] Reeve/IFAW, in prep.
[56] Personal communication from USAID and World Bank representatives at donors meeting in Madagascar (Dec 2001).
[57] Reeve/IFAW, in prep.

Is the Review effective?

The effectiveness of the Significant Trade Review is hard to gauge, since there has been no comprehensive 'review of the Review'. A study commenced by the Species Survival Network (SSN) in 2001, looking at significantly traded birds, indicates there are problems with the Review's implementation that need addressing. [58] These include regular quota overages with respect to species and countries that have been subject to recommendations under the Review. Looking at the bird trade alone between 1994 and 1999, the SSN study cited nine species and 13 countries for which quotas had been exceeded. In the case of Cameroon, for example, after the temporary trade suspension with respect to grey parrots (*Psittacus erithacus*) was lifted, the quota was again exceeded in 1998 and 1999 by a total of 7,068 specimens, but no action was taken.

The SSN study also found that in 15 reviews of significantly traded birds some of the exporting parties were omitted. Other problems cited were quota-setting in the absence of biological information; lack of peer review of field studies, which sometimes used questionable survey techniques; lack of uniform standards for non-detriment findings; and lack of follow-up on recommendations. (In a few cases, field projects promised by parties never materialized but exports continued.) There may also be a problem with implementation of Standing Committee-recommended trade suspensions by importing parties. Solomon Islands, a non-party, has been subject to a recommended import suspension for two species of butterflies, *Ornithoptera urvillianus* and *Ornithoptera victoriae*, since 1994, but some parties, notably France and Japan, have continued to import them.[59] These preliminary findings indicate that the Significant Trade Review may be less effective in practice than it appears on paper.

Proposed revision of the mechanism

The Significant Trade Review process has faced increasing criticism for being complex and difficult to understand, particularly by new parties to CITES. In December 2000 the Animals Committee decided to draft a new resolution for presentation to COP12 in November 2002, attempting to consolidate the current resolution with COP11 decisions and trying to streamline the process and

---

[58] Ann Michels, *History of Species Reviewed under Resolution Conf. 8.9 (Rev.): Part I: Aves* (SSN, Jul 2001).

[59] Trade data supplied by John Caldwell, UNEP–WCMC (Feb 2002).

make it more transparent.[60] The Secretariat was tasked with drafting a revised procedure which was presented to AC18 in April 2002.[61] The Secretariat's draft, in the interest of flexibility, proposed amalgamating current categories 1 and 2 (reducing the total number of categories to two) and abolishing the distinction between primary and secondary recommendations as well as the specific deadlines for their implementation. It also weakened the language on Standing Committee-recommended trade suspensions, such that they 'may' be included among strict measures for non-compliance with Animals and Plants Committee recommendations. In its presentation of the draft, the Secretariat alluded to the Standing Committee's reluctance of late to recommend trade suspensions, and the current initiative to examine other non-compliance measures available (see Chapter 6).

A working group of parties and NGO observers was tasked with revising the Secretariat's draft with a view to simplifying the mechanism without weakening its effectiveness, and providing incentives for countries to comply. The draft agreed by the Animals Committee and amended by the Plants Committee details a simpler process than the one currently in use, placing more emphasis on support to range states.[62] The initial selection of species is similar to the current procedure, but is based on 'priority concern' rather than an undefined 'safe' level of trade. Three categories of species are retained but revised:

1   *'species of urgent concern'*, for which the available information indicates that the provisions of Article IV, paragraph 2(a), 3 or 6(a) are not being implemented;
2   *'species of possible concern'*, for which it is not clear whether or not these provisions are being implemented;
3   *'species of least concern'*, for which the available information appears to indicate that these provisions are being met.

The distinction between primary and secondary recommendations is removed. Instead, different types of short-term and long-term actions are proposed for species of urgent concern and species of possible concern:

---

[60] CITES SC45 Doc. 16, 'Report of the Chairman of the Animals Committee', prepared for SC45 (Jun 2001).
[61] CITES AC18 Doc. 7.3, 'Revision of Resolution Conf. 8.9 (Rev.) and Decisions 11.106–11.108', prepared by the Secretariat for AC18 (Apr 2002).
[62] CITES COP12 Doc. 48.1 Annex 2 (provisional), 'Implementation of Resolution Conf. 8.9 (Rev.)', prepared by the Secretariat for COP12 (Nov 2002).

- *Recommendations for species of urgent concern* These should propose specific actions to address conservation and trade control problems, and may include cautious quotas or other temporary export restrictions, adaptive management procedures, taxon- and country-specific status assessments and field studies or evaluations of threats to populations.
- *Recommendations for species of possible concern* These should specify information required to enable categorization as either of urgent concern or least concern, and may include taxon- and country-specific status assessments, field studies or evaluations of threats to populations or cautious quotas as an interim measure.

Deadlines for implementation of recommendations are to be 'appropriate' to the actions recommended but should 'normally be no less than 90 days or no longer than two years'. Range state consultation is provided for at every stage. For species of least concern, the Secretariat is mandated to address problems identified through the review that are unrelated to Article IV implementation. This was included with illegal trade in mind. To improve transparency, a register of species in the review process, to include progress with the implementation of recommendations, is proposed. This may help to address the problem with lack of follow-up that was identified in the SSN study.

A worrying proposal with respect to non-compliance response that crept into the draft after AC18 is to relegate Standing Committee-recommended trade suspensions to measures of 'last resort'. The move, if approved at COP12, could undermine the non-compliance mechanism in the Significant Trade Review. Although a balancing provision urging more support to non-compliant range states is proposed, no specific funding provisions are included which will limit its usefulness in practice.

The proposal by the Animals and Plants Committees is undoubtedly clearer and simpler than the current mechanism. But it weakens the response to non-compliance, and fails to address concerns raised by delegates at AC18. One is the inclusion of adaptive management procedures among actions for species of urgent concern. This controversial tool provides for management based on previous experience, in essence trial and error. Criticized for its lack of precaution, several delegates were opposed to its inclusion. Another concern is the lack of specific deadlines for short and long-term actions. While the desire for flexibility and tailoring deadlines to the actions recommended is understandable, the current wording could allow unacceptable delays in action for species traded at high levels. Specific deadlines need to be maintained, ranging, for example, from 90 days for short-term actions, such as cautious quotas and trade restrictions, to two years for the longest-term actions, such as status assessments. The proposed revision also fails to address most of the problems identified in the SSN study, including the omission of exporting parties in the reviews, quota-setting in the absence of biological information, lack of peer review of field studies, and lack of uniform standards for non-detriment findings.

Suggestions for improving the mechanism

Linking national reporting with the Review

One issue of considerable concern is the adequacy of the data on which Significant Trade Reviews are based. Candidate species are selected on the basis of trade data compiled from annual reports. However, given the low rate, poor quality and delays in reporting, these data are incomplete and out of date. This shortcoming undermines the reliability of the initial selection, as well as the trade review studies and the setting of subsequent quotas to bring trade under control. Until annual reporting of trade data by parties is markedly improved, the whole process will continue to be undermined, and parties such as Comoros that fail to report could escape detection – and consequently sanctions – until trade reports from importing countries trickle into the system. Given that Comoros is a tiny country exporting large numbers of reptiles native to only a few islands, populations could be significantly reduced before CITES has had a chance to act.

Linking annual reporting with the Significant Trade Review could go some way to improving the situation by providing incentives to report, and connecting the two processes in the minds and practice of parties. One way of doing this would be to automatically set zero interim quotas during the reviews and any subsequent status assessments for countries that have failed to report for a specified period. The quotas could be reviewed once countries provide the missing reports. The provision of satisfactory and timely reports could also be introduced as an additional condition for lifting zero quotas recommended by the Animals Committee or suspensions of trade recommended by the Standing Committee for non-compliance.

Incorporating illegal trade

Trade data exclude illegal trade. Illegal trade can be significant, and in some cases can even exceed legal trade; sturgeon is a case in point. While illegal trade cannot be monitored with any degree of reliability – and in any case efforts should be aimed at prevention rather than monitoring – it needs to be given due consideration in the review process. In practice, the reviews conducted by TRAFFIC, IUCN and UNEP–WCMC take illegal trade into account, but the mandate to consultants for its examination is implicit rather than explicit, specifying biology, management and 'conclusions about the effects of international trade in the selected species', but not illegal trade.[63] Given the potential damage illegal trade can cause, it needs to be specified, not just implied, in the terms of reference for the reviews (recognizing the limitations of a desk study).

Verification

Another issue giving cause for concern is the dependence of the process on desk studies and knowledge of members of the Animals Committee and the Secretariat without on-site verification of parties' responses (with the exception of sturgeon, which is a special case). The response from Madagascar to Animals Committee recommendations concerning *Mantella aurantiaca* is a case in point. Information provided by the United States shows that Madagascar has far exceeded its export quotas on other species, questioning its capacity to obey a quota for *Mantella aurantiaca*. More pertinent, Madagascar has failed to implement monitoring with respect to other species that are subject to Animals Committee recommendations (an experimental management programme proposed in 1999 never materialized), and in any case does not have the capacity.[64] A brief on-site verification visit would have confirmed this.

Mozambique provides another illustration. In its response to Animals Committee recommendations on *Geochelone pardalis* (leopard tortoise), the Mozambique CITES Management Authority claimed that exports had been phased out to a single company which was farming leopard tortoise and was subject to a monthly monitoring system.[65] A brief visit to Mozambique by

---

[63] CITES Decisions 11.106, 11.117, 'Regarding Implementation of Resolution Conf. 8.9 (Rev.)' (2000).

[64] Reeve/IFAW (2002).

[65] CITES SC45 Doc. 12, 'Significant Trade in Specimens of Appendix II Species', prepared by the Secretariat for SC45 (Jun 2001); CITES Management Authority of Mozambique, 'Implementation of Animals' Committee Recommendations' (20 Feb 2001).

IFAW revealed that the exporter in question does not farm leopard tortoises and that there is no monitoring.[66] To give it its due, the Secretariat had not considered the Management Authority's response adequate and had requested more information. Mozambique was eventually subjected to a recommended suspension of imports of *Geochelone pardalis* in December 2001, but not until five months after the deadline for a response had passed.[67] Initially, Mozambique was omitted with respect to *Geochelone pardalis* from notifications of suspensions sent out in July and August 2001.[68] The recommended import suspension has since been lifted with no explanation of the basis for the decision.[69]

Mozambique appears to have deliberately misled the Animals Committee. On-site verification, were it feasible, would have quickly provided the information needed as well as a sound basis for sanctions. This case raises the question of whether other Management Authorities have attempted to mislead the Animals Committee and gone undetected. Without on-site verification of their claims, it is impossible to answer. While it is recognized that the limited finances currently available to CITES preclude on-site verification on a regular basis, its omission undermines the Review mechanism and predisposes it to abuse by unscrupulous Management Authority staff. If responses to non-compliance are to be appropriate and equitable, it needs to be given serious consideration in future revisions of the process. An evolution towards an ecosystem-based or regionally based approach may make incorporation of on-site verification into the mechanism increasingly viable.

Transparency, public comment and peer review

The Significant Trade Review has suffered from its increasing complexity with a lack of transparency, both to range states and NGOs (other than TRAFFIC and IUCN). The publication of regular updates through notifications posted on the website has improved the situation, as has the provision of a guide to the mechanism at COP11.[70] A register of species in the process, if

---

[66] Personal communication from Mozambique trader in question to Melissa MacDonald (Oct 2001).
[67] Notification to the Parties No. 2001/084, 'Implementation of Resolution Conf. 8.9 (Rev.)' (19 Dec 2001).
[68] Notifications to the Parties Nos. 2001/043, 2001/056, 'Implementation of Resolution Conf. 8.9 (Rev.)' (9 Jul and 10 Aug 2001).
[69] Notification to the Parties No. 2002/021, 'Implementation of Resolution Conf. 8.9 (Rev.)' (9 Apr 2002).
[70] CITES Doc. Inf. 11.2, 'A Guide to the Review of Significant Trade', prepared by Africa Resources Trust under contract to the Secretariat for COP11 (Apr 2000).

approved at COP12 and published on the website, should go even further to-wards enhancing transparency. Nevertheless, the mechanism as it stands excludes comments from non-range state parties and NGOs other than ver-bally through attendance at Animals and Plants Committee meetings when the consultants' reviews are presented. This precludes the incorporation of addi-tional information that could be valuable, and reduces transparency.

Publication of the consultants' reviews on the website at the end of the com-ment period for range states, inviting comments from non-range state parties and interested NGOs during a specified period – say, 30 days – would improve transparency and enhance the information base for Animals Committee recom-mendations in the absence of data from on-site visits. Subsequent publication of range state responses to Animals Committee recommendations, inviting pub-lic comment, could assist with countering misleading or false information and improve the knowledge base for non-compliance response. Lastly, in light of the SSN findings with respect to birds, field studies conducted in response to Animals Committee recommendations need to be subjected to peer review.

Incorporating the precautionary principle

The Significant Trade Review currently fails to incorporate the precautionary principle. This is a marked omission, given the uncertainty surrounding the status of many Appendix II listed species, as well as the extent of illegal trade, the unreliability of data on legal trade and the lack of on-site verification in the process. Such uncertainty demands that the precautionary principle be included and applied to provide a basis and guide for decisions at every stage. In other words, it should be explicit in the mechanism that, in deciding on categoriza-tion, interim quotas, Animals and Plants Committee recommendations and responses to non-compliance, parties should always act in the best interest of the conservation of the species.

A review of the Review

Given that the Review has now been operating for ten years since the introduc-tion of non-compliance response into the mechanism, and considering the implementation problems discovered in the SSN study with respect to birds, it is time the Significant Trade Review underwent a thorough assessment of its effec-tiveness. For such an assessment to be useful, it should include among other things random in-country checks on the follow-up of Animals Committee rec-ommendations; an assessment of whether Standing Committee-recommended trade suspensions have been implemented by importing countries; an examination of trade in species 'before' and 'after' they were subject to review; and a critical analysis of the basis for quota-setting and non-detriment findings with a view to applying uniform biological standards.

8 High-profile Appendix I species

Rhinos

At COP8 in March 1992, NGO observers lobbied parties to impose trade sanctions against China, South Korea (a non-party), Taiwan (a non-party but claimed by China as a province) and Yemen (a non-party) for their involvement in the rhino horn trade.[1] This reflected widespread concern about the precipitous decline of the rhino, caused primarily by continued trade in horn despite an Appendix I listing for all five species since 1977.[2]

Rhino horn, considered a 'magic remedy' by doctors of traditional medicine (TM), has been used for its fever-reducing, blood-cooling and detoxifying properties for more than 2000 years.[3] It was also used traditionally to make dagger handles in Yemen. A highly valued commodity, in 1990 in Taipei, the capital of Taiwan, African horn was retailing for an average of US$4,000 per kg and Asian horn for US$54,000 per kg.[4] The worldwide population of all wild rhinos was estimated at less than 10,500.[5]

The NGO lobbying effort led to a formal statement at COP8 by the Chairman of Committee I, Martin Holdgate, requesting that the Standing Committee and Secretariat, *inter alia*, propose 'maximum effective pressures on States' to comply with a 1987 resolution on trade in rhino products that remained unimplemented.[6] Resolution Conf. 6.10 had called for a prohibition on internal trade and destruction of rhino horn stocks, and had recommended that parties 'use all appropriate means (including economic, political and diplomatic) to exert pressure on countries continuing to allow trade in rhinoceros horn'.[7]

---

[1] Author's observation as an NGO participant at COP8.

[2] The South African population of *Ceratotherium simum simum* (southern white rhinoceros) was transferred to Appendix II with an annotation restricting trade to live animals and hunting trophies in 1994.

[3] Wang Xinxia, 'The Implementation of CITES in China', in James Cameron, Jacob Werksman and Peter Roderick (eds), *Improving Compliance with International Law* (Earthscan, 1996), pp. 204–10: 208.

[4] Esmond Martin, UNEP Special Envoy for Rhino Conservation, *Final Report* (20 Jan 1993) (hereinafter 'Martin, 1993a'), p. 20.

[5] *Taiwan Kills Rhinos* (EIA, 1993).

[6] Martin Holdgate, Chairman of Committee I, 'Statement on Rhinoceros Conservation', Com. I 8.13 (Rev.), COP8 (Mar 1992).

[7] CITES Resolution Conf. 6.10, 'Trade in Rhinoceros Products' (1987). The Resolution was repealed in 1994 and replaced with Resolution Conf. 9.14.

In June 1992 the Standing Committee made the rhino a special project leading up to COP9. Initially, the Secretariat was directed to gather information, urge market countries to control trade, and support range states.[8] UNEP was requested to take the lead in convening a meeting among donor, range and consumer states to raise funds for rhino conservation. (This meeting was held in June 1993.) Meanwhile, UNEP's Executive Director appointed rhino expert Esmond Martin as his special envoy to conduct a fact-finding mission in range and consumer states between September and December 1992, and to raise awareness through publicity. Following his reappointment in April 1993, Martin held high-level consultations with government officials in eight key states, attracting considerable media interest.[9]

A call by Israel at the June 1992 Standing Committee meeting for trade sanctions against China, Taiwan and South Korea was resisted.[10] But at its next meeting, in March 1993, after a contentious debate the Committee decided to write to the main consumer countries informing them that sanctions would be considered if they did not take necessary action.[11] At its subsequent meeting in Brussels in September 1993, the Standing Committee came under intense pressure from NGOs to implement trade sanctions with respect to both rhinos and tigers, the latter also a victim of the trade for TM. (Action with respect to tigers is detailed below.) On 7 September 1993, coincident with the Brussels meeting and following a petition by WWF–US and the National Wildlife Federation, the Secretary of the US Department of the Interior, Bruce Babbitt, announced the certification of China and Taiwan under the Pelly Amendment for engaging in trade in rhino and tiger parts and products that diminished the effectiveness of CITES.[12]

The Republic of Korea and Yemen had been notified of an intent by the United States to certify them, but since they were perceived to have taken effective action they avoided certification.[13] In January 1993 the government of the Republic of Korea had issued a decree making the display and sale of rhino horn, or its possession with intent to sell, a crime punishable by up to six

---

[8] SC28: Summary Report, Annex 2 (Jun 1992), p. 28.
[9] Martin (1993a); Esmond Martin, *Final Report of the UNEP Special Envoy for Rhinoceros Conservation* (Jul 1993) (hereinafter 'Martin (1993b')).
[10] SC28: Summary Report (Jun 1992), p. 7.
[11] SC29: Summary Report (Mar 1993), pp. 30–32.
[12] Following certification, the US President has discretionary power to impose trade sanctions against the certified country. See SC30: Summary Report (Sept 1993), pp. 14–15; US Fed. Reg. Doc. 94-4008 (24 Feb 1994).
[13] SC30: Summary Report, pp. 14–15.

months in prison and fine of 1 million won (then US$1,250). Inspections of oriental medicine clinics were stepped up, and in July 1993 South Korea acceded to CITES (another example of a free-rider becoming a 'forced rider').[14] Yemen did not immediately join CITES (it did not become a party until 1997), but on 2 December 1992 the Yemen Ministry of Supply and Trade had issued a decree prohibiting trade in rhino horn that had not been processed into dagger handles. (A ban on possession of daggers with rhino horn handles was considered unenforceable.) Traders were given two months to register stocks of raw rhino horn and another month to have them marked, after which any unmarked horns would be confiscated.[15]

China, then the world's largest exporter of patent medicines containing rhino horn, had banned their exports with effect from December 1992, but officials were strongly opposed to banning internal rhino horn sales. In discussions in October 1992 with the Special Envoy, they claimed that import/export corporations had bought their stocks legally before China joined CITES in 1981, so a ban on internal sales was unfair. But in response to NGO and Standing Committee pressure, on 29 May 1993 the Chinese State Council prohibited with immediate effect the manufacture of medicines containing rhino horn and tiger bones and, by the end of November, all internal and external trade in rhino horn, tiger parts and derivatives.[16] Registration of all rhino and tiger stocks was required, and rhino horn and tiger bone were removed from the official pharmacopoeia.[17]

The prohibition had been promulgated with a Notice following a fierce debate and strong opposition from public health sectors and the internal trade department. It was binding on all relevant administrative agencies and individuals throughout China, but questions were raised about the government's ability to enforce the provision, given that the trade in rhino products was largely out of its control. Chinese officials complained to the Special Envoy that neither adequate resources nor manpower had been allocated to the huge task of enforcing the Notice, which involved visiting every import/export corporation, TM factory and pharmacy to assess stocks of raw horn, rhino horn antiques (which were being ground into powder for medicine) and medicines containing horn, and arranging to seal them up in government stores.[18]

---

[14] Martin (1993b).
[15] Martin (1993a), p. 35.
[16] Martin (1993b), p. 6.
[17] CITES Doc. 42.10.4, 'Tiger Technical Missions', prepared by the CITES Tiger Technical Missions Team for SC42 (Sep/Oct 1999) (hereinafter 'Tiger Technical Missions report').
[18] Martin, (1993a, b); Wang Xinxia (see n. 3 above).

Clearly, the United States considered that China's action fell short of what was needed to avoid certification. At the September 1993 Brussels meeting, China protested to the Standing Committee about the US certification, declaring that it 'violated the sovereign principle of international law' and that any sanctions would be 'unfair and unacceptable'. It repeatedly objected to reference to Taiwan as a country.[19] Japan supported China and raised the spectre of GATT – that sanctions might conflict with the General Agreement on Tariffs and Trade.[20] (See Chapter 12 for more discussion on potential conflict with the WTO.)

In a very carefully worded decision reflecting the political sensitivity of taking action against China, the Standing Committee expressed concern at the failure by China and 'the competent authorities in Taipei' (i.e. Taiwan) to control illegal trade in both rhino horn and tiger specimens, and recommended, *inter alia*, that 'parties should consider implementing stricter domestic measures up to and including prohibition on trade in wildlife species'.[21] Switzerland had specifically requested that the words referring to sanctions should be 'assimilated to the text of Article XIV, paragraph 1'.[22] The Committee agreed four minimum criteria for implementing protection measures, to be met by consumer states before the end of November 1993:

1 the identification and marking of stocks of rhino horn;
2 the consolidation of both rhino horn and tiger bone stocks and their adequate control by the state;
3 the adoption and implementation of adequate legislative measures;
4 the provision for adequate enforcement of the above measures.

Influenced by strong opposition from consumer states, the criteria did not include the destruction of rhino horn stocks recommended by Resolution Conf. 6.10, even though the resolution was still in force.

The Standing Committee further recommended that a technical mission with a focus on implementation and enforcement be offered to consumer countries, followed by a high-level mission to assess progress.[23] Technical missions

---

[19] SC30: Summary Report, pp. 14, 15.

[20] Ibid. p. 16.

[21] 'Decisions of the Standing Committee on Trade in Rhinoceros Horn and Tiger Specimens', in ibid., p. 29.

[22] Ibid., p. 19.

[23] 'Decisions of the Standing Committee on Trade in Rhinoceros Horn and Tiger Specimens', in ibid., p. 29.

subsequently visited several consumer countries, including Japan, China, Taiwan, Hong Kong, South Korea and Yemen. The visits were followed by high-level missions led by the chairman of the Standing Committee (a post then held by Murray Hosking of New Zealand).[24]

Meanwhile, President Clinton reported to Congress in November 1993 that he was not imposing the sanctions permitted under the Pelly Amendment because China and Taiwan had both made good faith efforts to stop trade in rhino and tiger products. He noted, however, that the efforts had yet to result in diminished trade. An inter-agency task force was formed by the United States to provide technical assistance to China and Taiwan. The provision of law enforcement assistance was also authorized. The report to Congress laid out specific actions that could be taken by both states to show progress in ending illegal trade, such as consolidating stockpiles of tiger and rhino parts, creating a wildlife conservation unit and increasing enforcement penalties. A deadline of March 1994 was set for 'measurable, verifiable, and substantial progress' to be made if sanctions were to be avoided.[25] It was subsequently reported that during 1993 inspections had been carried out in 27 provinces in China, and that 33,000 markets, department stores and manufacturers had been visited. Over time, stocks of rhino and tiger parts and products were registered, stored, sealed and subjected to periodic inspection. But surveys by NGOs have indicated that products containing or claiming to contain rhino horn and tiger bone apparently remain available from a limited number of retail and wholesale outlets.[26]

Reports from the CITES missions were reviewed by the Standing Committee in March 1994. Consumer countries were described as 'reaching towards' the minimum criteria.[27] The Committee was severely split over whether to continue trade sanctions, and spent part of the time in a confidential conclave of voting members, attempting to resolve the issue.[28] However, despite NGO

[24] Robert Hepworth, 'Notes of Talk Delivered to Discussion Meeting on Enforcing Multilateral Environmental Agreements' (RIIA, London, 20 Oct 2000).

[25] DeSombre (see ch. 5, n. 38), citing 'Violations Relating to Endangered Species: Message from the President of the United States Transmitting a Report Concerning the People's Republic of China and Taiwan Engaging in Trade of Rhinoceros and Tiger Parts and Products that Diminishes the Effectiveness of the Convention on International Trade in Endangered Species of Wild Fauna and Flora (CITES), pursuant to 22 U.S.C. 1978 (b)', US Congress, House, 103rd Congress, 1st sess., House Document 103-162, 8 Nov 1993; US Fed. Reg. Doc. 94-4008 (24 Feb 1994).

[26] Tiger Technical Missions report, p. 35.

[27] SC31: Summary Report (Mar 1994), p. 21.

[28] Robert Hepworth (observer at SC31, Mar 1994) (n. 24 above).

criticism that the high-level mission had been too lenient, it was eventually decided to withdraw the recommendation for stricter domestic measures against China. It was merely noted that further action was still needed, and it was recommended that China report on this at the next meeting of the COP.[29] Taiwan and the Republic of Korea were subjected to further criticism for lack of progress, but the recommendations with respect to each of them differed markedly. With regard to Taiwan, the Standing Committee '[expressed] concern that the actions agreed by the authorities in Taipei towards meeting the criteria have not been implemented in an expedient manner and [agreed] to recommend that parties implement stricter domestic measures up to and including prohibition of trade in wildlife species now'. South Korea, however, was given until the next COP to demonstrate progress before parties should consider stricter measures.[30]

At the time, it was suspected that Taiwan was subjected to harsher treatment because it was the easier target, not least because it had no separate identity under CITES or the WTO. While this could well be true, it must not be forgotten that from the mid-1980s Taiwan had been the largest importer of African and Asian rhino horn. A ban on imports had been in place since 1985, but it was never enforced. In 1989 the Wildlife Conservation Act was passed which banned the internal sale and display of rhino horn without a special permit, but no permit was ever granted and rhino horn remained openly on sale.[31]

I can confirm from my own visits that, until Taiwan was subject to heavy outside pressure, it was a 'black hole' as far as trade in endangered species and their derivatives were concerned. Rhino horn was openly on sale and freely available until November 1992. There was no enforcement, no public or official awareness as to the effects of the trade, and no cooperation on the part of the authorities. UNEP's Special Envoy described a meeting with officials in October 1992 as 'very disappointing, as the Taiwanese were not giving the rhino horn problem much of a priority'.[32]

Public awareness took a sharp turn when a coalition of UK NGOs, among them the Environmental Investigation Agency and David Shepherd Wildlife Foundation, launched a campaign targeting Taiwan at a London press conference on 16 November 1992. They released a short, powerful advertising video in

---

[29] SC31: Summary Report (Mar 1994), pp. 12, 20–21.
[30] Ibid., p. 41; CITES Doc. SC.31.19 'Decisions of the Standing Committee on Trade in Rhinoceros Horn and Tiger Specimens' (Mar 1994).
[31] Martin (1993b).
[32] Martin (1993a), p. 22.

which blood dripped from a Taiwanese TV set showing film of rhinos being shot. The TV was labelled 'Made in Diewan' and the film advocated a consumer boycott of Taiwanese goods. US NGOs subsequently joined the UK groups, and the coalition took the campaign to Taiwan, holding press conferences and meetings in Taipei and generating substantial publicity and debate in the Taiwanese press (both positive and negative). Initially, the authorities reacted angrily to the campaign, threatening legal action against the groups and denying their charges of negligence.[33] But on 19 November 1992, three days after the London press conference, the government announced a total ban on the sale and display of rhino horn, the imposition of fines, and the immediate enforcement of the 1989 Wildlife Conservation Act. Rhino horns disappeared from medicine shop windows, and in early December Taiwanese police seized 40 kg of horn sent from Hong Kong at Taipei international airport.[34]

In May 1993 a survey of TM shops in Taipei by TRAFFIC found that those offering rhino horn for sale had declined from 72% in 1991 to 36%, and that both wholesale and retail prices had fallen. In June 1993 UNEP's Special Envoy and TRAFFIC-Taipei helped government officials draw up a strategy involving rewards for information on illegal trade, a ten-fold increase in fines, visits by the police to the Endangered Species Protection Unit in South Africa and the establishment of a special police task force.[35] Subsequently, on a widely publicized visit to Taiwan in November 1993, the late Michael Werikhe, a Kenyan conservationist known as the 'Rhino Man', found a marked improvement in attitude by the authorities, evident in information campaigns and a forthcoming revision of legislation. Throughout his visit, he was treated as a celebrity, even receiving an invitation to meet the President, which would have been unthinkable just a year before.[36]

Taiwan's response proved insufficient to avoid US sanctions. On 28 April 1994, shortly after the Standing Committee's recommendation to implement stricter domestic measures and on the basis of an evaluation of progress (which included a technical assistance mission to China and Taiwan), the United States acted on its certification and announced a prohibition of the importation of wildlife specimens or products from Taiwan. The prohibition was tempered with a continued commitment to provide assistance to eliminate

---

[33] 'Taiwan Denies Groups' Charges of Illegal Rhino Horn Imports', *Journal of Commerce* (17 Nov 1992); 'No Need for Legal Action in Rhino Row', *China News* (19 Nov 1992).

[34] Martin (1993a), p. 22.

[35] Martin (1993b), p. 4.

[36] Michael Werikhe, 'Taiwan', unpublished report on file with author (1993).

illegal trade. Congress urged Clinton to sanction China as well, but he refused on the basis that it had made progress.[37]

The major Taiwanese exports affected by the ban were reptile leather shoes and handbags; jewellery made from coral, mussel shells and bone; edible frogs' legs; live goldfish and tropical fish for the aquarium trade; and bird feathers. At the time, the most recent data (from 1992) indicated that annual wildlife imports from Taiwan to the United States amounted to about US$22 million.[38] According to Taiwanese officials, 53 companies would be affected by the ban. After an initial angry reaction, Taiwan redoubled its efforts to stop illegal wildlife trade. It agreed to inventory its rhino horns, consolidate stockpiles, instigate harsher penalties for convicted traffickers, enforce its wildlife protection laws and generally improve wildlife conservation. The Taiwanese government committed to spending US$37 million to implement the measures.[39]

On 27 October 1994 Taiwan amended its Wildlife Conservation Act along CITES lines. It also engaged in a public education programme and established a specialized Wildlife Protection Unit composed of police officers (which now cooperates actively with enforcement officers in African countries[40]). In response, the United States announced the lifting of its trade embargo on 30 June 1995, though Taiwan remained certified while the US Fish and Wildlife Service monitored its progress and provided training to Taiwan in law enforcement and CITES implementation practice.[41] In April 1997 the US Secretary of the Interior determined that Taiwan had made sufficient progress to warrant removal of the certification. China, however, remained certified.[42] Since the sanctions were lifted, Taiwan appears to have maintained its commitment to implementation and enforcement of CITES. It is one of the few countries to have provided assistance to the Kenya-based Lusaka Agreement Task Force, established to combat illegal wildlife trade in Africa (discussed in Chapter 9).

---

[37] Fed. Reg. Docs. 94-4008 (24 Feb 1994) and 94-10166 (28 Apr 1994); David S. Favre, 'Trade in Endangered Species' *Yearbook of International Environmental Law*, 5 (1994), p. 260; Sand (1997) p. 22 (see ch. 1, n. 3); DeSombre, p. 177.

[38] US Fed. Reg. Doc. 94-10166 (28 Apr 1994).

[39] DeSombre, p. 177.

[40] Adan Dullo, former Director, Lusaka Agreement Task Force, personal communication (1999).

[41] Sand (1997), p. 22, quoting US Department of Interior press release 'US Lifts Wildlife Trade Embargo on Taiwan' (30 Jun 1995); CITES Doc. 10.8, 'Secretariat Report', for COP10 (Jun 1997), p. 5.

[42] DeSombre, p. 178.

At COP9 in November 1994, trade sanctions in relation to the rhino horn trade were not discussed. A 'conservative' resolution on rhinoceros, prepared by IUCN, was approved, replacing Resolution Conf. 6.10.[43] Its tone was conciliatory rather than punitive. The previous direction to destroy stockpiles was replaced with a recommendation to mark and register legal stocks. Parties were 'urged' to implement comprehensive legislation and enforcement controls, including internal trade restrictions and penalties, and to cooperate among states to curtail illegal trade, while the Standing Committee was directed to continue to pursue actions to reduce illegal trade, ensuring, *inter alia*, that standardized indicators are developed to measure changes in the level of illegal hunting and the status of rhino populations in range states.[44]

Not surprisingly, given the nature of the resolution, there appears to have been little follow-up action under CITES since 1994, except for a workshop on the development of standardized indicators held by TRAFFIC under contract with the Secretariat in December 1999. Range states appear to have largely ignored a COP10 decision directing them to report to COP11 on their rhino conservation measures, despite a reminder sent to parties by the Secretariat in November 1999.

At COP11 the Secretariat rightly criticized the rhino resolution for having no reporting mechanisms and no role allocated to the Secretariat, making implementation hard to evaluate. As a result the resolution was amended with:

- a recommendation that the Secretariat provide technical advice to parties with inadequate legislation, enforcement or control of stocks;
- a requirement for range states to report at least six months before each COP meeting on population status, illegal hunting and trade, national legislation and law enforcement activities, according to a standard format to be developed by the Secretariat.[45]

It remains to be seen, however, if range states will comply, particularly since there are no sticks or carrots attached to the reporting requirement.

So has the rhino been 'saved'? The Secretariat reported a cautious picture to COP11 in 2000. It described the conservation status of several species as

---

[43] David S. Favre, 'Trade in Endangered Species', *Yearbook of International Environmental Law*, 5 (1994), p. 258; CITES Com. II 9.10 (Rev.), 'Summary Report of the Committee II Meeting', COP9 (Nov 1994), at p. 219.
[44] CITES Resolution Conf. 9.14, 'Conservation of Rhinoceros in Asia and Africa' (1994).
[45] CITES Resolution Conf. 9.14 (Rev.), 'Conservation of and Trade in African and Asian Rhinoceros' (2000).

remaining 'critical', though it reported some populations as having slightly increased, notably in South Africa, Namibia, India and Nepal. (The Kenyan population too has been increasing, at about 4% a year.) It went on to say that targeted anti-poaching work in some African range states appeared to have markedly reduced illegal hunting, and that dedicated anti-rhino-poaching units such as in Sumatra had proved effective, but that poaching remained of 'great concern to many Asian range states'. There was 'good reason to suspect that specialized criminal routes [were] being utilized to obtain, smuggle and finally market horns and products containing rhinoceros horn'.[46]

Through its contacts with the traditional medicine communities, the Secretariat reported that 'rhinoceros horn is still viewed as an important ingredient in treatments and cures for a number of diseases', with some practitioners not believing that there was an effective substitute.[47] However, since the action taken by CITES, UNEP and the United States, driven by NGO campaigns, general awareness among practitioners has increased markedly. New books published on TM now omit reference to using rhino horn as an ingredient.[48] In Yemen, during a visit in January 2001 Vigne and Martin saw no new rhino horn being made into dagger handles – the first time in 14 survey visits since 1978. Their report was cautiously optimistic. Although rhino horn traders said that horn could still be obtained from Djibouti, to where it was smuggled from Mombasa by boat or from Addis Ababa by train, they complained that the government ban on imports had affected their business. Overall there was a lack of rhino horn on the Yemeni market, prices had not risen, and water buffalo horn was being used as a substitute.[49]

Certainly the two species of African rhino appear to be recovering in most range states. A report released in June 2002 by the IUCN/SSC African Rhino Specialist Group states that the total estimated population had increased from 13,109 in 1999 to 14,770 in 2001. Of these, 11,670 were white rhinos (up from an estimate of 10,405 in 1999) and 3,100 were black rhinos (up from an estimate of 2,704 in 1999). Rhinos are also being re-established through government/ private-sector programmes in Uganda, Zambia and Botswana. While the overall picture is optimistic, however, rhinos in Cameroon and the Democratic

---

[46] CITES Doc. 11.32, 'Conservation and Trade in Rhinoceroses', prepared by the Secretariat for COP11 (Apr 2000).

[47] Ibid.

[48] Personal communication from doctor practising TM.

[49] Lucy Vigne and Esmond Martin, 'Closing Down the Illegal Trade in Rhino Horn in Yemen', *Pachyderm*, 30 (Jan–Jun 2001), p. 87.

Republic of Congo remain under serious threat, and declining budgets of conservation agencies in most range states give rise to concern.[50]

Poaching incidents and reports of illegal trade persist, albeit not on the scale of the 1980s and early 1990s. In February 2001 rhino horn was reported on sale for US$35,000 per kilo in a Sharjah market in the UAE, though the trader admitted that both rhino and tiger products were now 'difficult to get'.[51] In late November 2001 the carcasses of four rhinos were found in Tsavo National Park in Kenya, the first poaching of rhinos inside the country's parks for eight years.[52] The three species of Asian rhino, which number around 2,900, are particularly at risk.[53] A CITES technical team visiting tiger range states in Asia in 1999 'repeatedly heard of poaching of rhinoceros in Asia'.[54] Between mid-1998 and mid-2000, the Chitwan Valley, home to the Royal Chitwan National Park in Nepal, experienced an upsurge in poaching. In 1998 and 1999 at least 20 rhinos were killed illegally, whereas in 1994–7 under two had been poached on average every year. Improved anti-poaching strategies subsequently helped to stem the poaching, while an investigation resulted in the arrest of traders in Chitwan Valley and Kathmandu.[55] (The trail led to a woman in the Chinese embassy, who since 1990 had allegedly been exporting horns, along with tiger bones and other medicinal products, by road to China via Tibet.) More recently, however, civil unrest has caused a resurgence of poaching in Chitwan, with 18 rhinos poached between January and mid-April 2002.[56] A report released by WWF in August 2002 warns of an upsurge in poaching of Asian rhinos. It states that at least 86 have been killed in the past four years, mainly in India and Nepal.[57]

While it is certainly too early to claim the rhino has been 'saved', and CITES must not be complacent, especially in the face of increased poaching in Asia and declining conservation budgets in African range states, its action

---

[50] 'African Rhinos Edge Back from the Brink', *Environment News Service* (12 Jun 2002), referring to IUCN/SSC African Rhino Specialist Group report on rhinoceros populations.
[51] Joanna Langley, 'Trade in Endangered Species: For Sale: the World's Heritage', *Gulf News* (3 Feb 2001).
[52] 'Poachers Kill first Kenyan Rhinos in Eight Years', Reuters (6 Dec 2001).
[53] *Wanted Alive: Asian Rhinos in the Wild* (WWF, Aug 2002).
[54] Tiger Technical Missions report, p. 22.
[55] Esmond Martin, 'What Strategies are Effective for Nepal's Rhino Conservation: A Recent Case Study', *Pachyderm*, 31 (Jul–Dec 2001), p. 42.
[56] Ashok Kumar, personal communication, based on information from a reliable source (May 2002).
[57] *Wanted Alive: Asian Rhinos in the Wild* (n. 53 above).

between 1992 and 1994 does appear to have contributed to bringing some rhino populations back from the brink.

Tigers

The tiger has been listed on Appendix I since 1975 (the Siberian sub-species since 1987), but an upsurge in demand for tiger parts, alongside habitat loss, has driven populations even lower than those of the rhino. It has been estimated that just 5,000–7,000 are left in the wild, scattered in pockets in India and East Asia.[58] Tiger skins, bones and other body parts, especially the penis, are in demand for a variety of reasons, including traditional medicine (where tiger bone is used as a treatment for rheumatism), decoration, virility preparations, and symbols of power, luck and status. Live tigers, especially cubs, are also sought after as exotic pets, but to a lesser extent.[59]

In recent years, faced with the increasingly grave status of tigers and lobbying by NGOs for strong action, CITES has stepped up its activities to combat the trade, culminating in a threat of sanctions against India at COP11, together with a set of detailed recommendations to be carried out by CITES institutions and parties before COP12. A conservative resolution similar to the one on rhinos had been passed on tigers at COP9 in 1994, but continued illegal hunting and trade (and NGO pressure) prompted a further decision at COP10 in 1997, directing the Standing Committee to make tigers a priority issue, and to undertake technical and political missions to tiger range and consumer states.[60]

The Secretariat, at the request of the Standing Committee and with assistance from TRAFFIC and Environment Canada, conducted technical missions to 14 range and consumer states, producing a detailed and comprehensive report for SC42 in September/October 1999 with country-specific comments and recommendations. States visited included western as well as eastern consumers, namely Canada, Japan, the Netherlands, the United Kingdom and the United States. Range states that received missions, some of which were also consumers, were Cambodia, China, India, Indonesia, Malaysia, Myanmar, Nepal, the Russian Federation and Vietnam.[61]

---

[58] D. Banks, 'Tigers and Traditional Medicine – a Study', in *Proceedings of the EU Wildlife Enforcement Workshop, London 1–2 March 1998* (UK DETR, 1998), pp. 93–5: 93.

[59] Tiger Technical Missions report.

[60] CITES Resolution Conf. 9.13 (Rev), 'Conservation of and Trade in Tigers' (1997); Decision 10.66 'Regarding Trade in Tigers' (1997).

[61] Tiger Technical Missions report.

Three specific points were raised at SC42 by the Secretariat staff member who led the missions. First, there was very poor communication within and between range states; second, many range states had insufficient legislation to allow proper implementation of CITES; and third, specialized enforcement units were successful. He drew attention in particular to task forces in the US Fish and Wildlife Service, the CITES enforcement team at London's Heathrow airport and Inspection Tiger in the Russian Federation. As a result of the report, India, Japan and China, where problems were severe, were singled out for receiving a high-level political mission in early 2000.[62]

The political mission, led by the Standing Committee Chairman (then Robert Hepworth of the UK), reported to COP11 that it was favourably impressed with the way in which Japan and China, both consumer states, had responded to the technical mission's comments and recommendations. A complete ban on domestic trade was agreed in Japan, while China, with help from the political mission, managed 'to head off pressure' to resume use of their stockpiles of tiger parts and rhino horn, sealed in the aftermath of the internal trade ban in 1993. China, however, refused to destroy its domestic stocks of tiger parts and derivatives (one of the technical mission's recommendations), claiming they were legally acquired pre-convention material.[63]

India, the main tiger range state and source of illegal trade in tiger products, was strongly criticized by the political mission for poor enforcement, including corruption and collusion among staff and lack of cooperation among the relevant agencies; for funds not reaching field level; and for poor implementation of conservation schemes. Above all, the mission found no evidence of effective means being taken in India at any level to deter and detect tiger poaching and smuggling and other serious wildlife crime. This was despite the existence of Project Tiger, launched 27 years earlier by the then prime minister, since when US$8–10 million had been channelled into India from overseas governmental and non-governmental bodies for tiger conservation. The political mission recommended, *inter alia*, that all parties, non-parties and organizations stop funding tiger conservation in India until mechanisms were in place to disburse the funds efficiently, and that the COP11 meeting should direct the Standing Committee to recommend restrictions on trade in CITES listed species against India at SC45 if the Secretariat reported no progress in

---

[62] CITES Doc. 11.30 (Rev. 1), 'Conservation of and Trade in Tigers', COP11 (Apr 2000); SC42: Summary Report (Sep/Oct 1999), p. 18.
[63] SC42: Summary Report, p. 18.

enforcement and financial control. In particular, the mission specified the need for a specialized wildlife crime unit.[64]

Following strong resistance from India, supported by the United States, the final recommendations of a COP11 Tiger Working Group (which were subsequently approved as COP decisions) were significantly weaker than those of the political mission. The recommendation for a specialized wildlife crime unit was retained by the COP.[65] In relation to funding, however, parties, non-parties and other organizations were 'encouraged' to provide funds to India for tiger conservation, while India was 'encouraged' to demonstrate that measures were or would be in place for their efficient disbursement.[66] Any overt reference to trade sanctions, or to India in this regard, was removed. Instead, the Standing Committee was directed to report to COP12 on progress made by parties visited by the missions, with the provision that the report 'may contain recommendations regarding appropriate measures where no progress has been made'.[67] The United Kingdom, which had pressed particularly hard for sanctions with the support of the European Union and some NGOs, clarified that 'appropriate measures' meant the same as they did under the national legislation project, i.e. that they 'may include restrictions on commercial trade in specimens of CITES listed species'.[68] So, if no progress is apparent in tiger conservation and enforcement measures by COP12 in November 2002, India may once again find itself the subject of pressure for trade sanctions. And, given that the Standing Committee can make recommendations for 'appropriate measures' concerning any of the parties visited by missions where no progress has been made, the door is open to recommended trade sanctions with other non-compliant range and consumer states at COP12.

Although the COP watered down some of the political mission's recommendations in relation to India, its other suggestions were largely endorsed, becoming COP decisions. Perhaps the most far-reaching of these in terms of CITES enforcement was to create a Tiger Enforcement Task Force (TETF) with the objective of combating illicit trade in tigers and tiger parts and derivatives. The TETF, launched at a meeting hosted by India in April 2001, was

---

[64] CITES Doc. 11.30 (Rev. 1) (see n. 62 above); Robert Hepworth, 'Notes of Talk delivered to Discussion Meeting on Enforcing Multilateral Environmental Agreements' (RIIA, London, 20 Oct 2000).

[65] CITES Decision 11.49, directed to Parties on Tigers (2000).

[66] CITES Decision 11.48, directed to Parties on Tigers (2000).

[67] CITES Decision 11.82, directed to the Standing Committee on Tigers (2000).

[68] CITES Com. II 11.12, minutes of the 12th session of Committee II at COP11 (April 2000).

intended by the political mission to be the first of a new concept of ad hoc CITES Enforcement Task Forces (CETFs), targeting different fields of wild-life crime, to be convened by the Secretariat. Unfortunately, however, the COP could not accept this broader suggestion and narrowed down the remit and terms of reference to tigers alone. A full description of the TETF is contained in Chapter 9.

Other political mission recommendations approved by the COP included: a deadline of 31 August 2000 for range and consumer states to report their re-sponse to the technical mission's recommendations; a direction to the Secretariat to report to SC45 in June 2001 on their responses; and a direction to the Stand-ing Committee to consider the responses and 'decide whether further action is appropriate'.[69] The Standing Committee was also directed to continue its re-view of progress in range and consumer states, particularly those visited by missions, through a targeted programme considering control of illegal tiger trade, national legislative and enforcement measures, and implementation of the mission's recommendations.[70] Thus, between COP11 and COP12 (April 2000–November 2002), the Standing Committee was delegated a key decision-making role with respect to the tiger to ensure compliance with the technical mission's recommendations.

The Secretariat was also directed to seek invitations to the three tiger range states that remain non-parties to CITES (Bhutan, Democratic Republic of Ko-rea and Lao People's Democratic Republic) to encourage their accession; and to provide SC45 with an assessment of the effectiveness of legislative changes introduced in Japan.[71] Decisions approved at COP11 that were directed at par-ties concerned training for enforcement personnel; seeking cooperation with Interpol and the World Customs Organization (WCO); and investigating ille-gal trade and reporting it to the Secretariat. (The last decision was particularly directed at China, which 'remains a destination for tiger parts and derivatives'.) There was also a direction to China to circulate a list of former manufacturers of TM products containing parts of tiger or other Appendix I species to assist consumer country enforcement agencies; and a direction to range states to report to SC45 on their approach to involving local communities in tiger conservation, for example through ecotourism, and to draw on the experience of African states in all aspects of conservation, enforcement and ecotourism (presumably with the rhino in mind). Exchange visits of enforcement and

---

[69] CITES Decisions 11.47, directed to Parties; and 11.140, directed to the Secretariat on Tigers (2000).

[70] CITES Decision 11.81, directed to the Standing Committee on Tigers (2000).

[71] CITES Decisions 11.142 and 11.143, directed to the Secretariat on Tigers (2000).

management personnel between tiger range states and African range states were encouraged.[72]

These measures are highly detailed and represent the most concerted and extensive effort to date to bring an Appendix I group of species back from the brink of extinction in the wild. They rely less on sanctions and more on technical assistance than the measures taken for the rhino, though the threat of their use seems to have had a positive effect on India. As well as hosting the first TETF meeting and enforcement training course, India has recently established a Wildlife Crime Cell.[73] The success of the CITES initiative will depend on the continued political will of range and consumer states, their willingness to devote funds towards combating the illegal trade in tiger parts, and the availability of adequate funding for the TETF and its activities.

At SC45 in June 2001, the Secretariat advised that Myanmar was the only party not to have reported on its response to the technical mission recommendations. It also informed the Standing Committee that it had received no information to indicate that Japan's legislative changes had not been effective, and that Japan had engaged in an extensive public awareness campaign.[74] This information was contradicted by a report from the Japan Wildlife Conservation Society (which, although it could not attend the meeting, could distribute information), saying that products labelled as containing tiger parts continued to be widely available in Japan and that the problem had escalated with tiger bone derivatives being offered for sale over the internet. The NGO claimed that implementation of new legislation had been weak, and in some instances dealers had obtained a fresh stock of products.[75] In a survey carried out between January and April 2001, the group found tiger products, including drinks made from tiger bones and tiger penises, in 21 out of 65 stores offering Chinese herbal medicines. Under the April 2000 ban on domestic trade, only tiger products legally imported before that date and registered with the Environment Ministry can be sold, but as of June 2001 no products had been registered.[76] As already noted under country case studies of non-compliance, the Environmental Investigation Agency also released a report before SC45 documenting

---

[72] CITES Decisions 11.50, 11.52, 11.53, 11.54, 11.55 and 11.56, directed to Parties on Tigers (2000).

[73] SC46: Summary Report (Mar 2002), p. 16.

[74] CITES SC45 Doc. 21, 'Conservation and Trade in Specific Species', prepared by the Secretariat for SC45 (Jun 2001).

[75] 'Briefing Document for the 45th Meeting of the CITES Standing Committee' (SSN, Jun 2001).

[76] *Kyodo News* via COMTEX (13 Jun 2001).

a thriving trade in Thailand in both the import and export of tiger products and derivatives, and an established domestic industry manufacturing tiger products.[77] The Standing Committee, however, just noted the allegations from both NGOs. No action was recommended.[78]

By SC46 in March 2002, there had still been no response from Myanmar. No measures were recommended, even though the Secretariat reported that:

> it has intelligence that shows that Myanmar continues to be an important transit route for illicit trade in wildlife, including tiger parts and derivatives, and that specimens of Appendix I species are readily available for sale in towns along Myanmar's borders, particularly with China, the Lao People's Democratic Republic and Thailand.

Only one recommendation was made and approved specifically on the tiger at SC46 – that a technical mission be sent to Thailand to examine domestic control of trade in tiger specimens and general CITES implementation. Over 30 NGOs, including members of SSN and WWF, had sent a letter to the Chairman of the Standing Committee requesting such a mission. The Secretariat had also reported that it was continuing to receive information raising concerns about Thailand's domestic trade controls and the availability of medicinal products claiming to contain tiger ingredients, some allegedly manufactured in Thailand. No comment was made by the Secretariat to SC46 on Japan, though Cambodia was commended for initiatives on training and anti-poaching.[79]

The lack of specific recommendations regarding Myanmar is surprising, considering the mandate given by the COP to the Standing Committee to decide on appropriate action for non-responsive countries. While India appears to have responded to a veiled threat of trade sanctions, Myanmar has not. On the basis of the Secretariat's information, it would be more appropriate for the Standing Committee to recommend to COP12 'appropriate measures' in the form of trade sanctions for Myanmar, rather than India.

---

[77] Debbie Banks, Dave Currey and Faith Doherty, *Thailand's Tiger Economy* (EIA, Jun 2001).

[78] SC45: Summary Record (Jun 2001), p. 14.

[79] CITES SC46 Doc.15, 'Conservation of and Trade in Specific Species', prepared by the Secretariat for SC46 (Mar 2002); letter to Kenneth Stansell from 33 NGOs 'Re: CITES Tiger Decisions Taken at COP11' (19 Feb 2002); SC46: Summary Report, p. 16.

9 Enforcement, technical assistance and capacity-building

Enforcement, technical assistance and capacity-building are all means to respond to and prevent non-compliance. To be successful, they require resources and political commitment, which in the CITES context are all too often in short supply. This chapter attempts to give an overview of national enforcement capacity by taking a look at 15 selected parties, then examines efforts to improve enforcement at an international level, followed by a look at the programmes that have been developed to provide parties with technical assistance and capacity-building.

National enforcement

A snapshot of capacity in 15 countries

During their visits to range and consumer states, the tiger technical missions in effect conducted a review of wildlife law enforcement capacity in a variety of parties. Their findings, not surprisingly, are an eye-opener. There was a huge variation between parties concerning the national agencies involved, the techniques employed, and their capacity to enforce wildlife law and combat wildlife crime. The team identified corruption, collusion and nepotism (CCN) as three factors hampering progress with tackling illicit trade (see Box 9.1), forming the 'general impression that CCN is so extensive and ingrained in the cultures of some parties that it was hard to believe that any progress could be achieved unless such practices were first eradicated'.[1]

The following is a brief review of enforcement practices and capabilities in 15 CITES parties, 14 of which were visited by the tiger technical team in 1999. Most of the information has been extracted from the team's report, but where possible this has been supplemented with additional information. South Africa has been included on the basis of the author's own on-site research.

Cambodia The technical team identified numerous problems with wildlife law enforcement in Cambodia. In Ratanakiri province they found that 35 rangers were responsible for dealing with illegal wildlife exploitation and illegal

---

[1] Tiger Technical Missions report (see ch. 8, n. 17), p. 18.

Box 9.1: Some general observations of the Tiger Technical Missions team

- *Management and policy*: conservation remains a low priority for many countries.
- *NGOs*: in a number of states the involvement of NGOs was almost essential to wildlife law enforcement efforts; some governments have abdicated their responsibilities to a degree where NGOs control the enforcement of domestic wildlife laws almost entirely in some areas.
- *Corruption*: all too frequently, the team was advised that corruption played a major part in the inability of some range states to tackle wildlife crime effectively – not surprising, given the poor salaries of government employees and the potential profits of endangered species trafficking.
- *Collusion*: the team learned of instances where enforcement staff and government officials were actively cooperating with poachers and traders or deliberately ignoring illegal activities.
- *Nepotism*: the team heard of incidents in range states where appointment to positions in departments responsible for conservation and wildlife law enforcement relied more upon who you knew rather than on what you knew.

Source: CITES Tiger Technical Missions report (1999).

---

logging, yet they had only four motorbikes and three boats with which to patrol a huge area. (A foot patrol with the Vietnam border takes eight days.) They had very little equipment or funds to enable field patrols, were not armed, and relied on access to police communication. In contrast, possession of firearms was widespread among the population. Poaching was sophisticated. Gangs equipped with large-calibre, high-quality rifles, allegedly managed by Thai businessmen, were targeting elephant and tiger. One technique was to use a dead monkey as bait with a grenade underneath; the detonation killed the tiger but limited damage to its skin and skeleton. There was lack of coordination between Cambodian enforcement agencies, and press reports alleged poaching and collusion by soldiers. Salary scales of government and enforcement officials were often so low that many had a second job or engaged in private enterprise to supplement their income. Although staff from the Management Authority had attended a CITES training seminar in Thailand in 1998, knowledge of CITES appeared to be extremely limited among enforcement and implementation personnel. On the positive side, WWF had assisted the Ministry of Environment to establish a seven-member ranger team in Virachey National Park, which had limited equipment but considerable enthusiasm and was developing a scheme to use community volunteers.

Cambodia appears to have responded to the technical team's criticisms. At SC46 the Secretariat commended them for initiatives on training and anti-poaching.[2] Any effects in the field are, however, unknown.

Canada   The technical mission was complimentary of Canada's wildlife law enforcement effort. Despite having fewer than 35 operational officers (aside from headquarters staff) to cover a huge nation, the Wildlife Enforcement Division of Environment Canada was considered active and effective. It had maximized its potential through its close cooperation with Canada Customs, by providing training for customs officials, who play the primary role in shipment inspection, and by using innovative techniques such as equipping ports with digital cameras for identification. Environment Canada was also noted in the team's report as being internationally renowned for its identification manuals, which are a good aid to enforcement staff, and for assisting CITES training abroad. While not wishing to question the team's findings, and acknowledging that the Wildlife Enforcement Division seems to have maximized its potential effectiveness, 35 operational officers seems very few for one of the largest countries in the world.

China   The technical mission reported that 55,000 wildlife staff of the Forest Police Department in the State Forestry Administration (under the Ministry of Land and Resources) were primarily responsible for enforcing wildlife legislation. Police and customs officials are also empowered to enforce trade controls, while the military police play a major role in preventing illegal hunting and smuggling of state-protected wild animals in remote and national border regions.[3]

Smuggling of state-protected rare and endangered animals can result in the death penalty in China. Between 1986 and 1999 such a penalty was imposed 12 times. The technical team reported that the government had provided training for 500 CITES staff, police and customs officials, while another 160 had attended internationally organized training seminars. The effectiveness of China's enforcement effort, however, is hard to gauge from the team's report. Their only comment, apart from describing inspections carried out by officials following the 1993 ban on trade in rhino and tiger parts, is that

---

[2] CITES SC46 Doc. 15, 'Conservation of and Trade in Specific Species', prepared by the Secretariat for SC46 (Mar 2002).
[3] Wang Xi, 'China', in Terri Mottershead (ed.), *Environmental Law and Enforcement in the Asia-Pacific Rim* (Sweet & Maxwell Asia, 2002), p. 95.

Chinese enforcement agencies may not have an adequate appreciation of international wildlife crime. The agencies also appear to be unresponsive. Dutch police had tried to contact authorities in China, via Interpol, following the seizure of products apparently manufactured there, but had received little response.

In reply to the technical mission's recommendations, China announced at SC42 that it was considering the creation of a National Enforcement Co-ordination Committee for CITES, and that specialized enforcement units would be established at provincial level.[4] It would be interesting to know if this was carried through and, if so, how the committee and units are functioning.

In Hong Kong employees of the Agriculture, Fisheries and Conservation Department (AFCD) are primarily responsible for enforcement. Patrols in parks and reserves take place every day. Under the Hong Kong CITES legislation, the Animal and Plant (Protection of Endangered Species) Ordinance, the AFCD is given wide powers of search and seizure and fines are imposed for obstructing employees in their duties. In May 2001 the AFCD established the Endangered Species Resource Centre in Kowloon whose purpose is to raise awareness on CITES.[5]

India　The technical team found no fewer than 12 agencies in India with a potential role in combating poaching and/or smuggling. These include the state wildlife and forest departments, the Wildlife Protection Department (GOI), customs, the Ministry of Environment and Forests, the army, police, Indo-Tibetan border police, Border Security Force, coastguard, Railway Protection Force, Directorate of Revenue Intelligence, Foreign Post Office, Central Bureau of Investigation and the Interpol Unit of CBI.[6] At the time of their visit, however, the mission saw 'little evidence' of national coordination between these agencies. India subsequently refuted this allegation, stating that it had a special Coordination Committee for wildlife enforcement.

The primary role for wildlife protection in India is allotted to forest guards, foresters and rangers, about fifty of whom, the team reported, were being killed

---

[4]　SC42: Summary Report (Sep/Oct 1999), p. 18.
[5]　Terri Mottershead, 'Hong Kong', in Terri Mottershead (ed.), *Environmental Law and Enforcement in the Asia-Pacific Rim* (Sweet & Maxwell Asia, 2002), pp. 184–7.
[6]　Vivek Menon and Ashok Kumar, *Wildlife Crime: an Enforcement Guide* (Wildlife Protection Society of India/Natraj Publishers, 1998), p. 14.

every year in anti-poaching/illegal logging operations (compared with 8–12 poachers). The huge borders make control difficult, and while liaison with counterparts in neighbouring countries was found to be good in some places, it was fragmented in others. Delays in India's court systems were causing considerable problems. Although reward schemes were in place, India appeared to lack sufficient infrastructure to enable targeted follow-up to seizures and/or arrests.

NGOs were (and still are) providing much needed support. The Wildlife Protection Society of India (WPSI) was particularly commended for taking a lead in providing assistance, though the team regretted that all too often they were plugging gaps. Among other activities, WPSI has produced a practical and accessible enforcement guide on wildlife crime designed to assist wildlife law enforcement officers in India. The guide includes advice on CITES, Indian legislation, poaching and smuggling methods, investigation techniques, how to go to court, and information on identifying specimens.[7] Meanwhile, TRAFFIC maintains a wildlife crime database and has an informant network. Another NGO active in promoting effective enforcement but not mentioned by the team is the Wildlife Trust of India.

Overall, the team 'formed the clear impression that the lack of human resources, the lack of sufficient logistics, the size of the tiger habitat to be patrolled, the length of the borders where smuggling can take place and problems in the judicial system all combine to produce an insufficient deterrent'.[8] India, after an initially defensive reaction, has since hosted the first TETF meeting, was the first tiger range state to hold a training course on enforcement, (discussed in more detail below) and has established a Wildlife Crime Cell. The Cell, which falls under the Ministry of Environment and Forests, is still in its formative stages, comprising just one individual at the time of writing.[9]

Indonesia   Specialist personnel from the Department of Forestry and Nature Conservation (DFNC) known as 'Jagawana', combat poaching and wildlife crime together with the forest police and investigators. The field units were reported to have access to speedboats, pick-up trucks, motorbikes, rifles and revolvers. Undercover operations were permitted, and DFNC staff were observed to enjoy a relatively good working relationship with police, customs

---

[7] Ibid.
[8] Tiger Technical Missions report, p. 43.
[9] Vivek Menon, personal communication (Jul 2002).

and army. With the assistance of NGO funding, specialist rhino and tiger units had been deployed in some national parks. All CITES shipments had to be inspected prior to export, and customs officials had made a number of significant seizures. On the down side, the technical team flagged lack of motivation as a potential problem among enforcement staff, while there was evidence of some collusion between staff and illegal traders. The judicial process could be slow, and penalties handed down were seldom a deterrent. As already noted under the case study of Indonesia in Chapter 5, the team found CITES-listed species were readily available at a bird market in Jakarta and, commented that the 'brazen and open approach' to them indicated that enforcement of the law was 'not common or feared'.[10]

These last observations throw doubt on the real efficacy of the enforcement system, particularly given the difficulties anticipated in patrolling the world's largest archipelago (17,000 islands, 6,000 of which are inhabited) with a coastline of over 54,000 km. This doubt is born out by the recent report by the Indonesian NGO, KSBK, on parrot trade in Indonesia (discussed in the case study of Indonesia in Chapter 5), which reveals violations of trapping quotas; collusion with forestry department officials enabling trapping and sale of protected species (acknowledged by a senior forestry department official present at the KSBK news conference); and involvement of the military in transporting birds.[11]

Japan   The technical team reported that customs and police are the only enforcement agencies empowered by law, although others could be involved in inspection and overview of CITES trade. The team formed the impression that officials administering CITES controls did not have an extensive knowledge of international wildlife crime and illicit trade, which could 'adversely affect their ability to oversee controls and develop strategies'.[12] Wildlife crime was not viewed as a major problem, although, given the team's comment on lack of knowledge on the issue, this does not necessarily mean that there is no problem.

Malaysia   The primary enforcement agency is the enforcement division of the Department of Wildlife and National Parks (DWNP). Rangers carry out operational work, while officers who are graduate specialists conduct

---

[10] Tiger Technical Missions report, p. 49.
[11] 'Flying without Wing: Executive Summary' (KSBK, Jul 2002), <www.ksbk.or.id/prog/parrots_fly.htm>; 'Indonesian Army, Corrupt Officials Involved in Endangered Animal Trade: Report', *Associated Press* (4 Jul 2002).
[12] Tiger Technical Missions report, p. 55.

investigations, including undercover operations and import/export inspections. Employees were reported by the team to enjoy fringe benefits and public esteem. Staff demonstrated a high level of CITES knowledge. Multi-agency cooperation was observed, and customs officers had received some CITES training. Nevertheless, DWNP was considered to have insufficient resources to patrol borders effectively, and in the field there was lack of communication between forest and wildlife rangers.

Myanmar   Knowledge of CITES was limited among staff of the Management and Scientific Authorities and enforcement personnel. The Nature and Wildlife Conservation Division had relatively few staff dedicated to enforcement, though some anti-poaching units had been created in national parks. Routine involvement of the police, customs or the military in wildlife law enforcement was apparently uncommon. Border areas were not patrolled because of insurgents, and enforcement agency staff suffered from low salaries and limited resources and equipment. There was lack of coordination with enforcement agencies in neighbouring Thailand, despite a visible illegal trade at the border between the two countries. While a number of officials told the technical team that poaching and/or illegal wildlife trade was rare, according to other sources, poaching was common in some areas, wildlife products were on sale in rural markets, and there was smuggling to Thailand and China.

Nepal   The Nepalese Department of National Parks and Wildlife Conservation (DNPWC) is mandated to enforce wildlife laws in protected areas, and Forest Department staff oversee their enforcement elsewhere. A CITES unit set up under the DNPWC has the major responsibility for enforcing CITES regulations. Customs officers deal with border controls and police assist with investigations. Since 1994 there have been dedicated anti-poaching patrols aimed at protecting rhinos and tigers. The army has a large presence in protected areas, but the team noted no reports of involvement in poaching. The upsurge in rhino poaching in Chitwan Valley must have been ongoing at the time of the technical team's visit but went unobserved. The team reported that reward schemes were operated with NGO assistance. Workshops and seminars had taken place between Nepalese and Chinese authorities to establish joint actions relating, *inter alia,* to wildlife crime. There was also routine communication with counterparts in protected areas along the border with India. Nevertheless, patrolling borders appeared to be a particular problem. The technical team reported major problems with illicit trade transiting the country, particularly between India and China. Shahtoosh moves from China to India, while tiger parts move in the opposite direction. Other wildlife goods being trafficked across the Nepalese border include rhino horns, leopard skins and bones, golden monitor lizard skins, bear bile and musk deer pod.[13] Large tracts of land are difficult to patrol, and many border crossings at the time of the technical mission visit were unmanned.

The situation in Nepal seems to have declined since the team's visit. Nepalese conservationists have recently raised the alarm over increased poaching. As a result of the state of emergency, forest guards and army troops in protected areas were removed from their posts, leaving the field wide open to poachers. The Nepalese government was accused of hiding facts and failing to face up to public opinion.[14] Following an investigation into the bird trade, the Nepal Forum of Environmental Journalists was also critical of the government.[15] They found many species of wild-caught CITES-listed birds from India and Nepal on sale in Kathmandu markets. But owing to confusion over jurisdiction among government authorities and 'lack of seriousness', illegal traders were not being prosecuted. DNPWC jurisdiction is restricted to protected areas, the Forest Department cannot not take action in urban areas, and police stated that they do not have the mandate to take action over illegal traders until requested by the concerned authority. Also, penalties vary widely – from three months for cutting a tree in a protected area to a maximum of ten years in prison for trading or possessing rhino horns. A recently produced manual on enforcement of CITES regulations, jointly prepared by DNPWC and World Wildlife Fund–Nepal, is being seen as an indication that the government may be taking the situation more seriously. In addition to detailing Nepalese species listed under CITES, the manual spells out the respective roles of authorities, including customs officials, police, army, Forest Department, DNPWC, Natural History Museum and the post office administration, as well as NGOs and the public.

The Netherlands Enforcement of wildlife legislation is the responsibility of the General Inspection Service (Algemene Inspectiedienst or AID) within the Ministry of Agriculture, Nature Management and Fisheries (also the CITES Management Authority), as well as the customs service and police. The technical team noted a high level of awareness of CITES among enforcement

---

[13] Deepak Gajurel, 'Nepal's New Weapon against Illicit Wildlife Trade', *Environment News Service* (25 Jul 2002), <http://ens-news.com/ens/jul2002/2002-07-25-02.asp>.

[14] Ravi Sharma Aryal, quoted in *Kantipur Daily National News* (5 Jul 2002).

[15] Deepak Gajurel, 'Nepal's New Weapon against Illicit Wildlife Trade'.

agencies, reinforced by liaison and collaboration through a CITES project group which coordinates enforcement and training. This is important, since the Netherlands is a major transit point for wildlife shipments, particularly through the port of Rotterdam and Amsterdam airport.

Russian Federation   Six agencies were reported as being variously involved in wildlife law enforcement, including the Forest Service, customs, the police, and the State Committee on Environmental Protection. One problem highlighted was the delay in dealing with the Management Authority based in Moscow, a hangover from the Soviet Union's practice of centralizing power in the capital. The technical team was particularly impressed with Inspection Tiger, a specialized unit of the State Committee on Environmental Protection to combat tiger poaching. Between its founding in 1994 and 1999, it had taken action in over 1,550 instances of environmental crime and had seized 40 tiger skins and carcasses (though inadequate legislation meant that no prosecutions had followed, just administrative penalties). Inspection Tiger personnel were empowered to carry weapons and engage in covert operations, and had developed an efficient informer network. The unit was relatively well equipped, having received substantial donor assistance. The mere existence of Inspection Tiger brigades seemed to be acting as a deterrent. Staff had carried out joint operations and shared intelligence with the Federal Security Service (formerly the KGB).

Given the technical team's focus on tigers, its report comments little on enforcement capacity in general, although, considering the enormous problem in recent years with sturgeon, it can be fairly safely assumed that enforcement agencies were ill-equipped to counter the rise in illegal caviar trade after the fall of the Soviet Union.

South Africa   South Africa is made up of nine provinces, which enjoy a large degree of autonomy on matters relating to wildlife trade. Responsibility for wildlife law enforcement is divided between the nine different nature conservation authorities, South African National Parks (which is responsible for Kruger National Park) and the Endangered Species Protection Unit (ESPU) of the South African Police.

ESPU is one of the oldest specialized wildlife law enforcement units. It was established in June 1989 to prevent the use of South Africa as a conduit for ivory and rhino horn smuggled from neighbouring countries. Headquartered outside Pretoria, the specialized police unit now consists of 27 officers. (At one time it was 40 strong, but numbers have been reduced due to budget cuts.)

Officers investigate all aspects of wildlife crime, but the reduction in the unit's strength has inevitably reduced its capacity, forcing it to be selective in investigations. (For example, in 2001 effort was being invested in abalone and cycad investigations, but out of necessity other areas of wildlife crime were receiving less attention.)

Undercover operations have always been an important element in ESPU's work. As of November 2001, the unit had investigated 1,220 cases, made 1,668 arrests, and confiscated over 14 tonnes of ivory, 546 rhino horns, 46 tonnes of marine products (mainly abalone), 1,890 rare plants (mainly cycads) and 2,551 live birds and reptiles.[16] ESPU has trained wildlife law enforcement officers in other African countries, including a similar unit established in Namibia. It has also conducted training through the Lusaka Agreement (described below). In addition, it has initiated joint operations with officers in neighbouring countries. Nationally, the unit cooperates in investigations with officers in the provincial nature conservation authorities as well as national parks, but inter-agency jealousies have tended to get in the way, preventing realization of the full potential for cooperation. An attempt is being made to address this by allocating responsibility for liaison with different provinces to specific ESPU officers.

Despite its international recognition and contribution to enforcement in other African countries, ESPU faces the prospect of closure as part of a three-phase plan to close all specialized units of the South African Police. This, and a perceived lack of political will to address wildlife crime, is undermining the work of the unit. Given that South Africa is a major transit point for wildlife from other African countries to markets in Europe, the United States and the Far East, as well as a source of CITES-listed species and a market in its own right, the loss of ESPU would be a major step backwards – from both an international as well as a national perspective.

United Kingdom   CITES-related enforcement is primarily the responsibility of UK customs and police officers. Considerable success has been enjoyed by an eight-member CITES Enforcement Team, which has built up an international reputation since it was established by customs at Heathrow Airport in 1992. According to traders, Heathrow is now avoided as a transit point because of its strict controls. Customs Wildlife and Endangered Species Officers (CWESOs), formerly CITES Liaison and Intelligence Officers (CLIOs), have been appointed in each customs region. Most UK police forces have estab-

---

[16] ESPU statistics, 1989–Nov 2001.

lished Police Wildlife Liaison Officers (PWLOs) who carry out wildlife law enforcement duties alongside their normal work. Although the technical team noted central government's apparent commitment to fighting wildlife crime, it reported little specialized training for PWLOs and CLIOs who were hampered by lack of resources and the part-time nature of their positions. The team noted a lack of national coordination of enforcement action on a routine basis. Although police and customs worked well on a case-by-case basis, there was no routine communication or coordination of inquiries. The team also reported a general lack of international liaison by UK enforcement bodies, especially in the follow-up to seizures.

The newly established National Wildlife Crime Intelligence Unit (NWCIU) – set up in April 2002 following a Wolverhampton University study into wildlife crime commissioned by the Department for Environment, Food and Rural Affairs (DEFRA) – has the potential to address some of the technical mission's criticisms, particularly those concerning communication and international liaison.[17] The unit, which is part of the Specialist Intelligence Branch of the National Criminal Intelligence Service (NCIS), is to become a national focal point for gathering and analysing intelligence on serious wildlife crime related to priority species and their products. Its mandate is to identify trends and patterns in wildlife crime and links to other serious crime, as well as the main individuals involved; to develop intelligence sources; to provide a nucleus of expertise and knowledge; and to establish links with other domestic and international agencies dealing with wildlife law enforcement.[18]

In 1995, following a review of secondary wildlife controls by the UK CITES Management Authority, the Partnership for Action against Wildlife Crime (PAW) was launched.[19] PAW is a permanent body overseeing wildlife law enforcement and includes members from the Management Authority (DEFRA), police, customs, the Crown Prosecution Service and NGOs. As of May 2002,

---

[17] M. Roberts, D. Cook, P. Jones and J. Lowther, *Wildlife Crime in the UK: Towards a National Wildlife Crime Unit* (DEFRA, 2001). <www.defra.gov.uk/paw/publications/natcrime/default.htm>.

[18] 'National Wildlife Crime Intelligence Unit launched at NCIS', NCIS press release (22 Apr 2002), <www.ncis.gov.uk/press/2002/12_02>; ' "Big Time Wildlife Criminals to be Tracked Down by New Unit" – Meacher', DEFRA news release (22 Apr 2002), <www.defra.gov.uk/news/2002/020422b>.

[19] For a description of PAW and its activities see <www.defra.gov.uk/paw> and M. Brewer, 'The Partnership for Action against Wildlife Crime: What Is It and What Does It Do?' in *Proceedings of the EU Wildlife Law Enforcement Workshop 1–2 March 1998* (UK DETR, 1998), p. 18.

90 organizations had signed up to the Partnership. A Steering Group of government, police and customs officials guides PAW's activities.

The Partnership's objectives are to support the PWLO and CWESO networks; to draw attention to the growing problem of wildlife crime and the need for tough enforcement action; to facilitate an exchange of information, experience, specialist knowledge and expertise on wildlife issues; and to promote the use of DNA technology and other forensic techniques in investigations. It achieves this through its Working Groups – Legal, Publicity, Data Management and Exchange, and DNA and other Forensics Techniques. In 1997 PAW submitted proposals for changes in enforcement provisions in UK legislation. The Partnership has also contributed to the success of a number of operations against wildlife criminals in the UK, including Operation Charm, which targeted the illegal sale of TM products containing derivatives from rhinos and tigers and other endangered species. Planned activities include support for the new NWCIU; the continuing review of legislative proposals; awareness-raising among the judiciary; exploring sponsorship and funding for enforcement activities; encouraging police forces to designate full-time officers; support for providing police officers with a power of arrest for wildlife offences; support for making the offences 'notifiable'to enable the development of central records (neither of which is currently the case); identifying priority species for DNA research; and building a library of cases.

TRAFFIC recently stated that, although the formation of the NWCIU was a significant step forward in tackling illegal wildlife trade through the gathering of information on markets, criminals and networks, enforcers remained powerless to arrest criminals while penalties were so low. TRAFFIC saw the main problems in the UK as a lack of investment in wildlife law enforcement and minimal non-deterrent punishments under wildlife trade laws. On the basis of a report it had commissioned with WWF on international wildlife trade and organized crime, TRAFFIC recommended an increase in the maximum penalty under the Control of Trade in Endangered Species (Enforcement) Regulations (COTES) from two years' imprisonment to five, making offences arrestable.[20]

United States   CITES-related enforcement is primarily the responsibility of the US Fish and Wildlife Service Division of Law Enforcement. The tiger technical team commented that USFWS wildlife inspectors and special agents have

---

[20] 'Organized Gangs Move into Wildlife Trafficking', WWF news release (17 Jun 2002), <www.wwf.org.uk/News>; Cook et al./WWF-UK (see ch. 1, n. 16), p. 33.

an international reputation for effective enforcement. They work alongside other federal agencies as well as state game and fish wardens and Sheriff's Offices.

When fully staffed, the USFWS Division of Law Enforcement includes 252 special agents and 93 inspectors.[21] But because of a lack of funds, at the end of 2000 there were only 201 special agents (down from 216 at the end of 1999) and 90 inspectors. Most of these work in the field and report through seven regional law enforcement offices. A headquarters Office of Law Enforcement provides national oversight, support, policy and guidance for investigations and the wildlife inspection programme. It also trains law enforcement personnel, fields a special investigations unit, provides budget management and administrative support for the division, and participates in inter- and intra-agency teams addressing particular issues such as coral reef conservation, control of invasive species and protection of migratory birds.

The Office of Law Enforcement consists of four branches: Investigations, Special Operations, Training and Inspection, and Technical and Field Support. It is also responsible for the Clark R. Bavin National Fish and Wildlife Forensics Laboratory in Ashland, Oregon, opened in 1988.

The Branch of Investigations, staffed by senior special agents and wildlife inspectors, coordinates international enforcement efforts, liases with Interpol, and monitors significant cases, facilitating those involving more than one region, as well as fulfilling CITES obligations and providing international training (for which USFWS is highly regarded). In recent years it has trained enforcement officers from neighbouring Mexico and Canada, as well as from other CITES parties (China, Madagascar, Tanzania and Thailand) and the Lusaka Agreement Task Force.

The Branch of Training and Inspection trains new agents and inspectors at the Federal Law Enforcement Training Centre in Glynco, Georgia, and conducts annual in-service training at the National Conservation Training Centre in Shepherdstown, West Virginia. It also trains customs officers and officers from other US agencies, and has conducted a 'Law Enforcement for Managers' programme aimed at USFWS personnel managing law enforcement activities.

The Branch of Technical and Field Support provides national computer support for federal wildlife law enforcement efforts through the Law Enforcement Management Information System (LEMIS), operational since

---

[21] For a full description of USFWS law enforcement activities, see USFWS Division of Law Enforcement Annual Reports (1999 and 2000), <www.le.fws.gov/annual.htm>.

1983. An internet-based version of the system, LEMIS 2000, has also been implemented. The branch responds to requests for information on wildlife trade under the Freedom of Information Act.

The Branch of Special Operations specializes in undercover operations, often several years long, which are used to great effect against organized wildlife crime networks. Between 1981 and 2000 this branch had completed 16 major investigations resulting in over 800 convictions. Operation Chameleon, which established an undercover wildlife business in the San Francisco area called PacRim Enterprises, yielded charges against over twenty people in the United States and abroad over the five years it operated, and led to the jailing, among others, of Keng Liang 'Anson' Wong, a notorious Malaysian businessman and wildlife dealer. Wong, believed to be the kingpin in an international operation that smuggled reptiles from southeast and central Asia, New Zealand and Madagascar to the United States and other markets, was jailed for six years and fined US$60,000 in June 2001.[22] Operation Chameleon involved cooperation with enforcement agencies in Canada, Mexico, Germany and South Africa. A more recent undercover operation directed at smugglers of rare cycads led to arrests in late 2001 in the United States and South Africa.

As of the end of 2000, the Service's 90 inspectors staffed 13 designated ports of entry and 16 border, non-designated and special ports. They view import/export documents and where possible inspect shipments. But their numbers are too few to cope with the volume of wildlife trade in and out of the United States. In 1999 they processed 95,664 declared shipments of wildlife and wildlife products worth more than US$1 billion – an average of 262 a day. Only a proportion of these can be physically inspected.

Until 2001, when Congress approved a budget increase, the USFWS Division of Law Enforcement had not received any significant increases in funds for over a decade, causing shortfalls in funding. In its response to the ERM questionnaire, USFWS stated that the shortage of wildlife law enforcement personnel caused by funding shortfalls was a 'serious concern'.[23]

---

[22] 'Probe of International Reptile Trade Ends with Key Arrests', USFWS press release (15 Sep 1998); 'DOJ, DOI Announce Arrest of Renowned Reptile Smuggler', US Dept of Justice ENR (15 Sep 1998); 'Rare Reptile Smuggler Sentenced to Prison', *San Francisco Chronicle* (8 Jun 2001).

[23] US Fish and Wildlife Service response to ERM questionnaire in CITES Doc. 10.20, 'How to Improve the Effectiveness of the Convention: Comments from the Parties and Organizations on the Study', prepared for COP10 (Jun 1997), at p. 108.

Vietnam   The technical team reported that the prime responsibility for wildlife law enforcement in Vietnam lies with forest rangers, of which there are 8,500 throughout the country's 61 provinces. There are also 45 inspection stations at national and provincial borders. Five people in Hanoi deal with CITES administration and advise enforcement authorities. Salary scales of government and enforcement officials are so low that many have a second job or are engaged in private enterprise to supplement their income. Forest rangers are more poorly paid than police, army or customs staff. Nevertheless, there had been seizures of wildlife (1,159 in 1998).

Given Vietnam's history, the team found weapons were widely available, though armed conflict between enforcement officers and poachers was uncommon. There were no agreements allowing direct contact between enforcement personnel and their counterparts in neighbouring countries, despite trafficking along the borders. Team members heard of illegal activities along the Vietnam–China border allegedly involving Triad gangs, and there was evidence that Vietnam is regarded as a transit point for illegal wildlife trade from Cambodia and the Lao People's Democratic Republic (a non-party). There was rhino poaching, and illegal trade in primates was considered a major problem. There was also some suspicion of government personnel cooperating with traders. Donor aid and NGO support had enabled ten training courses to be run over the five years up to 1999 for customs, police, army frontier staff and forest rangers. Some 150 rangers had also received a day's input on CITES issues during a five- to seven-day workshop.

Specialized wildlife law enforcement units

CITES does not require parties to designate wildlife law enforcement units in the same way as it requires designation of Management and Scientific Authorities, but in recent years the Secretariat has acted within its limitations to promote their establishment. The need for such units has been a repeated theme of first the tiger technical missions, and subsequently the Secretariat and Tiger Enforcement Task Force. In support, the Secretariat has cited in particular the effectiveness of task forces in USFWS, the Russian Federation's Inspection Tiger and the UK's CITES Enforcement Team at Heathrow.[24]

In July 2001 the Secretariat provided parties with practical guidance for the structure and operation of specialized wildlife law enforcement units produced

---

[24] SC42: Summary Report (Sep/Oct 1999), p. 18.

by the TETF. The guidance emphasizes the 'absolutely essential' requirement for political will, along with proper authority to carry out duties. The importance of concentrating on priority and serious crime issues is stressed, as is the inclusion of personnel from other national agencies engaging in wildlife law enforcement. Anti-corruption work related to wildlife crime is considered 'desirable'. Other issues covered in the guidance include funding, training, incentives (adequate salaries commensurate with risk), structure, discipline, establishing informer networks, public recognition and personnel selection. Ideally, the unit should act as a central repository of intelligence on wildlife crime, should maintain an overview of serious cases, and should be responsible for liaison with regional and international law enforcement agencies such as Interpol, the WCO and the Secretariat. It is advised to establish the 'closest' working relationship with prosecution authorities. Raising awareness among the judiciary to promote appropriate sentencing and deterrence is also considered important. Close but 'appropriate' links with NGOs are recommended.[25]

Despite widespread recognition of their need, specialized wildlife law enforcement units are relatively few and far between. Countries known to have established them are India, Namibia, the Russian Federation, South Africa, Taiwan, the United Kingdom and the United States. (Some are described above in the snapshot of wildlife law enforcement capacity.)

International enforcement

Enforcement assistance from the Secretariat

The enforcement assistance activities of the Secretariat are consolidated under the four-person Legislation and Compliance Unit – formerly the Enforcement Assistance Unit, and before that the Enforcement Assistance and Permit Confirmation Unit. Its three professional members comprise two lawyers (one a former prosecutor) and a former police officer. Plans to employ a customs officer appear to have been shelved for the moment.

Since 1989, two resolutions have been passed expanding the enforcement remit of the Secretariat. Following the approval of Resolution Conf. 7.5 in 1989,[26] the Secretariat, with WWF support, developed a proposal for an Enforcement

---

[25] Notification to the Parties No. 2001/047, Annex 3, 'Guidance for Specialized Wildlife Law Enforcement Units' (9 Jul 2001).
[26] CITES Resolution Conf. 7.5 'Enforcement' (1989), now part of consolidated Resolution Conf. 11.3 'Compliance and Enforcement' (2000).

Project 'to assist the parties in both preventative and reactive CITES enforcement activities'. In addition to training seminars, the project included Secretariat missions to countries experiencing implementation problems and the printing of permits for parties having problems with the use of false documents.[27]

In 1994 Resolution Conf. 9.8 was approved, urging parties to provide funds to the Enforcement Project, and directing the Secretariat to utilize the funds towards three priorities:

1 the appointment of additional officers to the Secretariat to work on enforcement-related matters;
2 assistance in the development and implementation of regional law enforcement agreements;
3 training and technical assistance to parties.[28]

These priorities, now assimilated into Resolution Conf. 11.3, have been only partially realized. Initially the United Kingdom seconded a customs officer, Italy pledged to fund an assistant enforcement officer, and the Secretariat participated in training seminars jointly organized with USFWS and Interpol.[29] Now the number of professional enforcement officers in the Secretariat is reduced to one, while no assistance has been provided for the development and implementation of regional law enforcement agreements, despite the existence of the Africa-based Lusaka Agreement since 1994.

Much of the Secretariat's activities with assisting parties on enforcement have been described elsewhere in this book. In summary, they include missions to investigate infractions and other issues undermining CITES implementation in problem countries, and to provide advice on implementation and enforcement; analysis and provision of information to parties on infractions, illegal trade and wildlife crime through the TIGERS database and CITES Alerts; missions related to trade in specific species such as rhinos and tigers; needs assessment missions to determine enforcement requirements, in particular parties (a new development); training seminars on enforcement; and advice, intelligence and training through the Tiger Enforcement Task Force.

---

[27] CITES Doc. SC.23.24 'Enforcement of the Convention, including Plans for the Alleged Infractions Report', prepared by the Secretariat for SC23 (Apr 1991).
[28] CITES Resolution Conf. 9.8 'Enforcement' (1994), amended at COP10 (1997) then consolidated into Resolution Conf. 11.3, 'Compliance and Enforcement' (2000).
[29] CITES Docs. SC.36.10 and SC.37.8, 'Enforcement Issues', prepared by the Secretariat for SC36 (Jan/Feb 1996), and SC37 (Dec 1996).

Tiger Enforcement Task Force

Established following COP11 as a result of the political mission recommenda-tions on tiger trade (discussed in Chapter 8), the Tiger Enforcement Task Force (TETF) is coordinated by the Secretariat's Legislation and Compliance Unit, and consists of middle to senior-ranking officials drawn from law enforcement agencies and/or customs authorities in tiger range states and consumer states. It provides technical advice on wildlife crime and illicit trade and intelligence support to parties, with country representatives being responsible for opera-tions within their territory. The Legislation and Compliance Unit reports to the Standing Committee on TETF activities and disseminates information to parties. The Task Force may engage in training initiatives, and liases with Interpol, the WCO and 'appropriate' regional law enforcement groups, as well as drawing on the knowledge of TRAFFIC. It provides expert advice to parties, the Secre-tariat, the Animals Committee and the Standing Committee. A confidentiality clause in its terms of reference provides that intelligence will be disclosed only to Interpol, the WCO, relevant CITES Management Authorities and/or gov-ernment law enforcement agencies of a CITES party.[30]

The UK contributed £40,000 to help launch the Task Force, whose first meeting (a brainstorming session) was hosted by India in New Delhi on 2–5 April 2001.[31] Seven parties – Cambodia, Canada, China, India, Indonesia, Nepal and the Netherlands – and Interpol all nominated experts to be members of the TETF. Three areas were identified for initial concentration of effort:

1   intelligence gathering, analysis and dissemination;
2   guidance for specialized wildlife law enforcement units;
3   training.

TETF members identified a need in many states, particularly developing-country parties and those with economies in transition, for a system of recording and reporting information to the Management Authority during the initial stage of an incident. They produced a Preliminary Report Form (see Annex 4) and guidance on reporting and intelligence analysis, together with guidance for specialized wildlife law enforcement units already discussed

---

[30] CITES Decision 11.145, directed to the Secretariat on Tigers; Annex 4 to CITES Decisions 'Terms of Reference of the Tiger Enforcement Task Force' (2000).
[31] 'UK Action Boosts the Fight to Protect Tigers', press release by Foreign and Commonwealth Office and DETR (31 Oct 2000); 'New Task Force Set to Tackle Tiger Poaching', *Environment News Service* (3 Apr 2001).

above, which were distributed to parties in July 2001. The TETF also designed a two-week training course for enforcement personnel in tiger range states, aimed at developing skills to conduct anti-poaching operations, gather and use intelligence, target offenders, investigate cases of wildlife crime, collect evidence, liaise with other agencies and prepare cases for prosecution.[32] The first course was held at the National Police Academy in Hyderabad, India, in May 2002. Twenty-eight students attended from 12 countries. The course was practical, covering arrest techniques, border controls, CITES, covert operations, evidence gathering, fraud, forensic science, informants, interview techniques, intelligence, organized crime, personal safety, search and 'train-the-trainer' techniques. All students received an electronic version of the presentations to enable them to conduct further training.[33]

The establishment of the TETF is an important development in enforcement assistance and international cooperation. As the first international cooperative enforcement group formed under CITES, albeit ad hoc, it is being seen as a pilot project to test the concept of an enforcement task force dedicated to providing assistance to combat a specific type of illegal trade. It has made a promising start. However, it is limited by its terms of reference to issues concerning tigers and to participation by just tiger range and consumer states. The technical mission team had expressed concern that too narrow a focus could be counter-productive, since it risks giving the impression among potential consumers, poachers, smugglers and illegal traders that authorities are interested only in tigers. They commented that it might also prompt enforcement agencies to 'deploy their resources in a manner that will not be helpful in the longer term'.[34] The political mission had recommended that the TETF, as the first of its proposed ad hoc CITES Enforcement Task Forces, should also examine the connected illicit trade in leopard (whose bone is used as a substitute for tiger bone) and Tibetan antelope.[35] But the COP rejected this, along with the wider concept of CETFs. The TETF has clearly taken cognizance of the technical and political missions' opinions, since the guidance it has produced for parties on reporting and intelligence analysis as well as on specialized wildlife crime units is of general application. Nevertheless, the Task Force remains limited. To be truly effective, it needs to

---

[32] Notification to the Parties No. 2001/047, 'CITES Tiger Enforcement Task Force' (9 Jul 2001).

[33] 'Russian Tiger Goes to India Courtesy of CITES', CITES press release (4 Jul 2002).

[34] Tiger Technical Missions report.

[35] CITES Doc. 11.30, 'Conservation of and Trade in Tigers', COP11 (Apr 2000).

be formalized as a permanent entity with a broadened mandate and composition to enable it to incorporate other types of illicit trade and enforcement officers from other parties. Past efforts to establish such a group have been unsuccessful, largely through lack of Secretariat support, as the following section shows; but, given the success of the TETF, the time may have come for a change.

Failure to establish a permanent enforcement group

Since 1989 there have been several attempts to establish a permanent enforcement working group or committee within the CITES system, but all have failed. The initiative appears to date back to a proposal by the second Secretary General, Eugene Lapointe, at COP6 in 1987 that the Standing Committee should consider creating an Enforcement Committee to provide guidance to the Secretariat on their work on alleged infractions.[36] At COP7 the concept of a permanent Enforcement Committee, initiated by Canada, was endorsed and a working group established under the Standing Committee to prepare a resolution for COP8.[37] At SC21 in February 1990, the representative for Oceania (Murray Hosking of New Zealand) registered the strong interest of parties in Oceania and the region's 'strong support' for an Enforcement Committee. Showing a great deal of foresight, he suggested the name of the working group be changed to 'Working Group on the Establishment of a Committee on Compliance with the Convention', and summarized the main reasons for establishing such a committee as:

- the production of viable methods of combating smuggling;
- provision or coordination of enforcement training programmes;
- assistance in coordinating records of illegal wildlife activities.[38]

The tide then seems to have turned against the initiative, with the Secretariat at the centre of the opposition. In September 1990 David Brackett, the Secretariat Management Coordinator, gave a strongly worded negative response to a draft resolution circulated by Canada as chair of the Working

---

[36] CITES Com. II 6.9, 'Summary Report of the Committee II Meeting', COP6 (Jul 1987).
[37] CITES Plen. 7.8, 'Summary Report of the Plenary Session', COP7 (Oct 1989); CITES Com. 7.15, 'Report of the Working Group on the Establishment of an Enforcement Committee', COP7 (Oct 1989).
[38] SC21: Summary Report (Feb 1990), p. 22.

Group. The proposed enforcement committee was described as 'complex, probably unwieldy, and undoubtedly expensive'. The Secretariat opposed the involvement of such a committee in 'operational matters' since the 'parties have established a strong, professional Secretariat to provide for the operational needs of the Convention'.[39] Despite a positive response from the United Kingdom, Canada decided not to pursue the idea because of a lack of interest from other parties and the generally negative response from the Secretariat.[40]

In 1993 the Animals Committee developed a compromise proposal for the formation of a Law Enforcement Consultative Group – subsequently renamed the Law Enforcement Network – to be composed of enforcement officers nominated by the parties, directed by the Standing Committee and coordinated by the Secretariat. Its terms of reference were to include the provision of advice and technical assistance to parties and of recommendations on enforcement methods to detect and prevent illegal trade.[41] The Secretariat strongly opposed the formation of the network, its comments to the Standing Committee reflecting a bias against the initiative. Nine parties had responded to the Secretariat notification about the network proposal: five had supported it and one was neutral, but the Secretariat still recommended 'the network *not* be formed' (emphasis in original), favouring arguments by the minority of three parties opposed. The Secretariat concluded that the lack of response from the parties to their notification might indicate a 'reluctance to create a body within the CITES structure to assist with activities strictly related to enforcement',[42] although, given the parties' negligence in other areas – such as reporting trade and infractions – lack of capacity and/ or apathy would provide more plausible reasons for their lack of response. In the event, however, the Standing Committee endorsed the Secretariat's recommendation not to proceed.[43]

---

[39] CITES Doc. SC.23.20 Annex 2, Letter from D. Brackett, CITES Secretariat Management Co-ordinator, to J. Heppes, Chairman of the Working Group on Establishment of an Enforcement Committee (Sep 1990).

[40] D. Pollock, Doc. SC.23.20 Annex, Letter from the Director, Program Planning and Integration Branch, Canadian Wildlife Service, to Chairman of the Standing Committee (7 Jan 1991); SC23: Summary Report (Apr 1991), p. 11.

[41] Notification to the Parties No. 776, 'A Law Enforcement Network' (23 Nov 1993).

[42] CITES Doc. SC.31.13 'Proposal to Form a Law Enforcement Network', prepared by the Secretariat for SC31 (Mar 1994).

[43] SC31: Summary Report (Mar 1994), p. 44; CITES Doc. 9.25, 'Enforcement of the Convention', prepared by the UK for COP9 (Nov 1994).

At COP9 in 1994, a proposal by Ghana to establish a law enforcement consultative group again failed,[44] as did a further initiative by the United States at COP10 to set up a Working Group on Illegal Trade in CITES Specimens.[45] The US Management Authority subsequently complained about the 'active lobbying of Secretariat staff' with respect to their proposal, apparently referring in particular to the head of the CITES Enforcement Assistance and Permit Confirmation Unit.[46]

Reasons for the Secretariat's strong opposition to some form of permanent consultative body on enforcement are unclear. It could have been an unwillingness to countenance a perceived dilution of the Secretariat's powers. But the dismissal of two Secretariat staff members, including the head of the CITES Enforcement Assistance and Permit Confirmation Unit, following an internal investigation by the United Nations in 1998, invites speculation as to other reasons. Since the UN's report has not been released publicly, one can do no more than speculate. But one thing is clear: had it not been for active opposition by a far from neutral Secretariat, some form of permanent enforcement body could well have been part of the CITES institutional makeup by now.

The position of the Secretariat appears to have changed radically since COP10, as is witnessed by its support for the concept of CITES Enforcement Task Forces and its role in developing the TETF. Temporary in nature, the TETF is a different concept from a permanent enforcement body that can influence policy-making and the allocation of funding. However, given the changed climate in the Secretariat, the way could be open for its evolution into a permanent entity.

International cooperation

World Customs Organization and Interpol   Cooperation with Interpol and the WCO, formerly the Customs Cooperation Council, dates back to early COPs.[47] At COP9 in 1994, however, the Secretariat was directed to pursue closer

---

[44] CITES Doc. 9.25.1, 'Law Enforcement Consultative Group', submitted by Ghana to COP9 (Nov 1994); CITES Com. II 9.9 (Rev.), 'Summary Report of the Committee II Meeting', COP9 (Nov 1994).

[45] CITES Doc. 10.29, 'Working Group on Illegal Trade in CITES Specimens', submitted by the US to COP10 (Jun 1997).

[46] Eugene Lapointe, 'CITES under Siege: A Party Turns a Deaf Ear to the Majority: The Hostile Take-Over Bid', *Conservation Tribune*, special edn (IWMC–World Conservation Trust, Sep 1998), p. 5.

[47] CITES Doc.1.36, 'Collaboration between the Secretariat and the Customs Cooperation Council', prepared by the Secretariat for COP1 (Nov 1976); CITES Resolution Conf. 2.6, 'Trade in Appendix II and III Species' (1979).

international liaison with the two organizations.[48] Since then it has signed memoranda of understanding (MOU) with both.[49] The memoranda provide, *inter alia,* for an exchange of information and strengthened cooperation, joint publication of information materials to combat wildlife crime, and joint training for police, customs and other enforcement officers. The memorandum with the WCO also provides for a joint database on CITES offences.[50]

The WCO set up a working group on CITES which first met in 1996,[51] while in 1993 Interpol established the Subgroup on Wildlife Crime (now the Working Group on Wildlife Crime). The WCO CITES programme has produced a brochure together with the CITES Secretariat and has carried out other initiatives to raise awareness among members. Customs nomenclature has been amended to facilitate the implementation of customs controls for CITES-listed species; teaching material on CITES has been prepared for use by customs officers; and regional training seminars have been conducted, the first in eastern Europe in 1998. The WCO also publishes CITES Alerts concerning seizures and decisions affecting trade.[52] The joint database provided for in the MOU, however, has not materialized. Instead, CITES, the WCO and Interpol each maintain separate databases but have an agreement to share information as necessary.[53]

The main objective of the Interpol Working Group on Wildlife Crime is to contribute to the fight against illegal trade in endangered species by improving information exchange and encouraging international analyses. Its Ecomessage, originally developed by the Subgroup for the reporting of environmental crime to the Interpol General Secretariat by National Central Bureaus (NCBs), was subsequently distributed by the CITES Secretariat to Management Authorities, urging them to use it in communicating with their national NCB (see

---

[48] CITES Resolution Conf. 9.8, 'Enforcement' (1994).

[49] Notification to the Parties No. 967, 'Memorandum of Understanding between WCO and the CITES Secretariat' (7 Mar 1997) (MOU was signed 4 Jul 1996); CITES Doc. SC.41.14 Annex 2, 'Memorandum of Understanding between the General Secretariat of ICPO–Interpol and the Secretariat of the Convention on International Trade in Endangered Species of Wild Fauna and Flora (CITES)', signed 15 Oct 1998.

[50] Notification to the Parties No. 967 (see n. 49 above).

[51] CITES Doc. 10.8, 'Secretariat Report', COP10 (Jun 1997), p. 12.

[52] 'The Role of Customs Services and World Customs Organization (WCO)'s Enforcement Programme to Combat Environmental Crime', UNEP/Env.Law/MEAs/8, prepared by WCO for UNEP Workshop on Enforcement of and Compliance with MEAs (12–14 Jul 1999).

[53] John Sellar, personal communication (Jun 2002).

Annex 2).[54] As already discussed, the Ecomessage has since become the standard format for reporting infractions and illegal trade within CITES. Within Interpol, the General Secretariat in Lyons acts as a central collection and dissemination point for information supplied by the NCBs using the Ecomessage. But unforeseen problems have combined to make the system less useful than had been hoped. These include wide variations in what is legal and illegal in Interpol member countries, a lack of commonly agreed definitions of some terms, the involvement of a huge range of law enforcement agencies other than the police, and a general lack of knowledge of environmental crimes among many of them.[55] A renewed effort by the Interpol Working Group to promote use of the Ecomessage for reporting environmental crime is currently underway.[56]

The Interpol Analytical Criminal Intelligence Unit has carried out two analyses of wildlife crime: Project Noah, concerning the illegal trade in live reptiles, and Project Primate, a study of illegal trade in primates. Project Noah led to investigations in Kenya and South Africa. In 1996 the ESPU launched Operation Cobra in South Africa, resulting in several arrests and prosecutions of individuals connected with the reptile trade (though in many cases the penalties imposed were derisory). The Interpol Working Group has supported the development of regional working groups on wildlife crime, and revised the Practical Guide on cooperation between CITES Management Authorities and Interpol. A train-the-trainer course in environmental criminal investigations has been designed which includes training in the investigation of wildlife crime and a reference manual for law enforcement officers.[57] Regional 'train-the-trainer' workshops for investigators have been organized. An International Wildlife Crime Enforcement Network Address Book has also been produced with the WCO and CITES Secretariat.[58] An Environmental Crimes Unit is in the process of being created at the General Secretariat in Lyons, to be staffed initially by two full-time officers, one working on wildlife and the other on pollution.[59]

---

[54] Notification to the Parties No. 851, 'ICPO–Interpol: The Eco-Message' (18 Apr 1995).

[55] Brack et al (Feb 2002) (see Ch. 1, n. 23).

[56] Bill Clark, personal communication (Jun 2002).

[57] Environmental Criminal Investigations Training Programme (Interpol General Secretariat, 1999).

[58] Jytte Ekdahl, 'Interpol Wildlife Crime Subgroup: Role and Activities', in *Proceedings of the EU Wildlife Enforcement Workshop, London 1–2 March 1998* (UK DETR, 1998), pp. 77–80; 'International Criminal Police Organization', UNEP/Env.Law/MEAs/7, prepared by Interpol for UNEP Workshop on Enforcement of and Compliance with MEAs (12–14 Jul 1999).

[59] Bill Clark (see n. 56 above).

UN Environment Programme   In 1998 international cooperation on enforcement moved up the political agenda, with an initiative to combat environmental crime launched by G8 Environment Ministers at a meeting at Leeds Castle in the UK.[60] Following up on the initiative, the governments of the United Kingdom, Canada, Germany and Japan funded a UNEP-hosted Workshop on Enforcement of and Compliance with MEAs in Geneva in July 1999, at which CITES was discussed, along with the Basel Convention and Montreal Protocol. Recommendations included, *inter alia*:

• guidelines for cooperation at regional and global level related to compliance and enforcement;
• encouraging collaborative law enforcement projects between countries sharing borders;
• bringing together customs agencies, environmental law enforcement units and police on a regional basis to improve understanding and launch cooperative actions.[61]

A second workshop was convened in December 1999 at which draft proposals for guidelines for effective national environmental enforcement and international cooperation and coordination in combating environmental crime were discussed.[62] A Compliance and Enforcement of Environmental Conventions Unit was established under UNEP, and a list of Enforcement Focal Points compiled and distributed. But the initiative seems to have slowed down. There is little evidence that the unit is still active, and follow-up work appears to have been focused on the guidelines. At UNEP's Governing Council meeting in February 2002 two sets of guidelines were adopted, one on 'Compliance with and Enforcement of Multilateral Environmental Agreements', and the other on 'National Enforcement, and International Cooperation in Combating Violations, of Laws Implementing Multilateral Environmental Agreements'.[63] The guidelines are non-binding, general in nature and dependent on voluntary

---

[60] See Communiqué from G8 Environment Ministers' Meeting, Leeds Castle (3–5 Apr 1998).
[61] 'Report on the Workshop on Enforcement of and Compliance with Multilateral Environmental Agreements (MEAs)', UNEP/Env.Law/MEAs.RPT (30 Jul 1999).
[62] 'Report of the Working Group of Experts on Compliance and Enforcement of Environmental Conventions – preparatory session', UNEP/EC/WG.1.5 (16 Dec 1999).
[63] UNEP Governing Council Decision SS.VII/4, 'Compliance with and Enforcement of Multilateral Environmental Agreements', UNEP(DEPI)/MEAs/WG.1/3, annex II (Feb 2002).

action by MEA members. Those on compliance and enforcement of MEAs tend to state the obvious and existing practice among most MEAs, particularly those negotiated more recently. An older MEA such as CITES, however, could benefit from some of the suggestions, notably those on National Implementation Plans, Compliance Plans for problem states (using the UAE as a test case), and regional or sub-regional environmental action plans or strategies for MEA implementation.

The guidelines may serve some purpose, depending on the political will of states to implement them, but MEA compliance and enforcement would be better served if UNEP were to concentrate on building enforcement capacity and creating and supporting practical mechanisms for inter-agency cooperation at national and international level. This could be achieved through more targeted action, such as assisting with the establishment of adequately funded and trained specialized wildlife/environmental crime units, and acting as a mediator to bring national law enforcement agencies together (police, customs and others involved in wildlife law enforcement) in regions that still lack mechanisms for cross-border cooperation. A precedent for this exists with the UNEP-sponsored Lusaka Agreement discussed below.

INECE Another initiative to promote networking and enforcement cooperation is the International Network for Environmental Compliance and Enforcement (INECE). INECE evolved out of a MOU between the US Environmental Protection Agency and the Dutch Environment Ministry, entered into in 1985 to promote mutual exchange and transfer of ideas. The exchange began to expand into a network with the first International Enforcement Workshop, held in Utrecht in 1990 and organized by the US and Dutch governments to broaden their bilateral exchanges. In 1992 UNEP became a third key anchor of the partnership, the aim of which was to promote effective environmental compliance and enforcement programmes. The name INECE was adopted in 1997 to signal commitment to an ongoing network. INECE has now evolved into an international partnership of government officials, international organizations and NGOs. Involved are the World Bank and several associate organizations, including Interpol, the WCO, IUCN, NGOs with relevant programmes, regional enforcement networks and regional development banks. INECE activities, which focus on networking, capacity-building and enforcement cooperation, are coordinated by an Executive Planning Committee of about 25 persons selected to represent all regions. The committee includes representatives from NGOs with active programmes for environmental compliance and enforcement on an international scale. Since 1990, international conferences on environmental compliance and enforcement have been held at two-year intervals.[64]

Regional cooperation

A number of regional mechanisms for enforcement cooperation were established in the 1990s. In 1991, as a result of the Utrecht International Enforcement Workshop, EU member states initiated IMPEL, the European Network for Implementation and Enforcement of Environmental Law.[65] AC-IMPEL, the equivalent for central and eastern European countries targeted for future accession to the European Union, was also established. In 1994 the Africa-wide Lusaka Agreement was adopted, and in 1995 the North American Wildlife Enforcement Group (NAWEG) was set up.

Africa: the Lusaka Agreement Task Force   The Lusaka Agreement on Cooperative Enforcement Operations Directed at Illegal Trade in Wild Fauna and Flora was adopted in Lusaka, Zambia, on 9 September 1994 and entered into force on 10 December 1996.[66] It was founded by African wildlife law enforcement officers attending a NGO-funded conference on cross-border cooperation in wildlife law enforcement in Lusaka in 1992. The agreement's core provision – an inter-agency Task Force composed of wildlife law enforcement officers seconded from designated National Bureaus – was the brainchild of the first head of the ESPU, Pieter Lategan. Officers attending the conference from a variety of agencies including police, customs, national parks authorities and the army, embraced the idea, and, with assistance from the CITES Secretariat and USFWS representatives attending the meeting, drafted the first version of the agreement.[67]

Under the agreement, parties commit to seconding at least one officer from their designated National Bureau to the Lusaka Agreement Task Force

---

[64] See INECE website <www.inece.org/>.

[65] Ibid.; 'Report on the Workshop on Enforcement of and Compliance with Multilateral Environmental Agreements (MEAs)' Annex VI Background Paper, UNEP/Env.Law/ MEAs.RPT (30 Jul 1999). See also Michael Faure and Gunter Heine, *Criminal Enforcement of Environmental Law in the European Union* (Maastricht: IMPEL Working Group on Criminal Prosecution in Environmental Cases, 1998).

[66] Lesotho, Kenya, Swaziland, South Africa, Uganda and Tanzania signed the Lusaka Agreement on 9 Sep 1994. See 'Lusaka Agreement on Co-operative Enforcement Operations Directed at Illegal Trade in Wild Fauna and Flora: Lusaka Final Act' (UNEP, 1994).

[67] R. Reeve and L. A. Carter, *Proceedings of the First African Wildlife Law Enforcement Cooperation Conference,* 9–11 Dec 1992 (Zambia Ministry of Tourism).

(LATF). The main function of the LATF is to conduct cross-border investigations into illegal wildlife trade at the request of and in cooperation with the Bureaus. It goes beyond an Interpol-type organization, which just facilitates exchange of intelligence, in that its officers can participate in operations, including undercover operations, within the territories of parties, subject to party consent. LATF officers are also granted privileges and immunities, including exemption from visa requirements and entry restrictions, enabling them to move freely and quickly between parties when necessary. Negotiated under UNEP auspices, the agreement is open to accession by all African states, of which six have become parties: Congo (Brazzaville), Kenya, Lesotho, Tanzania, Uganda and Zambia. Ethiopia, South Africa and Swaziland are signatories.

The agreement has had a rocky ride. Despite setting a precedent for combating organized wildlife crime across borders and strengthening enforcement of CITES on a regional basis, its implementation in the early days was a lengthy and at times difficult process. Although it entered into force relatively quickly, it then remained in limbo for over two years for lack of funds. Major donors were unforthcoming with funding to establish the Task Force, despite several approaches, and parties, all of which are developing countries with limited financial resources, could not afford the initial assessed annual contributions.[68] It did not help that South Africa, a key country in the founding and negotiation of the agreement, failed to ratify it. Then, in March 1999, after reassessing and reducing their contributions and agreeing to delay the secondment of officers to headquarters, the Governing Council of parties decided to make the LATF operational from 1 June 1999 with their own financial contributions. Tanzania was the first to come forward with funds, on the basis of which the director, intelligence officer, liaison officer and support staff were appointed and the headquarters established in Nairobi at the main offices of the Kenya Wildlife Service.[69] The only donor funds available at the time were small grants from UNEP and the UK-based David Shepherd Wildlife Foundation. Since then, funding for training, equipment and special operations has gradually been forthcoming from other donors and NGOs, including Norway, USFWS, Taiwan and IFAW. Three more field officers have also been seconded to headquarters from

---

[68] 'Report of the Consultative Meeting of the Governing Council of the Parties to the Lusaka Agreement Held in Nairobi, Kenya on 21–22 Oct 1998', UNEP/Env.Law/LAGC.2/3 (UNEP).
[69] 'Report of the Second Meeting of the Governing Council', 15–19 Mar 1999, UNEP/Env.Law/LAGC.2/8 (UNEP).

Congo, Uganda and Zambia, which brought the complement of senior LATF officers to five. Sadly, the death of LATF's first Director, Adan Dullo, in March 2002 reduced the number to four.

It should be emphasized that, in addition to launching LATF on their own funds, parties are providing core funding – a major achievement, given their limited resources. Use of donor funding has been restricted to special operations, training and equipment.[70] Initially, the Task Force concentrated its efforts on training and intelligence gathering, providing training for wildlife law enforcement officers from 11 countries, and supplying intelligence to national bureaus, leading to successful operations. Its first cooperative operation resulted in the seizure of ivory in Kenya, and the second in the arrest of poachers in Tanzania.[71] A communications system has been established and a database is being set up, and with the expansion of the Task Force more cooperative operations are possible. LATF played a key role in the seizure in June 2002 of six tonnes of ivory smuggled from Zambia to Singapore, seen as the biggest achievement of the organization's short history.[72]

The Lusaka Agreement initiative has had a mixed reception in CITES. Initially, the Secretariat provided much-needed technical support in its drafting and assisted throughout the negotiations. This was largely due to the support and enthusiasm of its enforcement officer, John Gavitt, on secondment from USFWS.[73] The Standing Committee endorsed the draft agreement in 1993 and urged its adoption and financial support.[74] However, after COP9 in 1994 the Secretariat distanced itself, making no effort to comply with the directive in Resolution Conf. 9.8 to provide assistance with the agreement's development and implementation. One of the reasons could be the Secretariat's general lack of support for enforcement initiatives at the time, witnessed by its opposition to an enforcement working group. But it was almost certainly influenced by opposition to the agreement from a few southern African states, particularly Namibia and Zimbabwe, dating back to sub-regional divisions over the ivory

---

[70] Musa Lyimo, Deputy Director (now Acting Director), LATF, personal communication (2001).

[71] Adan Dullo, former Director, LATF, personal communication (1999).

[72] Odhiambo Orlale, 'Recovered Ivory Originated from Zambia', *Daily Nation* (10 Jul 2002), <www.nationaudio.com/News/DailyNation/Today/News/News68.html>.

[73] See L. A. Carter and R. Reeve, *Proceedings of Working Group 2 Meeting for the Development of the Lusaka Agreement*, 26–27 Jun 1993 (Zambia Ministry of Tourism/ Kenya Ministry for Tourism and Wildlife).

[74] See 'Decisions of the Standing Committee on Trade in Rhinoceros Horn and Tiger Specimens', in SC30: Summary Report (Sep 1993), p. 30.

trade and evident since the beginning of the initiative. Botswana, Namibia and Zimbabwe, all strong proponents of the ivory trade, did not participate in the negotiations, despite invitations and available funding.[75] At COP9 differing opinions spilled over in public when Namibia objected to the 'underlying philosophy' of the agreement and Lusaka Agreement states criticized Namibia for comments that were misrepresentative and factually incorrect.[76] Namibia and Zimbabwe have continued to oppose the agreement, though Botswana has shown signs of interest. According to a former European Commission official, their opposition was one reason for the Commission's reluctance to approve a funding application to support the agreement's implementation.

Informal discussions with a member of the Namibian CITES delegation indicated that part of Namibia's objection was the encroachment on sovereignty which the delegation perceived as inherent in the way the LATF operates. 'We don't want South African policemen stomping all over our territory' was the comment. Another reason given was the perceived involvement in negotiations by the Environmental Investigation Agency – an NGO known for its strong stance against the ivory trade and long-standing criticism of pro-trade southern African states. But, while EIA was a co-sponsor of the first two meetings that gave birth to the agreement, its involvement ended in 1993 when UNEP assumed responsibility for the negotiations. In an attempt to encourage widespread participation and to divorce themselves from the 'NGO tag', countries decided to exclude all NGOs from the negotiating meetings, as well as subsequent Governing Council meetings. Despite this move, however, which in the long term may have unfortunate consequences for the transparency and understanding of the agreement among the public and NGO community, the 'NGO tag' has persisted. It was still being floated as a problem in the way LATF was perceived in informal discussions with Secretariat staff at COP11, in spite of the public signing of a MOU by the Task Force Director and the CITES Secretary General.

In the wake of controversy over the Lusaka Agreement, the Southern African Development Community (SADC) developed a Protocol on Wildlife Conservation and Law Enforcement (the SADC Protocol) and promoted it as an alternative for wildlife law enforcement cooperation.[77] The Protocol,

---

[75] Author's observation as member of UNEP coordinating secretariat for the Lusaka Agreement negotiations.

[76] Committee II: Summary Report, CITES Com. II, 9.9, 9.12 (Rev.), COP9 (Nov 1994).

[77] CITES Doc. SC.41.6.1 (Rev.) Annex 2, 'Report of the Secretariat's Mission to Verify Compliance with Decision 10.1, Part A by Botswana, Japan, Namibia and Zimbabwe', SC41 (Feb 1999).

however, has a much wider scope, addressing primarily cooperation in wildlife management and sustainable use. Its provisions for cooperation on wildlife law enforcement are less specific than in the Lusaka Agreement. They do not provide for cross-border operations on illegal trade, but rely mainly on Interpol NCBs to provide a mechanism for cooperation and information sharing. In discussions of the Protocol at the second meeting of the Governing Council, Lusaka Agreement parties came to the conclusion that the two agreements were not mutually exclusive.[78] The Protocol was signed in Maputo, Mozambique, in August 1999 by 14 states, including three that are also parties to the Lusaka Agreement: Lesotho, Tanzania and Zambia. As of February 2001, with ratification by two-thirds of the signatories being required for it to enter into force, only three countries – Botswana, Mauritius and Namibia – had ratified the Protocol.[79]

Whether the development of the SADC Protocol was born from genuine commitment to cooperation, was a direct product of the Lusaka Agreement's opponents, or was simply politically expedient, given that some countries involved were pressing to sell their ivory stocks and needed to show a commitment to cooperative law enforcement, is open to question. At SC41 in February 1999, Botswana, Namibia and Zimbabwe all put forward their involvement in developing the SADC Protocol as evidence of their commitment to a mechanism like the Lusaka Agreement (one of the prerequisites to obtaining Standing Committee approval for sale of their ivory stocks and discussed further in chapter 4 above). This was accepted by the Secretariat and Standing Committee, even though the protocol was in draft form and quite different from the Lusaka Agreement.

In 1994, after the Lusaka Agreement was adopted, a leading commentator on CITES remarked: 'In this author's opinion, it is doubtful that the agreement will ever be ratified or implemented.'[80] Given the track record of previous African environmental treaties, such as the Bamako Convention[81] and the 1968 African Convention on Conservation of Nature and Natural Resources, his pessimism was understandable. The Lusaka Agreement's survival in the face of strong opposition can be attributed to LATF's founding officers Nick Carter,

---

[78] 'Report of the Second Meeting of the Governing Council', UNEP (see n. 69 above).

[79] 'SADC Wildlife Protocol Promises Better Wildlife Management', *Wildnet Africa News* (20 Feb 2001).

[80] David S. Favre, 'Trade in Endangered Species: Enforcement Developments', *Yearbook of International Environmental Law*, 5 (1994), p. 260.

[81] Convention on the Prohibition of International Trade in Waste with Africa (Bamako, 1991).

Adan Dullo and Musa Lyimo, as well as parties and a few steady supporters. The late Nick Carter, liaison officer from 1999 until his death in March 2000, was awarded the Goldman Environmental Prize in 1997 for his contribution to the Lusaka Agreement. Without his persistence in the wilderness years from 1994 to 1999, followed by Adan Dullo's work establishing the Task Force, it could well have gone the way of its predecessors.

North America: NAWEG As a regional network of senior North American wildlife law enforcement officials, the North American Wildlife Enforcement Group (NAWEG) includes members from the federal wildlife agencies in Canada, Mexico and the United States. Its efforts are focused on improving capacity to enforce CITES and national wildlife legislation in North America. If approved, NAWEG may serve as the regional link to the WCO and Interpol Working Group on Wildlife Crime. The network works in close cooperation with the Commission for Environmental Cooperation (CEC), a Council of cabinet-level environment officials assisted by a secretariat, which was established pursuant to the North American Agreement on Environmental Cooperation, a side-agreement to the North American Free Trade Agreement (NAFTA). NAWEG also participates as a member of the North American Working Group on Environmental Enforcement and Compliance Cooperation (EWG), constituted in 1996 by the CEC Council to serve as a regional forum for cooperation.[82]

Technical assistance

Early recognition

Technical assistance has a dual purpose: to help bring non-compliant parties into compliance, and to prevent non-compliance. The need for technical assistance was recognized early in the Convention's history, but finding the funds to support it has been an uphill task. At COP3 in 1981, the Secretariat, after achieving limited success in requests for external funding, reported to the COP that, although most exporting countries were 'Third World nations crucially dependent on outside assistance...in most multilateral and bilateral programmes of technical assistance and cooperation, wildlife management and conservation is either totally omitted or ranked as low priority'.[83] A resolution was

---

[82] 'NAWEG' brochure distributed at COP11 (Apr 2000).
[83] CITES Doc. 3.20, 'Technical Cooperation, Training and Implementing Legislation: Report from the Secretariat', COP3 (Feb/Mar 1981).

adopted, which is still in force, appealing to parties to include technical assistance in CITES matters in bilateral and multilateral development aid programmes.[84] Despite this, funds available to CITES for technical assistance are paltry compared with other MEAs such as the Montreal Protocol, serving to limit this form of non-compliance response (discussed further in Chapter 10 on weaknesses in the CITES compliance system).

Identification manual

Assistance with identification of specimens of listed species was one of the earliest forms of technical assistance to parties.[85] In 1977, on the basis of a Special Working Session resolution, the Secretariat and a Committee of Experts started the preparation of an *Identification Manual*.[86] The manual, which now runs to several volumes, is available in English, French and Spanish. It is continually updated and there are plans to make it available on the website. Prior to COP11, when its functions were transferred to the Secretariat, the regular update was carried out under the guidance of the Identification Manual Committee, whose terms of reference included the provision to parties of assistance in the development of national or regional identification manuals as well as advice on identification of specimens, and assistance in preparing seminars for enforcement officers on identification.[87]

Assistance with national reporting and drafting legislation

Other forms of technical assistance available for some time have been with the production of annual reports and drafting of national legislation. Guidelines for annual reporting were first produced in 1982, and subsequently the Secretariat offered to computerize parties' reports from export permits. Guidelines to assist with drafting national legislation, issued by the IUCN Environmental

---

[84] The resolution also appealed to parties for secondments to the Secretariat and developing countries. See CITES Resolution Conf. 3.4, 'Technical Cooperation' (1981).
[85] Article XII.2(f) provides that one of the functions of the Secretariat is the periodic publication and distribution to the parties of current editions of the Appendices and any information that will facilitate identification of specimens of species included in those Appendices.
[86] Wijnstekers (see ch. 3, n. 2), p. 474.
[87] CITES Resolution Conf. 9.1 (Rev.), Annex 4, 'Establishment of the Identification Manual Committee of the Conference of the Parties' (1997).

Law Centre, have been available to parties since 1981.[88] In response to requests for advice on developing implementing legislation, the Secretariat has variously drafted model law, developed a legislation checklist, directed requests for assistance to UNEP regional offices (e.g. for certain Latin American countries), conducted missions and provided written comments on draft legislation.

Capacity-building

Training seminars and Secretariat missions

In 1989 the Secretariat organized its first 'capacity-building' training seminars, but only at European level because of a lack of funds.[89] Previously, training of officers from Management Authorities had been on an ad hoc basis during technical missions by Secretariat staff, with the exception of a 1983 regional seminar organized for American states by the United States.[90] By 1997 the Secretariat had organized 74 training seminars in which over 4,000 people – mainly Management Authority staff and enforcement officers – had participated. Funding was provided by individual parties, Interpol, the WCO and NGOs.[91] At COP11, the Secretariat reported that in 1999 it had organized or participated in nine training seminars, giving priority to those organized for regions or sub-regions. It also took part in several missions to assist parties in the field, some of which have already been described in other parts of this book such as the tiger technical missions, missions to assist with drafting legislation and others to promote MIKE.[92]

Since COP11, capacity-building through training seminars and missions has continued. In April 2001 the Secretariat sought external funding for over 12 training seminars and workshops, of which national legislation and assistance to Scientific Authorities are the main areas of focus.

---

[88] Cyrille de Klemm, *Guidelines for Legislation to Implement CITES*, IUCN Environmental Policy and Law Paper No. 26 (IUCN, 1993). This revises and updates G. Edmonds, *Guidelines for National Implementation of the Convention on International Trade in Endangered Species of Wild Fauna and Flora*, IUCN Environmental Policy and Law Paper No. 17 (IUCN, 1981).

[89] CITES Doc. 7.7, 'Thirteenth Annual Report of the Secretariat', COP7 (Oct 1989).

[90] CITES Doc. SC.35.12, 'Enforcement', prepared by the Secretariat for SC35 (Mar 1995).

[91] CITES Doc. 10.32, 'Training', prepared by the Secretariat for COP10 (Jun 1997).

[92] CITES Doc. 11.9.1, 'Annual Report of the Secretariat', COP11 (Apr 2000).

Legal capacity-building programme

The premiss of the new legal capacity-building programme under the national legislation project (described in full in Chapter 6) is to train national experts to develop laws in their own countries rather than relying on consultants. Implementation of the programme is organized in a series of building blocks. The first is the development of technical documents, including a questionnaire on the national legal system and a checklist of provisions required under the Convention and through resolutions. The second is a series of regional workshops to develop regional models of law. The third is the provision of support to lawmakers and enforcement bodies. Three target groups have been identified: policy-makers and senior government officers responsible for formulating environmental policies; legal officers and draftsmen responsible for preparing draft legislation; and Management Authorities and enforcement agencies.[93] The programme is an ambitious undertaking. Nine regional workshops are planned with a total estimated budget of US$687,000.[94] Initially these were to be held between June 2000 and March 2003, but at the time of writing just two workshops have been conducted, one in West Africa, attended by 18 French-speaking African countries, and one in Hong Kong for countries in East, South and Southeast Asia.

While training national experts is urgently needed and deserves full support, it is important that the capacity-building programme does not detract from the use of trade sanctions under the national legislation project for persistent non-compliance. To realize the project's full potential, the two types of response need to be balanced. All too often, the problem lies not so much with national experts as with senior politicians and government officials from ministries with political clout, who rate wildlife legislation low on the parliamentary agenda. (But they sit up when trade sanctions are threatened.) The national legislation project has proved that trade sanctions can precipitate a remarkably rapid response from governments that have failed to act for years. Italy, where civil servants supported trade restrictions as the only way to kickstart government action, is another good example.

---

[93] CITES Doc. 11.21.1, 'National Legislation Project', prepared by the Secretariat for COP11 (Apr 2000).

[94] 'CITES Projects and Activities', distributed to potential donors by the Secretariat (19 Apr 2001).

Information management and assistance to Scientific Authorities

In addition to the legal capacity-building programme, new training programmes under development by the Secretariat in cooperation with different partner organizations concern information management and assistance to Scientific Authorities. A series of training workshops on information management are to be implemented in partnership with UNEP–WCMC.[95] In cooperation with IUCN, the CITES Secretariat has embarked on a programme based on a provision in Resolution Conf. 10.3, which encourages 'parties, the Secretariat and interested non-governmental organizations to develop and support workshops/seminars designed specifically to improve the implementation of CITES by Scientific Authorities'.

To stimulate compliance with Resolution Conf. 10.3, IUCN organized a workshop in Hong Kong in October 1998, funded by external sources, on the making of non-detriment findings by Scientific Authorities, the result of which was a draft manual on the subject. As a follow-up, funding has been allocated from the core CITES budget to support a programme of six workshops between 2000 and 2003, organized in close cooperation with IUCN. The workshops are being held in particular countries or regions targeted for their large volumes of trade, as well as for problems with non-detriment findings and other implementation difficulties; at the same time, an attempt is being made to cover all the major groups of fauna and flora in trade. Along with non-detriment findings, the workshops cover other responsibilities allocated to Scientific Authorities through COP resolutions and decisions. A manual dealing with these tasks is being developed by the Secretariat, together with specific identification materials for species traded from individual countries or particular sub-regions.[96]

---

[95] CITES Doc. 11.57, 'CITES Information Management Strategy', prepared by the Secretariat for COP11 (Apr 2000).

[96] CITES Doc. 11.40, 'Assistance to Scientific Authorities for Making Non-Detriment Findings', prepared by the Secretariat for COP11 (Apr 2000).

Part IV
Weaknesses, lessons and potential conflict

10 Weaknesses in the CITES compliance system

National implementation

In June 2001, in context of a recommendation to discard a species-specific focus and take a more coordinated approach, the Secretariat identified ten essential elements for effective CITES implementation:

1 adequate national legislation to regulate CITES trade;
2 adequate national legislation to protect and regulate the harvest of species of conservation concern;
3 adequate national legislation to enable enforcement and penalize offenders;
4 economic incentive policies, incorporated into legislation where necessary, to promote compliance;
5 sufficient provision and training of administrative and enforcement personnel;
6 provision of effective scientific advice for both administrative and enforcement personnel;
7 trade monitoring and analyses, combined with information management systems, to aid policy-making;
8 education and awareness-raising campaigns directed towards traders and the public;
9 support of the judiciary in adequately responding to crimes and helping to deter offenders;
10 inter-agency cooperation and exchange of information at national, regional and international levels.[1]

The elements would be equally at home in a list of weaknesses in the CITES compliance system. Within the limited resources available to CITES, attempts are being made to address many of these elements, but with widely varying degrees of success. The head of the Secretariat Legislation and Compliance Unit recently listed the main problems related to CITES implementation at a national level as:

---

[1] CITES SC45 Doc. 21, 'Conservation of and Trade in Specific Species', prepared by the Secretariat for SC45 (Jun 2001).

- lack of or insufficient national legislation, particularly regarding penalties;
- issuance of irregular documents;
- lack of, or insufficient, border control;
- fraud;
- lack of, or insufficient, coordination and communication between the Management Authority, Scientific Authority and enforcement agencies;
- insufficient communication with the Secretariat;
- lack of, or insufficient, control of domestic trade (since domestic trade has implications for international trade).[2]

Legislation

As of March 2002, around 50% of parties still had legislation that failed to provide for some or all of the four basic requirements identified under the national legislation project:

1   a Management Authority and a Scientific Authority;
2   prohibition of trade in violation of CITES;
3   penalties for such trade;
4   confiscation of specimens illegally traded or possessed.

This failure to apply minimum standards does not reflect well on parties. It means in effect that 50% were still in violation of the Convention ten years after the project started (down from 75% in that time). Some have the excuse of being newcomers to CITES (since the beginning of 2000 there have been 12 new parties), but most are persistent non-compliers, aware since either 1994 or 1997 that their legislation was inadequate. With 50% of parties still to enact national legislation after ten years, the project can only be regarded as a qualified success, though it is hoped the new requirement for Legislation Plans may elicit more response.

The capacity-building programme will begin to reap results only in the longer term. And for the benefits to endure, it will need to ensure that national experts trained under the programme pass on their expertise by becoming trainers themselves and organizing in-country programmes. Such an approach is costly and time-consuming, and will need political will at national level to carry it through. Whether that is present – or can be generated – is a moot question. In the

---

[2] Marceil Yeater, 'Enforcement and the CITES National Legislation Project', in Monika Anton, Nicholas Dragffy, Stephanie Pendry and Tomme Rozanne Young (eds), *Proceedings of the International Expert Workshop on the Enforcement of Wildlife Trade Controls in the EU, 5-6 Nov 2001* (TRAFFIC/IUCN, 2002).

meantime, to prevent the project losing momentum, follow through with threatened trade sanctions to deal with persistent non-compliers is essential.

National institutions

A key institutional weakness at national level is the lack of specialized wildlife law enforcement units in all but the few parties where they have been established voluntarily. Among the scientific and management institutions that exist, there is enormous variation in capacity, funding and competence from party to party. As already discussed, several have failed to designate their Scientific Authorities. Among those authorities that have been designated, lack of coordination is a common complaint. In some cases, the Scientific Authority is marginalized or its advice ignored, Madagascar being a case in point. In some developing-country parties the Scientific Authority comprises just one person in a grossly underfunded scientific institution with no capacity to carry out non-detriment findings. Occasionally the opposite is the case. In Uganda most of the limited resources are vested in the Scientific Authority, which has powers of inspection (though only one inspector), while the Management Authority is a one-man operation issuing permits.

The programme to build capacity in Scientific Authorities is encouraging, but one-off training seminars and a manual will not address the fundamental lack of human resources that exists in the less developed range states. More sustained training programmes are required, both for administrative and scientific staff. In Malaysia, the tiger technical mission found that personnel were well informed on CITES matters. This was attributed to the Malaysian government's policy of sponsoring staff in the Department of Wildlife and National Parks to attend universities abroad for further education such as masters degrees. In Spain a masters course on CITES has been developed. A sponsorship programme for staff in Management and Scientific Authorities to attend such a course could provide long-term benefits for the Convention's implementation at national level, as long as its reach was wide enough and the programme could be sustained into the future.

Management and Scientific Authorities in developing-country parties are also handicapped by a lack of equipment, particularly computers, and limited access to telecommunications. They often need to turn to NGOs for help; prior to COP11, I was asked to provide the representative of a Scientific Authority in a southern African party with preparatory documents from the CITES website because he had no access to the internet, and the documents mailed by the Secretariat had failed to reach further than one person's desk in the Management

Authority. If computers are provided, they are often reserved for senior officials not involved in day-to-day permitting or enforcement matters. While the Secretariat is attempting to address this lack of capacity through the information management strategy, as already pointed out, it will be a long time, if ever, before all national CITES officials (not just senior staff) have equivalent access to information. In the short to medium term, the gap will probably widen between the internet haves and have-nots, placing many developing-country parties at an increasing disadvantage, with the website as the central core for data and information dissemination.

Another issue of concern is poor regional communication and response by Scientific and/or Management Authorities to requests by regional members of CITES technical committees. The Animals Committee Chairman reported in June 2001 that there was 'hardly any response to requests from members of the Committee, while parties attend AC meetings only to take care of issues of interest to them'. He expressed a hope that regional and inter-regional contacts would improve in the future.[3]

CITES has never had access to sufficient funding to enable it to engage in really effective and sustained national institutional strengthening – to the extent, for example, that the Montreal Protocol's Multilateral Fund has supported through Country Programmes. An idea to be explored (and discussed further in Chapter 13) is the formulation of national CITES Action Plans, based on a country-by-country review of national implementation and enforcement capacity – in effect, an extension of the tiger technical missions. To work, these would have to pay equal attention to the needs of, and input from, wildlife law enforcement agencies as well as Management and Scientific Authorities. Of course, they would need funding, political will and follow-up. Many will say this is impossible, but the regime needs to aim high if it is to succeed in strengthening itself at its weakest points.

Reporting on trade and infractions, and verification

Much has been said already about the failure of parties to report their trade data on an annual basis and the detrimental effects of this on the Convention's information base and the ability of CITES institutions to make informed decisions. This is a key weakness that demands concerted action, and a new approach. A useful start would be to review the experience gained in reporting from other conventions and international institutions, such as the Montreal

---

[3] CITES SC45 Doc. 5.16, 'Report of the Chairman of the Animals Committee' to SC45 (Jun 2001).

Protocol, Ramsar Convention, International Labour Organization and Climate Change Convention (discussed in the following chapter). The review would provide the basis for proposing a mechanism to stimulate improved reporting by parties on a sustained basis.

More attention also needs to be paid to the requirement for biennial reporting. If parties had fulfilled this obligation to provide information on legislative, regulatory and administrative measures taken to enforce CITES, a substantial information base on national implementation and enforcement measures, updated every two years, would exist by now (although, if it were based solely on information provided by parties, it would probably present a picture biased towards positive action). Ideally, such an information base would accept information from other sources such as NGOs and provide a foundation for building capacity in parties to enable full implementation and enforcement of the Convention, which ought to be in their interest. But this would require funds on a big scale, and political will, neither of which is much in evidence.

Change in Secretariat policy on infractions reporting is another issue that has weakened the compliance system through loss of accountability and public access to information. While the TIGERS database and CITES Alerts are constructive and necessary developments, they need to be balanced with a requirement for the public reporting of infractions and the resources necessary to support it, respecting confidentiality where necessary.

Another area of weakness lies in the ad hoc nature of verification through on-site missions. A valuable tool, Secretariat missions tend to be reserved for high-profile species and countries presenting serious problems through non-compliance. Ideally, on-site verification needs to be formalized as a regular tool, for example through periodic review of implementation and enforcement in parties, or to check compliance with Animals and Plants Committee recommendations in the Significant Trade Review mechanism, targeting countries likely to present the biggest problems.

Enforcement

Achilles' heel of CITES

Enforcement is the Achilles' heel of CITES. Effective enforcement turns the Convention from paper reality into actuality. Ineffective enforcement undermines its very objective and every initiative to improve CITES implementation, from the national legislation project to the Significant Trade Review. Model legislation is all very well, but without enforcement its worth is no more than the paper on which it is written; monitoring populations and trade are all very well, but without enforcement CITES may be fiddling while Rome burns. Meanwhile, lack of cooperation and coordination among national, regional and international wildlife authorities, law enforcement agencies and NGOs, plays into the hands of organized wildlife crime networks, whose cooperation and co-ordination at all levels is more sophisticated. These observations are axiomatic, but nevertheless, they are all unfortunate features of the CITES regime.

There has been a great deal of rhetoric and numerous resolutions since CITES came into force on the need for stronger enforcement measures and the need to control illegal trade.[4] Recent developments, such as the creation of the TETF and improved international cooperation with WCO and Interpol, are encouraging. But the reality, particularly when it comes to national enforcement and inter-agency cooperation, fails to match the rhetoric. Generally speaking, they fall far short of the practical needs to combat organized wildlife crime. This is amply demonstrated by the snapshot of enforcement capacity in 15 countries in the previous chapter. Regional cooperation is also inadequate. Existing mechanisms are restricted to Africa, Europe and North America, the Lusaka Agreement covering just six African countries. The majority of CITES parties do not belong to a regional cooperation mechanism. And, although good cooperation exists between CITES institutions and TRAFFIC and IUCN, it needs to be broadened to other NGOs that are knowledgeable about wildlife trade and wildlife crime.

In 1992 an enforcement officer seconded to the Secretariat by USFWS highlighted the following problems:

- lack of proper funding for training of enforcement personnel;
- lack of proper coordination between CITES Management Authorities and CITES enforcement officials;
- lack of understanding of the importance of enforcing wildlife laws at levels of government responsible for funding conservation programmes;
- in some countries, political pressure directed at keeping enforcement programmes underfunded owing to the immense profits derived from poaching and illegal trade.[5]

---

[4] See the preamble in several CITES resolutions: Resolution Conf. 3.9 (Rev.), 'International Compliance Control' (1994); Conf. 6.4 (Rev.), 'Controls on Illegal Trade' (1994); Conf. 7.5, 'Enforcement' (1989); Conf. 9.8 (Rev.), 'Enforcement' (1997); and Conf. 11.3, 'Compliance and Enforcement' (2000).

[5] John Gavitt, 'CITES and Problems with Enforcement' in R. Reeve and L. A. Carter (eds), *Proceedings of the First African Wildlife Law Enforcement Cooperation Conference*, 9–11 Dec 1992 (Zambia Ministry of Tourism).

In its 1996 study, ERM commented that 'effective national enforcement of CITES is hard to achieve, even for the richest countries...'. ERM found that parties responding to its questionnaire were experiencing difficulties in several areas:

- domestic financial limitations;
- insufficient scientific information;
- lack of adequate legislation and regulatory mechanisms;
- the low ranking of CITES and wildlife conservation in national political priorities;
- the lack of trained personnel at all levels, but especially in the customs service and at field level;
- the need for appropriate equipment (e.g. computers and software) and facilities;
- inadequate public information.[6]

As the former CITES Secretary General stated in 1998, 'wildlife crime is not, nor is likely ever to be, a top priority for the enforcement authorities'.[7] In 1999, the Working Group on CITES at the first UNEP Enforcement Workshop identified lack of political will as a factor facilitating wildlife crime, alongside the lack of cooperation between agencies and inadequate resources for enforcement.[8]

Parties lack political will when it comes to even simple practical measures. A request from the Secretariat to Management Authorities in 1991 to provide the name of an enforcement body to assist the Secretariat with coordinating CITES enforcement activities produced replies from just seven parties.[9] A more recent example is the poor response by parties to requests for information on elephant poaching and, in the context of ETIS, on illegal trade. While lack of capacity is to some extent an excuse, frequently underlying this is a lack of political will. There are many other manifestations of this which have already been discussed in the previous chapter – the lack of a permanent institution in

---

[6] ERM report (see ch. 3, n. 106), p. 50.

[7] I. Topkov, 'Summary and Conclusions', in *Proceedings of the EU Wildlife Enforcement Workshop, London 1-2 March 1998* (UK DETR, 1998), p. 107.

[8] Report of the CITES Working Group, UNEP Workshop on Enforcement of and Compliance with MEAs, Geneva (12–14 Jul 1999).

[9] Notification to the Parties No. 630, 'CITES Enforcement Co-ordination' (8 Apr 1991); CITES Doc. SC.31.13, 'Proposal to Form a Law Enforcement Network', prepared by the Secretariat for SC31 (Mar 1994).

CITES in which enforcement officers can participate and influence policy decisions, despite repeated efforts to establish one; the lack of a specific requirement under CITES that parties designate national wildlife law enforcement agencies; the unwillingness of the COP to support the concept of ad hoc CITES Enforcement Task Forces while restricting the TETF's mandate to tigers; the presence of just one professional enforcement officer in the CITES Secretariat; and the equivocal support afforded to the Lusaka Agreement in the early stages of its implementation.

Bias towards science and management

Within the CITES regime, enforcement has always been a 'poor relation' to science and management, from both an institutional and a financial point of view. This is probably rooted in the origins of CITES and the expertise of participants in the Convention's negotiations – hence the binding requirements to designate Management and Scientific Authorities, but no equivalent requirement to designate specialized wildlife law enforcement agencies, a major omission that has weakened the regime immeasurably. The bias towards science and management is evidenced by funding priorities of parties and the nature of CITES institutions.

Funding priorities   An analysis of spending on externally funded projects shows a marked bias towards species-specific studies and monitoring (see Tables 3.2 and 3.3). Between 1997 and 1999, twice as much was spent on species-related studies of status and trade than on activities designed to improve implementation and enforcement. In the 2000–2002 triennium the imbalance has been redressed to a certain extent, with far more projects directed towards improving enforcement and implementation being proposed for funding (though whether they were actually funded is a different issue). But by far the biggest externally funded project is the scientifically driven monitoring programme for elephants, MIKE, the estimated cost of which is US\$4 million between 2000 and 2002 (over 55% of the total sought for external funds).

While projects and programmes involving monitoring and leading to improved wildlife management deserve support, particularly in relation to the Significant Trade Review, they need to be balanced with equivalent funding for implementation and enforcement. One of the objectives of the Strategic Vision through 2005 is to 'encourage the proper funding of CITES implementation and enforcement by parties, and the adoption of national mechanisms that have resource users make a greater contribution to such funding'. But the action points proposed to achieve this – to 'evaluate existing mechanisms for obtaining funds from resource users for conservation benefit...' and to 'ensure adequate funding for necessary research and investigation on CITES species'[10] – completely miss the main objective.

Exclusion of enforcement expertise The nature of CITES institutions, which effectively exclude law enforcement expertise, serves to reinforce the bias in funding priorities. The existence of three committees – on animals, plants and nomenclature – integrates and institutionalizes scientific expertise in these areas within the regime. But there is no equivalent integration and institutionalization of wildlife law enforcement officers (other than through the ad hoc and species-specific TETF).

The concept of epistemic communities in political science is useful here. An epistemic community is 'a network of professionals with recognized expertise and competence in a particular domain and an authoritative claim to policy-relevant knowledge within that domain or issue-area'.[11] Studies have shown that epistemic communities contribute to the evolution of knowledge within international regimes and enable them to learn through participating in advisory and regulatory bodies. In other words, the application of specialized knowledge to policy-making depends on the ability of groups possessing this knowledge to gain and exercise bureaucratic power. The community of scientists with specialized knowledge relating to CITES-listed species can influence policy-making, and therefore funding priorities, within the CITES regime because it can exercise bureaucratic power through the technical and scientific committees. Wildlife law enforcement officials, and experts on other aspects of implementation and compliance such as reporting, have no equivalent means to exercise power and influence the regime since there is no dedicated permanent committee to address these issues. And, as already seen in the previous chapter, efforts to establish one have not been warmly received.

The exclusion of the enforcement community was patently obvious at COP11. Just eight delegations (5% of parties at the time) included enforcement officers.

---

[10] CITES Decision 11.1, Annex 1, 'Strategic Vision through 2005', Objective 1.9 (2000).

[11] Peter Haas, 'Introduction: Epistemic Communities and International Policy Coordination', *International Organization*, 46 (1992), p. 3.

Cooperation and coordination

Despite advances in the last decade, lack of coordination and cooperation between governmental, inter-governmental and non-governmental organizations – between national CITES authorities and enforcement agencies; between national agencies and international organizations (Interpol, WCO and the CITES Secretariat); between national agencies on a regional basis across borders; and between all of them and NGOs – is a recurring issue. One of the objectives in the Strategic Vision for the Convention through 2005 is to strengthen enforcement capacity and improve coordination among Management Authorities and other agencies such as police and customs.[12] Yet there is little evidence of serious initiatives to realize this objective. The problem remains apparent in developed and developing countries alike. Lack of political will, inter-agency jealousies and underfunding of wildlife law enforcement all conspire to exacerbate it. It is an issue that the G8 initiative had the potential to influence considerably, but, given UNEP's failure to follow up recommendations of the 1999 workshop other than the enforcement guidelines, the potential has not been fully realized.

So saying, examples of good coordination and cooperation do exist and could be replicated. At a regional level, the LATF and NAWEG provide models for regions still lacking cooperation mechanisms – something UNEP is ideally placed to facilitate. At a national level, the UK's PAW provides an excellent model for other parties. One of its strengths is in the involvement of a wide variety of non-governmental organizations. NGOs are a valuable source of information, and people with information on illegal trade are often more inclined to approach a NGO than an official government agency. Yet cooperation between NGOs, other than TRAFFIC and IUCN, and the Secretariat and Management Authorities is (with a few exceptions) generally lacking, and in many countries, particularly where transparency and principles of good governance have yet to make their mark, NGOs are seen as a threat rather than potential partners.

Lack of cooperation between enforcement officers and prosecutors, leading to non-prosecution of wildlife criminals or the needless loss of cases, is another common problem which attracts little attention, and one that was emphasized repeatedly at a Commonwealth regional workshop in Botswana in 1999, which brought together investigators and prosecutors from 12 African countries. Another obstacle to successful prosecutions identified by this workshop was the poor understanding of CITES provisions and relevant national laws by

---

[12] CITES Decision 11.1, Annex 1, 'Strategic Vision through 2005', objective 1.3 (2000).

prosecuting lawyers, and the lack of awareness of wildlife crime among the judiciary. A key recommendation of the workshop was for a 'train-the-trainer' course, followed by in-country training in professional enforcement to prevent, investigate and prosecute environmental crime that would bring together investigators and prosecutors.[13] But the recommendation was not followed up by the UK's DETR, which funded the workshop. This is a common complaint. Too often training is in the form of short workshops with a narrow reach and no consistent follow-up. True capacity-building requires sustained long-term training based on a cascade approach – training national trainers who go on to train enforcement officers and prosecutors in their own countries. Although designed just for investigators, the Interpol environmental criminal investigations training programme provides a good model.

Judicial awareness and non-deterrent penalties

Lack of awareness among the judiciary is another widespread problem receiving little attention. Even if stringent penalties are provided for in wildlife legislation (which is often not the case), they may not be reflected in judgments, which frequently hand down non-deterrent fines. In the United Kingdom, for example, the maximum penalty of two years' imprisonment under COTES has never been imposed; nor has the seven-year maximum under the Customs and Excise Management Act for a wildlife trade offence.[14] In 2000, following the confiscation of 138 shahtoosh shawls worth £353,000 (over US$500,000) from the Renaissance Corporation, a UK court fined the company just £1,500.[15] In Kenya in May 2000, a Swiss-American dealer, Thomas Price, was caught exporting hundreds of frogs, snakes and lizards from Mombasa with fake permits.[16] He was fined KSh14,000 (US$180), less than the value of some of the snakes on his price list, despite evidence he had been sending out similar shipments for some years. The fine did nothing to deter his activities; he was recently arrested again for a similar offence, for which he was fined KSh 20,000 (US$250) and deported.[17] In South Africa, prosecutions under ESPU's Operation Cobra, which ran from 1996 to 1998, resulted in derisory fines or simply a

---

[13] Proceedings of the Commonwealth Africa Regional Workshop on the Use of and Enforcement of the Criminal Law in the Prevention of Environmental Crime, Gaborone, Botswana (8–12 Nov 1999).

[14] Cook et al./WWF–UK (see ch. 1, n. 16), p. 29.

[15] Ibid., p. 22.

[16] 'Suspected Reptiles Exporter Arrested', *Daily Nation* (30 May 2000).

[17] Rosalind Reeve, *The Reptile Trade in Kenya* (IFAW, 2002).

caution. It was considered an unproductive use of resources to continue investigations into the reptile trade while non-deterrent penalties were being imposed[18] (though this may have changed following two recent cases described below).

At an IUCN/TRAFFIC workshop analysing legislation and wildlife trade controls in the European Union held in November 2001, a number of wildlife crime cases were reported. Not one involved penalties that were near the maximum allowed by law. In most cases the assessments, even including court costs and other costs such as specimen care, were no more than a quarter of the maximum penalty. It was observed that the basic problem limiting wildlife trade enforcement in the EU was not so much national legislation but 'the lack of will among judges to enforce these provisions'. Even if a minimum penalty was specified, judges considering the crime minor would exercise their independence by, for example, applying rules of evidence strictly against the prosecutor. A case in Germany was cited where, despite proof of the existence of worldwide organization on the part of wildlife smugglers, the court refused to find 'common intention to commit the offences', which was necessary to impose penalties on the group and to apply enterprise-based liability generally. Only a few primary defendants were convicted on separate offences, and, although prison sentences were imposed, well over a year later the individuals involved had still not begun to serve them.[19]

In a few countries the situation does seem to be changing. Since the beginning of 2001 there have been some record-setting judgments that could act as precedents for future cases. The jailing of Anson Wong in the United States for six years is a case in point. Another is the record-setting fine of US$10.4 million against US Caviar & Caviar and the jailing of three executives. In August 2001, in the Cape in South Africa, two Czechs were fined R84,500 each (then about US$12,000) for poaching Appendix II-listed tortoises.[20] The fines were considered a major breakthrough, but they were surpassed in December 2001 when two Slovaks were each fined R168,000 (then about US$14,000, owing to the depreciating rand), also for poaching Cape tortoises.[21] In January 2002 in Jamaica, two Hondurans were each fined J$1 million (US$22,100) or 12

---

[18] ESPU officer, personal communication (Oct 2001).

[19] Tomme Rozanne Young, 'National Wildlife Trade Regulation in EU Member States', in Monika Anton, Nicholas Dragffy, Stephanie Pendry and Tomme Rozanne Young (eds), *Proceedings of the International Expert Workshop on the Enforcement of Wildlife Trade Controls in the EU, 5–6 Nov 2001* (TRAFFIC/IUCN, 2002).

[20] 'A Major Breakthrough for Environmental Law Enforcement', Western Cape Nature Conservation Board press release (31 Aug 2001).

[21] 'Big Fines, Harsh Words for Tortoise Smugglers', *Pretoria News* (13 Dec 2001).

months in prison for illegally fishing conch, with additional fines or six months in jail for possession of a hawksbill turtle – the highest penalties ever imposed for an environmental crime in Jamaica.[22] In the United Kingdom, again in January 2002, bird smuggler Raymond Humphrey was sentenced to six and a half years in prison, the highest ever sentence imposed for wildlife smuggling in the UK. He had been arrested at Heathrow airport with 22 CITES-listed birds concealed in two suitcases. The birds had been stuffed into tubes with their feet bound by electrical tape.[23] These cases indicate that wildlife crime is beginning to be taken seriously in some jurisdictions, but they remain the exception rather than the norm.

International institutions

It is perhaps paradoxical that the international institutions in CITES should be considered under weaknesses of the regime, given the apparently successful partnership between the Secretariat and Standing Committee in dealing with cases of non-compliance. But the way in which CITES operates institutionally departs from other more recently established regimes in a number of ways. Some of these may be desirable; however, others can serve to undermine the regime and stunt its development.

Recalling Lang's three minimum institutional requirements for a satisfactory system of compliance control – a secretariat, a 'reviewing' and/or 'recommendatory' body composed of individual experts or government representatives to evaluate and interpret data and facts, and a main political body to 'take measures'[24] – it is evident that CITES diverges from these requirements in two ways. First, since the abolition of the Technical Committee, CITES has lacked a separate reviewing/recommendatory body. Instead, with the exception of Significant Trade Reviews, these functions are carried out by the Secretariat, assisted by outside institutions, which also undertakes verification missions. Over the years, the Secretariat has become strong and pro-active. This can be an asset if the institution's muscle is exercised appropriately and neutrally, but the history of the CITES Secretariat indicates this has not always been the case.

The other divergence from Lang's minimum requirements is in the way the political bodies operate. While Lang envisages the main political body taking

---

[22] 'Jamaica Imposes Record Fines on Turtle Poachers', *Environment News Service* (24 Jan 2002).

[23] TRAFFIC website, <www.traffic.org.>.

[24] Lang (see ch. 2, n. 18), p. 694.

measures, under CITES, decisions on compliance have increasingly been delegated by the COP to the Standing Committee, a political body for which implementation is just one issue on a busy, growing agenda, including finance, administration and time-consuming, often controversial, species-specific issues (and which also lacked transparency, until its recent decision to allow NGO participation).

The Secretariat: a chequered history

Compared with secretariats serving other major MEAs, the CITES Secretariat has a number of unique features. One is in the close relationship it has developed with selected NGOs, which was actually provided for in the terms of the Convention. The 1971 Ramsar Convention on wetlands is the only other major MEA with such close NGO links, its secretariat (the Ramsar Bureau) being provided by IUCN.[25] Another unique feature is the Secretariat's pro-active role in compliance, developed from its mandate in Article XII to make recommendations on implementation of the Convention. In none of the more recently negotiated major MEAs, including the Basel Convention, Montreal Protocol, Climate Change Convention and Biodiversity Convention, has the Secretariat been given a recommendatory function. Generally this has been reserved for committees of experts or governmental representatives, such as the Montreal Protocol's Implementation Committee or, when it enters into force, the Kyoto Protocol's Compliance Committee, with the secretariat's role restricted to information exchange. The CITES Secretariat, on the other hand, has made extensive use of its recommendatory powers. With a few exceptions, notably on annual reporting, its recommendations to the Standing Committee and COP have invariably been followed in recent years, though sometimes with amendments to allow parties more latitude.

The provision of extensive powers to the Secretariat is a double-edged sword. On the one hand, it has strengthened the compliance system, but on the other, it has led the Secretariat on occasions to stretch its powers and take a parti pris position on issues, causing controversy and even open conflict with parties and NGOs. This is clearly evident from the Secretariat's turbulent history.

The first CITES Secretary General, Peter Sand, an international lawyer of considerable repute, was appointed in 1978 and worked extremely hard to provide the Secretariat, and CITES itself, with a sound foundation, overseeing the

---

[25] Convention on Wetlands of International Importance Especially as Waterfowl Habitat (Ramsar, 1971).

regime's early growth and development. But, following Sand's announcement of his resignation at the New Delhi COP in 1981, the Secretariat entered a phase that was to end in dispute at COP7 in 1989 and the subsequent departure of Sand's successor, Eugene Lapointe, in contentious circumstances.

Evidence of uneasiness in relations between the Secretariat, UNEP and the Standing Committee, and the unwillingness of the Secretariat to subordinate itself to the Standing Committee, can be found in the report of SC18, held in February/March 1989. Responding negatively to a review of the Secretariat's organizational structure and the roles of CITES institutions, the Secretary General criticized the composition of the working group and the presentation of the report, and complained about lack of consultation with the Secretariat. He also had 'difficulty with the concept of the Standing Committee providing "instructions" to the Secretariat' and 'could not agree' with the recommendation that the Standing Committee or the COP set priorities for funding projects. The SC report notes that the UNEP representative's views 'did not coincide entirely with those of the Secretary General', and that the representative reminded the Committee that UNEP's Executive Director is the Secretariat of the Convention. Meanwhile, the representative of France 'felt it was necessary to make a clear distinction between the policy role of the Standing Committee and the management role of the Secretary General'. The meeting concluded that the Standing Committee had a role in providing overall direction to the Secretariat, but not in day-to-day direction. The observer for Israel raised the concern that the Secretariat was relying heavily on funding from trade groups, especially those trading in Appendix I species. It was suggested that guidelines for the acceptance of funding be developed by Israel, while a proposal for the long-term goals and objectives of the Secretariat be prepared by the Secretary General for consideration at COP7.[26]

COP7, held in Lausanne, Switzerland, in October 1989, was a difficult meeting. Many conservationist NGOs were lobbying hard for the listing of the African elephant on Appendix I and the consequent banning of the ivory trade. Parties were deeply divided. Feelings were running high. Some NGOs accused the Secretariat of partiality in the ivory trade dispute, of playing a questionable role in the 1986 registration of large quantities of ivory without having to declare the country of origin (in effect, legalizing large stockpiles of illegally obtained ivory), and of publicly lobbying through the media against an Appendix I listing.[27]

---

[26] SC18: Summary Report (Feb/Mar 1989), pp. 11–14.

[27] Sand (1997) (see ch. 1, n. 3), n. 45, p. 29; *A System of Extinction* (EIA, Oct 1989).

Parties rejected a number of Secretariat proposals at COP7 and engaged in a heated debate over whether external funding should be sought from wildlife trade groups. As already discussed, this led to a strengthened monitoring of the Secretariat's budget process by enhancing oversight powers of the Standing Committee.[28] There was yet more controversy over the Secretariat's role in recommending the sale by Guyana of over 10,000 skins from Appendix II-listed caiman lizards, believed to have been obtained illegally from other countries including Brazil, from which all wildlife exports were banned. (The proceeds of the sale were to be used for conservation projects in Guyana.) The United States complained to the COP that the Secretariat had known about the issue since July 1988 but had not consulted parties. Furthermore, the Secretariat had called a press conference to discuss the subject before the matter had been raised with the Standing Committee. The Secretary General countered that Guyana had decided to sell the skins only in June 1989, since when there had been no meeting of the Standing Committee. But other concerns about the sale were raised by Brazil, Germany and Kenya. The discussion resulted in the COP referring the matter to the Standing Committee and UNEP, with the recommendation that clear guidelines be established.[29]

The issue provoked an equally heated debate in the Standing Committee. The United States repeated its concerns, raising several questions relating to the sale price, the selection of the trader, the percentage that went back to the trader and the apparent lack of a sales and conservation agreement. The representative of South and Central America and the Caribbean complained of lack of communication with him about an issue involving his region, and the observer from Kenya added that at least three channels of communication had not been used: to the Standing Committee, the Animals Committee and the COP. The representative of North America suggested that the Standing Committee agree (which it did) that there was no proof of illegal activity or breach of the Convention on the part of the Secretariat, but that there 'were perceptions of improper activity', and that guidelines on the role of the Secretariat in the sale of goods should be developed.[30] The guidelines agreed at SC21 provided, *inter alia,* for notification by the Secretariat to the Standing Committee and the appropriate regional representative of each request to assist with disposal of confiscated material, and for full disclosure to the public and transparency in the sale. They also directed that the Secretariat should not become directly

---

[28] David S. Favre, 'Trade in Endangered Species', *Yearbook of International Environmental Law*, 1 (1990), p. 195.

[29] See CITES Plen.7.3 (Rev), Report of the Plenary Session (Oct 1989).

[30] SC21: Summary Report (Feb 1990), p. 8.

involved in identifying potential buyers and handling financial transactions unless there was no other way of ensuring the proceeds went to conservation projects.[31]

Meanwhile, a group of 18 national and international NGOs requested publicly that the UNEP Executive Director replace Eugene Lapointe. In the spring of 1990 it was announced, with no specific reasons given, that the Secretary General would step down.[32] Lapointe, a Canadian lawyer, appealed to the UN administration in New York, and in 1993 obtained damages amounting to a year's salary, which the UN Appeals Board recommended be debited from the UNEP Executive Director's own salary account.[33] Lapointe has since established an NGO, the IWMC–World Conservation Trust, which lobbies actively in favour of trade and sustainable use, fielding a large delegation comprising 18 observers at COP11. In communications he signs himself as the former CITES Secretary General.

In 1991 Ambassador Izgrev Topkov of Bulgaria was appointed by UNEP to replace Lapointe. There was also considerable change in the Secretariat's staff under the direction of UNEP that year, causing controversy within the Standing Committee. The Committee did not support the replacement of Lapointe, and questioned the authority of UNEP to control staffing decisions within the Secretariat.[34] The extent of the tension is illustrated by an Annex to the minutes of SC22, dated 14 August 1990, in which the representative of South and Central America and the Caribbean, the late Felipe Benavides, describes a meeting between the Standing Committee and UNEP's Executive Director, Dr M. Tolba. Benevides refuted several points made by Dr Tolba concerning the Secretariat and referred to a legal opinion he had commissioned, which had established that the 'procedure' for dismissing the Secretary General had not been followed correctly, after which the Executive Director 'attacked' him for having qualified his behaviour as 'bizarre' and left the room, 'slamming the door'.[35] Following this breakdown in relations, the respective roles of the UNEP Executive Director and the Standing Committee in personnel decisions were subsequently clarified. But the tendency of members of the Secretariat to

---

[31] Ibid., Annex 2, 'Guidelines for Secretariat Involvement in the Sale of CITES Specimens' (Feb 1990).

[32] David S. Favre, 'Trade in Endangered Species', *Yearbook of International Environmental Law*, 1 (1990), p. 195.

[33] Sand (1997), n. 45, p. 29.

[34] David S. Favre, 'Trade in Endangered Species', *Yearbook of International Environmental Law*, 2 (1991), p. 206.

[35] SC22: Summary Report, Annex 3 (14 Aug 1990).

fail to take a neutral position on issues was still apparent, as is illustrated by the Secretariat's continued active opposition to some kind of CITES enforcement working group or committee through to COP10 in 1997, discussed in chapter 9.

It was at COP10 that problems with the Secretariat were again raised, this time by the Chair of the Standing Committee, Murray Hosking. This is evident from the report to COP11 by Hosking's successor, Robert Hepworth, which referred to 'difficulties within the Secretariat' reported at COP10 by the previous chairman. These 'difficulties' led to a majority of the Standing Committee agreeing on the need for an independent inquiry. Meanwhile, two senior and long-serving Secretariat staff members (both heads of units) were suspended from duty. Following the inquiry and a further investigation by the UN Office of Internal Oversight (UNOIOS), the UNEP Executive Director informed the Standing Committee in June 1998 that the contracts of the two suspended officers were to end and that the Secretary General would be assigned to other duties.[36] The UNOIOS report was not released to the public, or to the COP, and the 'difficulties within the Secretariat' were not clarified to parties and observers at COP11. Rumours at the time, however, raise questions over whether they concerned mismanagement, possibly even corruption. Other problems intimated concerned externally funded projects, and unduly strong affiliations of the two staff members with the regions for which they were coordinators.

A look at external funding received from wildlife trade/industry sources between 1994 and 1999 reveals that in the triennium 1994–6 wildlife trade/industry organizations contributed over US$160,000, US$90,000 of which came from the Unione Nazionale Industria Conciaria (the Italian tanning union).[37] In the next triennium (1997–9), after the 'difficulties' in the Secretariat had been reported by the Standing Committee Chairman, the only donation from wildlife trade/industry organizations was US$1,500, from the International Wood Products Association – more than 99% less than the funds received from trade and industry between 1994 and 1996.[38]

In April 1999, the fourth CITES Secretary General, Willem Wijnstekers, formerly with the European Commission, took up his post. Several other posts

---

[36] CITES Doc. 11.8, 'Matters relating to the Standing Committee: Report of the Chairman', prepared for COP11 (Apr 2000).

[37] See CITES Doc. 10.14, 'External Funding', prepared by the CITES Secretariat for COP10 (Jun 1997).

[38] CITES Doc. 11.10.4, 'External Funding', prepared by the Secretariat for COP11 (Apr 2000).

in the Secretariat were advertised at the same time, including newly created positions in the Enforcement Assistance Unit (now the Legislation and Compliance Unit). Reflecting the way in which the Secretariat was perceived at the time, Wijnstekers made a statement to the Standing Committee in which he emphasized his intention to enhance policy transparency and 'restore the confidence of the parties – and of the Standing Committee in particular – in the Secretariat'.[39]

It was hoped that these changes would mark a new era of transparency, accountability and neutrality. Certainly, the current Secretariat is more transparent in its operations than its predecessor. The CITES website is a vast improvement on the past, with reports of Committee meetings finally being published along with preparatory documents albeit tardily. On the issue of neutrality and accountability, however, the jury is still out. There have been some decisions and incidents where the Secretariat appears to have overstepped its remit, and on a couple of occasions ruffled party feathers. One was the decision to revise the infractions report to COP11 (described in Chapter 4); another was its decision to circulate 'Provisional Assessments' of parties' proposals to COP11 for amendments of the Appendices well in advance of the usual distribution of its formal recommendations.

The Provisional Assessments prompted complaints from Kenya, the United States and several NGOs. As the United States pointed out, they were published without peer review or analysis by scientists with expertise in the species concerned, and before comments were available from IUCN and other bodies. Furthermore, the Secretariat declared in the assessments that it 'supports' or 'cannot support' the proposals. The United States commented that 'it might be more helpful if the Secretariat noted any deficiencies in proposals, in terms of the listing criteria in Resolution Conf. 9.24, and made recommendations to parties on how to improve proposals, and reported on the results of its consultations with other bodies and with scientific experts'.[40] Kenya rightly pointed out that the Secretariat was risking influencing parties undecided on their positions through the provision of partial information. In relation to its joint proposal with India to relist the African elephant populations in Botswana, Namibia and Zimbabwe on Appendix I, Kenya 'was surprised, not only by the content, but also by the tone of the Secretariat's comments'. In a strongly

---

[39] 'Statement by Mr Willem Wijnstekers, Secretary-General Designate, to the 41st Meeting of the Standing Committee', Annex 1, SC41: Summary Report (Feb 1999), p. 52.
[40] 'US Response to Provisional Assessments Provided in Notification to the Parties 1999/97', US Fish & Wildlife Service (31 Jan 2000).

worded letter to the Secretary General, the Director of Kenya Wildlife Service stated: 'We respect that there may be some individuals within the Secretariat who do not agree with our views on elephant conservation and trade, but we were extremely disappointed to see this difference of personal opinion reflected in the Secretariat's official assessments'.[41]

The Secretariat was also criticized for the political nature of its assessments; for setting higher standards of proof than required by the listing criteria in Resolution Conf. 9.24; for not taking into account the precautionary principle; and for suggesting that it would support some proposals if amendments were made.[42] It stated, for example, that it would support the (highly controversial) proposals by Norway and Japan to down-list certain populations of minke whales to Appendix II if they were amended to include zero quotas.[43] Following criticism from parties as well as NGOs, the Secretariat back-tracked on this position, describing it in its final recommendations as 'cumbersome and unrealistic'.[44]

Yet another incident where the Secretariat's behaviour was questioned was over a unilateral change in the wording of a species listing. This provoked the Earth Negotiations Bulletin (which reports on MEA meetings) to ask: 'Who's the Alpha Male?' Reporting on the December 2000 Plants Committee meeting, ENB commented:

> Despite the Secretariat's self-description as 'humble servants to the parties', many believe that it is subtly stretching its powers to a level of involvement not witnessed in other international environmental fora. In the Plants Committee, the Secretariat came under fire for having unilaterally altered the wording in listing monkey-puzzle tree populations (*Araucaria araucana*), with the unintended result of split-listing the species. Furthermore, it declined a private request by the Chair to restore the original wording, and the issue came out in the open during a Plenary session where the Committee decided to send a letter to the Standing Committee reaffirming the original intent of a COP-11 decision. There was a widespread feeling among par-

---

[41] Nehemiah Rotich, letter to Willem Wijnstekers commenting on the Secretariat's Preliminary Assessments (29 Jan 2000).

[42] 'WCL Comments on the Secretariat's Provisional Assessments of the Proposals Circulated in Notification No. 1999/97', Wildlife & Countryside Link (24 Jan 2000).

[43] Notification to the Parties No. 1999/97, 'Provisional Assessments by the Secretariat of Amendment Proposals' (29 Dec 1999).

[44] 'Consideration of Proposals for Amendment of Appendices I and II', prepared by the Secretariat for COP11 (Apr 2000).

ticipants that the 'old guard' of the Secretariat, noted for its European composition, is not fully receptive to guidance by the parties.[45]

The Secretariat's tendency to unilateralism must be addressed. This is an important issue in the light of the central reviewing and recommendatory role ascribed to the Secretariat in the absence of any oversight by a committee of independent experts on implementation, enforcement and compliance. For example, in June 2001 the Secretariat informed the Standing Committee that it was to embark on a review of all resolutions with the intention of proposing to the COP 'amendments in order to: clarify parts that are unclear; solve current problems with implementation of the resolutions; and eliminate parts that are no longer necessary'. It added that it did not expect the Standing Committee to be involved.[46] Subsequently, the Standing Committee expressed concern about the Secretariat independently reviewing resolutions, and requested that a list of those to be amended be notified to parties with an explanation of reasons.[47] In April 2002 the Secretariat published a list of 23 resolutions for which it is considering preparing proposals for amendment or repeal at COP12.[48] A review of resolutions is undoubtedly needed, given the complexity of CITES regulations, compounded by duplication and lack of clarity in places. But it has major implications. It needs to be handled neutrally, not used as a convenient mechanism to remove inconvenient provisions. Yet there is no mechanism in place for independent review of the Secretariat's recommendations. The Standing Committee does not have the time or expertise, and the COP is inappropriate.

The Secretariat should not be judged solely on the basis of its turbulent history. Its staff members work hard on a tight budget and can claim much of the credit for the development of an active compliance system. Nevertheless, for the sake of its reputation and the proper operation of the Convention, the Secretariat's periodic tendency to stretch its powers needs to be addressed by parties. The line between pro-activity and overstepping one's remit is a fine one, and must be trodden carefully. Safeguards need to be put in place to ensure that mistakes of the past are not repeated. One way to achieve this would be through operational guidelines addressing issues such as accountability,

---

[45] 'A Brief Analysis of the CITES Technical Committees Meetings', *Earth Negotiations Bulletin*, 21/17 (18 Dec 2000). See <www.iisd.ca/CITES/CITPA/>.
[46] CITES SC45 Doc. 19, 'Implementation of Existing Resolutions (Decision 11.136)', prepared by the Secretariat for SC45 (Jun 2001).
[47] SC46: Summary Report (Mar 2002), p. 8.
[48] CITES Notification to the Parties No. 2002/024 'Revision of Existing Resolutions' (9 Apr 2002).

transparency, neutrality and conflict of interest, while at the same time ensuring that the compliance system is not compromised. An additional safeguard would be the establishment of a Compliance Committee with the power to review Secretariat recommendations.

The Standing Committee

The Standing Committee is a political body whose powers have increased extensively since it was established, to the extent that it has become a 'mini-COP', conducting the business of the Convention between COP meetings. Up to now its operation has been far from transparent, as witnessed by the exclusion of NGOs from its meetings (with the exception of IUCN and TRAFFIC) and inaccessibility of reports. But the recent decisions to extend NGO participation and publish reports on the website have opened the Committee to public scrutiny, and should eventually reap benefits for the regime from a broadened input.

With just 17 potential members,[49] only 14 of which can vote, the Standing Committee is a small body relative to the 158-strong COP. Yet its decision-making role between meetings of the COP, particularly with respect to implementation and compliance, has gradually strengthened over the years as more business has been delegated. Since 1989, within the broad mandate of COP resolutions, the Standing Committee has been solely responsible for deciding on measures against non-compliant countries, including trade sanctions, on the basis of Secretariat recommendations. It is rare nowadays that problem countries are discussed at any length by the COP, probably from a desire to avoid singling out parties at the large and highly publicized COP meetings. The resolution on Bolivia in the 1980s proved to be an exception. The Standing Committee has also been delegated far-reaching decision-making powers with respect to actions on high-profile species. Examples are its key role in approving sanctions over rhino horn trade; its somewhat controversial role in approving the 1999 ivory auctions; and its mandate to decide measures in relation to tiger range and consumer states.

While the Standing Committee's decision-making responsibilities have broadened, the number of regional representatives in relation to the size of the COP has decreased. Just 9% of parties now have the right to vote and exercise the Committee's considerable powers (excluding the Depositary's right to vote

---

[49] From COP11 to COP12, the Standing Committee was composed of 16 members, there being no previous host country.

in a tie). In comparison, at the time of the Standing Committee's establishment in 1979 there were six regional representatives out of 51 parties (12%).[50] Guidelines exist on the duties of regional representatives. These include maintaining a 'fluid and permanent communication' with parties in their region and with the Secretariat, and communicating with parties before meetings of the Standing Committee, *inter alia* to request their opinions, and again after the meetings to inform them of the results.[51] While this falls short of an overtly expressed duty to *represent* the opinions of other parties in the region at Committee meetings, it can be argued that it is implicit.

Perhaps not surprisingly, this duty is not always fulfilled. This was plainly evident at SC41 in February 1999, when the ivory sales were approved. Three of the four parties wanting to trade ivory (Japan, Namibia and Zimbabwe) were members of the Standing Committee: Japan and Namibia were regional representatives with votes, while Zimbabwe was there by virtue of its role as host of COP10. However, instead of representing its region, Japan represented Japan – an ivory consumer – not even paying lip service to India's strongly held position opposing the trade. Namibia represented Namibia and the ivory trade lobby, and, though several southern African states supported the ivory sales, not all did, Zambia being a case in point.[52] Had the decision on compliance with the conditions for selling ivory (Decision 10.1) been reserved for the COP, the objections of range states, as voting members, would at least have been heard and counted. But by delegating the decision to regional representatives on the Standing Committee, these states were effectively disenfranchised. Since only one of the nine opposing range states attending SC41 (Burkina Faso) was a regional representative with a vote,[53] the decision to approve the sales was almost a foregone conclusion. Set against a background of years of divided debate and active lobbying by pro-ivory trade states and their relative strength within the Standing Committee, to refuse them at that point would have been a political time bomb – though, given the valid objections over compliance with the conditions in Decision 10.1, it would have been the more defensible

---

[50] See Resolution Conf. 2.2, 'Establishment of the Standing Committee of the Conference of the Parties' (1979); and CITES Doc. 3.6, 'Report of the Secretariat', COP3 (Feb/Mar 1981).

[51] CITES Decisions 11.74 and 75 Directed to the Standing Committee 'Regarding Duties of the Regional Representatives' (2000).

[52] Author's observation as observer party representative at SC41.

[53] The other eight range states opposed to the sales of ivory going ahead on the basis that Decision 10.1 conditions had not been fulfilled were Chad, Congo-Brazzaville, Ghana, Kenya, India, Liberia, Mali and Zambia.

decision from a substantive viewpoint. Substantive issues aside, however, the procedure leading to the sales invites questions about how regional representatives fulfil their duties, and how to deal with conflict of interest. The behaviour of Japan and Namibia at SC41 indicates that a duty to represent other parties' opinions and positions needs to be made explicit to prevent more vocal and/or economically powerful parties dominating the agenda with their own concerns. In cases of clear conflict of interest, the regional representative(s) concerned could be asked to step down and hand over to the alternate(s).

Another issue is the relatively slow turnover of members of the Standing Committee. Since regional representatives serve for two intervals between COP meetings, they can be members for up to five years. If they host a meeting of the COP, they can perpetuate their membership for another four to five years (as next host party, then previous host party). Japan did this, and as a result was a member of the Standing Committee, exerting considerable influence, for over ten years (from 1989 to 2000). One solution would be to reduce the term served by regional representatives to one interval between COP meetings. An argument against this is that it reduces continuity and the institutional memory of the Committee. But if parties serve as alternates before they become full voting members, the validity of this argument diminishes.

It must also be questioned whether the Standing Committee is able to give adequate time and attention to implementation and enforcement questions, and whether as a political body it is appropriate for it to act in an expert capacity. Controversial species-specific issues can sometimes dominate a Standing Committee meeting. At SC41, for example, discussion over the ivory trade filled nearly half the available time, with the result that many agenda items, including ones on enforcement, were cut short or referred to the next meeting. While SC41 was perhaps exceptional in this respect, the fact remains that implementation and enforcement issues have to compete for air time in a multifaceted and busy schedule.

The missing leg: a Compliance Committee

In February 1990 the Standing Committee representative for Oceania, Murray Hosking, was ahead of his time with his suggestion that the proposed Enforcement Committee (originally put forward by Secretary General Eugene Lapointe) be changed to a Committee on Compliance. Unfortunately, the initiative was squashed by the Secretariat and all attempts to resurrect it have failed.

The lack of a committee dedicated to issues concerning compliance, implementation and enforcement is a significant gap in the institutional makeup of CITES. Some of the reasons for its necessity have already been pointed out. These include:

- the prevailing opinion that, for a satisfactory system of compliance control, some form of reviewing and/or recommendatory body is needed in addition to a secretariat;
- the lack of expertise on current committees to deal with enforcement and compliance;
- the unsuitability of the Standing Committee as a political body to assume a reviewing and recommendatory role that requires specific expertise;
- the lack of a forum for experts on compliance control and enforcement within CITES, effectively excluding them from decision-making and perpetuating the secondary role of these issues within the regime (the argument of epistemic communities);
- the need for review by independent experts nominated by the parties of recommendations made by the Secretariat (often on the basis of advice from subcontracting NGOs, TRAFFIC and IUCN) on issues of compliance, implementation and enforcement;
- the ability to withstand criticism of controversial decisions, e.g. trade sanctions, if they have the backing of independent experts;
- the need to enhance the importance of, and attract funding for, projects designed to increase the capacity for implementation and enforcement, and therefore improve compliance;
- the need to devote more time to these issues than the Standing Committee – a political body – is able to give with its busy agenda.

CITES was adopted at a time when a separate compliance committee was not considered an institutional necessity. But experience in modern regulatory MEAs has changed this view. The following chapter, devoted to lessons from other compliance systems, clearly demonstrates this. In its expansion of the mandate of the Technical Expert Committee to review implementation and enforcement issues in 1981, CITES was ahead of its time. But since the Committee's abolition in 1987, a key element of oversight of recommendations to the political bodies has been lost.

In the aftermath of COP11, a new initiative arose from the Animals Committee to establish some form of Implementation Committee. Reviewing the resolutions, decisions and Action Plan, it became clear that a substantial number of implementation and legal issues had been delegated to the Animals Committee, whose members are elected on the basis of their expertise in zoological matters. It seemed 'inappropriate to ask these biologists to e.g. try to establish how best to mark tins of caviar'.[54] A proposal was therefore put to the Chairman of the Standing Committee to look into the possibilities of establishing a technical committee composed of experts on implementation and legal matters, freeing up the Animals Committee to focus on zoological issues. The result was a document prepared by the Secretariat for SC45 advocating the re-establishment of a committee, similar to the old Technical Committee, responsible for considering implementation matters. In its arguments, the Secretariat pointed out the lack of relevant expertise in the current committee structure to deal with several decisions arising from COP11, e.g. enforcement and legislative measures concerning trade in bear, tiger and musk deer specimens, labelling systems, and recommendations on trade in time-sensitive research samples. It also cited precedents that now exist for an implementation committee in other MEAs.[55]

Support from the Standing Committee was tentative. It agreed that the Secretariat should develop a proposal for COP12 with the guidance of a working group convened by the United States, but instructed it to take into account interventions by Committee members in preparing its proposal:

- it could not be an enforcement committee, since that idea had been rejected by the COP;
- there was concern about the cost, so budgetary implications needed to be clear;
- the cost could be minimized by the way in which the committee conducted its work, especially if no meetings were required;
- needs could be met through establishing temporary ad hoc groups, or a committee with a changing membership, rather than a permanent committee.[56]

Since SC45, the Standing Committee and Secretariat seem to have exchanged their initial positions. At SC46 in March 2002, the Standing Committee agreed on the need to establish a mechanism for considering technical and implementation issues, with input from Management Authorities and technical experts.

---

[54] CITES SC45 Doc. 16, 'Report of the Chairman of the Animals Committee', prepared for SC45 (Jun 2002).

[55] CITES SC45 Doc. 8, 'Establishment of an Implementation Committee', prepared by the Secretariat for SC45 (Jun 2001).

[56] SC45: Summary Report (Jun 2001), p. 6.

Draft terms of reference produced by the working group were revised.[57] They proposed a Technical Subcommittee on Implementation Issues of the Standing Committee, to be made up of regional representatives with relevant expertise in CITES implementation, and chaired by an individual from a Management Authority. The subcommittee's proposed mandate was very narrowly drawn. It was to have no authority to initiate new tasks on its own, being restricted to advice, guidance and drafting resolutions on technical and procedural implementation issues specifically directed to it by the Standing Committee, including, *inter alia*, the marking, labelling and identification of parts and derivatives; interpretation of the Convention, resolutions and decisions; implementation of new or proposed listings; and adjustment to changing trade patterns and technology.[58] The Standing Committee, however, could not conclude discussion of the proposed subcommittee, and referred it to SC47, to be held immediately prior to COP12.

Meanwhile, the Secretariat has changed its view on the need for a permanent committee. In a document prepared for SC46, it states that the best approach would be for technical and implementation issues to be referred to the Secretariat either directly by the COP or by one of the existing permanent committees. The Secretariat, it states, could undertake the work with the help of experts, or establish a working group of party representatives and experts drawn from NGOs and the private sector. It cites as a major consideration in changing its view the apparent consensus among countries involved in UNEP discussions on international environmental governance against the creation of additional subsidiary bodies under MEAs. Other considerations cited are finance, the need for different types of experts for different implementation issues, and the desirability of simplifying procedures. The Secretariat concludes by stating that it is 'opposed in principle to the proposal emanating from the working group'.[59]

In preparation for COP12, the United States has put forward a discussion document on committees and on enhancing implementation.[60] It expresses its strong opinion on the need for an ongoing forum to discuss implementation issues that 'includes and is led by the parties'. It considers that under the current

---

[57] SC46: Summary Report (Mar 2002), p. 2.

[58] CITES SC46 Doc. 6.1, 'Draft Terms of Reference: The Technical Subcommittee on Implementation Issues of the Standing Committee', prepared at SC46 (Mar 2002).

[59] CITES SC46 Doc. 6, 'Establishment of an Implementation Committee', prepared by the Secretariat for SC46 (Mar 2002).

[60] COP12 Doc. 13.2, 'Establishment of Committees: Enhancing Implementation of the Convention', prepared by the USA for COP12 (Nov 2002).

situation numerous implementation issues are not being addressed or resolved, and that the Secretariat proposal to SC46 is unlikely to change the situation because of constraints of budget, workload and expertise. Two of the options it proposes are: (1) to establish a joint implementation subcommittee under the Animals and Plants Committees; and (2) to merge the Animals and Plants Committees into a single scientific committee and establish a second administrative/policy-making committee to address implementation matters, an option that mirrors the current COP committee structure.

These developments lay the foundation for what could prove to be a lively debate at SC47 and COP12. On the one hand are the unresolved draft terms of reference for an Implementation Subcommittee, narrow and cautious and in any case not supported by the Secretariat. On the other is the Secretariat's proposal that it deal with implementation issues on an ad hoc basis. Meanwhile, the United States clearly wants parties to hold the reins on these matters. Its proposal for a separate administrative/policy-making committee holds out most hope for the future, although what is really needed is not a committee dealing purely with matters of technical implementation, but a permanent Compliance Committee, mandated to review and make recommendations to the COP and Standing Committee on issues relating to compliance, including capacity-building to improve implementation and enforcement by parties, and determinations of non-compliance and recommendations on consequences (e.g. trade restrictions or suspension of rights and privileges). Ideally such a committee should be composed of independent experts (or government representatives with relevant expertise) who could be organized into different branches or subgroups (like the Kyoto Protocol Compliance Committee, discussed in the following chapter). There is no reason (other than lack of political will among parties) why the second administrative/ policy-making committee proposed by the United States could not be recast as a Compliance Committee, drawing in expertise currently excluded from existing institutions, and absorbing members of the Tiger Enforcement Task Force into an expanded enforcement subgroup. However, given the past response to proposals for an enforcement group, and the Secretariat's stated opposition to a new permanent committee, the chances of this being realized are slim.

Funding mechanism

The funds available to CITES, which, even including external funding, amount to less than US$10 million a year, are paltry in comparison with funds available even to other MEAs.[61] The Multilateral Fund of the 1987 Montreal Protocol on Substances that Deplete the Ozone Layer received contributions of US$240 million when it was first established by an amendment in 1990 to disburse funds to developing countries; the four successive replenishments of the Fund, occurring every three years, total over US$1.5 billion. By early 2001 a total of over US$1.1 billion had been allocated to developing countries with a consumption of ozone depleting substances (ODS) lower than 0.3kg per capita ('Article 5 parties'), for the purpose of institutional strengthening, project preparation, and implementation of investment projects. As of 2000, nearly 2,500 such projects were being implemented in developing countries to help shift their use to non-ODS. Implementation of the Montreal Protocol has also been assisted by funding provided by the Global Environment Facility (GEF) to countries with economies in transition, mainly in central and eastern Europe and the former Soviet Union, which do not qualify for support under the Multilateral Fund. As of 2000, the GEF had allocated US$148 million for 14 such countries.[62]

The GEF, a financing body dedicated specifically to the environment, is the major international funding source for environmental projects. Formed initially as an experimental facility in 1990, it was restructured and established permanently in 1994. It has four focal areas for project spending: biodiversity, global warming, international watercourses and ozone depletion.[63] By mid-1999 the GEF had allocated more than US$2 billion for more than 500 projects in 120 countries;[64] for its second replenishment in 1998, the GEF Trust Fund received US$ 2.75 billion.[65] The GEF provides the financial mechanism for the UNFCCC and the CBD, and when they enter into force will do the same for the 1997 Kyoto Protocol negotiated under the UNFCCC (which sets emissions targets

---

[61] For an overview of financial mechanisms for MEAs, see Peter H. Sand, 'Carrots Without Sticks? New Financial Mechanisms for Global Environmental Agreements', *Max Planck Yearbook of United Nations Law*, 3 (1999), pp. 363–88 (hereinafter 'Sand (1999)').

[62] Duncan Brack, 'Funding Ozone Protection: The Multilateral Fund of the Montreal Protocol', prepared for Multilateral Fund Secretariat (2001); 'Matrix on Trade Measures Pursuant to Selected MEAs', WT/CTE/W/160, note by the WTO Secretariat (19 Sep 2000).

[63] See Article I, paras 2 and 3, 'Instrument for the Establishment of the Restructured Global Environment Facility' (1994).

[64] Joy Hyvarinen and Duncan Brack, 'Global Environmental Institutions: Analysis and options for change' (RIIA, Sep 2000). See <www.riia.org/Research/eep/eep.html>.

[65] The New Delhi Statement of the First GEF Assembly (15 Apr 1998). See GEF website at <www.gefweb.org/>.

for greenhouse gases) and the 2000 Cartagena Protocol on biosafety negotiated under the CBD.[66] As of 2000, the GEF had approved biodiversity projects
amounting to over US$600 million.[67] Such a sum dwarfs the funds available to
CITES, as do the sums being discussed in connection with the Kyoto Protocol.
Pending further negotiations under the Protocol, the Prototype Carbon Fund,
proposed by the World Bank as a closed-end mutual investment fund to which
industrialized countries and the business sector would be expected to contribute, has been set at US$100–120 million. Minimum contributions of US$10
million for public sector and US$5 million for private sector participants have
been proposed.[68]

In contrast with these huge sums available to implement other major MEAs,
assistance for CITES implementation from multilateral funds (other than the
CITES Trust Fund) has been almost non-existent. The only CITES-related
biodiversity conservation project known to have been funded so far by GEF is
a project in Gabon, involving the training of local wildlife conservation officers, the production of an identification manual and development of methods to
allow local communities to monitor changes in wildlife populations with a
view to sustainable management.[69] The need to gain access to GEF funds for
CITES implementation has been recognized for sometime. In response to the
ERM questionnaire sent to CITES parties as part of the study on the effectiveness of the Convention, 95% of replies called for more use to be made of the
GEF for CITES-related activities.[70] But one of the difficulties has been that the
criteria established for the tranche of GEF money reserved for biodiversity
projects favour ecosystem-oriented projects rather than a species approach.[71]
Access is also dependent on a closer working relationship with the CBD. ERM
notes that 'it is hard to see how this could be achieved effectively without some
degree of subordination of CITES to the CBD',[72] but, given the strength of the
CITES regime, this is (hopefully) unlikely.

---

[66] Article 21.3, UNFCCC; Article 39, CBD; Article 28, Cartagena Protocol; Article 11,
Kyoto Protocol.

[67] 'Matrix on Trade Measures Pursuant to Selected MEAs' (see n. 62 above).

[68] Investors would contribute to the Fund on the basis of bilateral 'participation
agreements'. The funds would be reinvested in projects for reducing or offsetting carbon
emissions in developing countries and eastern Europe. In return, investors would receive
carbon offset certificates. See Sand (1999).

[69] See OECD (ch. 1, n. 3 above), p. 41.

[70] See ERM report (ch. 3, n. 106 above), Annex E, Table Q.94.

[71] OECD, p. 40.

[72] ERM report, p. 66.

A number of recent CITES COP recommendations have called for the exploration of access to GEF funds. A COP10 resolution on cooperation with the CBD, still in force, calls on parties to explore opportunities for GEF funding.[73] A subsequent COP11 decision directs the CITES Secretariat, in cooperation with the Secretariat of the CBD, to approach the GEF Secretariat 'to determine which projects for the sustainable management of [CITES-listed species] are eligible for financing from GEF'.[74] Also, as part of the Action Plan to implement the Strategic Vision through 2005, approved at COP11, it is proposed that dialogue be initiated through UNEP to access GEF funding for CITES priorities. UNEP is one of the three implementing agencies of the GEF, along with the UN Development Programme (UNDP) and the World Bank. There is no evidence that these initiatives have born any fruit, or indeed that they have been started. In any case, it must be recognized that occasional multilateral project-based finance is no substitute for a stable and adequate funding mechanism. The Strategic Vision states that 'Present funding barely covers the Convention's primary expenditures... if CITES is to continue to play a major role in species conservation, a more stable flow of financial resources is required'. While the Action Plan calls for the development of new funding mechanisms, no indication is given as to how this might be achieved.[75]

It is clear that far more extensive funding is needed if CITES is to move forward and achieve anywhere near the level of implementation seen for example under the Montreal Protocol. The increase in activities directly related to implementation and enforcement needs since COP11 is encouraging. But it fails to go far enough. A programme to provide technical assistance and sustained capacity-building to developing country parties, aimed in particular at improving national enforcement capacity and national reporting as well as enhancing cooperation among relevant national agencies, and a programme to support regional cooperation initiatives are just some examples of urgent, but under-recognized and underfunded needs which should be classed as priorities. It would be more beneficial overall for the Convention – and for the species whose survival it is supposed to ensure – if the Secretariat were directed to determine the eligibility for GEF funding of cross-cutting projects to build capacity for CITES implementation and enforcement as opposed to yet more

---

[73] CITES Resolution Conf. 10.4 'Cooperation and Synergy With the Convention on Biological Diversity' (1997).

[74] CITES Decision 11.129, 'Regarding Financing the Conservation of Species of Wild Fauna and Flora' (2000).

[75] CITES Decision 11.1, Annex 1 'Strategic Vision through 2005', Goal 7 and Objectives 7.3 and 7.4 (2000).

species-specific projects on sustainable management, and for parties to lobby the GEF to allocate biodiversity funds to CITES. Given the ecosystem approach to GEF biodiversity funding, cross-cutting programmes to improve parties' overall capacity for implementation and enforcement could be more eligible for funding than species-specific proposals.

Under the principle of common but differentiated responsibility of states, developed from the application of equity in international law and expressed in different forms in all recent major MEAs, the main importing countries with the largest consumer markets for wildlife would be expected to bear the burden of increased CITES funding.[76] Ideally, this would be achieved through a dedicated mechanism similar to the Multilateral Fund, with payments linked to import levels and the primary recipients being developing country parties. But the Montreal Protocol is the only MEA to possess its own significant funding mechanism, and in today's political climate such a mechanism under CITES is unlikely to be approved. Access to GEF funds is a more realistic option, but to achieve this a more than tentative exploration on the part of CITES parties and the Secretariat will be needed. As more MEAs are negotiated and come into force, competition for GEF funds will increase. As well as providing financial mechanisms for the Kyoto and Cartagena Protocols, the GEF is expecting to play a role in assisting the Stockholm Convention on persistent organic pollutants. To compete, CITES will need to make its voice heard, something in which NGOs could be instrumental if they chose to be.

---

[76] Principle 7 of the Rio Declaration states the principle of common but differentiated responsibility thus: 'states shall cooperate in a spirit of global partnership to conserve, protect and restore the integrity of the Earth's ecosystem. In view of the different contributions to global environmental degradation, states have common but differentiated responsibilities. The developed countries acknowledge the responsibility that they bear in the international pursuit of sustainable development in view of the pressures their societies place on the global environment and of the technologies and financial resources they command.'

11 Learning from other compliance systems[1]

Reporting and verification in other MEAs

The importance to compliance systems of national reporting and verification, preferably through independent review by experts of the information submitted by parties, cannot be over-emphasized. The more reliable and usable the data, submitted regularly and on time, the more able is the regime to monitor and improve implementation and compliance. Yet, while most MEAs are reliant on self-reporting by parties on the implementation of their commitments, reporting rates vary widely and are often low, sometimes under 50%,[2] while the information is variable in quality and not always reliable. A few of the MEA regimes, in particular the Montreal Protocol, the UNFCCC, the Kyoto Protocol and the Ramsar Convention, have developed methods to improve the quality and/or timeliness of reporting, which provide lessons for CITES. In addition, under the UNFCCC, a system of in-depth review of national data by independent experts has been developed, which will be extended to the Kyoto Protocol when it enters into force. Lessons on reporting and review may also be drawn from the International Labour Organization (discussed below), particularly the usefulness of NGO observations on national reports and the procedure for review by experts followed by public scrutiny.

Montreal Protocol

The Montreal Protocol, which commits parties to reductions and phase-outs in the production and consumption of ozone depleting substances (ODS), has an unusually high reporting rate among MEAs. At the 13th meeting of the parties (MOP) in October 2001, parties were commended for achieving a reporting rate of over 95% for 1999 data (though not all parties had reported by the deadline of

---

[1] This chapter draws heavily on Kal Raustiala, *Reporting and Review Institutions in 10 Multilateral Environmental Agreements* (UNEP, 2001) (hereinafter 'Raustiala'); and Duncan Brack, 'International Environmental Disputes: International Forums for Non-compliance and Dispute Settlement in Environment-related Cases', prepared for UK DETR (March 2001); see <www.riia.org/Research/eep.html> (hereinafter 'Brack (2001a)'). Note that the page numbers for 'Raustiala' refer to an electronic version of the report and may differ in the final printed copy.
[2] Raustiala, p. 27.

30 September 2000). The reporting rate for 2000 data was better; as of 13 October 2001 (13 days past the deadline), 101 out of 175 parties (58%) had submitted data. This relative success in persuading parties to report has been achieved by capacity-building through funding, combined with the threat of losing 'Article 5' status (awarded to developing countries with a consumption of ODS lower than 0.3 kg per capita), and therefore access to funds for non-reporting. At the most recent meeting of the Montreal Protocol Implementation Committee (described below) in July 2002, the Ozone Secretariat reported that a higher percentage of developing countries than non-Article 5 parties were reporting.[3] The key to improving the capacity to comply with reporting requirements was the decision by the Executive Committee of the Multilateral Fund to include institutional strengthening as part of its activities – the aim being to establish dedicated national ozone offices (ozone focal points) in each Article 5 party.[4]

Within three months of becoming a party, and then on an annual basis, all parties must provide statistical data on the production, import and export of ODS controlled by the Protocol. They must also report the amounts used for chemical feedstocks, amounts destroyed, and imports and exports of recycled substances. Parties that are permitted special use of controlled ODS under the essential-use exemption must also report on this use. Reporting requirements vary, depending on the extent to which a party has ratified the amendments to the Protocol (which have added new controlled ODS and phase-out schedules).

Additionally, developing countries operating under Article 5 whose country programmes have been approved by the Executive Committee of the Multilateral Fund must report annually to the Fund on all controlled ODS and on administrative and supportive action in the implementation of their country programmes.[5] In addition to allocating funds to each Article 5 party to create an ozone focal point, the Fund arranges for experts to advise the focal points on data reporting. UNEP has also developed a handbook on data reporting to assist parties. If a country classed as an Article 5 party, and therefore eligible for Multilateral Fund assistance, does not provide its initial report within one year of completion of the country study, it will lose its status and consequently its access to the Fund (a powerful incentive to report); before 1 January 1999 it also risked losing its eligibility for the ten-year

---

[3] Duncan Brack, personal communication (Jul 2002).
[4] Duncan Brack, 'Funding Ozone Protection: The Multilateral Fund of the Montreal Protocol', prepared for the Multilateral Fund Secretariat (2001).
[5] Raustiala, p. 63.

grace period in implementing ODS control measures because of its non-classification as an Article 5 party.[6]

To elicit subsequent reports, the Ozone Secretariat uses persuasion, backed by an unspoken threat that funds will be rescinded if countries do not comply.[7] Since developing countries from the Multilateral Fund and countries with economies in transition from GEF are receiving funds for capacity-building, there is no reason why they should fail to report by the deadline, but some do, and these are considered to be in non-compliance. To date, no funds have actually been withheld from Article 5 parties for non-reporting, though the GEF has withheld funds from the Russian Federation for this reason.[8] The Implementation Committee went as far as deciding to recommend to the MOP that the Democratic Republic of Korea lose its status as an Article 5 party if data were not submitted by 30 September 1998, but since Korea responded before the deadline the Committee's decision was not put into effect.[9]

Ramsar Convention

Another MEA that has achieved unusual success with national reporting is the 1971 Ramsar Convention on Wetlands.[10] In addition to initial data on designated wetlands sites, at each COP parties must submit national reports detailing implementation activities undertaken in the three years since the last COP. About two-thirds of the national reports are on time and complete. With the inauguration of the website, reports were made public, generating additional publicity which has improved their quality. The Ramsar Bureau has also created an interactive electronic form for reports, with the aim of making them easier to prepare and post on the website.

The most interesting aspect of reporting under Ramsar is a new development with the potential to revolutionize national reporting under MEAs. In a move that other secretariats should watch closely, the Ramsar Bureau is seeking to redefine the reporting process as a by-product or natural outcome of a national planning process related to the implementation of the Convention's

---

[6] To create an incentive for developing countries to become parties, 1 Jan 1999 was set as the final date when they could benefit from the 10-year delay in implementing ODS control measures.

[7] Madhava Sarma, former Executive Secretary, Ozone Secretariat, personal communication (1999).

[8] Duncan Brack, personal communication (May 2002).

[9] Implementation Committee Recommendation 20/(f).

[10] Raustiala, pp. 37–40.

substantive commitments. At Ramsar COP7, a resolution was passed inviting parties to adopt national targets for the Ramsar Strategic Plan, and calling for the establishment and maintenance by parties of an ongoing record of implementation for national planning and reporting purposes.[11] Subsequently, the Bureau has produced an innovative national planning tool, containing specific objectives and a set of questions related to implementation. It is also creating an interactive electronic form of the tool. Thus, instead of one-off reporting every three years, primarily for international consumption, there will be a dynamic ongoing framework for strategic planning and action by national governments, which will also fulfil the obligation to report.

The idea that reporting can be redefined as an activity that is helpful in substantive implementation at the national level is potentially of great importance. It should increase the incentives for governments to report fully, accurately and on time by making reporting a directly beneficial activity.

Climate Change Convention and Kyoto Protocol

The UNFCCC contains a comparatively well-developed system of national reporting which has been extended to the 1997 Kyoto Protocol.[12] UNFCCC Annex I parties (developed countries and those with economies in transition) must submit, within six months of entry into force of the Convention and periodically thereafter, a 'national communication' to the COP describing steps taken or planned to implement the UNFCCC. The communications must contain a specific estimate of the effects that policies and measures will have on emissions and removals. Since 1996, Annex I parties have also had to submit to the COP an annual inventory of anthropogenic emissions by sources and removals by sinks, supported by a National Inventory Report with information on national circumstances and methods pertinent to the review and analysis of the inventory.[13] Non-Annex I parties are also required to submit national communications but have up to three years after entry into force to submit the first communication. Least developed country parties can make their initial communication at their discretion.[14]

The UNFCCC Secretariat prepares a compilation and synthesis of national communications, identifying errors, omissions and inconsistencies. Information

---

[11] Resolution VII.27.
[12] Raustiala, p. 77.
[13] Molly Anderson, *Verification of the Kyoto Protocol: Filling in the Detail*, VERTIC Briefing Paper 02/02 (May 2002).
[14] UNFCCC, Article 12.

provided by parties is not challenged. The Annex I reporting process has been underway for several years, while the first compilation and synthesis for non-Annex I parties was prepared in 1999. Compliance with reporting requirements is moderate. For example, by the deadline of April 1998 only four out of 36 Annex I parties had submitted emissions inventories data to the Secretariat for 1990–6. By June 1999 the number had increased to 25, but less than half had submitted their national greenhouse gas inventories that were due in April that year.[15] Data submitted are published on the UNFCCC website.

The Kyoto Protocol, which commits Annex I parties to targets and timetables to reduce greenhouse gas emissions, requires Annex I parties to incorporate in their annual inventories of emissions and removals 'supplemental information' needed to ensure compliance with their emissions targets.[16] They must also incorporate into their national communication 'supplemental information' necessary to demonstrate compliance with their commitments under the Protocol. Detailed guidelines have been prepared on the preparation and submission of inventories and national communications by Annex I parties as part of the Marrakesh Accords, due to be agreed at the first meeting of the parties to the Kyoto Protocol after its entry into force (COP/MOP-1).

The UNFCCC, in addition to self-reporting by parties, employs a system of in-depth reviews (IDRs) carried out by outside experts.[17] Established by a decision of the first Conference of the Parties, the process submits to an in-depth review the national communications of Annex I parties by a review team of experts nominated by parties and international organizations and drawn from a pre-approved roster. Experts are not allowed to participate in review teams for their own country's national communication. The reviews, to be undertaken within a year of the receipt of the national communication by the Secretariat, aim at providing a 'thorough and comprehensive technical assessment of the implementation of the Convention' by individual parties.[18]

The IDR process initially provided for country visits as an option, with the consent of the party concerned; but in practice IDRs have invariably involved

---

[15] Raustiala, p. 78.

[16] Kyoto Protocol, Article 7. For a guide to the Kyoto Protocol provisions, see Michael Grubb, Christiaan Vrolijk and Duncan Brack, *The Kyoto Protocol: A Guide and Assessment* (RIIA/Earthscan, 1999). See also Farhana Yamin, 'The Kyoto Protocol: Origins, Assessment and Future Challenges', *RECIEL*, 7:2 (1998), p. 113.

[17] Raustiala, pp. 77–81.

[18] Decision 2/CP.1, 'Review of First Communications from the Parties Included in Annex I to the Convention'. All documents relating to the climate change regime can be obtained from the website <www.unfccc.de>.

a country visit. Consisting of between three and six persons and coordinated by the UNFCCC Secretariat, the review teams visit the country's capital for usually four to five days near the beginning of the IDR, and meet with relevant government officials, members of the academic and scientific community and business and environmental NGOs. Thus, as with the ILO (see below), an opportunity is provided for NGO input to the reporting process at the review stage. The end product (until review of inventories was separated) was a report produced to a standard format, including, *inter alia,* detailed information on inventories of greenhouse gas emissions and removals, policies and measures, projections of emissions, expected impacts of climate change, and adaptation measures, which is published on the UNFCCC website.[19] At COP4 in 1998, parties decided the review should be separated into two distinct parts: a technical review of inventory information, and a review of non-inventory information in national communications. New reporting and review guidelines were adopted in 1999, as well as a common reporting format. Countries were encouraged to trial the new reporting guidelines for their 2000 and 2001 annual inventory submissions and to volunteer for expert review in accordance with the new review guidelines.[20]

IDRs have provided a sound basis of technical information on which to assess the implementation of the UNFCCC by developed country parties. Their usefulness, and in particular the value of on-site visits, is reflected in a comment from the United States: 'our own domestic preparation for the country visit caused us to re-examine many of the underlying materials that were used in the preparation of the [national] communication. In short, the review process, while still only in its formative stages, clearly serves a valuable purpose.'[21] Nevertheless, it has been questioned whether the full potential of IDRs has been realized. While they standardize reported data, enabling comparability between countries, filling information gaps and increasing transparency, parties appear to pay little attention to the reports at meetings, and NGOs generally pay only limited attention. However, according to Raustiala, private actors have shown greater interest, and a small secondary market in the content of the reports has developed in certain major industrialized countries.[22]

---

[19] Rosalind Reeve, 'Practical Experience with Visiting Mechanisms in International Environmental Law', in *Visits under Public International Law: Theory and Practice, Proceedings of an APT Workshop, 23–24 September 1999* (Association for the Prevention of Torture, Nov 2000).

[20] Anderson (see n. 13 above), p. 2.

[21] FCCC/IDR.1/USA, 'Report on the In-depth Review of the National Communication of the United States of America'.

[22] Raustiala, p. 80.

The true value of the IDR process will probably be realized only through the Kyoto Protocol, which extends the existing process and addresses a shortcoming, namely its inability to identify and communicate to parties problems influencing compliance and potential non-compliance.[23] Under the Kyoto Protocol, the expert review teams are required to prepare a report for the COP/MOP assessing implementation of commitments by each Annex I party and identifying potential problems and factors influencing fulfilment of the commitments. The reports will be circulated to all parties by the Secretariat, which will list 'questions of implementation' identified in the reports for further consideration by the COP/MOP and Compliance Committee (described below). Detailed guidelines have been prepared on the scope, timing and procedures of the expert reviews as part of the Marrakesh Accords for agreement at COP/MOP-1.

Each Annex I party is to be subject to an initial comprehensive review prior to the first commitment period (2008–2112) or within a year of entry into force of the Kyoto Protocol for that party. Expert teams will carry out an in-country visit and review complete inventories for all years as well as national systems and methodologies for estimating emissions and removals, national registries (a form of 'bank' recording the various units issued, transferred or cancelled under the Kyoto flexibility mechanisms), and the first national communication. Thereafter, Annex I parties will be subject to a desk-based or centralized review of annual inventories (among other implementation issues) on an annual basis, with at least one in-country visit in the commitment period, and a periodic in-country review of national communications. If a party's national communication is not submitted within six weeks of the due date, the delay shall be brought to the attention of the COP/MOP and Compliance Committee and made public. Expert review teams will also have a role in reviewing information submitted by parties requesting reinstatement after suspension of their eligibility to use the Kyoto mechanisms (discussed further below).

Non-compliance response in other MEAs

Modern non-compliance procedures operating or being developed under recent MEAs, or 'compliance procedures and mechanisms', as they are referred to under the Kyoto Protocol, have all established (or are proposing to establish) a committee dedicated to compliance issues. While it is recognized that there cannot be a single formula for all regimes, some form of implementation or compliance committee reporting to the main political body, in addition to

---

[23] Kyoto Protocol, Article 8. See also Yamin (n. 16 above), p. 124.

the Secretariat, is now an accepted institutional necessity for regulatory MEAs which commit parties to specific undertakings (as opposed to the CBD with its generalized obligations). This section examines the non-compliance procedures in operation under the Montreal Protocol and Convention on Long-Range Transboundary Air Pollution, as well as the procedures and mechanisms relating to compliance recently agreed under the Kyoto Protocol. Several other MEAs now in force are currently developing non-compliance procedures/compliance mechanisms, including the Basel Convention, the Espoo Convention on environmental impact assessment, and the Aarhus Convention on access to information, public participation and access to justice in environmental matters. Other recently adopted regulatory MEAs that commit parties to developing non-compliance/compliance procedures once they enter into force are the Cartagena Protocol, the Rotterdam Convention on hazardous chemicals and pesticides, and the Stockholm Convention on persistent organic pollutants.[24]

Montreal Protocol

The Montreal Protocol was the first MEA to include explicitly from the start a formal mechanism for handling and identifying cases of non-compliance.[25] The non-compliance procedure (NCP) developed under Article 8 of the Protocol and adopted by decision involves the Secretariat, an Implementation Committee and the MOP.[26]

The Montreal Protocol Implementation Committee is composed of government representatives from ten parties, two members from each of the UN's

---

[24] Article 34, Cartagena Protocol; Article 17, Rotterdam Convention; Article 17, Stockholm Convention.

[25] Article 8, 'Non-compliance', provides that 'Parties, at their first meeting, shall consider and approve procedures and institutional mechanisms for determining non-compliance with the provisions of this Protocol and for treatment of parties found to be in non-compliance.'

[26] The Montreal Protocol non-compliance procedure was adopted by Decision IV/5 and Annexes IV and V of the 4th Meeting of the Parties to the Protocol, UNEP/OzL.Pro.4/15 (25 Nov 1992). It was reviewed in 1998 pursuant to Decision IX/35; see Annex II of the report of the 10th MOP, UNEP/OxL.Pro.10/9, and will be reviewed again in 2002, but any changes will likely be minor since parties seem satisfied with it. See also Raustiala, pp. 64–9; Jacob Werksman, 'Compliance and Transition: Russia's Non-Compliance Tests the Ozone Regime' *Heidelberg Journal of International Law*, 56 (1996), pp. 750–73: 754; and Patrick Széll, 'The Development of Multilateral Mechanisms for Monitoring Compliance' in Winfried Lang (ed.), *Sustainable Development and International Law* (Graham and Trotman, 1995), pp. 97–109: 99.

five geographical regions elected by the MOP for two years. Meetings are also attended by representatives of the Ozone Secretariat, as well as the secretariat, chair, vice chair and implementing agencies (the World Bank, UNEP, UNDP and UNIDO) of the Multilateral Fund, and the GEF. The Committee meets at least twice a year, and, although its meetings are closed, proceedings are available afterwards. It receives reports from the Ozone Secretariat on the status of compliance with the Protocol's phase-out schedules, and other obligations based on reports from the parties themselves. In its report, the Secretariat cites parties that have deviated from control measures under the Protocol where the deviations cannot be explained by factors such as essential use exemptions (as well as cases of previous non-compliance, where the party is meeting the benchmarks for moving back into compliance agreed by meetings of the parties).

Parties potentially in non-compliance are informed that their cases will be considered by the Implementation Committee at its next meeting and requested to attend and explain their situation. The Committee can also consider reports on implementation/non-compliance from parties concerning other parties, or from a party itself. It can review reported government data but cannot verify it unless invited by the party concerned. Parties believed to be in non-compliance are asked to formulate a plan of action, including performance targets or benchmarks, which, once agreed by the MOP, are reviewed by the Implementation Committee in subsequent meetings. The Committee reports its recommendations for specific cases to the MOP, which can 'decide upon and call for steps to bring about full compliance'.[27] An 'indicative list of measures' may be taken by the MOP with respect to a non-compliant party, including 'appropriate assistance', 'issuing cautions' and 'suspension...of specific rights and privileges under the Protocol', which can include those dealing with finance and trade.[28] The Committee's final report is public, but excludes information received in confidence.

The Montreal Protocol NCP is widely considered to have been a success by parties and academic observers.[29] The first cases in 1995 (Belarus, Bulgaria, Poland, the Russian Federation and Ukraine) all made what were treated by the Secretariat as formal submissions of non-compliance (i.e. 'self-accusations'). The Implementation Committee responded by developing compliance plans and subsequent reviews. All five parties eventually moved towards compliance. Important to the success of the process was a decision by the GEF to

---

[27] NCP, para. 9.

[28] Decision IV/5 and Annex V of the Report of the 4th Meeting of the Parties.

[29] Raustiala; Jacob Werksman, 'Responding to Non-Compliance under the Climate Change Regime', draft OECD Information Paper on file with author (1998).

withhold additional funds for new ozone-related projects in parties involved in the NCP until their compliance plans were approved by the Implementation Committee. The Committee worked out individual plans with each country and the GEF funds were then distributed in tranches, the release of funds being dependent on a positive report from the Implementation Committee. In the case of the Russian Federation, the most serious non-complying party (and the only producer), a World Bank special initiative mobilized additional funding to ensure production sector phase-out for chlorofluorocarbons (CFCs) and halons, which was achieved by the end of 2000, four years later than its obligation under the Protocol. Nine more former planned economies (Azerbaijan, Czech Republic, Estonia, Latvia, Lithuania, Kazakhstan, Tajikistan, Turkmenistan and Uzbekistan) have since been placed before the Implementation Committee by the Secretariat and treated similarly.[30]

The main objective of the NCP is to create a multilateral, non-confrontational and discursive process. In this it appears to have been singularly successful. Every non-compliant country identified so far is moving back into compliance with 'relatively few diplomatic feathers ruffled along the way (despite a walkout by the Russian delegation of the 1995 meeting of the parties)'.[31] But until recently the procedure has not had to deal with non-compliance on the part of developing-country parties operating under Article 5 of the Protocol, a test the regime is only just beginning to meet as their obligations to phase out ODS come into effect. ODS control measures for Article 5 parties began on 1 July 1999 with a freeze on production and consumption of CFCs at the end of a ten-year grace period. At the 13th MOP in October 2001, five Article 5 parties were found to be in non-compliance with their control measures (Argentina, Belize, Cameroon, Ethiopia and Peru) and asked to submit a plan of action with time-specific benchmarks to return to compliance.[32] A further 15 Article 5 parties (Bangladesh, Chad, Comoros, Dominican Republic, Honduras, Kenya, Mongolia, Morocco, Niger, Nigeria, Oman, Papua New Guinea, Paraguay, Samoa and Solomon Islands) were presumed to be in non-compliance on the basis of their reporting but had not responded to the Secretariat's request for data. They were cautioned that parties would consider measures if they failed to return to compliance in a timely manner (as are all parties found to be in non-compliance) and a decision was taken to 'closely monitor' their progress.[33]

---

[30] Brack (2001a), p. 15, and personal communication; Report of the 13th Meeting of the Parties to the Montreal Protocol, UNEP/OzL.Pro.13/10 (Oct 2001).

[31] Brack (2001a), p. 15.

[32] Decisions XIII/21, XIII/22, XIII/23, XIII/24 and XIII/25.

[33] Decision XIII/16.

Reasons given by parties for their lack of compliance were the low price of CFCs on the world markets, making industry reluctant to convert to alternatives, and unanticipated delays in preparing projects for the Multilateral Fund or in their approval, or in the disbursement of funding by the implementing agencies.

It was anticipated that the response of these non-compliant Article 5 parties to MOP recommendations would provide the most exacting test of the NCP to date. So far the procedure has stood up well. At the July 2002 meeting of the Implementation Committee data showed that a majority of the Article 5 parties listed in 2001 had moved back into compliance.[34]

LRTAP Convention

The compliance system devised under the 1979 Convention on Long-Range Transboundary Air Pollution (LRTAP Convention) largely follows the Montreal Protocol NCP. It involves the Secretariat reporting to an Implementation Committee, established in December 1997, which in turn reports to the Executive Body of parties, which may decide action to bring about compliance. Initially, the Implementation Committee was established under Article 7.3 of the Protocol on Further Reduction of Sulphur Emissions (the Second Sulphur Protocol) by a decision of the Executive Body setting out its structure and functions. Shortly afterwards, however, the Executive Body decided to expand the remit of the Implementation Committee to all the Protocols under the Convention addressing different types of emissions. Since the Protocols treated compliance in different ways, however, various legal bases were needed to apply a single compliance system, which was eventually established with a further Executive Body decision. The first two cases to be considered by the Implementation Committee were Slovenia, concerning problems over compliance with the Second Sulphur Protocol, and Norway, relating to compliance with the VOC (Volatile Organic Compounds) Protocol. Both cases arose from self-notification of the problems and requests for advice on how to deal with them, in part deliberately to assist the non-compliance system to evolve and develop.[35]

---

[34] Duncan Brack, personal communication (Jul 2002).

[35] Széll (see n. 26 above); update by personal communication from Patrick Széll, Mar 2001. For the LRTAP compliance system, see EB Decision 1897/2, Annex 3, Report of the Fifteenth Session of the EB, Doc. ECE/EB.AIR/53.

Box 11.1: Article 18 of the Kyoto Protocol

The Conference of the Parties serving as the meeting of the Parties to this Protocol shall, at its first session, approve appropriate and effective procedures and mechanisms to determine and to address cases of non-compliance with the provisions of this Protocol, including through the development of an indicative list of consequences, taking into account the cause, type, degree and frequency of non-compliance. Any procedures and mechanisms under this Article entailing binding consequences shall be adopted by means of an amendment to this Protocol.

Kyoto Protocol

A great deal of work has gone into the formulation of a compliance mechanism under the Kyoto Protocol. The work has been conducted through the Joint Working Group on Compliance, established in November 1998 as part of the Buenos Aires Plan of Action. Aiming for completion at the sixth conference of the parties to the Climate Change Convention (COP6) in November 2000, the Plan set out a schedule for reaching agreement on the operational details of the Kyoto Protocol, including a mechanism to promote compliance and deal with cases of non-compliance as provided for by Article 18 (see Box 11.1).

It was anticipated even before serious negotiations began that a system responding to non-compliance under the Kyoto Protocol would need to be strong and comprehensive, not least because of the complex issues to be solved and the complexity of parties' obligations.[36] For this reason, the Montreal Protocol NCP has provided only a partial model, although a common element that observers agreed on was the need for some kind of standing implementation committee separate from the COP, with limited membership, to deal with questions of non-compliance.[37]

At COP6 in The Hague in November 2000, talks on the Kyoto Protocol collapsed as parties failed to reach agreement on operational details, with compliance presenting one of several obstacles. Differences were apparent

---

[36] Jacob Werksman, 'Responding to Non-Compliance under the Climate Change Regime', Information Paper for the OECD on file with author (1998).
[37] Jacob Werksman, 'Designing a Compliance System for the UN Framework Convention on Climate Change', in James Cameron, Jacob Werksman and Peter Roderick (eds), *Improving Compliance with International Environmental Law* (Earthscan, 1996), pp. 85–147: 104; Hermann E. Ott, 'Elements of a Supervisory Procedure for the Climate Regime', *Heidelberg Journal of International Law*, 56/3 (1996), pp. 732–49: 746.

between countries favouring a strong mechanism, with penalties for failure to meet targets in reducing emissions, and those less keen on legally binding consequences.[38] Negotiations were suspended and resumed at COP6 Part II in Bonn in July 2001. In the meantime, the United States announced in March 2001 that it would not implement the 'fatally flawed' Kyoto Protocol. The decision had the effect of uniting most of the world in opposition to the US attitude and strengthening parties' determination to reach agreement – which they did.

The Bonn Agreements included a package of draft decisions which were forwarded to COP7 in Marrakesh in October/November 2001. Some of the texts remained to be finalized, one being the draft decision on compliance, which turned out to be the most challenging issue on which to reach agreement. Legally binding consequences were still a source of controversy, with the European Union and many developing countries supporting a strong regime and Umbrella Group countries (comprising most non-EU OECD countries plus Russia and Ukraine) attempting to weaken it. Japan and Russia in particular used their negotiating power towards this end (a power strengthened by the need for their participation in the Protocol to enable it to enter into force following the US withdrawal).

The final agreement on compliance steered a course between the two positions by deferring to the first meeting of the parties after entry into force (COP/MOP-1) a decision on whether the consequences for parties in non-compliance were legally binding. The compromise text notes in a preambular paragraph that 'it is the prerogative of the Conference of the Parties serving as the meeting of the parties of the Kyoto Protocol to decide on the legal form of the procedures and mechanisms relating to compliance'.[39] If the COP/MOP decides to makes the consequences legally binding, an amendment of the Protocol would be required (see Box 11.1).

Despite the compromise, the mechanism agreed in Marrakesh is still the strongest of any multilateral environmental agreement.[40] At the centre of the

---

[38] On the negotiations, see Christiaan Vrolijk, *A New Interpretation of the Kyoto Protocol: Outcomes from The Hague, Bonn and Marrakesh*, RIIA Briefing Paper (Apr 2002), <www.riia.org/Research>; Michael Grubb and Farhana Yamin, 'Climate Collapse at The Hague: What Happened, Why and Where Do We Go From Here?', *International Affairs*, 77:2 (Apr 2001), pp. 261–76; 'Summary of the Seventh Conference of the Parties to the UN Framework Convention on Climate Change: 29 Oct–10 Nov 2001', *Earth Negotiations Bulletin* (12 Nov 2001), <www.iisd.ca/climate/cop7/>.

[39] Decision 24/CP.7, 'Procedures and Mechanisms Relating to Compliance under the Kyoto Protocol'.

[40] For details of the Kyoto Protocol compliance mechanism, see Annex to Decision 24/CP.7 in the Marrakesh Accords.

mechanism is a 20-person Compliance Committee consisting of two branches: a facilitative branch and an enforcement branch. In essence, the facilitative branch promotes compliance while the enforcement branch deals with cases of non-compliance. The Compliance Committee reports on its activities to the COP/MOP. Members are to be experts serving in their individual capacities. Each branch will be composed of a member from each of the five UN regional groups, one from the small island developing states, two from Annex I parties and two from non-Annex I parties. Members of the enforcement branch are to have legal experience.

The *facilitative branch* will provide advice and facilitation to parties in implementing the Protocol and promoting compliance, taking into account the principle of common but differentiated responsibilities. It will address questions of implementation relating to Article 3.14 (minimizing adverse impacts on developing countries) and supplementarity (that the Kyoto mechanisms – emissions trading, joint implementation and the clean development mechanism – be supplemental to domestic measures). With the aim of promoting compliance and providing an early warning system for potential non-compliance, it will also provide advice and facilitation on emissions targets (assigned amounts which should not be exceeded), national systems and methodologies for estimating greenhouse gas emissions and removals, and submission of annual inventories. The 'consequences' that can be applied by the facilitative branch are limited to advice, financial and technical assistance, including technology transfer and capacity-building, and formulation of recommendations to the party concerned.

The *enforcement branch* is more judicial in nature. It will determine:

- compliance with emissions targets;
- compliance with requirements for annual inventories, and national systems and methodologies;
- a party's eligibility to use the Kyoto mechanisms.

The consequences of non-compliance differ in the three types of case. In cases of non-compliance in relation to annual inventories, national systems and methodologies, the enforcement branch will make a declaration of non-compliance, and will require submission of a compliance action plan within three months of the non-compliance determination. The compliance plan must include an analysis of the causes of non-compliance, measures to be implemented and a timetable for implementation not exceeding 12 months. Regular progress reports on implementation of the plan are to be submitted to the enforcement branch.

If the enforcement branch determines that an Annex I party fails to meet the eligibility requirements to use the Kyoto mechanisms, which include submission of an annual inventory, it shall suspend the eligibility. A party may submit a request to reinstate its eligibility, either through an expert review team or directly to the enforcement branch. The enforcement branch then decides through an expedited procedure on whether eligibility can be reinstated.

The consequences of a determination that emissions targets have been exceeded are:

• deduction from the party's assigned amount for the next commitment period of a number of tonnes equal to 1.3 times the amount of excess emissions (i.e. compensation for excess emissions at a penalty rate of 30%);
• submission within three months of a compliance action plan designed to meet the emissions target in the next commitment period, giving priority to domestic measures;
• suspension of eligibility to participate in emissions trading.

Annual progress reports on implementation of the compliance action plan to meet the emissions target (which cannot exceed three years or the end of the next commitment period) are to be submitted to the enforcement branch.

The compliance mechanism can be triggered in three ways: through 'questions of implementation', identified by the Secretariat from expert review team reports; by any party with respect to itself; and by any party with respect to another party. There are detailed procedures and timetables for handling cases. Except for 'self-accusations', each branch is required to undertake a preliminary examination to ensure that the case is supported by sufficient information, is not trivial or ill-founded, and is based on the Protocol's requirements. Parties are entitled to request hearings of cases under the enforcement branch, and a timetable is laid down for submissions, the hearing and the decision, which must include conclusions and reasons. Final decisions, and decisions not to proceed after a preliminary examination, shall be publicly available. Enforcement branch hearings shall be held in public, and information considered by either branch shall be made public, unless decided otherwise by the relevant branch.

Parties may appeal within 45 days to the COP/MOP against decisions of the enforcement branch relating to emissions targets. A three-quarters majority is needed to override a decision, in which case the matter will be referred back to the enforcement branch. Enforcement branch decisions shall stand pending the appeal, and become definitive if within 45 days no appeal has been made.

International Labour Organization[41]

The International Labour Organization (ILO) is a specialized agency of the United Nations that administers roughly 180 labour-related treaties, ranging from bans on white lead paint and other occupational health hazards, to workplace protection from air pollution, radiation and toxic chemicals. It was founded in 1919, primarily to improve living and working conditions by building a comprehensive international labour code. A cornerstone of its activity is a unique system of supervision of the implementation of ILO standards, which has evolved over eight decades. By far the oldest compliance system managed by international organizations, according to commentators it has proved extremely effective and provides lessons for MEAs.[42]

Institutionally, the ILO consists of a yearly plenary assembly (the International Labour Conference), a Governing Body and a permanent secretariat (the International Labour Office). It is characterized by a unique tripartite structure of government, labour and employer representatives. Workers and employers are part of national delegations to the International Labour Conference and are also represented as members of the Governing Body. Compliance issues are examined by two tiers of institutions: first by relatively small technical bodies, and then by the larger political organs. There are essentially two types of procedure: a regular procedure, which routinely reviews implementation of ILO standards, and a series of ad hoc procedures, which can be triggered on an adversarial basis to consider alleged cases of non-compliance.

National reporting and regular review

The *regular procedure* involves a review of national reports by an independent technical body, the Committee of Experts on the Application of Conventions and Recommendations, in a closed session. The Committee of Experts is composed of 20 members who meet annually in their personal capacities to undertake an independent and technical evaluation of the reports and the degree to which national legislation and practices conform to international obligations. The

---

[41] Information on the ILO has been taken mostly from Cesare Romano, *The ILO System of Supervision and Compliance Control: A Review and Lessons for Multilateral Environmental Agreements* (International Institute for Applied Systems Analysis, 1996) (hereinafter 'Romano').

[42] Romano; Peter H. Sand, *Lessons Learned in Global Environmental Governance* (World Resources Institute, 1990), p. 33, citing E. A. Landy, *The Effectiveness of International Supervision: Thirty Years of ILO Experience'* (Stevens & Sons, 1966) which documents ILO case histories.

absence of publicity and observers has apparently depoliticized this regular review and enhanced the Committee's reputation for objectivity and competence. The reports, as a general rule, are due every five years. Copies are sent by governments to national organizations of employers and workers, who may submit observations on the reports to the Committee of Experts (which they frequently do). The involvement of non-state actors in the reporting process at this stage is considered valuable. It gives them an opportunity to report on aspects of implementation that governments may choose to omit, and enhances the overall credibility of the data-gathering process.

The Experts' report is then considered by the Conference Committee on the Application of Conventions, a tripartite political body that receives parties' observations. A new report is submitted to the plenary Conference, singling out states with particular implementation problems. The Conference Committee comprises some 200 members, and its procedure is public. It provides a forum for the discussion of problems with implementation and exposes the debate to public scrutiny. States have on occasions reacted strongly to being singled out in Conference Committee reports. The United States even withdrew from the ILO for three years. The ability of the review system to withstand such strong political opposition has been attributed to the credibility of the Committee of Experts' and its firm reputation.[43]

Ad hoc non-compliance procedures

The ILO's four adversarial ad hoc procedures were developed to deal with non-compliance. They can be initiated by a member state or by a workers' or employers' association, and in three of the four procedures involve intermediary recommendatory bodies, which report to the Governing Body.

Representation procedure   The representation procedure is a 'soft' and strictly political procedure. In effect, it represents 'a preliminary but not legally necessary step' in the ILO supervisory system.[44] Employers' and workers' associations can make a representation to the International Labour Office concerning a member's compliance with one of the ILO conventions. The Governing Body then sets up an Examining Committee if it considers the representation receivable. The Committee – a political body composed of Governing Body members – meets in private and reports to the Governing

---

[43] Romano, p. 8.
[44] Romano, pp. 10–11.

Body with recommendations. The final outcome is publication of the representation and any reply from the government concerned. From 1985 to 1995, about thirty cases reached the Governing Body under this procedure.

Complaints procedure   The quasi-judicial complaints procedure is more intrusive. It deals with formal complaints of alleged breaches of ILO conventions. A complaint may be filed with the International Labour Office by any member against any other member, as long as they have both ratified the convention concerned. Alternatively, the procedure can be triggered by the Governing Body, or by a delegate to the Conference in his or her personal capacity. The Governing Body then consults with the government concerned, and may set up a Commission of Inquiry composed of three members, usually judges sitting in their personal capacities. In some cases Commissions of Inquiry have carried out on-site visits, during which they are not accompanied by government representatives. The Commission of Inquiry considers the case in camera and reports to the Governing Body, which may recommend action to the Conference if a member state fails to implement its recommendations. The Commission's reports are published. If its conclusions are rejected by a state, the state can refer the complaint to the International Court of Justice (ICJ), whose decision is final. Between 1960 and 1995 more than twenty complaints were filed; nine were submitted to a Commission of Inquiry; and none was referred to the ICJ. In most cases, the governments concerned accepted the Commission's report.

Freedom of association procedure   The special procedure established to examine complaints concerning freedom of association is the most frequently used of the ad hoc procedures. It can be made against states that have not ratified the relevant conventions, and can be triggered by a member state (against itself or another member), a workers' or employers' organization or the International Labour Conference. A nine-member tripartite Governing Body Committee on Freedom of Association, meeting in private, analyses the receivability of a complaint and reports to the Governing Body, which can refer the case to the Fact-Finding and Conciliation Commission, composed of nine independent experts appointed by the Governing Body. The Commission then reports back to the Governing Body with recommendations. By 1995 the Committee on the Freedom of Association had examined more than 1,800 cases, six of which had been referred to the Commission. Many of the cases related to the imprisonment of trade unionists.

A fourth ad hoc procedure enables the ILO Director General to undertake special studies on discrimination in employment. But it is rarely used, probably because a study can be carried out only if the government concerned agrees to it.

Effectiveness of the ILO compliance system

The ILO was awarded the Nobel Peace Prize in 1969 in recognition of its achievements in the protection of human rights. A large part of its achievement is considered to be due to its compliance system, the backbone of which is the regular review procedure. Between 1964, when the Committee of Experts began to monitor members' responses, and 1995, the ILO's supervisory bodies registered 2,107 cases of progress, i.e. where national legislation and practice were changed to meet the requirements of a ratified convention, following supervisory body reports.

Several features contribute to the effectiveness of the ILO compliance system. One is the benefit of small, specialized bodies to review compliance as opposed to an open-ended membership. Another is the division of functions between the technical Committee of Experts, composed of individuals chosen on the basis of their competence, and the political Conference Committee, which achieves a balance in the treatment of cases. Last, but far from least, is the key role played by non-state actors. They can initiate all ad hoc procedures and participate in all major ILO committees. In practice, most cases have been triggered by non-state actors, and it is these that have submitted the majority of observations under the regular review procedure. Without their involvement, the system would probably be virtually obsolete.

North American Agreement on Environmental Cooperation[45]

The North American Agreement on Environmental Cooperation (NAAEC), one of two NAFTA side accords (the other being on labour), is focused primarily on promoting environmental cooperation in North America and on ensuring that domestic environmental laws are properly enforced. To this end, it employs an innovative approach to induce compliance. Any citizen in a NAFTA party can submit a complaint to the Commission for Environmental Cooperation (CEC) alleging that a party is 'failing to effectively enforce its [domestic] en-

---

[45] Information on the NAAEC has been taken from Raustiala, pp. 99–101.

vironmental law'.[46] The CEC Secretariat first determines if a submission meets admissibility criteria; if so, it requests a response from the party concerned. Then, in conjunction with the CEC Council, it decides whether to investigate the claim further. Composed of environment ministers from the three parties, the Council can approve an investigation by majority vote. The results of the investigation, known as a *factual record*, can be made public by a two-thirds vote of the Council.

Between 1994 and April 2002, 33 citizen submissions were brought concerning a whole range of issues, including an abandoned lead smelter in Mexico, the spotted owl in the United States, noise pollution by Mexico City Airport, water resource protection in California, mining in British Columbia and a hazardous waste landfill in Mexico.[47] Most were brought by environment and conservation NGOs, while a few involved individual citizens. Fourteen of the submissions were against Mexico (42%), 11 were against Canada (33%) and eight were against the United States (24%). The outcome of the 33 submissions, as of 24 April 2002, was as follows:

- Nine cases had led or were leading to a factual record (four against Canada, four against Mexico and one against the US);
- One case (against Mexico) was awaiting a decision of the Council as to whether it would approve the CEC Secretariat's recommendation for a factual record;
- Four cases were under review by the CEC Secretariat (three against Mexico and one against Canada);
- Nineteen cases were terminated for various reasons (in a case against Canada, the Secretariat recommended a factual record but the Council decided against it).

Thus, over eight years since 1994, 27% of citizen submissions have led, or were leading, to an investigation and factual record. This compares with 10% of submissions as of March 2001, indicating a marked increase in the success rate.

A similar procedure, but with a higher legal standard, can be triggered by a NAFTA party in cases of a 'persistent pattern of failure to effectively enforce domestic environmental law'. If diplomatic efforts cannot resolve the problem, the Council may convene an arbitral panel, which, if it agrees with the allegation, can propose a plan of action together with the parties involved. If

---

[46] NAAEC Article 14.
[47] See CEC website at <www.cec.org>.

the complaining party believes that the plan of action is not being implemented adequately, a monetary penalty may be imposed. The penalty is paid to the CEC, which must use it to improve environmental enforcement in the losing party. Further non-implementation by the losing party can lead to trade sanctions. To date this process has not been triggered.

The NAAEC Secretariat also has substantial powers to review party performance. On an annual basis, it prepares a report on actions taken by each party in connection with its obligations under the NAAEC, 'including data on the party's environmental enforcement activities'.[48] The Secretariat can also initiate an investigation into, and prepare a report on, any matter related to the NAAEC, unless two-thirds of the parties object.

---

[48] NAAEC Article 12.

12 Relationship with the WTO

CITES has not been deterred in its use of trade sanctions by the establishment of the World Trade Organization (WTO) in 1995 and the concurrent strengthening of the multilateral trading system (MTS). If anything, use of this non-compliance response tool has increased in recent years, despite speculation that such measures may conflict directly with the provisions of the General Agreement on Tariffs and Trade (GATT). This chapter examines the potential for conflict in light of the trade and environment debate, evolving GATT/WTO case law, and the Doha Ministerial Declaration mandating negotiations on the relationship between MEAs and the MTS.

Interface between the multilateral trading system and the environment

Policy areas for international trade and environmental protection operate within discrete regimes, each a subset of the international legal order. They differ fundamentally in the manner of their construction, the language of obligation and the means available for effecting compliance. Yet, the two regimes are inherently connected. Practical aspects of the interface can be seen in everyday issues. Barriers to markets are created by numerous measures for environmental protection, such as regulations on pesticide residues in food, the use of recyclable boxes for the sale of cut flowers, the manner in which fish and animals are caught or trapped, eco-labelling of products, trade in ODS or hazardous waste and, last but not least, trade in endangered species. At the Rio Conference on Environment and Development in 1992, there was a political consensus that many environmental problems are bound up with issues surrounding international trade law and its regulatory structure. One of the objectives of the Rio Principles was to make the regimes regulating trade and environment mutually supportive. Ten years later, although the interrelationship between the MTS and environment has become increasingly important – and controversial – this is far from being achieved.

The signing in 1994 of the Marrakesh Agreement Establishing the World Trade Organization marked the completion of the Uruguay Round of trade negotiations lasting eight years. It also marked a significant extension in the scope of the MTS through the adoption of a set of agreements administered by the WTO, which are centred around the GATT and cover areas such as agriculture, textiles, services, intellectual property, technical barriers to trade, health standards and dispute settlement.

To date, the trade and environment debate has been shaped largely by jurisprudence emerging from the GATT/WTO dispute settlement system. The Uruguay Round did not include in its negotiations the relationship between international trade and environment. Instead, trade ministers in Marrakesh agreed to establish a WTO Committee on Trade and Environment (CTE), mandated to identify relationships between trade and environment measures and to make recommendations on whether any modifications to the MTS were required.[1] After two years of negotiations from 1994 to 1996, the CTE failed to agree recommendations on the need for any modifications; and until the Doha Ministerial Conference in November 2001, when it was instructed to begin trade and environment negotiations (discussed further below), it settled merely for an analytical role. In the vacuum that resulted, conclusions on WTO policy relating to the environment have had to be drawn from GATT/WTO case law.

The adoption of the Dispute Settlement Understanding (DSU) as part of the package of WTO agreements in effect 'legalized' the dispute settlement procedure, which operated more or less informally prior to 1994. It also strengthened the MTS considerably, through:

- the establishment of new institutions, including a Dispute Settlement Body (DSB) and a standing Appellate Body;
- the introduction of reverse consensus for the adoption of dispute panel and Appellate Body reports, which means that reports almost always become binding[2];
- a provision enabling the DSB to authorize withdrawal of trade concessions by the party whose complaint has been upheld from the party in breach.

This swift rule-based mechanism, backed by sanctions and envied by environmental policy-makers, has shaped the trade and environment debate on a case-by-case basis.

Before considering these cases and the relationship between MEAs and the MTS, in particular whether CITES trade suspensions would be considered

---

[1] The Marrakesh Ministerial Decision on Trade and Environment (WTO, 14 Apr 1994).

[2] Under the pre-WTO dispute settlement procedure, consensus was required to adopt panel reports. The losing party could therefore veto their adoption. Under the DSU, a consensus is required to reject reports.

WTO-compatible, it is necessary first to examine the relevant GATT provisions.

The aim of the MTS is to liberalize trade between WTO members. Its core principles and provisions are to be found in the following articles of the GATT:

- *GATT Articles I ('General Most-Favoured Nation Treatment') and III ('National Treatment on Internal Taxation and Regulation')* prohibit discrimination in trade:
  - Article I requires WTO members to grant every other member the most favourable treatment it grants to any country with respect to imports and exports of 'like products'; i.e., WTO members may not discriminate between 'like products' produced and traded by other members;
  - *Article III* requires imported and domestic 'like products' to be treated identically with respect to internal taxes and regulations;
- *GATT Article XI ('General Elimination of Quantitative Restrictions')* prohibits any restrictions other than duties, taxes or other charges on imports from and exports to other WTO members, including quotas, import or export licences or other measures.

Thus, WTO members are not permitted to discriminate between other WTO members' traded products, or between domestic and international production, and are obliged to eliminate all restrictions other than tariffs. Successive trade negotiating rounds have both reduced tariff and non-tariff barriers to trade and extended the core GATT principles to ever wider ranges of traded goods and services – so that essentially the same principles are built into all the other WTO agreements that have developed alongside the GATT.

There are, however, ten *general exceptions* to GATT obligations outlined in Article XX, which under particular circumstances permit trade restrictions for various reasons, including the pursuit of environmental protection. The relevant provisions of Article XX state that:

> Subject to the requirement that such measures are not applied in a manner which would constitute a means of arbitrary or unjustifiable discrimination between countries where the same conditions prevail, or a disguised restriction on international trade, nothing in this Agreement shall be construed to prevent the adoption or enforcement by any contracting party of measures:
>
> ...
>
> (b) necessary to protect human, animal or plant life or health;
>
> ...

(g) relating to the conservation of exhaustible natural resources if such measures are made effective in conjunction with restrictions on domestic production or consumption.

WTO members wanting to apply trade restrictions for environmental purposes can therefore argue that their actions are justified under Article XX. In general, however, Article XX has been construed narrowly. Until the case brought by Canada against the EC over a French ban on imports of asbestos and products containing asbestos, every unilaterally imposed trade-related environment measure (TREM) that had been challenged under the GATT/WTO failed to pass the tests set by the panels and Appellate Body in their interpretation of Article XX.[3] In seven out of nine cases, the environmental measures in question were found not to be justifiable, either because:

- the measures were not 'necessary' (Article XX(b)) to the achievement of the environmental goal, because the panel believed that there were less trade-restrictive or GATT-inconsistent measures available; or because
- the measures were not 'relating to the conservation of exhaustible natural resources' (Article XX(g)), because the policies in question were extra-jurisdictional; i.e., they attempted to modify the behaviour of other WTO members and could not therefore be considered as being aimed primarily at conserving the natural resources of the country applying the trade measures; or because
- the measures represented 'arbitrary or unjustifiable discrimination' (Article XX chapeau), either because there were less discriminatory methods available that could have been employed, or because they were applied in a discriminatory way.

---

[3] Nine dispute panel findings are generally considered to be the main trade–environment cases, though others are also relevant: *US – Restrictions on Imports of Tuna (1991); US – Restrictions on Imports of Tuna (1994); US – Taxes on Automobiles (CAFE case) (1994); US – Standards for Reformulated and Conventional Gasoline (1996); EC – Measures Concerning Meat and Meat Products (Beef Hormones) (1998); US – Import Prohibition of Certain Shrimp and Shrimp Products (Shrimp–Turtle) (1998); Australia – Measures Affecting Importation of Salmon (1998); EC – Measures Affecting Asbestos and Asbestos-Containing Products (2000); US – Import Prohibition of Certain Shrimp and Shrimp Products (Shrimp–Turtle) (2001).* The first three cases were GATT panel findings not adopted by the GATT Council; although the panel reports have no legal status, they tend to provide precedents. The others were WTO panel findings, all referred to the Appellate Body. See <www.wto.org> for reports.

In contrast with the narrow interpretation of Article XX, the term 'like products', which is not defined in the GATT, has been interpreted broadly, with negative consequences for TREMs. The interpretation of 'like products' has become one of the most difficult issues in the trade and environment debate. Panels have allowed differences in intrinsic characteristics and end use to distinguish products but have excluded differences in process and production methods (PPMs).[4] Since PPMs are frequently a greater source of damage to the environment than the products themselves, environmental policy-makers have argued strongly for their recognition as distinguishing characteristics; examples of PPMs include polluting methods of production, and fishing techniques involving an unacceptable incidental catch of other species. Others argue for their recognition on the basis of unfair competition from countries seen as pollution havens for their lax environmental standards and poor working conditions. But trade policy-makers have argued equally strongly (and more successfully) for the exclusion of PPMs on the basis that ad hoc dispute panels would be delegated extraordinary discretion in deciding which were acceptable, opening the door to unacceptable abuses of trade rules. They also argue, along with developing countries, that enforcing similar PPMs in different countries could deny the very basis of competitive advantage, and in any case would be inappropriate, since different countries have different assimilative capacities.[5]

WTO dispute cases related to trade and environment, all of which have been referred to the Appellate Body, show a trend towards increasing acceptance of TREMs under certain circumstances, and even PPMs. The arguments of the Appellate Body (which consists of international lawyers) have proved more sophisticated than the somewhat erratic GATT/WTO panels (consisting of trade specialists), integrating environmental principles and principles of public international law more fully than in pre-WTO cases handled solely by GATT panels. A gradual modification of the approach to TREMs is evident, culminating in the first endorsement of their use by the Appellate Body in the 2001 *US shrimp–*

---

[4] Some PPMs directly related to the characteristics of products are covered by the Agreement on Technical Barriers to Trade (TBT Agreement) and the Agreement on the Application of Sanitary and Phytosanitary Measures (SPS Agreement), e.g. pesticide use on food crops, cattle raised on growth hormones. WTO members may regulate such PPMs within the disciplines of these agreements.

[5] Thomas J. Schoenbaum, 'International Trade and Protection of the Environment: The Continuing Search for Reconciliation', *American Journal of International Law*, 91 (1997), p. 288; Duncan Brack, *Trade and Environment after Seattle*, RIIA Briefing Paper (Mar 2000).

turtle case. Opinions in recent cases have significant implications for future use of both TREMs and PPMs on a unilateral basis, and, as will be argued below, MEAs.

In the 1996 *US gasoline standards* case, the first dispute referred to the Appellate Body under the DSU, the Appellate Body overturned key aspects of the panel's original arguments, redefining the tests for Article XX(g). The US measures were found to qualify under Article XX(g) as legitimate environmental policy measures, but ultimately failed the requirements of the chapeau because the United States had failed to consult with affected states to resolve the potential *inequitable application* of the baseline emission standards, amounting to unjustifiable discrimination and a disguised restriction on trade.[6]

The Appellate Body used a similar argument in the 1998 *US shrimp–turtle* case. In overturning the panel's reasoning, it found that US measures banning shrimp imports from countries not certified as having enforced mandatory use of turtle excluder devices (TEDs) on shrimp trawlers fell within Article XX(g) but failed the chapeau's provisions because the *way in which they were applied* amounted to unjustifiable and arbitrary discrimination. While the United States had negotiated a multilateral agreement with countries in the Caribbean/western Atlantic region and given them a three-year phase-in time to fit TEDs, no serious efforts had been made to negotiate similar agreements with other countries, who were given a phase-in period of only four months.[7] In response to the finding, the United States changed its shrimp import policy from country-by-country certification to shipment-by-shipment certification. A challenge by Malaysia failed when the Appellate Body upheld a compliance panel decision that the US measures were justified under Article XX in light of good faith efforts by the United States to negotiate with Indian Ocean and Southeast Asian states on a sea turtle protection agreement, as well as the additional flexibility provided by the revised certification scheme.[8]

The final *shrimp–turtle* ruling, the first to endorse a TREM that distinguishes between physically identical products on the basis of an environmentally harmful

---

[6] James Cameron and Karen Campbell, 'Challenging the Boundaries of the DSU through Trade and Environment Disputes', in James Cameron and Karen Campbell (ed.), *Dispute Resolution in the World Trade Organization* (Cameron May, 1998).

[7] Duncan Brack, 'The US Shrimp–Turtle Case: Implications for the Multilateral Environmental Agreement – World Trade Organization Debate', *Yearbook of International Environmental Law*, 9, (1998) (Oxford University Press, 2000).

[8] *US shrimp–turtle*, Appellate Body report (compliance review), WT/DS58/AB/RW (22 Oct 2001); *Bridges Weekly Trade Digest*, 5:19 (22 May 2001), and 5:36 (23 Oct 2001), <www.ictsd.org>.

PPM, is a landmark case, and of particular relevance to the debate around MEAs and the WTO (see further below). But some WTO members have already criticized the result, claiming the Appellate Body overstepped its mandate by allowing the TREM to stand.

In between the two rulings by the Appellate Body in the *shrimp–turtle* case was another significant case influencing the trade and environment debate – the 2000 *EC asbestos* dispute. This case is notable as being the first time a dispute panel has found that a trade restriction can be justified by GATT Article XX(b), in this instance because of the health risks of exposure to asbestos fibres, which are potentially carcinogenic. The Appellate Body upheld the decision on appeal by Canada, but reversed the panel's underlying and deeply suspect argument on 'like' products. In reaching its conclusion, the panel had argued that products containing asbestos and non-asbestos-containing substitutes were 'like products', their end use (as building materials) being the only relevant factor distinguishing them. It had found that the French decree, though 'saved' by Article XX, discriminated between asbestos and its substitute products and so violated GATT Article III.[9] The Appellate Body observed that, in 'examining the "likeness" of products, panels must evaluate all of the relevant evidence'. It went on to say: 'We are very much of the view that evidence relating to the health risks associated with a product may be pertinent in an examination of "likeness" under Article III:4 of the GATT 1994.'[10]

MEAs and the multilateral trading system

The use of trade restrictions under MEAs has become one of the main items of debate within the 'trade and environment' agenda in recent years. Multilaterally approved trade measures have been used in international regimes for over a century, but since the birth of the WTO there has been extensive discussion on the compatibility of trade measures taken under environmental regimes and the GATT and other WTO agreements. While it is often necessary to regulate trade to protect the environment, it is not seen as necessary to protect the environment to facilitate trade (though it can be argued that this is somewhat short-sighted). Thus, trade agreements rarely address environmental matters;

---

[9] *EC Asbestos* case, Dispute Panel report, WT/DS135/R (18 Sep 2000); Duncan Brack, 'Environmental Treaties and Trade: Multilateral Environmental Agreements and the Multilateral Trading System', in Gary P. Sampson and W. Bradnee Chambers (eds), *Trade, Environment and the Millennium (second edition)* (United Nations University Press, 2001) (hereinafter 'Brack (2001b)').

[10] *EC Asbestos* case, Appellate Body report, WT/DS135/AB/R (12 Mar 2001).

but several MEAs contain TREMs, not merely for use as sanctions but as integral to their very purpose. Paradigm examples of such MEAs are the Montreal Protocol, CITES, the Basel Convention and, more recently, the Cartagena Protocol on biosafety, the Rotterdam Convention on trade in hazardous chemicals and the Stockholm Convention on persistent organic pollutants.[11]

There are broadly three sets of reasons why trade restrictions have been incorporated into MEAs:

1   to provide a means of monitoring and controlling trade in products where the uncontrolled trade would lead to or contribute to environmental damage;
2   to provide a means of complying with other requirements of the MEA;
3   to provide a means of enforcing the MEA, by forbidding trade with non-parties or non-complying parties.[12]

Examples of the first kind of TREM are import and export permits, certificates or licences required under CITES and the Montreal Protocol for shipments of listed species and ODS; the system of prior informed consent for shipments of hazardous waste and listed chemicals used, respectively, in the Basel and Rotterdam Conventions; and the advanced informed agreement procedure for shipments of 'living modified organisms' (LMOs) required under the Cartagena Protocol. The only real experience with the second category of TREMs is with the Montreal Protocol, which requires parties to control consumption and production of ODS. Since the Protocol defines consumption as production plus imports minus exports, parties have employed a variety of trade restrictions to exercise control over trade and so satisfy their control schedules, including voluntary industry agreements, product labelling, import licences, excise taxes, quantitative restrictions on imports and total or partial import bans. The Kyoto Protocol might lead to similar measures affecting trade, since it allows Annex I parties (developed countries and those with economies in transition) to take action 'in accordance with national circumstances' in a range of potential areas, including energy efficiency, renewable energy sources and removal of market distortions.[13] The third category of TREMs represents

---

[11]   Brack (2001b); Thomas J. Schoenbaum, 'International Trade and Protection of the Environment: The Continuing Search for Reconciliation', *American Journal of International Law*, 91 (1997), p. 281.

[12]   For a more detailed consideration see Steve Charnovitz, 'The Role of Trade Measures in Treaties', in Agata Fijalkowski and James Cameron (eds), *Trade and the Environment: Bridging the Gap* (Cameron May, 1998); and Brack (2001b).

[13]   For further discussion see Duncan Brack, Michael Grubb and Craig Windram, *International Trade and Climate Change Policies* (RIIA/Earthscan, 1999).

the most drastic interference with international trade. Examples in use include the trade suspensions under CITES employed against non-compliant parties and non-parties (the implications of which are discussed further below), and the bans on trade under the Montreal Protocol between parties and non-parties in ODS, products containing ODS and products made with ODS (though parties have decided the last category is impracticable to enforce).

While international trade law and international environmental law have evolved largely in isolation from each other, in recent years the negotiation of new MEAs has been strongly influenced by the perceived need to co-exist with a strengthened MTS. The threat of a conflict with WTO rules has been raised in almost all recent MEA negotiations, generally by those opposed to the principle of the MEA and/or its effective enforcement. This 'political chill' effect has resulted in attempts to write 'savings clauses' into new MEAs with the object of subordinating them to WTO disciplines. Both the Cartagena Protocol and the Rotterdam Convention contain a preambular savings clause – but also another provision that the MEA is not subordinate to any other agreement, leading to conflicting interpretations of their relationship with the WTO.[14]

In theory, the two bodies of law could be compatible. The WTO agreement recognizes in its preamble that trade should be conducted 'while allowing for the optimal use of the world's resources in accordance with the objective of sustainable development, seeking both to protect and preserve the environment and to enhance the means for doing so...'[15] On the face of it – and with liberal interpretation – Article XX could accommodate MEA trade measures, as long as they are applied in a non-discriminatory way. But in practice, the relationship between MEAs and the MTS has proved elusive. The debate is suffused with uncertainty and speculation, and whether there is a real as opposed to a perceived conflict is unclear.

The relationship between MEAs and the MTS featured strongly in the CTE's discussions in its first two years of existence during the run-up to the Singapore WTO Ministerial Conference in 1996. Members put forward various proposals to resolve the perceived conflict between the two bodies of law, including the establishment of a degree of oversight by the WTO of the negotiation and operation of trade provisions in future MEAs, and an amendment

---

[14] Brack (2001b); for analysis of the impact of these preambular statements see Christoph Bail, Robert Falkner and Helen Marquard (eds), *The Cartagena Protocol on Biosafety: Reconciling Trade in Biotechnology with Environment and Development?* (RIIA/ Earthscan, 2002).

[15] 1994 Agreement Establishing the World Trade Organization, preamble, para 1.

to GATT Article XX to create a presumption of compatibility with MEAs. But no consensus was reached on the need for modifications to trade rules.[16]

The GATT/WTO dispute settlement system has never had to consider the compatibility of an MEA trade measure, since there has never been a case involving a direct conflict.[17] It is therefore impossible to say for certain what the outcome would be. Tentative conclusions can be drawn from GATT/WTO case law, but caution needs to be exercised in extrapolating from arguments used in cases of trade measures imposed unilaterally to those involving the application of trade measures mandated by or in pursuance of the requirements of multilateral agreements. The arguments of the Appellate Body may be more sophisticated and environmentally conscious than those of past panels, but their interpretation of GATT provisions provides no certainty that all MEA trade-related measures would be considered WTO-compatible. In the 1998 *US shrimp–turtle* case, the Appellate Body commented:

> Perhaps the most conspicuous flaw in this measure's application relates to its intended and actual coercive effect on the specific policy decisions made by foreign governments, Members of the WTO[18]

and

> it is not acceptable, in international relations, for one WTO Member to use an economic embargo to *require* other Members to adopt essentially the same comprehensive regulatory programme, to achieve a certain policy goal, as that in force within that Member's territory, *without* taking into consideration different conditions which may occur in the territories of those Members.[19]

MEA TREMs directed against non-parties would have precisely this effect, hence the uncertainty and nervousness caused by the Appellate Body's opinion.

---

[16] For a more extensive discussion, see Duncan Brack, 'The Use of Trade Measures in Multilateral Environmental Agreements', in *Sustainability, Trade and Investment: Which Way Now for the WTO?* RIIA Conference (2000); and Brack (2001b).

[17] In January 1997 Zimbabwe apparently threatened to apply to the WTO for compensation for the loss of international ivory markets arising from the Appendix I listing of the African elephant under CITES, but the case became irrelevant when at COP10 in Harare Zimbabwe's elephant population was downlisted to Appendix II and an experimental trade in its ivory stockpile permitted. See Brack (2001b), n. 8.

[18] *US shrimp–turtle,* Appellate Body report, WT/DS58/AB/R (12 Oct 1998), para. 161.

[19] Ibid., para.164.

In initially finding against the United States, the panel and Appellate Body stressed the desirability of multilateral approaches to environmental protection. The Appellate Body opposed the US action not primarily because it was a restriction on trade, but because of the 'arbitrary and unjustifiably discriminatory' way in which it was applied, the United States having made serious efforts to negotiate a multilateral agreement only with countries in the Caribbean/western Atlantic region.

In its final 2001 ruling in the *US shrimp–turtle* case, the Appellate Body confirmed the panel's view that, while the United States had an obligation to make 'serious good faith efforts' to reach agreement at international level before resorting to unilateral measures, there was *no requirement for an actual agreement*. Quoting Rio Principle 12, that 'Environmental measures addressing transboundary or global environmental problems should, as far as possible, be based on international consensus', the Appellate Body stated that a multilateral approach is strongly preferred, but went on to say:

> it is one thing to prefer a multilateral approach in the application of a measure that is provisionally justified under one of the subparagraphs of Article XX of the GATT 1994; it is another to require the conclusion of a multilateral agreement as a condition of avoiding 'arbitrary or unjustifiable discrimination' under the chapeau of Article XX.[20]

This represents a huge leap in the Appellate Body's reasoning, with potentially important implications for MEA TREMs, and arguably runs counter to their statements in the first *shrimp–turtle* case.

While it is still unclear how WTO rulings on MEA-mandated trade measures would go, there seems an increasing possibility that many would be accepted. Specific trade measures between parties, such as import and export licenses and requirements for prior informed consent, would very likely be considered WTO-compatible since all parties have agreed to them. It is less clear how trade measures used against non-parties and in response to non-compliance would be viewed. While the Appellate Body's first opinion in the *shrimp–turtle* dispute implied they might still rule against them, the final ruling opens the door to their acceptance. The US measure – a unilaterally imposed ban, without specific endorsement by an MEA, and based on a PPM – is among those least likely to be found acceptable, much less likely than a

---

[20] *US shrimp–turtle*, Appellate Body report (compliance review), WT/DS58/AB/RW (22 Oct 2001), para. 124.

TREM agreed multilaterally under an MEA, provided it is not applied in a discriminatory way,

The relationship between environmental treaties and the world trading system ought to be one of the easiest questions to resolve, given that the environmental regulations in question are well defined and multilateral in nature. But this is far from the case, as evidenced by the CTE's first failed attempt to address the issue. All that could be agreed on in the report to the WTO Singapore Ministerial Conference was that potential conflicts should be resolved in a 'mutually supportive' manner, respecting the objectives of both the WTO and the MEA.

The inclusion of environmental issues in the new round of trade liberalization talks launched at the WTO Ministerial Conference in Doha, Qatar, in November 2001 (mainly at the insistence of the European Union and only reluctantly agreed by the majority of members), has re-fuelled the debate on MEAs and the MTS. Some commentators see it as a new beginning; others see it as a move to subordinate MEAs to the WTO.[21] In the preamble of the Doha Ministerial Declaration outlining the Work Programme for the talks, ministers affirm their commitment to sustainable development using stronger language than ever before in a WTO text, expressing the conviction that acting for the protection of the environment and the promotion of sustainable development and the aims of an open and non-discriminatory MTS *can and must* be mutually supportive. They reaffirm the rights of countries to take measures to protect human, animal or plant life or health, or the environment, subject to the Article XX chapeau, and encourage continued cooperation between the WTO and relevant international environmental organizations. Most importantly, environment-related negotiations were launched in four areas:

1 fisheries subsidies;
2 the relationship between WTO rules and trade obligations set out in MEAs;
3 procedures for information exchange between MEA secretariats and relevant WTO committees, including criteria for granting observer status;
4 the reduction or elimination of tariff and non-tariff barriers to environmental goods and services.[22]

The CTE was also instructed to give particular attention, *inter alia,* to labelling requirements for environmental purposes, and to make recommendations for future action, including the desirability of negotiations.[23]

---

[21] For conflicting opinions, see Steve Charnovitz, *Bridges*, 5:9 (Nov/Dec 2001) and Victor Menotti, *Bridges*, 6:3 (Mar/Apr 2002), <www.ictsd.org>.
[22] Doha Ministerial Declaration, paras 29 and 31.
[23] Ibid., para. 32.

The mandate for the talks on the relationship between MEAs and the MTS has been narrowly drawn. Negotiations are limited to specific trade obligations set out in MEAs, and to their application between members that are also parties to the MEA. They are also precluded from prejudicing the WTO rights of any member that is not a party to the MEA in question, which would seem to remove discussion of a blanket protection of MEA trade-related measures applied to members that are non-parties. A work programme for the negotiations in a special session of the CTE has been agreed. At the time of writing in July 2002, two meetings have been held. So far talks have focused on the structure and scope of the negotiations. A deep division is evident between the European Union, the strongest proponent of an amendment to Article XX to create a presumption of compatibility with MEAs, and most other members. An EU paper presented to the first session, attempting to bring disputes involving non-parties into the negotiations and proposing, *inter alia*, that consensus be sought on the extent to which 'specific trade obligations' should be considered automatically in conformity with the WTO, was considered to go far beyond the scope of the Doha mandate.[24] At the second session, delegates broadly agreed that the outcome of the negotiations should bind only those WTO members that are MEA parties.[25]

Whether the Doha negotiations will provide a tangible and beneficial outcome for MEAs and the environment is open to question. Members seem to be lagging behind the Appellate Body when it comes to environmental issues, including TREMs. Limiting negotiations to specific obligations, coupled with the strong opposition by most members to widening the mandate, seems to remove the possibility that all TREMs taken under an MEA could be automatically deemed compatible with the MTS. By only binding parties to the outcome, the possibility of protecting MEA-mandated TREMs from a WTO challenge by a non-party (in practice, more likely than a challenge by a party) is removed. Such a narrow mandate, and the fact that negotiations are being conducted 'unilaterally' within the WTO and not 'multilaterally' with MEA representatives on an equal footing with trade negotiators, mean that several issues – including potential conflict with some of the trade measures taken under CITES – will remain unresolved.

---

[24] *Bridges*, 6:3 (Mar/Apr 2002).
[25] Ibid., 6:5 (Jun 2002).

Potential conflict with CITES measures

CITES relies on a wide range of trade measures to achieve its objectives, which on the face of it conflict with several GATT provisions, particularly those in Articles I, III and XI.[26] They include:

* bans on commercial trade and temporary trade suspensions;
* requirements for export and import permits, export quotas, labelling systems, and the tagging and marking of wildlife products;
* differential treatment depending on whether the same species is captive-bred, ranched, artificially propagated or traded from the wild;
* differential treatment on the basis of a split-listing.

Quotas, permit requirements, the prohibition on trade in Appendix I species for primarily commercial purposes, and temporary trade suspensions all violate GATT Article XI (elimination of quantitative restrictions), which prohibits all restrictions other than duties, taxes and charges. Meanwhile, differential trade rules for the same species of wildlife depending on its origin and treatment are potentially in conflict with GATT Articles I and III.

Prior to the final *US shrimp–turtle* ruling, extrapolating from the arguments and findings of earlier GATT/WTO case law, there was a high degree of uncertainty over which CITES trade measures, if any, could be 'saved' by Article XX in the event of a dispute.[27] But the *shrimp–turtle* case has changed the picture. The clear implication of both rulings by the Appellate Body is that trade measures agreed and applied multilaterally, in a way that does not distinguish arbitrarily or discriminate between countries, are permissible. This suggests quite strongly that CITES permit, labelling and tagging requirements would be judged WTO-compatible. It would be difficult to argue that they represented arbitrary or unjustifiable discrimination when all parties involved have agreed. A similar argument can be made for other trade measures agreed and applied multilaterally, such as quotas, bans on commercial Appendix I trade and differential trade rules for the same species. This view also finds support in the CTE's endorsement of multilateral solutions based on international cooperation

---

[26] For an overview, see Barney Dickson, 'CITES and GATT/WTO – The Potential for Conflict', presented at the UK Workshop on CITES and WTO Trade Rules, Hughes Hall, Cambridge, 29 September 2000.

[27] Duncan Brack, 'The US Shrimp–Turtle Case: Implications for the Multilateral Environmental Agreement–World Trade Organization Debate', *Yearbook of International Environmental Law*, 9 (1998) (Oxford University Press, 2000).

and consensus as the best way for governments to tackle transboundary or global environmental problems.[28] PPM-based measures for the differential treatment of the same species also gain increased acceptability from the final *shrimp–turtle* ruling, as long as they are applied in a non-discriminatory way.

Trade suspensions adopted as a non-compliance response are a different matter. As already noted, reasoning used by the panel and Appellate Body in the 1998 *US shrimp–turtle* case suggests that they still might rule against this kind of measure, since both expressed disapproval of the use of trade measures to coerce other governments into changing their policy. Trade suspensions under CITES are designed to compel selected parties – and non-parties – to change their policy. They are intentionally discriminatory between countries that are in compliance with CITES provisions and those that are not in compliance, and they are agreed not by the COP but by a small proportion of parties (the Standing Committee) acting on behalf of the COP. The final *shrimp–turtle* ruling, however, suggests that suspensions against parties might be acceptable if it could be demonstrated that the non-compliance response system is applied to all parties in a non-discriminatory way, and that serious good faith efforts had been made to settle the problem by negotiation first. It is conceivable that suspensions recommended against non-parties may even be acceptable under these circumstances.

The country case studies discussed earlier in this book demonstrate that the CITES non-compliance response system has not always been applied equitably. In the 1980s easy targets like Equatorial Guinea, El Salvador and Bolivia were subject to sanctions, but economically and politically powerful importing countries like Japan and some of the EU member states escaped. A non-discriminatory approach demands similar treatment for all non-compliant states. The trade suspensions imposed on Italy and Greece in the 1990s demonstrate a more equitable application of the system in recent years, though the reluctance to impose sanctions against China compared with the response to Taiwan on rhino horn trade shows that economic and political power still wield influence.

Implications for the CITES compliance system

Some may think it unwise, even dangerous, to speculate by extrapolating from arguments used in GATT/WTO cases involving unilateral measures. Temporary trade suspensions under CITES have proved remarkably effective in

---

[28] WTO: Report of the CTE to the Singapore Ministerial Conference, WT/CTE/1 (8 Nov 1996).

bringing countries into compliance, at least on paper. While their use has shown no signs to date of being influenced by a strengthened MTS, there is a danger that the Standing Committee may be deterred, purely on the basis of speculation, from agreeing a trade suspension or other restriction as a non-compliance measure, particularly in the case of non-parties.

Most WTO members are also parties to CITES. A challenge by a CITES party of a trade suspension seems unlikely, especially if the measure is based on a consensus of the Standing Committee (which, according to current practice, is usually the case). The question also arises as to who would be the respondent party, given that the WTO dispute settlement system is designed to resolve bilateral disputes. Nevertheless, in the event that such a challenge occurred, WTO policy indicates it would probably recommend an attempt in the first instance to resolve the dispute within the CITES system. The CTE has agreed that, if a dispute arises between WTO members who are both parties to an MEA, they should consider first trying to resolve it through the dispute settlement mechanisms available under the MEA (though whether a panel could decide not to handle a dispute is a moot point).[29] This may betray a misunderstanding of the difference between dispute settlement and compliance systems with respect to MEAs. To date, no MEA has invoked its dispute settlement provisions as disputes seldom, if ever, arise in a bilateral context. If a dispute were to arise within CITES over a recommended trade suspension, the mechanism provided would in any case be deficient to deal with it. Article XVIII simply states that, if a dispute cannot be resolved by negotiation, parties may submit it 'by mutual consent' to arbitration by the Permanent Court of Arbitration in The Hague. Theoretically, the challenging party could just refuse consent, leaving the WTO as the only alternative forum for resolving the dispute.

To help deflect a WTO challenge by a party subject to a trade suspension, it would be beneficial for CITES to strengthen its dispute settlement provisions. Rather than attempt to amend Article XVIII (a futile exercise, given the length of time for amendments to enter into force), it would be more practical to introduce a new alternative procedure. One option would be an ILO-type ad hoc procedure, allowing reference of disputes to a body established by and reporting to the Standing Committee and not dependent on the consent of the disputing party. The quasi-judicial complaints procedure provides perhaps the best model. Another option would be to hold a hearing similar to those provided for under the procedures of the enforcement branch of the Kyoto

---

[29] Ibid.

Protocol Compliance Committee. A permanent institution competent to hold such hearings would be needed, a role that could be fulfilled by a Compliance Committee were one to be established under CITES.

In the event of a WTO challenge by a non-party, the WTO would provide the only possible forum for settlement of the dispute, bringing the two international regimes into direct conflict. The potential for such a conflict will not be lessened by the Doha negotiations, and its outcome is by no means certain. International treaty law provides no clear answer as to whether CITES or the WTO would prevail. The Vienna Convention on the Law of Treaties states that 'the earlier treaty applies only to the extent that its provisions are compatible with those of the later treaty', an expression of the principle of *lex posterior* (the later treaty will prevail).[30] According to this scenario, the 1994 WTO Agreement (which includes the GATT) would take precedence. But another principle of customary international law, *lex specialis,* provides that the more specific treaty, in this case CITES, would prevail.

As more and more countries join CITES, the risk of a non-party challenge is diminishing. As of 1 January 2002, just 12 of the 144 WTO members were not party to CITES (one being the European Community, whose member states are all parties).[31] A qualitative analysis of CITES imports from non-parties between 1996 and 2000 reveals that only three of the 11 non-CITES-party WTO members have a notably significant trade – Taiwan, Solomon Islands and Haiti (in descending order of significance).[32] The Solomon Islands is currently subject to a recommended trade suspension under the Significant Trade Review with respect to three species (although some parties, particularly France and Japan, continued to import two of the species, *Ornithoptera urvillianus* and *Ornithoptera victoriae*, both butterflies, after the trade suspension was recommended). So a risk of a challenge, albeit small, does exist. Potential respondents could be parties that implement Standing Committee recommendations for a trade suspension. As already discussed, the chance that a non-party challenge would be resolved in the favour of CITES has increased following the final *shrimp–turtle* ruling, particularly if it can be shown that good faith efforts were made to resolve the issue first and that there was a non-discriminatory approach in applying the trade restrictions. There is also likely to be strong political pressure to settle the issue 'out of court'. The risk that a CITES trade

---

[30] Article 30.3.
[31] WTO members not party to CITES as of 1 Jan 2002: Albania, Angola, Bahrain, Croatia, European Community, Haiti, Kyrgyz Republic, Lesotho, Maldives, Oman, Taiwan, Solomon Islands, <www.wto.org>; <www,cites.org>.
[32] Trade data supplied by John Caldwell, UNEP–WCMC (Feb 2002).

suspension could be ruled WTO-incompatible is therefore even smaller than the risk of a challenge arising in the first place. However, given the dominance and strength of the WTO, and the recent decision to exclude non-party issues from the CTE trade environment negotiations, a challenge cannot be ruled out altogether.

Currently, CITES-related trade represents a miniscule proportion of the world trade in goods, which stood at US$6.2 trillion in 2000.[33] But commercial timber and fish species are increasingly coming under the CITES remit, despite strong opposition from both industries. The listing of sturgeon species on Appendix II in 1997 was a major step in this respect, and at COP11 a UK proposal to list the basking shark on Appendix II came very close to being approved. With the listing of these commercially valuable species, the economic stakes in CITES will increase. The world timber trade has been estimated at about US$150 billion annually and the legal caviar trade at US$100 million.[34] The likelihood of a WTO challenge increases along with the economic stakes, and demands a pro-active rather than a reactive approach to avert challenges that might undermine the CITES compliance system. Strengthening the Convention's dispute settlement mechanism along the lines of the Kyoto Protocol enforcement branch hearings or ILO ad hoc complaints procedure would be one way to avert a challenge by a party; while a proposal by UNEP Executive Director Klaus Töpfer for an 'early warning system' of impending MEA-related disputes, and attempts to cement closer links between the MEA secretariats and the WTO, could help to avert non-party challenges.[35]

---

[33] 'World Trade Slows Sharply in 2001 amid the Uncertain International Situation', WTO Press/249 (19 Oct 2001); see <www.wto.org>.
[34] Brack et al. (Feb 2002) (see ch. 1, n. 23); 'CITES Moves to Block Caviar Smuggling Operations', CITES press release (16 Nov 2001).
[35] 'UNEP and WTO Promote Synergies between Trade and Environment', *Bridges Weekly Trade News Digest* (27 Oct 2000), <www.ictsd.org>.

Part V
Looking to the future

13 Conclusions and recommendations

Policing international trade in endangered species is a complex task, involving action and cooperation between governmental and non-governmental stakeholders at all levels, both between states and within states. At the centre is CITES. In the absence of an international wildlife law enforcement agency, the CITES compliance system is the key to ensuring that parties implement and enforce the Convention. Following the success of the Montreal Protocol's non-compliance procedure, modern regulatory MEAs now mandate the negotiation of specific procedures and mechanisms to induce compliance and deal with non-compliance. The most detailed to date can be found in the compliance system agreed under the Kyoto Protocol, the most complicated of any MEA. But CITES pre-dates these developments. There is no provision in the Convention for negotiating procedures and mechanisms to address non-compliance. Instead its compliance system has evolved through 'soft law' and practice over nearly three decades on the basis of broad provisions, mandating:

- parties to report annually on CITES trade and biennially on implementation and enforcement measures;
- the Secretariat to review national reports, communicate problems on implementation to parties and make recommendations;
- parties to respond with remedial action and report to the COP;
- the COP to review parties' responses and make recommendations.[1]

Since these skeleton provisions were agreed, several different procedures have been developed to address different forms of non-compliance. The Standing Committee is now the primary institution to recommend 'measures' for non-compliance response on the basis of Secretariat advice. The Secretariat, meanwhile, has assumed a full review and recommendatory role, which under modern compliance systems is usually assigned to an implementation or compliance committee.

In the interest of order and clarity, the conclusions and recommendations that follow mirror the structure used to describe the CITES compliance system in the main text.

---

[1] Articles XII and XIII.

Primary rule system

Trade provisions

Since the purpose of this book was not to dissect CITES trade provisions, but rather to analyse the system that influences parties to comply with them, comments will be restricted to four key issues that affect compliance.

The first is the dependence of the CITES permit system on customs controls at national borders. As these borders dissolve with the tendency towards regional economic integration and reduced customs controls, the permit system risks becoming increasingly irrelevant. The problems with implementation and enforcement in the European Union caused by the abolition of internal border controls provide salutary lessons. But although the general issue was raised three years ago at a Standing Committee meeting, discussion was postponed and little seems to have happened since, perhaps because it would involve questioning the future of the core provisions of CITES. Nevertheless, the potential effect of regional economic integration on CITES trade controls needs to be faced, and sooner rather than later if CITES is to maintain its relevance.

The second issue, which needs addressing, is the vulnerability of permits to fraud. This is beginning to happen with the increasing use of labelling and marking systems for CITES species in trade, but these requirements will need to be extended, ideally to all specimens, to enable better tracking and trade controls.

The other issues concern exemptions from permit requirements and special provisions, which have long created problems. As one loophole has been narrowed through interpretation and definition, another has opened up. Two of the most obvious ones that need to be closed are the lack of a definition and specific provisions for 'ranched' Appendix II specimens (and those described as 'F'), and the lack of controls over quotas. Both loopholes are increasingly being used, in the first instance to get around trade controls on wild-caught specimens, and in the second as a means to control trade in the absence of non-detriment findings.

International institutions

By allocating considerable review and recommendatory powers to the Secretariat, a non-elected body, and delegating the COP's decision-making role on case-by-case non-compliance to the Standing Committee, CITES departs from accepted institutional requirements. It could be argued that this has strengthened the system by enabling the use of trade sanctions as a non-compliance response; the COP is reluctant to target parties at its meetings and would be unlikely to recommend measures as strong as those decided by the Standing Committee. Maintaining the Standing Committee (distinct from the COP) as the decision-making body on a case-by-case basis has a clear advantage, despite its recent reluctance to act against large numbers of parties found to be in non-compliance over-reporting and national legislation. Nevertheless, if the Committee is to fulfil this role in a non-discriminatory way and achieve a degree of objectivity, its regional representatives need an explicit mandate to represent the opinions of parties in their region, as opposed to national interests – as was evident for example in the ivory sale debate in 1999 – and to defer to alternates on issues involving a clear conflict of interest.

The system as it stands concentrates too much power in the hands of the Secretariat, power that is unparalleled among other MEAs except at regional level. The Secretariat is functioning more efficiently and transparently than it has in a long time, but its turbulent history provides little guarantee that problems will not arise again. Too much power runs the obvious risk of abuse. Other disadvantages are loss of control by parties over the review and recommendatory process, and vulnerability of the system to criticism over controversial decisions through lack of an independent body of experts from which recommendations emanate. As a political body lacking specific expertise on compliance issues and with a busy agenda, the Standing Committee is ill-equipped to fulfil this reviewing and recommendatory role. Instead, there is a clear need for a Compliance Committee of independent experts (or government representatives with relevant expertise), which could review issues relating to compliance, and make recommendations to the Standing Committee for action on a case-by-case basis and to the COP on issues where broad-based resolutions or decisions are needed, such as national legislation or annual reporting. The Committee could also play a valuable role in overseeing matters such as the current review of COP resolutions and decisions by the Secretariat, and implementation of COP recommendations relating to compliance and directed to the Secretariat to ensure their fulfilment. Apart from acting as a safety net, it would curb the Secretariat's apparent tendency to unilateralism.

To fully realize its potential, the proposed Compliance Committee would need to be constituted in subgroups, along the lines of the Kyoto Protocol, which could make recommendations on a range of measures on implementation and enforcement, from capacity-building to recommended trade suspensions. Given the importance to CITES of national enforcement, one of the subgroups could comprise enforcement officers acting in an advisory capacity – in effect, the TETF expanded to include participation by other parties. In addition to the advantages mentioned, a Compliance Committee would provide more legitimacy for recommended trade suspensions, and would strengthen their chances of surviving a WTO challenge by a non-party.

Funding

CITES is chronically underfunded compared with the commitments it is expected to implement. Expectations have grown but the budget has stood still, and parties show no willingness to increase their contributions. Until recently, external funding has been biased towards species-specific projects, but under the new Secretary General a shift is evident towards more cross-cutting projects to improve implementation, for example through building capacity in Scientific Authorities and to develop national legislation. Nevertheless, projects directed towards improving enforcement capacity are still at a relative disadvantage, particularly with such a huge proportion of external funding being devoted to the monitoring programme for elephants, MIKE. The Convention is also disadvantaged as a whole by its apparent inability to access GEF funding.

A re-examination of the Convention's funding mechanism is needed. A financial mechanism along the lines of the Montreal Protocol's Multilateral Fund, supported by contributions from developed consumer countries and devoted to building capacity for implementation and enforcement of CITES in developing-party range states, would be an ideal solution. In the current political climate, however, and given the long-standing lack of party political will when it comes to increasing CITES funding, this is unlikely to be realized. A more realistic option is to direct the Secretariat to determine the eligibility for GEF funding of cross-cutting capacity-building projects in developing-country parties, supported by active lobbying by parties themselves in the GEF Assembly and Council for a proportion of biodiversity funds to be allocated to CITES.

Compliance information system

National reporting and review

Until the threat of trade sanctions at COP11, the proportion of parties reporting their CITES trade data on time was declining. Waving the 'stick' of a recommended trade suspension has generated improved compliance; but since the stick has not been applied, and most likely will not be, the benefit will almost certainly be short-lived. A new approach to annual reporting needs to be formulated. The first step would be to review techniques used to elicit reports from parties in other conventions, as well as methods to improve the quality of reports given that this also presents a problem in the CITES context. Again the Montreal Protocol provides a potential model, in particular the institutional strengthening provided by the Multilateral Fund combined with the threat of losing access to the Fund. Such an approach would undoubtedly improve reporting by CITES parties, but it needs access to resources that CITES does not and is not likely to have. The approach being developed under the Ramsar Convention – to integrate reporting into a dynamic ongoing framework for strategic planning and action by national governments – is a more realistic option, at least in the short term, and should be watched carefully for lessons that could be applied in the context of CITES.

Biennial reporting by parties on their measures to implement and enforce CITES is virtually non-existent, except to the extent that some include this information on an ad hoc basis in their annual reports. If it worked properly, the system would provide a regular update of the state of compliance in parties. In the UNFCCC the equivalent requirement for national communications is taken much more seriously. The in-depth reviews of the communications carried out by independent teams with in-country visits are building an extensive and, importantly, reliable database for the Convention. When extended to the Kyoto Protocol, they will also provide a basis for identifying potential non-compliance. Given the dependence of CITES on national measures, biennial reporting needs to be implemented, and to be ascribed far more importance than it is at present. Periodic in-depth review of the reports involving in-country visits by independent teams, which consult, among others, a broad range of NGOs, would improve not only the quality and amount of information available on which to base compliance related decisions, but also probably the quality of reporting over time. Given the cost implication of an IDR process, however, an alternative to be considered would be the publication of the reports on the CITES website, inviting comments from other parties and NGOs – or, as in the ILO, the distribution of reports to relevant national NGOs for review and comment.

Information on infractions, illegal trade and wildlife crime

The development of the TIGERS database to process reports on wildlife crime and illegal trade and the introduction of CITES Alerts have undoubtedly improved the efficiency of intelligence processing and dissemination. But the reduction in public access to information through the radical revision of the infractions report is regrettable. These reports were valuable, both as a publicly available source of information and as a means to encourage the countries cited to address the problems identified. If the Secretariat does not have the human or financial resources to maintain production of the reports before each COP, the resources could and should be sought externally to enable reinstatement of the reports in the detailed format used prior to COP11.

Non-compliance response system

Problem countries

The use of recommended trade suspensions in CITES listed species has been remarkably effective against non-responsive countries with major implementation problems, at least to the extent that a paper study can determine. Most parties targeted for major problems appear to have moved into compliance, while non-parties have been induced to join the Convention or, in the case of Grenada, to clamp down on illegal trade. In some of the early cases where in-country verification missions appear not to have been carried out, it is difficult to be sure that the national measures taken were effective. In the later cases, however, following the introduction of the non-compliance procedure in 1989, Secretariat verification missions to assess problems, develop recommendations and monitor compliance with conditions for lifting recommended trade suspensions have been used more frequently. More reliance can therefore be placed on the conclusion that countries responded and trade sanctions were effective. The UAE was the only country that failed to respond to trade sanctions, at least the first time round. The most recent recommended trade suspension against the UAE, however, seems to be proving more effective, although final conclusions cannot be drawn until the Secretariat has verified progress with implementation of the Action Plan.

While evidence suggests that the non-compliance procedure for countries experiencing major implementation problems has been successful, the way in which the procedure has been applied has been to some extent discriminatory, at least in the early days. Trade suspensions were recommended for easy developing country targets, while non-compliant parties such as Japan and some of the EU member states escaped. The balance was redressed to some extent in the 1990s with trade sanctions recommended against Italy and Greece. Yet the decision to recommend trade sanctions against Taiwan but not China over rhino horn trade in 1994 indicates that discrimination can still be a problem. Given the recent opinions of the WTO Appellate Body that trade-related environment measures may be acceptable if applied in a non-discriminatory way, it will be important for CITES to ensure in future that this is the case.

Problem issues

Of the problem issues for which non-compliance response mechanisms have been agreed, only the national legislation project has achieved notable success. Even so, the response of parties was slow until recommended trade restrictions began to be applied to persistently non-compliant parties with significant levels of trade. Targeted parties responded rapidly, all of them enacting CITES legislation except for Fiji, which has pledged to have legislation in place before the end of 2002. The introduction of CITES Legislation Plans for the large number of parties analysed in Phases I and II of the project but still without adequate implementing legislation is a promising development and is likely to accelerate the rate of compliance, provided the threatened trade suspensions are put into effect as and when parties pass their respective deadlines. The development of a legal capacity-building programme since COP11 is important for building long-term compliance and harmonization of national CITES legislation (which needs to include, among many other features, more deterrent penalties). But given the anticipated length of time before it reaps results, and the need to sustain pressure at a political level to ensure parliamentary support for enacting updated legislation, the threat of recommended trade suspensions will need to be maintained for cases of persistent non-compliance.

In comparison with the national legislation project, attempts to deal with non-compliance in relation to annual reporting and non-designation of Scientific Authorities have been less effective. Parties have proved reluctant to recommend trade suspensions for non-reporting, the Standing Committee having failed to implement a clear COP decision to recommend a suspension of CITES trade with parties that have not reported for three consecutive years. Although the threat alone has prompted many parties to produce their reports, future use of the tool has been undermined by not carrying it through. As argued above, a new approach to annual reporting other than an occasional threat of trade sanctions is needed if the reporting rate, and quality of reporting, are to be improved on a consistent and sustained basis.

Implementation of the mechanism adopted by the COP in 1997, whereby parties were advised not to accept export permits from parties that had not designated Scientific Authorities for a specified length of time, stopped in its tracks in March 1999 with no explanation given. The mechanism was entirely dependent on the Secretariat, with no need for approval by the Standing Committee. One can only surmise there was a policy change within the Secretariat, but, given that the COP recommendation, which is still in effect, left no room for discretion, implementation should have continued. Instead, efforts have been focused on a capacity-building programme for Scientific Authorities, which was agreed by the COP at the same time as the trade restriction. Capacity-building in this area is clearly needed, but the 'stick' should have been maintained to induce non-compliant parties to designate their Authorities.

The mechanism to address non-payment of dues to the CITES Trust Fund, the latest 'issue' to become a cause for possible sanctions, remains untested. Since requests to parties for a time-frame for payment produced little response, the Standing Committee agreed that parties should be asked to submit a compliance plan for payment by a specified deadline. However, since no penalties were agreed for non-compliance, it is questionable whether the measure will be effective.

Significant Trade Review

The Significant Trade Review has evolved into one of the main mechanisms within CITES for inducing compliance, but on a selective basis with respect to non-detriment findings and trade in individual Appendix II species. An assessment of its effectiveness is difficult, since there has been no comprehensive review of the programme since recommended species-specific trade suspensions were introduced as a non-compliance response in 1992. Many species and countries have been and still are affected by sanctions, at least on paper, but preliminary studies indicate that the recommended import suspensions may not always be implemented and that recommended export quotas are regularly exceeded. A comprehensive 'review of the Review' is called for, not just desk-based, but supported by random in-country visits to give some idea of how effective the programme has been on the ground. The aim would be to provide reliable data to support a revision of the Review process based on empirical observations, as opposed to relying on literature-based conclusions.

Meanwhile, the forthcoming revision of the Significant Trade Review at COP12 in November 2002, with a view to simplification and clarification of the mechanism, provides a more immediate opportunity for improving the procedure. Recommendations include:

- introducing on-site verification of compliance with Animals and Plants Committee recommendations, at least for cases giving most cause for concern;
- linking annual reporting with the review, for example by requiring reporting as one of the conditions for lifting zero quotas;
- incorporating the precautionary principle into the review process;

- improving transparency by publishing consultants' reviews on the CITES website;
- extending the net for information that is included in the consultants' reviews by allowing for a comment period by other parties and NGOs;
- requiring peer review of field studies;
- specifying as opposed to implying, in the terms of reference, that illegal trade be included in the consultants' reviews.

It is important that any revision of the Review mechanism does not lose sight of the importance of recommended trade suspensions as a responce to non-compliance. The Animals and Plants Committees have proposed more support for non-compliant states – formerly just an afterthought tacked on to the end of the review procedure. Support to range states for implementing Animals and Plants Committee recommendations, to ensure, for example, that quotas are not exceeded or field studies are carried out, is a clear need, but no specific funding provisions have been included in the proposed clause, limiting the chances that support will be forthcoming. Recommended trade suspensions are therefore likely to remain the primary means of response.

Recent developments indicate that the Significant Trade Review may be evolving towards a more ecosystem-based or country-based approach. In addressing the decline of sturgeon species, the Animals Committee made basin-by-basin recommendations as opposed to addressing each country separately. Although problems are far from being solved, progress has been made in developing unified strategies for management. The Secretariat verified progress through on-site missions. This approach holds out some promise for the future, making it more difficult for traders to shift their operations to other countries not subject to recommended import suspensions. But the country-based approach that has been initiated with a test review of Madagascar is less advisable and needs to be reconsidered. By crossing into the territory of the non-compliance procedure for countries with major implementation problems, the distinction between the two non-compliance responses has become blurred. To have parallel procedures in the same Convention for dealing with non-compliance by parties makes no sense. Besides, in the case of Madagascar, delays in completing the review might prevent urgently required action. It would be more appropriate, given prevailing circumstances in the country, for CITES to support the trade moratorium announced by the new administration by urging parties to suspend imports, then to examine ways of building capacity to implement and enforce CITES in Madagascar once the political situation is resolved.

High-profile Appendix I species

The ad hoc response to non-compliance over implementing the ban on trade in rhino horn seems to have been successful. It involved technical and political missions, the appointment of a UNEP special envoy and the threat of trade sanctions (actually carried out in the case of Taiwan, a non-party), backed by increased security of rhino habitat, strong NGO campaigns and publicity. Targeted consumer countries moved towards compliance, though problems are still apparent given China's refusal to destroy domestic stocks and the continued availability of products claiming to contain rhino horn from some outlets, at least as of 1999. The traditional medicine community appears generally supportive of the campaign, but a market for rhino horn persists and CITES cannot be complacent. Some African rhino populations appear to be recovering, but Asian species remain critically endangered. Poaching incidents still occur, most seriously in recent times in Nepal.

The replication of the ad hoc response over rhino horn trade to address trade in tiger parts is more difficult to judge. It hinges more on missions and the provision of assistance – most notably through the Tiger Enforcement Task Force – than on recommended trade suspensions. Some countries appear to have responded to recommendations, notably India after averting the threat of trade sanctions at COP11. Others, however, particularly Myanmar, have not responded, and on the basis of NGO information Japan too may still present problems, while three tiger range states remain non-parties.

The Secretariat has recommended that the species-specific focus be discarded in favour of a more coordinated approach to addressing non-compliance, since several of the countries involved have general problems with CITES implementation and enforcement, involving many CITES-listed species. Also, a species-specific approach might give the impression that other species are less important. This is a valid point. A possible way to handle a 'coordinated approach' is through national CITES Action Plans (discussed further below). But where an Appendix I species is facing a crisis, there is still mobilization of a species-specific campaign to induce compliance and generate awareness.

Enforcement

It is a truism that enforcement is the Achilles' heel of CITES. A field researcher with Wildlife Conservation Society working in central Africa recently commented, 'law enforcement is the bedrock of conservation, and until everyone in the international community understands this, the poachers are going to keep coming'.[2] Unfortunately, the message has yet to get through to many actors in the CITES regime. The evidence is considerable. Enforcement is relatively under-funded compared with species-specific management and monitoring. MIKE, which absorbs a huge amount of funding, is the latest case in point. The establishment of specialized wildlife law enforcement units is not a required national measure under the Convention, as is the need to designate Management and Scientific Authorities. And lastly, wildlife law enforcement expertise is excluded from the CITES regime through lack of a forum for officers, except for the species-specific TETF, attempts to establish a permanent enforcement working group having failed. It all adds up to lack of political will, a repeated theme of commentators on the issue.

The emergence of regional mechanisms for intergovernmental cooperation on wildlife law enforcement, particularly the Africa-based Lusaka Agreement and NAWEG, are encouraging developments that could and should act as precedents for other regions. But so far there seems to be little evidence of other regions taking an initiative. A Lusaka-type agreement would be particularly valuable in the Asian region, where, according to the report of the tiger technical mission, enforcement problems abound. UNEP's experience in negotiating the Lusaka Agreement puts it in an ideal position to take a lead, the first step being to facilitate a meeting of wildlife law enforcement officers from countries in the Asian region. The recommendations of the 1999 UNEP-hosted enforcement workshop to encourage collaborative law enforcement projects between countries sharing borders, and to bring together law enforcement officers on a regional basis to launch cooperative actions, provide added support for an Asian regional initiative. But to date UNEP has only followed up on the workshop's recommendation for a set of MEA enforcement guidelines whose practical use is somewhat questionable. UNEP needs encouragement (and funding) to implement the outstanding workshop recommendations, which could have tangible outcomes in the fight against wildlife crime if they were realized.

Meanwhile, attention to building national capacity to enforce CITES is long overdue. Ideally, what is needed is a requirement for parties to establish specialized wildlife law enforcement units, backed by guidance and funds to build capacity and expertise. But this would need an amendment of the Convention, which is unlikely to be achieved, and in any case is impractical because of the inevitable delay for its entry into force. Another approach would be to include a

---

[2] Peter Walsh, field researcher with Wildlife Conservation Society, in Tim Friend, 'Warfare on Gorillas', *USA Today* (8 Jul 2002).

requirement for specialized wildlife law enforcement units in national CITES Action Plans, backed by access to funds for capacity-building from GEF. The capacity-building programmes would need to include components aimed at improving judicial awareness of wildlife crime with a view to the imposition of deterrent penalties, and at bringing wildlife crime investigators together with prosecutors in joint training sessions, perhaps as part of a wider capacity-building programme using a cascade ('train-the-trainer') approach.

Expansion of non-compliance response measures

The Secretariat's suggestions for an expanded range of non-compliance response measures, including suspension of rights and privileges and financial penalties, are pragmatic. The Standing Committee's lukewarm response is unfortunate, and may betray a lack of understanding of compliance systems or, alternatively, a fear that Committee members themselves may become subject to penalties. The Committee's call for more incentives to induce compliance is supportable. The use of 'sticks' in CITES clearly needs to be balanced with more supportive measures through technical assistance and capacity-building. The need for this support has been recognized since the early days of the Convention, and technical assistance in the form of guidelines on legislation and reporting, and Secretariat expert missions, has been made available to parties, along with training seminars and, most recently, efforts to build capacity on legislation and in Scientific Authorities. But these efforts are not enough. More sustained capacity-building is needed, for example:

- a sponsorship programme for the masters course on CITES in Spain;
- regular train-the-trainer refresher courses in each region, bringing together all relevant authorities, including law enforcement agencies and prosecutors;
- implementation of the capacity-building component of the information management strategy to close the gap between the internet 'haves' and 'have-nots'.

But this approach requires funds, multilateral rather than bilateral. CITES parties, particularly consuming countries, will need to increase their contributions to the Trust Fund or launch a concerted effort to access the GEF. Given that the political will to do this appears weak, a penalty-type non-compliance response needs to be maintained; and, given the Standing Committee's reluctance to recommend trade suspensions for certain issues, it would benefit from encompassing an expanded range of measures along the lines of those suggested by the Secretariat.

National CITES action plans

An approach to building national capacity for the implementation and enforcement of CITES that deserves serious consideration is the formulation of national Action Plans. Such Plans would ideally need to:

- set definite timetables and targets;
- pay equal attention to the needs of Management and Scientific Authorities and wildlife law enforcement agencies;
- include a requirement to establish specialized wildlife law enforcement units;
- incorporate incentives for annual and biennial reporting, possibly along the lines of the Ramsar Convention;
- be subject to verification that timetables and targets are being met;
- be adequately funded, recognizing the principle of common but differentiated responsibilities (i.e., consumer country parties should pay).

If CITES parties are unprepared to fund the Plans, the GEF could be explored as a possible funding source. Losing access to funds could provide an added incentive to induce compliance.

A coordinated non-compliance mechanism

Several non-compliance procedures are operating in CITES side by side, having evolved separately to address country-specific, issue-specific or species-specific problems. The recent blurring of the distinction between the Significant Trade Review and the procedure for addressing major implementation problems on a country-specific basis indicates that some coordination, clearly allocating roles between institutions, is needed. At the centre of a new coordinated system could be the proposed Compliance Committee. This could operate in tandem with the Animals and Plants Committees on the Significant Trade Review, perhaps playing a role in overseeing verification of their recommendations and, in cases of non-compliance, making recommendations for Standing Committee action. Meanwhile, country-based and issue-based non-compliance response, as well as ad hoc responses to urgent Appendix I cases, would most appropriately be handled by the Compliance Committee and

Standing Committee, the Secretariat providing a role in information collection, analysis and dissemination and verification.

Action by the proposed Compliance Committee would most appropriately be triggered by:

- Secretariat reports compiled from biennial reports on implementation and compliance, supplemented with information from a wide range of NGOs and subject to some kind of expert review, and information from UNEP–WCMC's review of annual trade reports;
- a party in respect of another party;
- a party in respect of itself.

Some pathway for NGO submissions, perhaps subject to admissibility criteria and resulting in an inquiry into the case of non-compliance publicized through the CITES website, could be beneficial. The representation procedure under the ILO and the citizen submissions under the North American Agreement on Environmental Cooperation provide potential models.

Most of the existing non-compliance procedures have as a common factor the use of recommended trade suspensions in CITES-listed species or the threat of their use. Compliance plans are also becoming more commonly used, most recently for the national legislation project, as well as to bring the UAE back into compliance, and to address non-payment of dues to the Trust Fund. A new coordinated procedure would need to embrace both the concept of compliance plans and the continued use of recommended trade suspensions, but, as has already been argued, the range of responses needs to be extended to include a variety of positive and negative incentives to enable a broader response to different types of non-compliance. A coordinated procedure would also need to build in monitoring of the compliance action plans by the Secretariat, much as happens already, with penalties for failing to meet targets and timetables. Some kind of appeals procedure along the lines of the hearings provided for in the Kyoto Protocol compliance mechanisms would be advisable, not least since it would help to deflect attempts by parties to challenge recommended trade restrictions in the WTO.

Relationship with the WTO

There has long been speculation on the outcome of a conflict between an MEA trade-related environment measure (TREM) and the WTO. As a treaty entirely dependent on TREMs to achieve its objective, CITES is one of the

MEAs at the centre of the debate. Certainly, the potential exists for a conflict. While in theory the two bodies of law should be compatible, earlier GATT/WTO case law provided no certainty this would be judged the case by a WTO dispute panel. And the narrow mandate of negotiations on the relationship between MEAs and the multilateral trading system under the WTO Committee on Trade and Environment (CTE) launched in Doha seems to have removed the possibility that all MEA TREMs will automatically be considered WTO-compatible. But case law emerging from disputes referred to the Appellate Body, in particular the final ruling in the *US shrimp–turtle* case, provides cause for more optimism and has increased the chance that MEA TREMs would be considered acceptable under the WTO if they were applied in a non-discriminatory way – even TREMS used as a non-compliance response, and possibly even TREMs applied against non-parties.

Disputes over trade sanctions between WTO members that are also parties to CITES should be handled ideally within CITES, a solution supported by the CTE. Given the unsuitability of the current dispute settlement provision under CITES, a new alternative procedure under the proposed Compliance Committee, or an ad hoc procedure under the Standing Committee, would, as already argued, help to deflect a challenge. However, since a panel may not be able to refuse a case, a provision to enable reference of disputes to the MEA in question may need to be included in the Dispute Settlement Understanding. The current Doha round of trade negotiations provides an opportunity for this. A dispute involving a non-CITES-party WTO member subject to a recommended trade restriction would be dependent solely on the WTO for settlement. Although the chance of this happening is small, given that most WTO members are parties to CITES, it exists. Whether a recommended trade restriction applied against a non-party would pass the tests being developed by the Appellate Body is uncertain. Although the chance for its acceptance has increased with the *shrimp–turtle* ruling, it would have to be demonstrated that the measure has been applied in a non-discriminatory way, which was not always the case in the past. A more coordinated non-compliance procedure under CITES with recommendations emanating from an independent body of experts, such as the proposed Compliance Committee, would probably increase the acceptability of a measure recommended against a non-party.

Closing comment

A crucial element to the future development of the compliance system under CITES is political will. This chapter has made several suggestions as to how the system could be strengthened and improved. But while CITES often attracts publicity, giving it quite a high profile in the minds of the public, generally speaking this is not matched by political action, and universally speaking it fails to be matched by funding. An expanding agenda does not equate with a budget that stands still. Capacity-building needs funds. Parties will have to face the fact, sooner rather than later, that CITES needs considerably more money if compliance is to be achieved – if not through the Trust Fund, then through the GEF. Political will somehow needs to be activated. If all the actors in CITES were to bury their differences, even just temporarily, and work together to generate the will, the chances are it could happen.

Part VI
Annexes

Annex I
Key dates of CITES meetings

Conferences of the Parties

COP1	Berne, Switzerland, 2–6 November 1976
COP2	San José, Costa Rica, 19–30 March 1979
COP3	New Delhi, India, 25 February–8 March 1981
COP4	Gaborone, Botswana, 19–30 April 1983
COP5	Buenos Aires, Argentina, 22 April–3 May 1985
COP6	Ottawa, Canada, 12–24 July 1987
COP7	Lausanne, Switzerland, 9–20 October 1989
COP8	Kyoto, Japan, 2–13 March 1992
COP9	Fort Lauderdale, Florida, USA, 7–18 November 1994
COP10	Harare, Zimbabwe, 9–20 June 1997
COP11	Gigiri (Kenya), 10–20 April 2000
COP12	Santiago, Chile, 4–15 November 2002

Standing Committee meetings

SC1	Bonn, Federal Republic of Germany, 22 June 1979
SC2	Bonn, Federal Republic of Germany, 29 January 1980
SC3	Nairobi, Kenya, 26 April 1980
SC4	New Delhi, India, 25 February–6 March 1981
SC5	Gland, Switzerland, 16 July 1981
SC6	Christchurch, New Zealand, 21 October 1981
SC7	Gland, Switzerland, 21–23 June 1982
SC8	Gaborone, Botswana, 18 April 1983
SC9	Gaborone, Botswana, 28 April 1983
SC10	Gland, Switzerland, 3–4 November 1983
SC11	Gland, Switzerland, 3–5 July 1984
SC12	Buenos Aires, Argentina, 27 April 1985
SC13	Lausanne, Switzerland, 28 October–1 November 1985
SC14	Ottawa, Canada, 27–31 October 1986
SC15	Ottawa, Canada, 20 July 1987
SC16	Ottawa, Canada, 24 July 1987

SC17	San José, Costa Rica, 25–28 & 31 January 1988
SC18	Lausanne, Switzerland, 27 February–3 March 1989
SC19	Lausanne, Switzerland, 19 October 1989
SC20	Lausanne, Switzerland, 20 October 1989
SC21	Lausanne, Switzerland, 5–8 February 1990
SC22	Nairobi, Kenya, 8–10 August 1990
SC23	Lausanne, Switzerland, 8–12 April 1991
SC24	Lausanne, Switzerland, 20–21 January 1992
SC25	Kyoto, Japan, 1 & 12 March 1992
SC26	Kyoto, Japan, 10 March 1992
SC27	Kyoto, Japan, 13 March 1992
SC28	Lausanne, Switzerland, 22–25 June 1992
SC29	Washington, DC, USA, 1–5 March 1993
SC30	Brussels, Belgium, 6–8 September 1993
SC31	Geneva, Switzerland, 21–25 March 1994
SC32	Fort Lauderdale, Florida, US, 5 November 1994
SC33	Fort Lauderdale, Florida, US, 17 November 1994
SC34	Fort Lauderdale, Florida, US, 18 November 1994
SC35	Geneva, Switzerland, 21–24 March 1995
SC36	Geneva, Switzerland, 30 January–2 February 1996
SC37	Rome, Italy, 2–6 December 1996
SC38	Harare, Zimbabwe, 7–8 June 1997
SC39	Harare, Zimbabwe, 20 June 1997
SC40	London, UK, 3–6 March 1998
SC41	Geneva, Switzerland, 8–12 February 1999
SC42	Lisbon, Portugal, 28 September–1 October 1999
SC43	Nairobi, Kenya, 8 April 2000
SC44	Nairobi, Kenya, 20 April 2000
SC45	Paris, France, 18–22 June 2001
SC46	Geneva, 11–15 March 2002
SC47	Santiago, Chile, 1–2 November 2002

Annex 2
Interpol ECOMESSAGE

Information to be supplied

1. Subject: Code name/Reference number
                     Legal description of the offence
2. Place and method of discovery
3. Date/time
4. a) Products (wastes)
      Substances (radioactive)
      Species and description of the specimen (wildlife)
   b) Quantity and estimated value
5. Identity of person(s) involved
   a) Date of arrest
   b) Family name (maiden name)
   c) First name(s)
   d) Sex
   e) Alias
   f) Date and place of birth
   g) Nationality
   h) Address
   i) Information contained in the passports and ID
   j) Profession
   k) If any, function in one of the companies mentioned in 6
   l) Other information
6. Companies involved
   a) Type
   b) Name
   c) Activities
   d) Address and phone/fax of headquarters
   e) Registration number
   f) Business address and phone/fax
7. Means of transportation and route
8. a) Country and town of origin
   b) Country of provenance

c) Country(ies) of transit
d) County and town of destination
9. Identification of documents used
10. Law enforcement agency
11. Modus operandi
12. Additional information
13. Information requested

Annex 3
Countries and species affected by Standing Committee recommended import suspensions under the Significant Trade Review as of 9 April 2002[1]

Standing Committee's recommendations to all parties to suspend imports of specimens of the species indicated from each state listed

Party/non-party	Species	Date of recommendation	Additional conditions and remarks
Antigua and Barbuda	*Strombus gigas*	SC41, February 1999	
Argentina	*Lama guanicoe*	SC29, March 1993	On the condition that all permits are confirmed by the Secretariat before being accepted by the country of import, the suspension does not apply to: a) specimens that form part of the registered stock in Argentina;
		SC41, February 1999	b) products obtained from the shearing of live animals carried out under the approved management programme, appropriately marked and registered; and c) non-commercial exports of limited quantities of wool for industrial testing, up to 500 kg annually.
Barbados	*Strombus gigas*	SC41, February 1999	
Democratic Republic of the Congo	*Hippopotamus amphibius*	SC45, June 2001	
	Poicephalus robustus	SC45, June 2001	
	Geochelone pardalis	SC45, June 2001	

---

[1] Taken from Notification to the Parties No. 2002/021 Annex 2.

Party/non-party	Species	Date of recommendation	Additional conditions and remarks
Dominica	*Strombus gigas*	SC41, February 1999	
Indonesia	*Cacatua sulphurea*	SC30, September 1993	
	Ptyas mucosus	SC30, September 1993	
		SC41, February 1999	The suspension does not apply to 102,285 marked skins acquired before the current trade prohibition entered into force on the following conditions: a) the export of the skins should not be permitted unless the Secretariat confirms receipt of a copy of the export permit concerned issued by the Management Authority of Indonesia; and b) import of specimens from this registered stockpile should be permitted only after confirmation of the validity of the Indonesian export permit by the Secretariat.
Kazakhstan	*Saiga tatarica*	SC45, June 2001	
Lithuania	*Lynx lynx*	SC29, March 1993	
Madagascar	*Coracopsis vasa*	SC32, November 1994	
	Chamaeleo spp. (except *Chamaeleo lateralis, C. oustaleti, C. pardalis and C. verrucosus*)	SC32, November 1994	
	Phelsuma spp. (except *P. laticauda, P. lineata, P. madagascariensis, P. quadriocellata*)	SC32, November 1994	
Malawi	*Hippopotamus amphibius*	SC45, June 2001	
Mali	*Poicephalus robustus*	SC45, June 2001	

Party/non-party	Species	Date of recommendation	Additional conditions and remarks
Mozambique	*Cordylus tropidosternum*	SC45, June 2001	
Nicaragua	*Dendrobates auratus*	SC45, June 2001	
	Dendrobates pumilio	SC45, June 2001	
Peru	*Aratinga erythrogenys*	SC29, March 1993	
Republic of Moldova	*Lynx lynx*	SC29, March 1993	
Russian Federation	*Saiga tatarica*	SC45, June 2001	
Rwanda	*Hippopotamus amphibius*	SC45, June 2001	
Solomon Islands	*Corucia zebrata*	SC45, June 2001	
	Ornithoptera urvillianus	SC32, November 1994	
	Ornithoptera victoriae	SC32, November 1994	
Suriname	*Dendrobates tinctorius*	SC45, June 2001	
Togo	*Poicephalus robustus*	SC45, June 2001	
Trinidad and Tobago	*Strombus gigas*	SC41, February 1999	
Ukraine	*Lynx lynx*	SC29, March 1993	
United Republic of Tanzania	*Agapornis fischeri*	SC29, March 1993	
	Poicephalus cryptoxanthus	SC32, November 1994	
	Poicephalus meyeri	SC32, November 1994	
	Poicephalus rufiventris	SC32, November 1994	
	Tauraco fischeri	SC32, November 1994	
	Geochelone pardalis	SC32, November 1994	This suspension does not apply to specimens of this species produced from ranching/captive-breeding operations, for which the level of annual export quotas has to be agreed between the Management Authority and the Secretariat.
	Malacochersus tornieri	SC29, March 1993	This suspension does not apply to specimens of this species produced from ranching/captive-breeding operations, for which the level of annual export quotas has to be agreed between the Management Authority and the Secretariat.

Party/non-party	Species	Date of recommendation	Additional conditions and remarks
	Gongylophis colubrinus	SC32, November 1994	This suspension does not apply to specimens of this species produced from ranching/captive-breeding operations, for which the level of annual export quotas has to be agreed between the Management Authority and the Secretariat.

Annex 4
Preliminary report form[1]

 (to be used for reporting incidents of wildlife crime, illegal trade, poaching of endangered species or significant intelligence*)

1. Date ....

2. Place ....

3. Species ....

4. Type of event ....

5. Suspect(s):

....

....

....

6. Evidence:

....

....

....

7. Modus operandi:

....

....

....

8. Actions:

....

....

....

9. Other relevant information:

....

....

....

10. Person reporting ....

11. Date form submitted ....

The categories of incidents and intelligence to be reported should be decided at national/provincial level, and guidance should be given as to whom the form should be submitted.

---

[1] Produced by the CITES Tiger Enforcement Task Force and taken from Notification to the Parties No. 2001/047 'CITES Tiger Enforcement Task Force', 9 July 2001.

The following guidance should be used to assist in the completion of the form and as a memory aid for staff at the scene of the incident.

Date: indicate, as appropriate
- date of discovery
- date of incident
- date information received

Place: indicate, as appropriate
- full address (if known)
- nearest town or landmark
- map reference
- GPS coordinates
- type of place, e.g. forest, commercial building, private dwelling, railway station, airport etc.

Species: indicate, as appropriate
- common name
- quantity
- age
- sex (if known)
- live or dead
- type of specimen, e.g. skin, trophy head, medicinal product, leather articles etc.

Type of event: indicate, as appropriate
- poaching
- taking
- death
- seizure
- trade
- intelligence

Suspect: indicate
- full name
- age, including date and place of birth (if known)
- address
- nationality (ID and passport No. if known)
- occupation
- description
- whether previous offender

Evidence: provide brief details of initial results, e.g.
- witnesses
- documents
- carcasses (whether any parts removed, e.g. horn or tusk) and plants
- scene of crime results (weapons, nets, lights, traps, poison, footprints, tyretracks, photographs)

Modus operandi: manner in which the crime was committed, e.g.
- vehicle(s) used (provide registration number if possible)
- apparent cause of death
- method of killing, smuggling or concealment
- route used

Actions: provide details of initial work done by law enforcement agency or others at scene, e.g.
- arrest
- post-mortem
- filing or registration of case
- seizure
- search

Other relevant information: give details such as
- intelligence gathered
- any further action required

Person reporting: indicate
- full name
- rank or title
- organization